HOUSEBROKEN
THERE'S A NEW DAWG IN TOWN

by Steve Watkins

**Andrews McMeel
Publishing**

Kansas City

For information, write Andrews McMeel Publishing, an Andrews McMeel Universal company, 4520 Main Street, Kansas City, Missouri 64111.

04 05 06 07 08 BBG 10 9 8 7 6 5 4 3 2 1

ISBN: 0-7407-4673-1

Library of Congress Control Number: 2004103566

Foreword

As someone who was picked on as a kid, I was always sensitive to the dynamics of cartoons. Usually the plots revolved around one character constantly tormented by another, with the tormentor being rewarded despite his obnoxious behavior.

For example, when I watched *Looney Toons*, I always saw Wile E. Coyote as minding his business, tending to the daily activities of life in the desert, when the pestering Road Runner would appear and constantly "beep" at him. I felt that the actions of the Road Runner were highly irritating, and I did not fault the Coyote for attempting to end the interruption. Some may not favor his homicidal attempts at silencing the bird while employing an endless supply of Acme products, but I understood. But who stood victorious in the end? The annoying Road Runner, while the poor Coyote usually found himself on the receiving end of a dynamite explosion.

Similarly, the comics page is littered (no pun intended) with cartoon dogs suffering in abusive relationships with cats. Garfield kicks Odie on a regular basis. Bucky the cat treats Satchel the dog like "Rainman." Even Snoopy gets his doghouse trashed by his unseen cat neighbor.

It seemed to me that if cats were the ruling class of cartoons, then the disenfranchised dogs were the "minorities." As an African-American, I felt that a dog character that would stand up for himself would be the proxy of all minorities. Thus DJ Dog was born. He says what he thinks and (when he thinks) thinks what he says. One critic of the strip has said derisively *"Housebroken* is about a dog who thinks he's black." In a comic strip world where cats dominate, he'd be a fool to think he was white.

To Mom and Dad

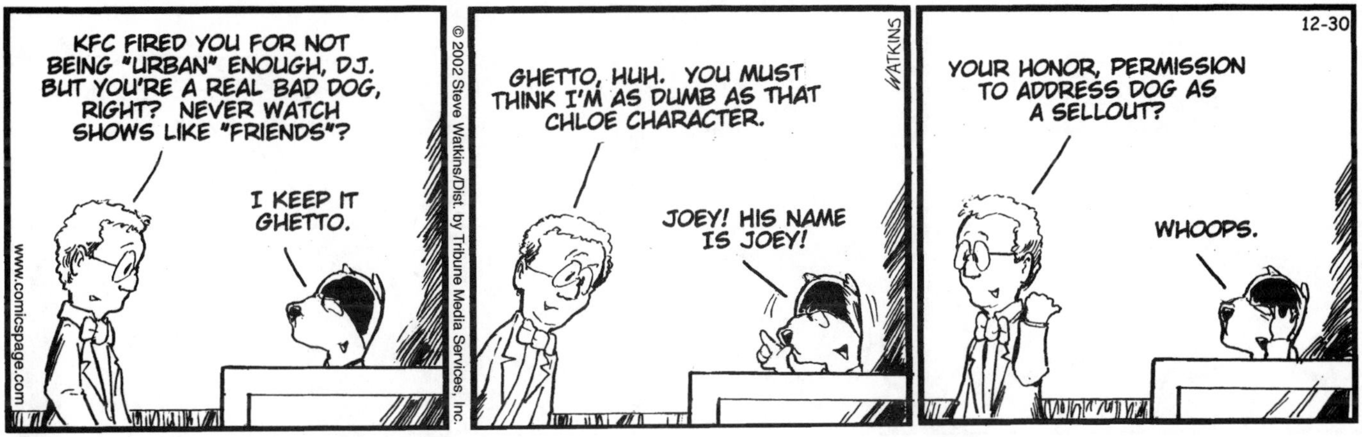
KFC FIRED YOU FOR NOT BEING "URBAN" ENOUGH, DJ. BUT YOU'RE A REAL BAD DOG, RIGHT? NEVER WATCH SHOWS LIKE "FRIENDS"?
I KEEP IT GHETTO.
GHETTO, HUH. YOU MUST THINK I'M AS DUMB AS THAT CHLOE CHARACTER.
JOEY! HIS NAME IS JOEY!
YOUR HONOR, PERMISSION TO ADDRESS DOG AS A SELLOUT?
WHOOPS.
12-30
WATKINS
© 2002 Steve Watkins/Dist. by Tribune Media Services, Inc.
www.comicspage.com

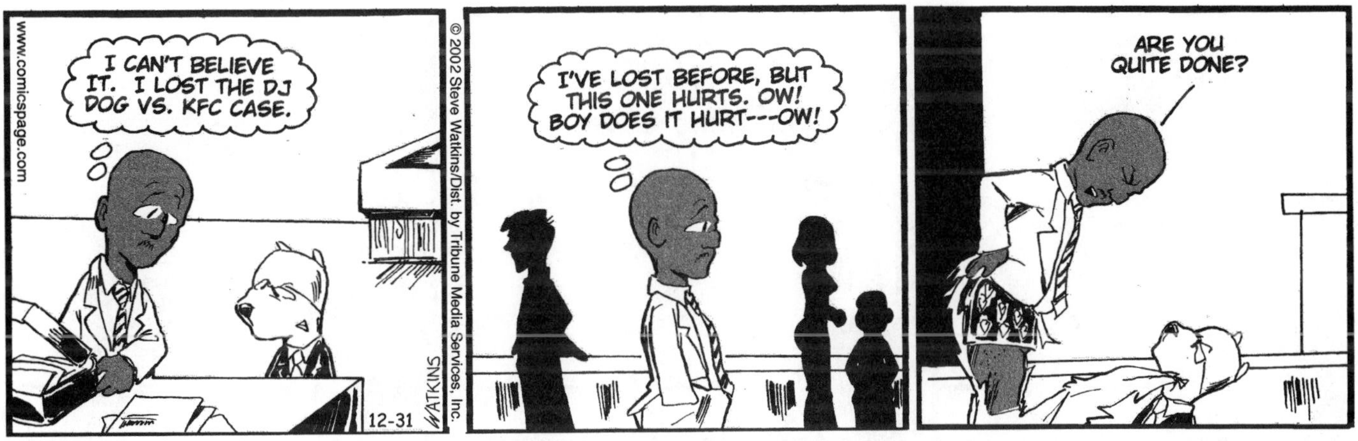
I CAN'T BELIEVE IT. I LOST THE DJ DOG VS. KFC CASE.
I'VE LOST BEFORE, BUT THIS ONE HURTS. OW! BOY DOES IT HURT---OW!
ARE YOU QUITE DONE?
12-31
WATKINS
© 2002 Steve Watkins/Dist. by Tribune Media Services, Inc.
www.comicspage.com

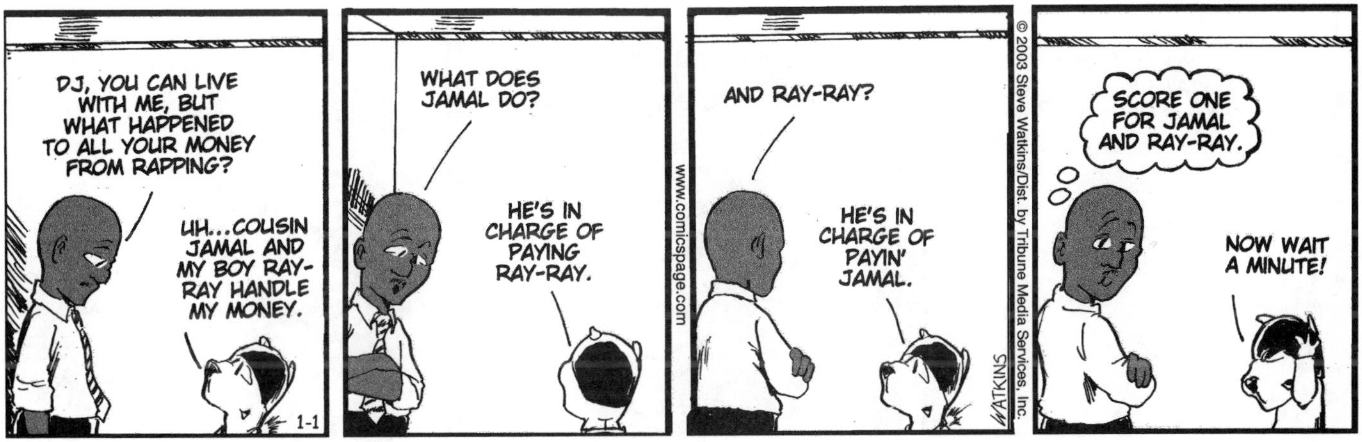
DJ, YOU CAN LIVE WITH ME, BUT WHAT HAPPENED TO ALL YOUR MONEY FROM RAPPING?
UH...COUSIN JAMAL AND MY BOY RAY-RAY HANDLE MY MONEY.
WHAT DOES JAMAL DO?
HE'S IN CHARGE OF PAYING RAY-RAY.
AND RAY-RAY?
HE'S IN CHARGE OF PAYIN' JAMAL.
SCORE ONE FOR JAMAL AND RAY-RAY.
NOW WAIT A MINUTE!
1-1
WATKINS
© 2003 Steve Watkins/Dist. by Tribune Media Services, Inc.
www.comicspage.com

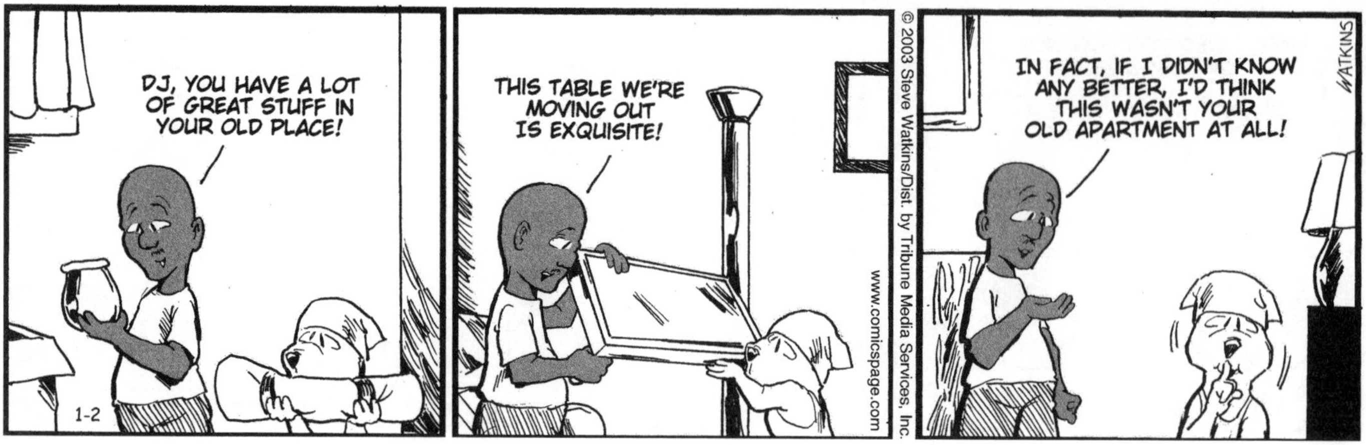
DJ, YOU HAVE A LOT OF GREAT STUFF IN YOUR OLD PLACE!
1-2
THIS TABLE WE'RE MOVING OUT IS EXQUISITE!
© 2003 Steve Watkins/Dist. by Tribune Media Services, Inc.
www.comicspage.com
IN FACT, IF I DIDN'T KNOW ANY BETTER, I'D THINK THIS WASN'T YOUR OLD APARTMENT AT ALL!
WATKINS

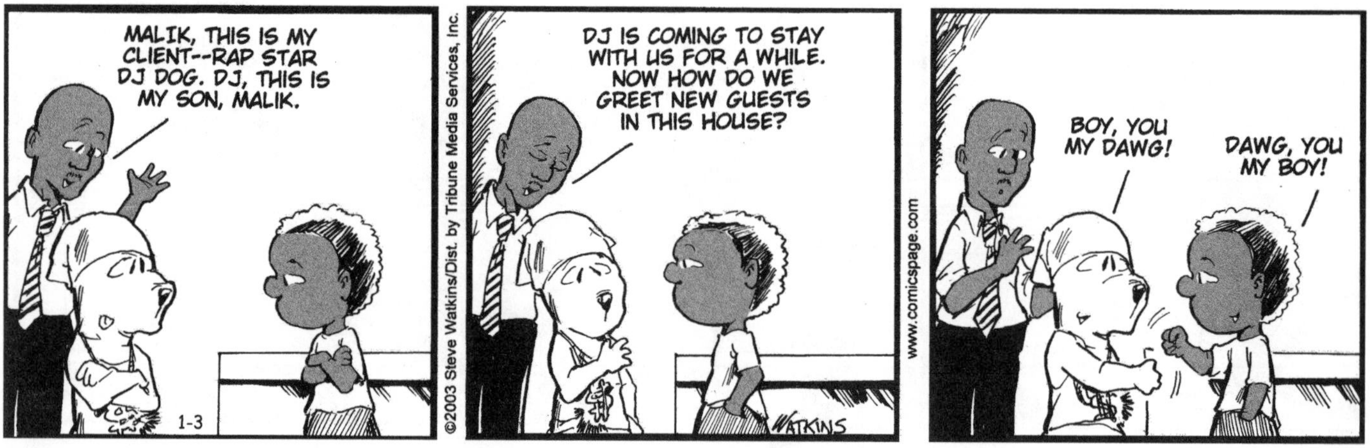
MALIK, THIS IS MY CLIENT--RAP STAR DJ DOG. DJ, THIS IS MY SON, MALIK.
1-3
©2003 Steve Watkins/Dist. by Tribune Media Services, Inc.
DJ IS COMING TO STAY WITH US FOR A WHILE. NOW HOW DO WE GREET NEW GUESTS IN THIS HOUSE?
WATKINS
www.comicspage.com
BOY, YOU MY DAWG!
DAWG, YOU MY BOY!

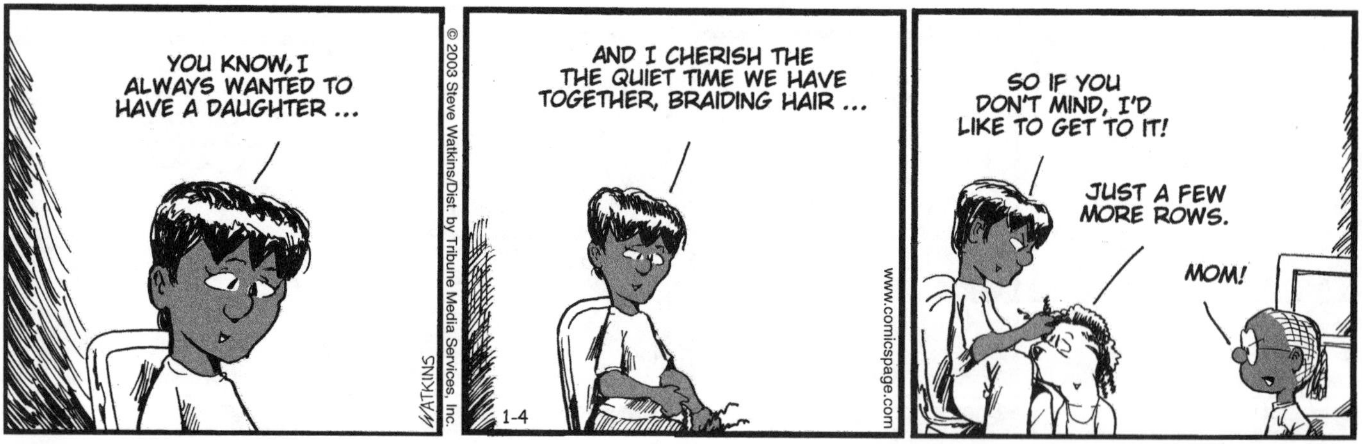
YOU KNOW, I ALWAYS WANTED TO HAVE A DAUGHTER ...
WATKINS
© 2003 Steve Watkins/Dist. by Tribune Media Services, Inc.
AND I CHERISH THE THE QUIET TIME WE HAVE TOGETHER, BRAIDING HAIR ...
1-4
www.comicspage.com
SO IF YOU DON'T MIND, I'D LIKE TO GET TO IT!
JUST A FEW MORE ROWS.
MOM!

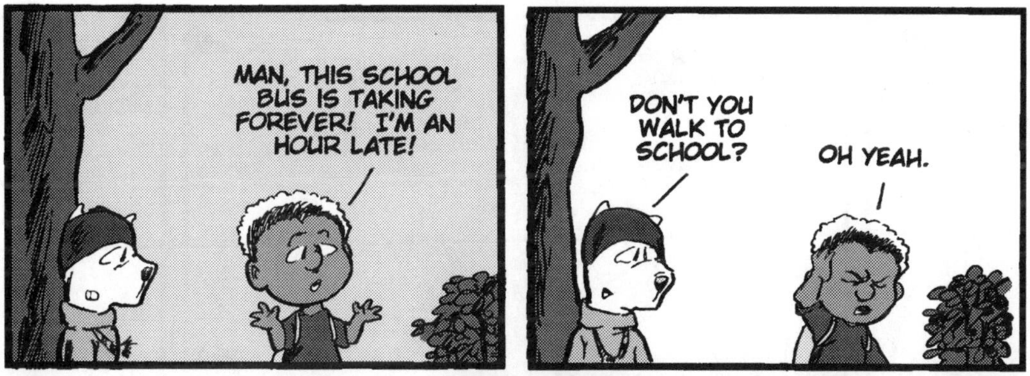
MAN, THIS SCHOOL BUS IS TAKING FOREVER! I'M AN HOUR LATE!
DON'T YOU WALK TO SCHOOL?
OH YEAH.

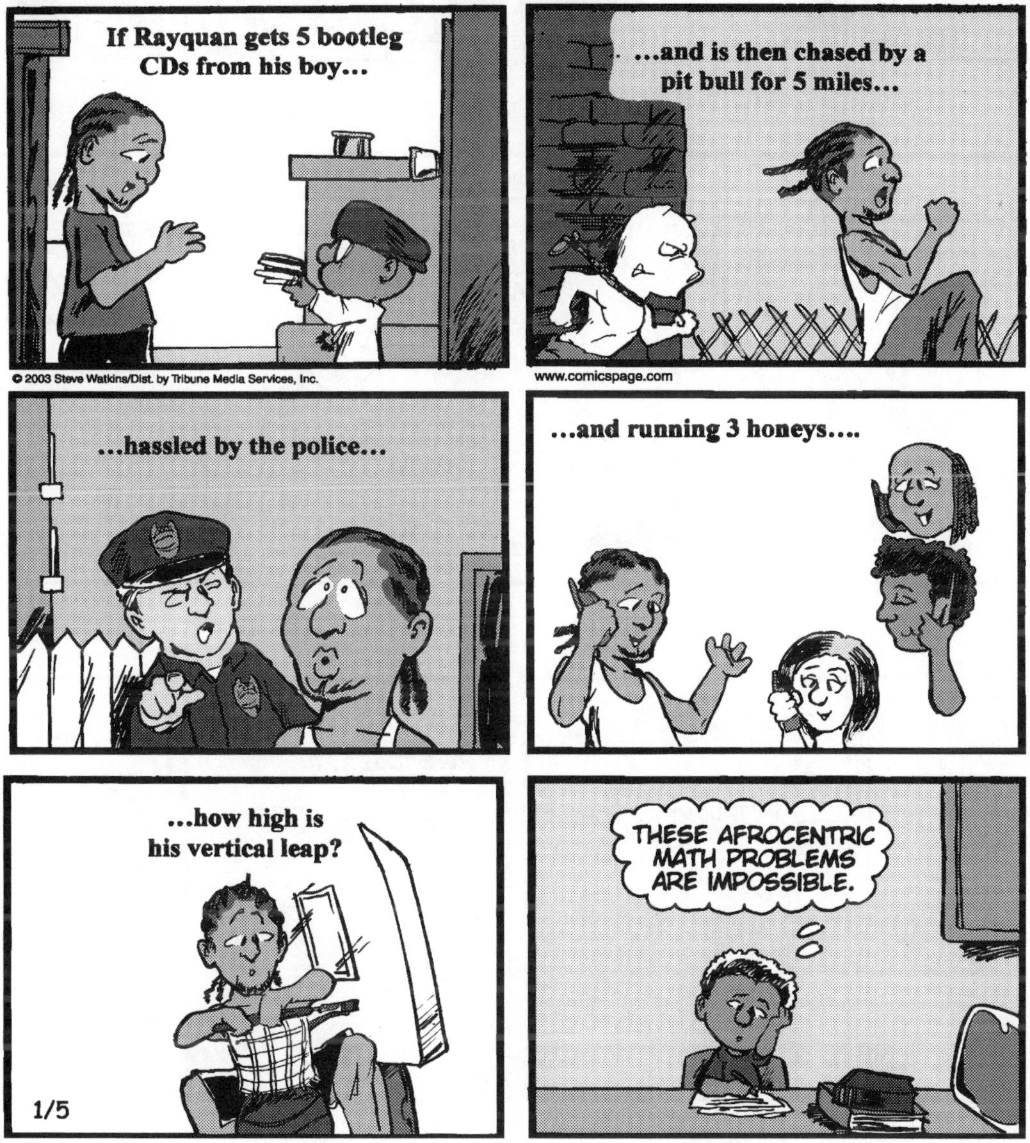
If Rayquan gets 5 bootleg CDs from his boy...
...and is then chased by a pit bull for 5 miles...
© 2003 Steve Watkins/Dist. by Tribune Media Services, Inc.
www.comicspage.com
...hassled by the police...
...and running 3 honeys....
...how high is his vertical leap?
1/5
THESE AFROCENTRIC MATH PROBLEMS ARE IMPOSSIBLE.

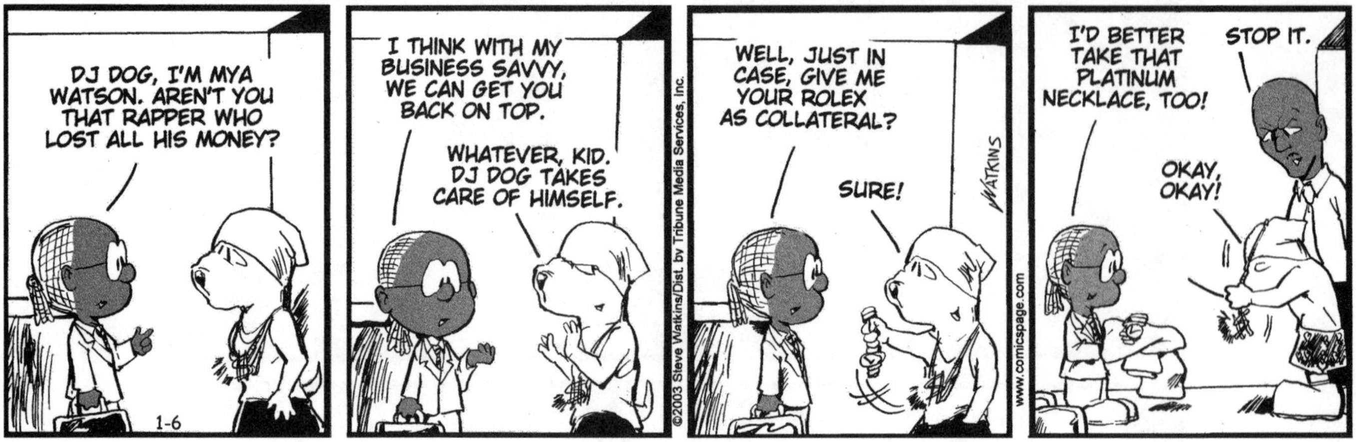
DJ DOG, I'M MYA WATSON. AREN'T YOU THAT RAPPER WHO LOST ALL HIS MONEY?
1-6
I THINK WITH MY BUSINESS SAVVY, WE CAN GET YOU BACK ON TOP.
WHATEVER, KID. DJ DOG TAKES CARE OF HIMSELF.
©2003 Steve Watkins/Dist. by Tribune Media Services, Inc.
WELL, JUST IN CASE, GIVE ME YOUR ROLEX AS COLLATERAL?
SURE!
WATKINS
www.comicspage.com
I'D BETTER TAKE THAT PLATINUM NECKLACE, TOO!
STOP IT.
OKAY, OKAY!

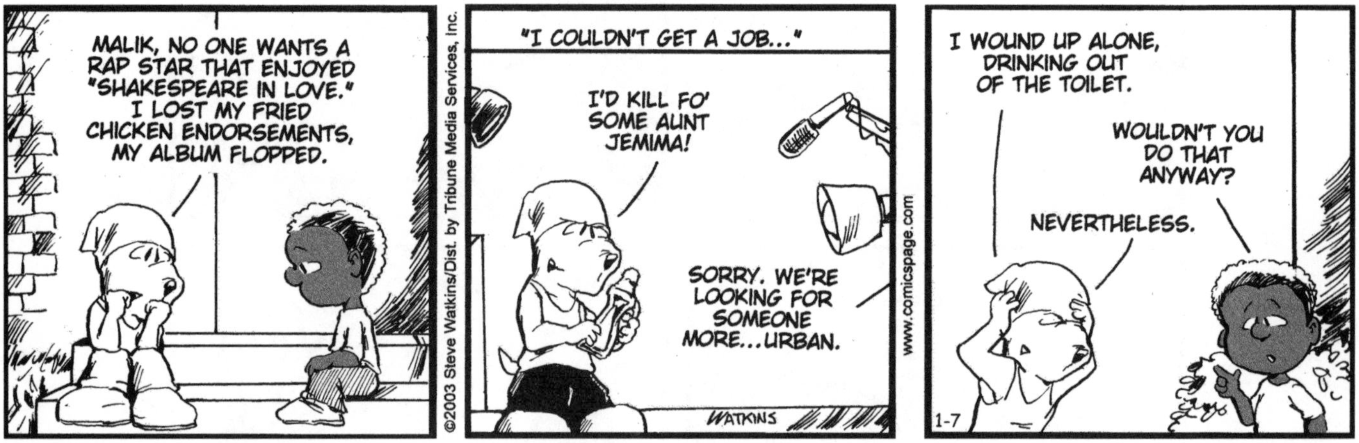
MALIK, NO ONE WANTS A RAP STAR THAT ENJOYED "SHAKESPEARE IN LOVE." I LOST MY FRIED CHICKEN ENDORSEMENTS, MY ALBUM FLOPPED.
©2003 Steve Watkins/Dist. by Tribune Media Services, Inc.
"I COULDN'T GET A JOB..."
I'D KILL FO' SOME AUNT JEMIMA!
SORRY. WE'RE LOOKING FOR SOMEONE MORE...URBAN.
WATKINS
www.comicspage.com
I WOUND UP ALONE, DRINKING OUT OF THE TOILET.
WOULDN'T YOU DO THAT ANYWAY?
NEVERTHELESS.
1-7

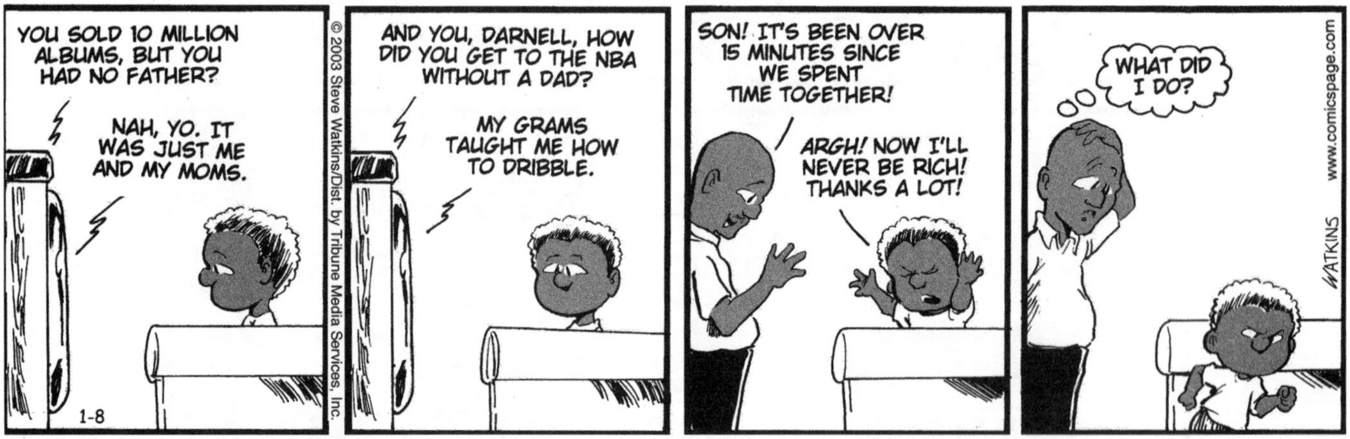
YOU SOLD 10 MILLION ALBUMS, BUT YOU HAD NO FATHER?
NAH, YO. IT WAS JUST ME AND MY MOMS.
1-8
© 2003 Steve Watkins/Dist. by Tribune Media Services, Inc.
AND YOU, DARNELL, HOW DID YOU GET TO THE NBA WITHOUT A DAD?
MY GRAMS TAUGHT ME HOW TO DRIBBLE.
SON! IT'S BEEN OVER 15 MINUTES SINCE WE SPENT TIME TOGETHER!
ARGH! NOW I'LL NEVER BE RICH! THANKS A LOT!
WHAT DID I DO?
WATKINS
www.comicspage.com

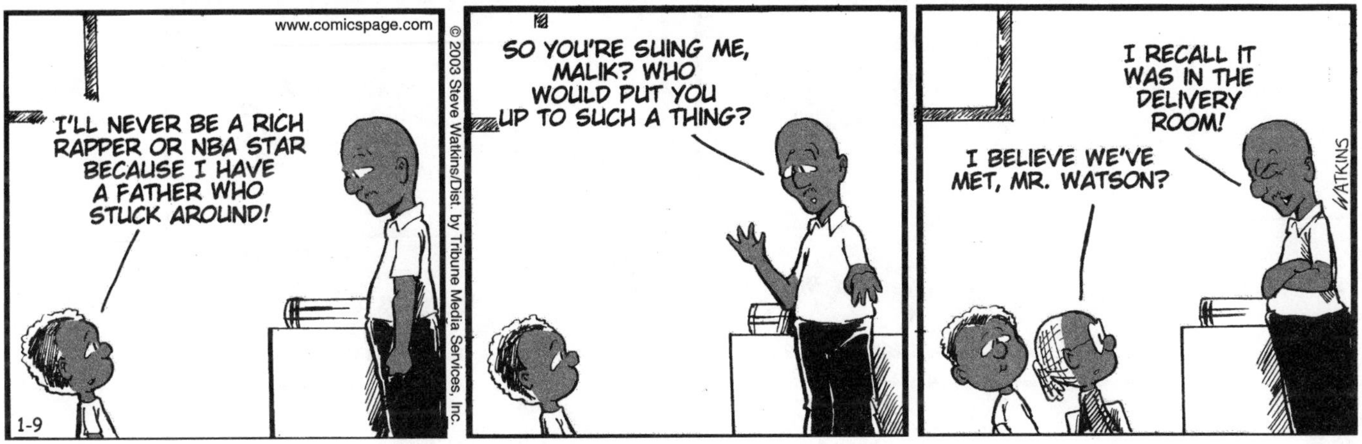
www.comicspage.com
I'LL NEVER BE A RICH RAPPER OR NBA STAR BECAUSE I HAVE A FATHER WHO STUCK AROUND!
1-9
© 2003 Steve Watkins/Dist. by Tribune Media Services, Inc.
SO YOU'RE SUING ME, MALIK? WHO WOULD PUT YOU UP TO SUCH A THING?
I BELIEVE WE'VE MET, MR. WATSON?
I RECALL IT WAS IN THE DELIVERY ROOM!
WATKINS

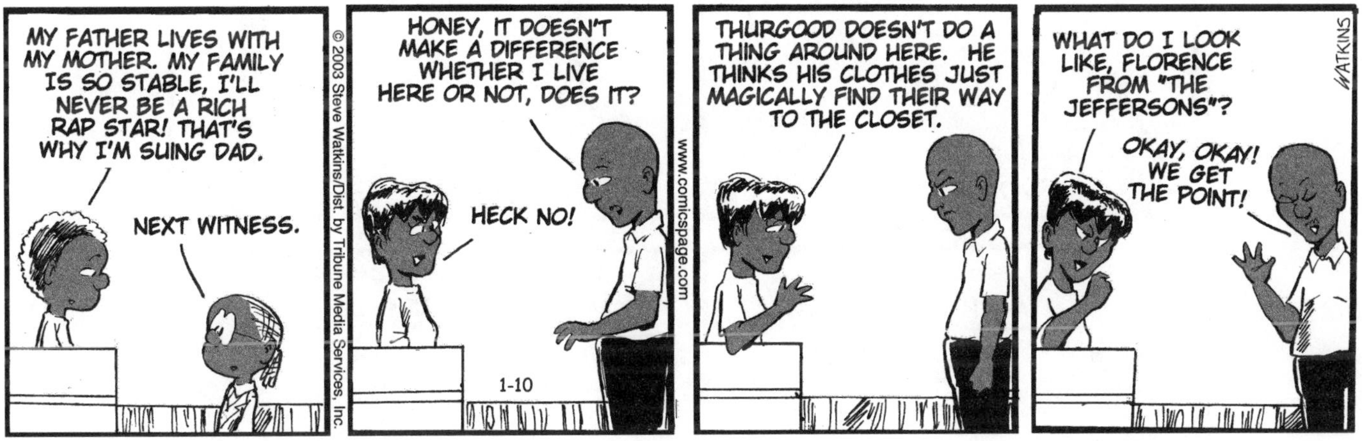
MY FATHER LIVES WITH MY MOTHER. MY FAMILY IS SO STABLE, I'LL NEVER BE A RICH RAP STAR! THAT'S WHY I'M SUING DAD.
NEXT WITNESS.
© 2003 Steve Watkins/Dist. by Tribune Media Services, Inc.
HONEY, IT DOESN'T MAKE A DIFFERENCE WHETHER I LIVE HERE OR NOT, DOES IT?
HECK NO!
1-10
www.comicspage.com
THURGOOD DOESN'T DO A THING AROUND HERE. HE THINKS HIS CLOTHES JUST MAGICALLY FIND THEIR WAY TO THE CLOSET.
WHAT DO I LOOK LIKE, FLORENCE FROM "THE JEFFERSONS"?
OKAY, OKAY! WE GET THE POINT!
WATKINS

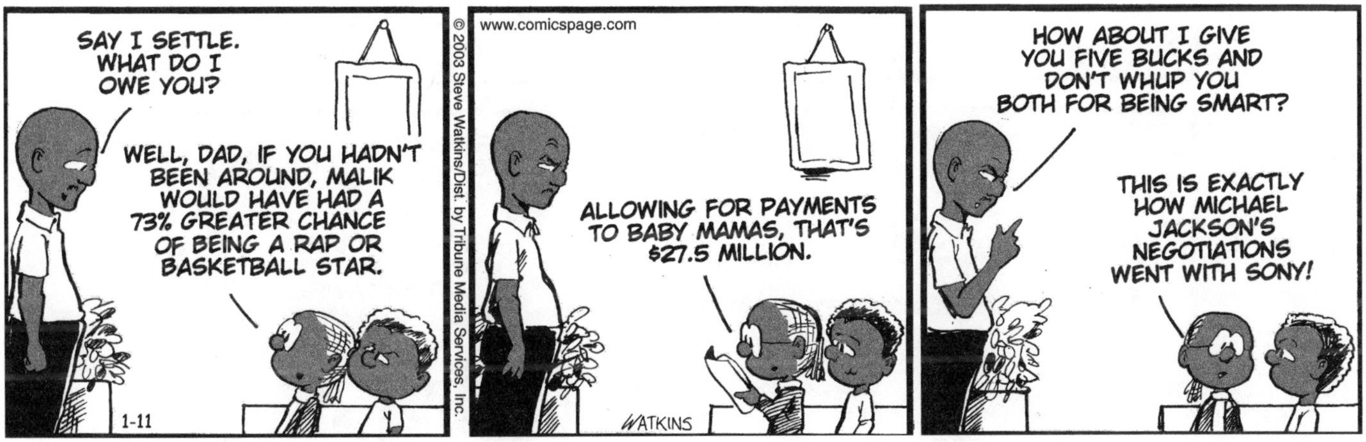
SAY I SETTLE. WHAT DO I OWE YOU?
WELL, DAD, IF YOU HADN'T BEEN AROUND, MALIK WOULD HAVE HAD A 73% GREATER CHANCE OF BEING A RAP OR BASKETBALL STAR.
1-11
© 2003 Steve Watkins/Dist. by Tribune Media Services, Inc.
www.comicspage.com
ALLOWING FOR PAYMENTS TO BABY MAMAS, THAT'S $27.5 MILLION.
WATKINS
HOW ABOUT I GIVE YOU FIVE BUCKS AND DON'T WHUP YOU BOTH FOR BEING SMART?
THIS IS EXACTLY HOW MICHAEL JACKSON'S NEGOTIATIONS WENT WITH SONY!

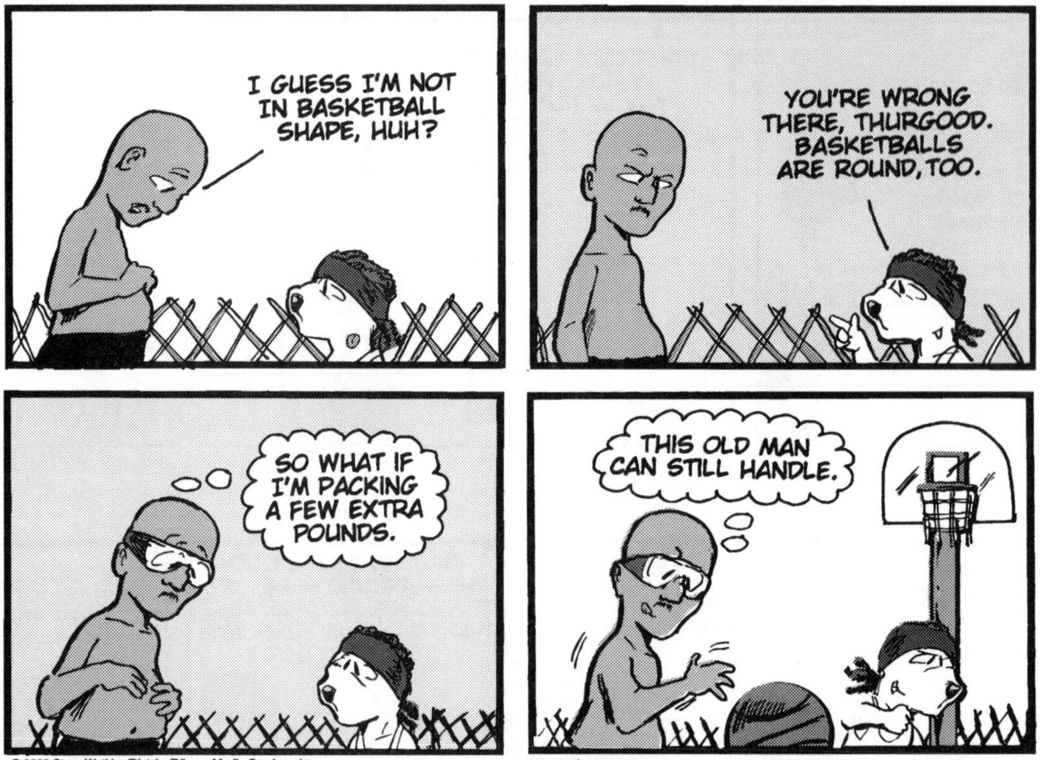
I GUESS I'M NOT IN BASKETBALL SHAPE, HUH?
YOU'RE WRONG THERE, THURGOOD. BASKETBALLS ARE ROUND, TOO.
SO WHAT IF I'M PACKING A FEW EXTRA POUNDS.
THIS OLD MAN CAN STILL HANDLE.

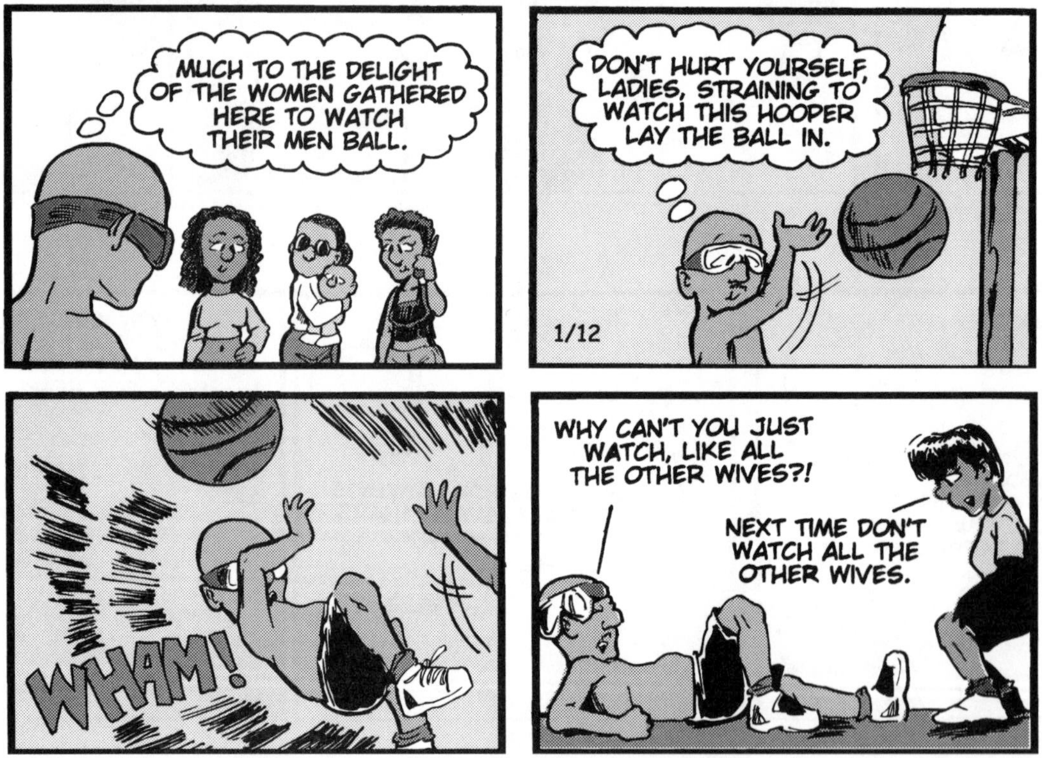
MUCH TO THE DELIGHT OF THE WOMEN GATHERED HERE TO WATCH THEIR MEN BALL.
DON'T HURT YOURSELF, LADIES, STRAINING TO WATCH THIS HOOPER LAY THE BALL IN.
1/12
WHAM!
WHY CAN'T YOU JUST WATCH, LIKE ALL THE OTHER WIVES?!
NEXT TIME DON'T WATCH ALL THE OTHER WIVES.

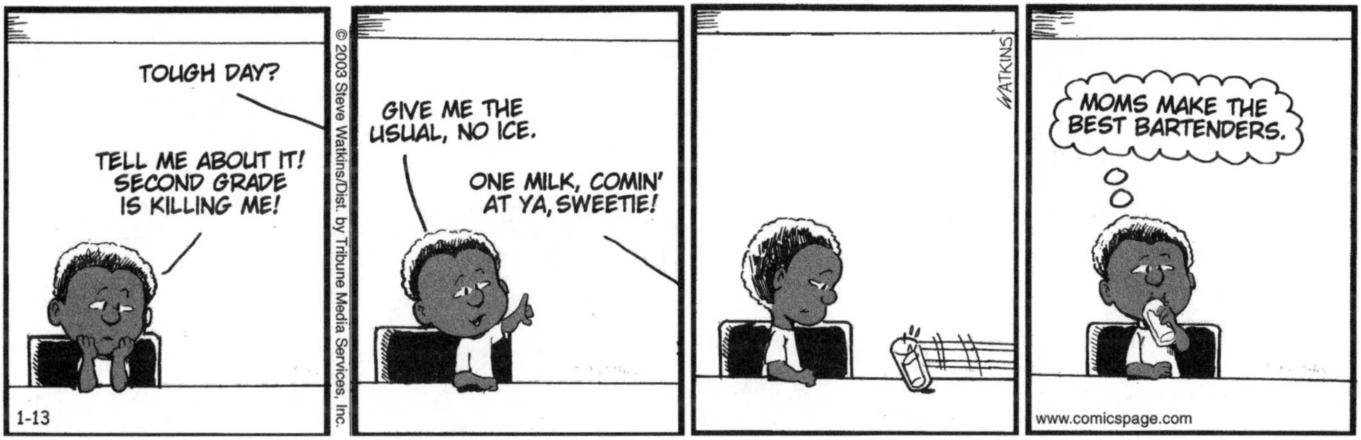
1-13
TOUGH DAY?
TELL ME ABOUT IT! SECOND GRADE IS KILLING ME!
© 2003 Steve Watkins/Dist. by Tribune Media Services, Inc.
GIVE ME THE USUAL, NO ICE.
ONE MILK, COMIN' AT YA, SWEETIE!
WATKINS
MOMS MAKE THE BEST BARTENDERS.
www.comicspage.com

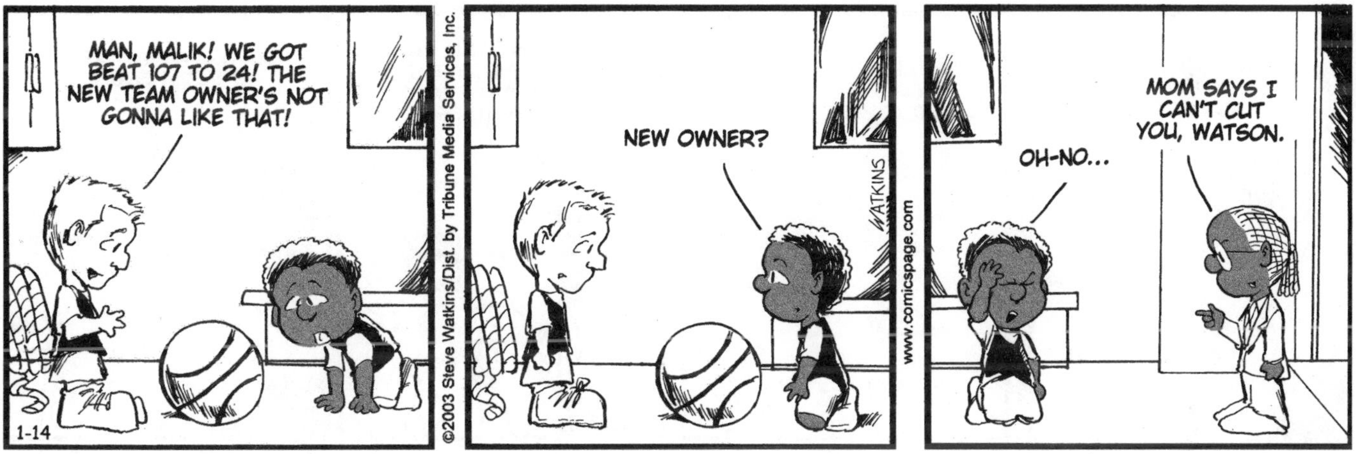
1-14
MAN, MALIK! WE GOT BEAT 107 TO 24! THE NEW TEAM OWNER'S NOT GONNA LIKE THAT!
©2003 Steve Watkins/Dist. by Tribune Media Services, Inc.
NEW OWNER?
WATKINS
www.comicspage.com
OH-NO...
MOM SAYS I CAN'T CUT YOU, WATSON.

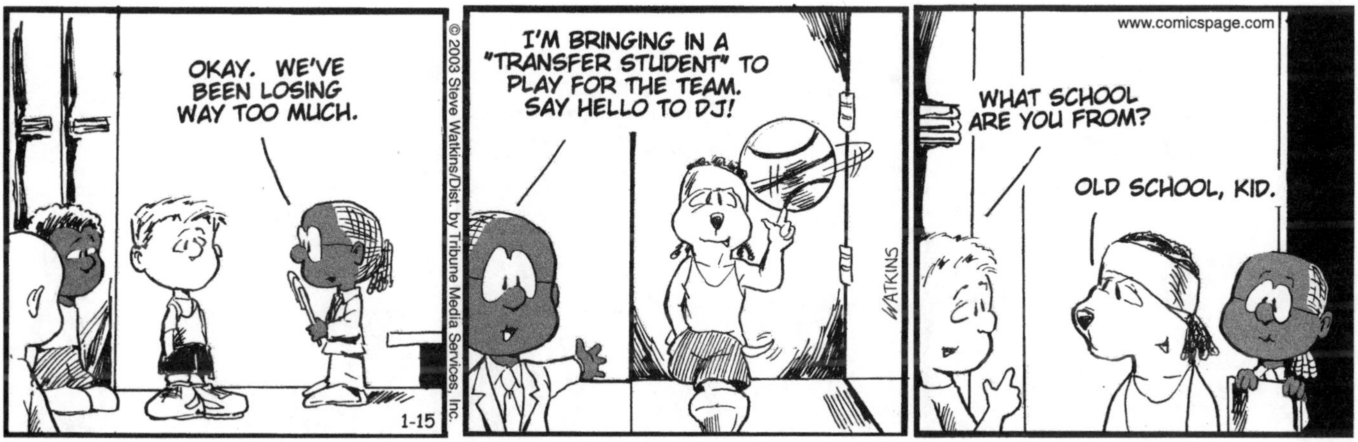
OKAY. WE'VE BEEN LOSING WAY TOO MUCH.
1-15
© 2003 Steve Watkins/Dist. by Tribune Media Services, Inc.
I'M BRINGING IN A "TRANSFER STUDENT" TO PLAY FOR THE TEAM. SAY HELLO TO DJ!
WATKINS
www.comicspage.com
WHAT SCHOOL ARE YOU FROM?
OLD SCHOOL, KID.

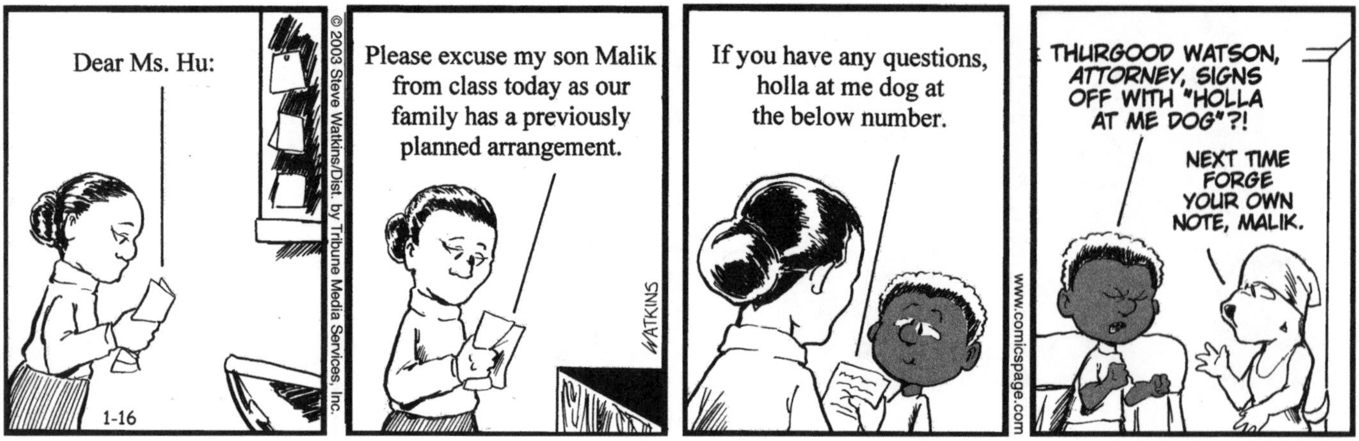
Dear Ms. Hu:
1-16
© 2003 Steve Watkins/Dist. by Tribune Media Services, Inc.
Please excuse my son Malik from class today as our family has a previously planned arrangement.
WATKINS
If you have any questions, holla at me dog at the below number.
www.comicspage.com
THURGOOD WATSON, ATTORNEY, SIGNS OFF WITH "HOLLA AT ME DOG"?!
NEXT TIME FORGE YOUR OWN NOTE, MALIK.

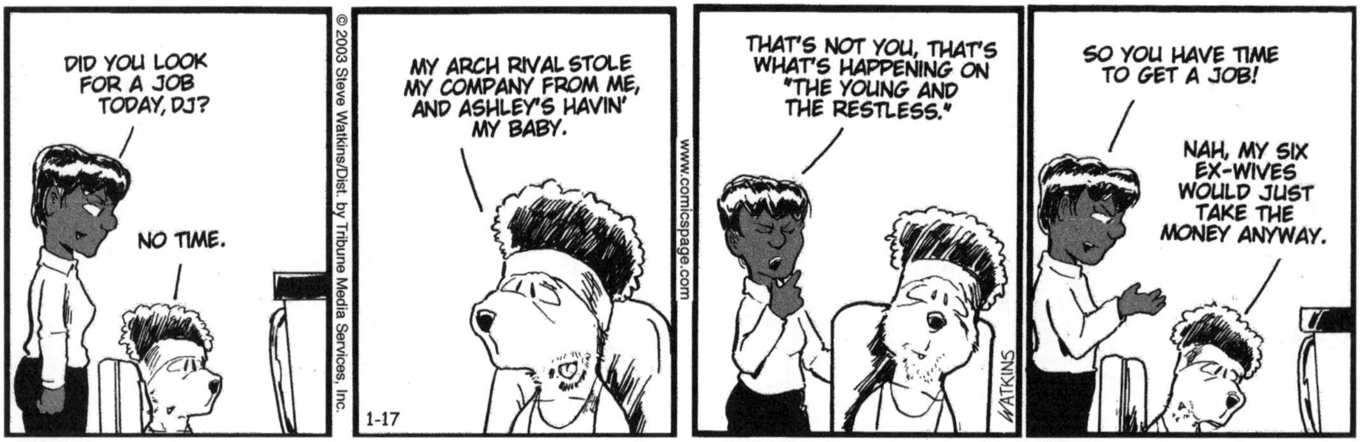
DID YOU LOOK FOR A JOB TODAY, DJ?
NO TIME.
© 2003 Steve Watkins/Dist. by Tribune Media Services, Inc.
MY ARCH RIVAL STOLE MY COMPANY FROM ME, AND ASHLEY'S HAVIN' MY BABY.
1-17
www.comicspage.com
THAT'S NOT YOU, THAT'S WHAT'S HAPPENING ON "THE YOUNG AND THE RESTLESS."
WATKINS
SO YOU HAVE TIME TO GET A JOB!
NAH, MY SIX EX-WIVES WOULD JUST TAKE THE MONEY ANYWAY.

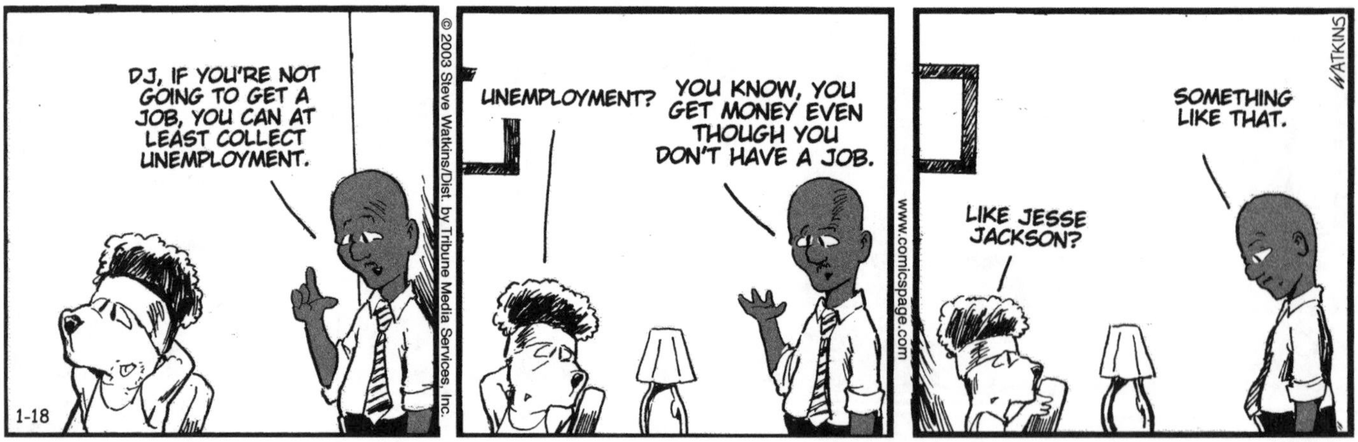
DJ, IF YOU'RE NOT GOING TO GET A JOB, YOU CAN AT LEAST COLLECT UNEMPLOYMENT.
1-18
© 2003 Steve Watkins/Dist. by Tribune Media Services, Inc.
UNEMPLOYMENT?
YOU KNOW, YOU GET MONEY EVEN THOUGH YOU DON'T HAVE A JOB.
www.comicspage.com
LIKE JESSE JACKSON?
SOMETHING LIKE THAT.
WATKINS

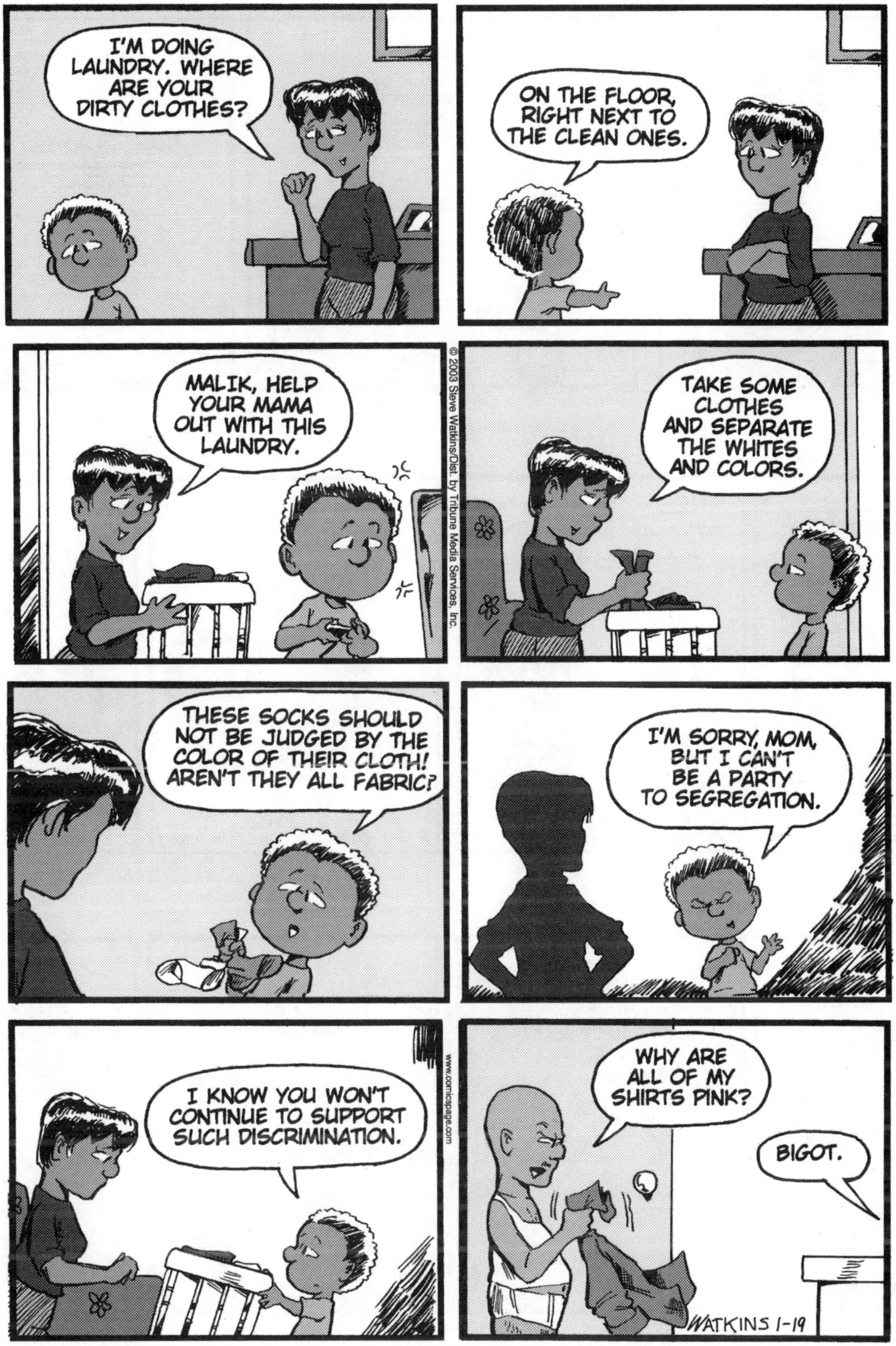
I'M DOING LAUNDRY. WHERE ARE YOUR DIRTY CLOTHES?
ON THE FLOOR, RIGHT NEXT TO THE CLEAN ONES.
MALIK, HELP YOUR MAMA OUT WITH THIS LAUNDRY.
TAKE SOME CLOTHES AND SEPARATE THE WHITES AND COLORS.
THESE SOCKS SHOULD NOT BE JUDGED BY THE COLOR OF THEIR CLOTH! AREN'T THEY ALL FABRIC?
I'M SORRY, MOM, BUT I CAN'T BE A PARTY TO SEGREGATION.
I KNOW YOU WON'T CONTINUE TO SUPPORT SUCH DISCRIMINATION.
WHY ARE ALL OF MY SHIRTS PINK?
BIGOT.
WATKINS 1-19

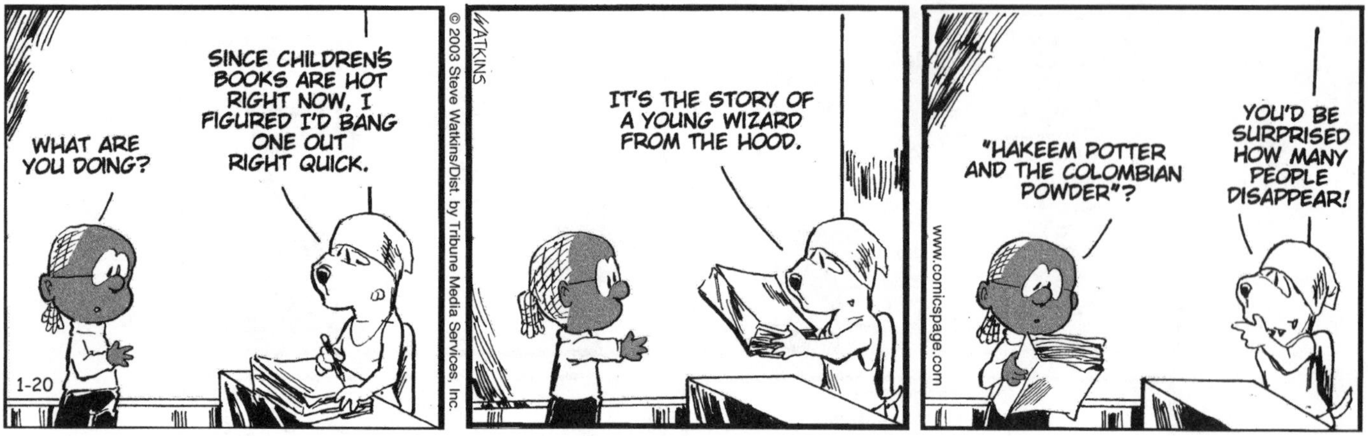
WHAT ARE YOU DOING?
SINCE CHILDREN'S BOOKS ARE HOT RIGHT NOW, I FIGURED I'D BANG ONE OUT RIGHT QUICK.
1-20
© 2003 Steve Watkins/Dist. by Tribune Media Services, Inc.
WATKINS
IT'S THE STORY OF A YOUNG WIZARD FROM THE HOOD.
"HAKEEM POTTER AND THE COLOMBIAN POWDER"?
YOU'D BE SURPRISED HOW MANY PEOPLE DISAPPEAR!
www.comicspage.com

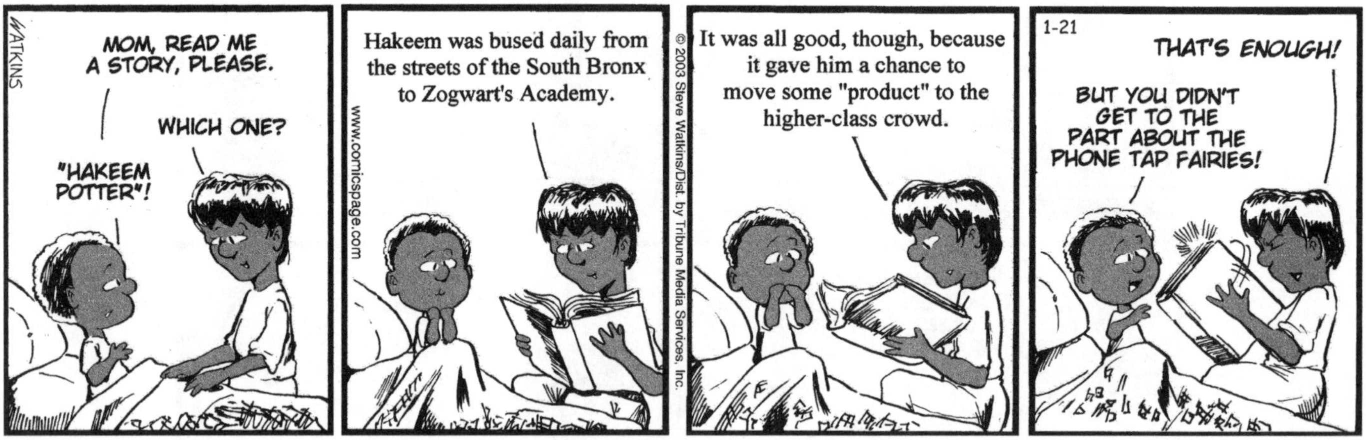
WATKINS
MOM, READ ME A STORY, PLEASE.
WHICH ONE?
"HAKEEM POTTER"!
Hakeem was bused daily from the streets of the South Bronx to Zogwart's Academy.
www.comicspage.com
© 2003 Steve Watkins/Dist. by Tribune Media Services, Inc.
It was all good, though, because it gave him a chance to move some "product" to the higher-class crowd.
1-21
THAT'S ENOUGH!
BUT YOU DIDN'T GET TO THE PART ABOUT THE PHONE TAP FAIRIES!

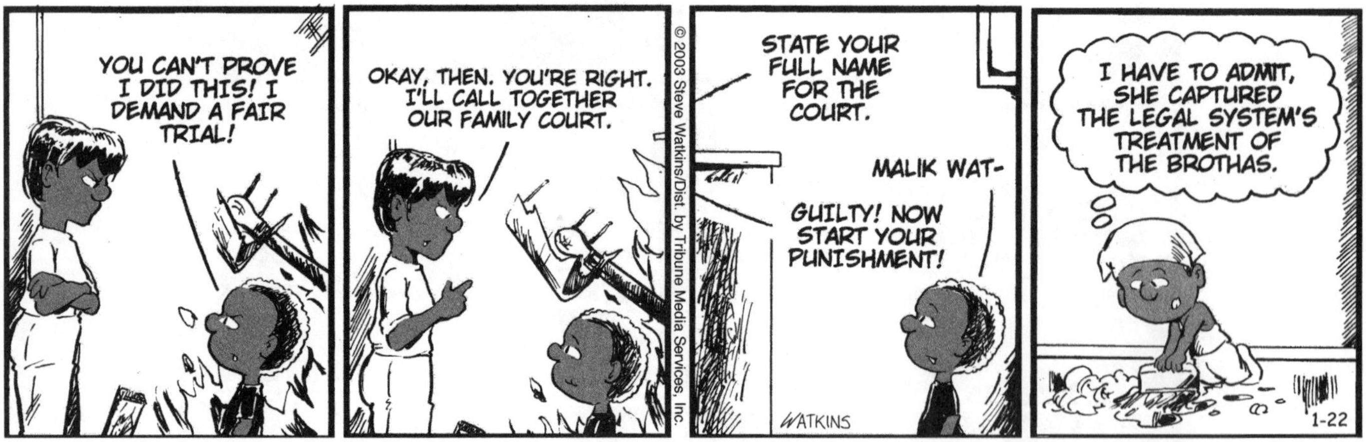
YOU CAN'T PROVE I DID THIS! I DEMAND A FAIR TRIAL!
OKAY, THEN. YOU'RE RIGHT. I'LL CALL TOGETHER OUR FAMILY COURT.
© 2003 Steve Watkins/Dist. by Tribune Media Services, Inc.
STATE YOUR FULL NAME FOR THE COURT.
MALIK WAT-
GUILTY! NOW START YOUR PUNISHMENT!
WATKINS
I HAVE TO ADMIT, SHE CAPTURED THE LEGAL SYSTEM'S TREATMENT OF THE BROTHAS.
1-22

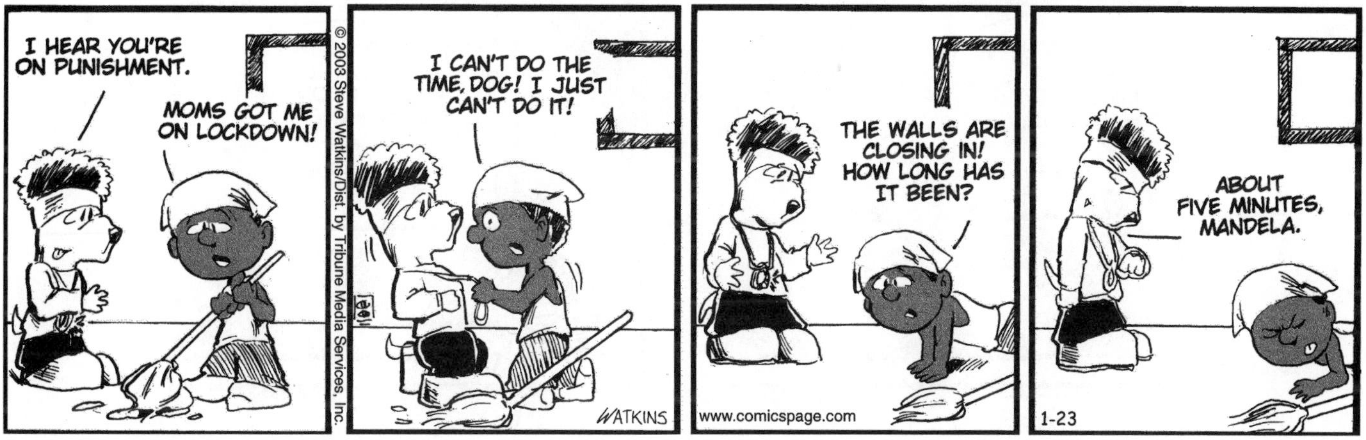
I HEAR YOU'RE ON PUNISHMENT.
MOMS GOT ME ON LOCKDOWN!
© 2003 Steve Watkins/Dist. by Tribune Media Services, Inc.
I CAN'T DO THE TIME, DOG! I JUST CAN'T DO IT!
WATKINS
THE WALLS ARE CLOSING IN! HOW LONG HAS IT BEEN?
www.comicspage.com
ABOUT FIVE MINUTES, MANDELA.
1-23

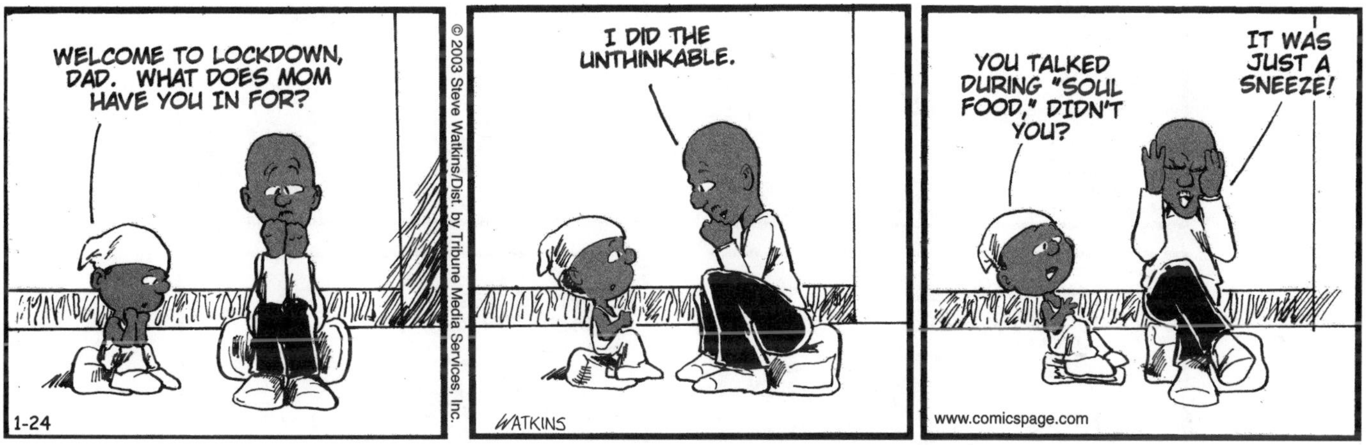
WELCOME TO LOCKDOWN, DAD. WHAT DOES MOM HAVE YOU IN FOR?
1-24
© 2003 Steve Watkins/Dist. by Tribune Media Services, Inc.
I DID THE UNTHINKABLE.
WATKINS
YOU TALKED DURING "SOUL FOOD," DIDN'T YOU?
IT WAS JUST A SNEEZE!
www.comicspage.com

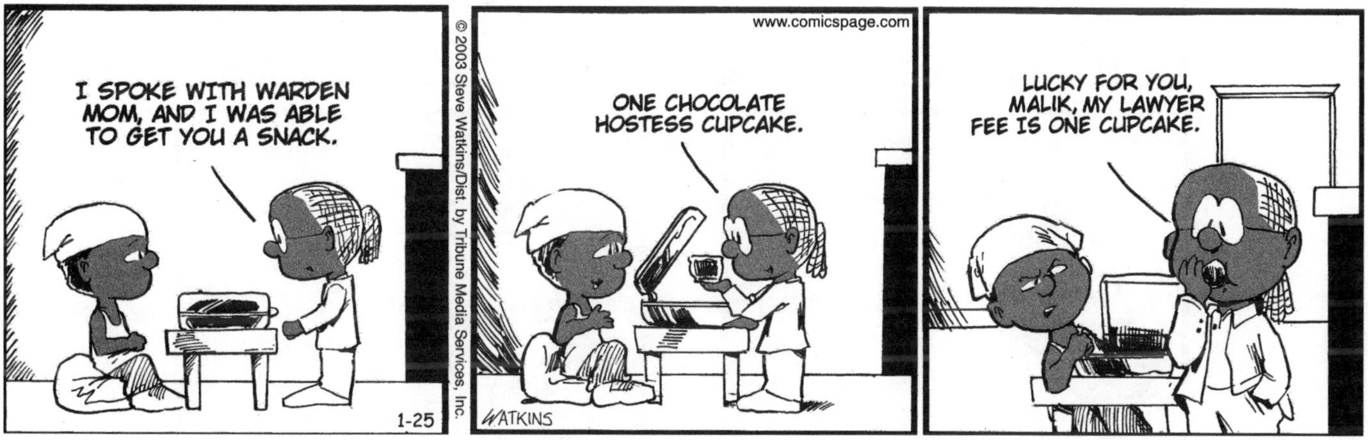
I SPOKE WITH WARDEN MOM, AND I WAS ABLE TO GET YOU A SNACK.
1-25
© 2003 Steve Watkins/Dist. by Tribune Media Services, Inc.
www.comicspage.com
ONE CHOCOLATE HOSTESS CUPCAKE.
WATKINS
LUCKY FOR YOU, MALIK, MY LAWYER FEE IS ONE CUPCAKE.

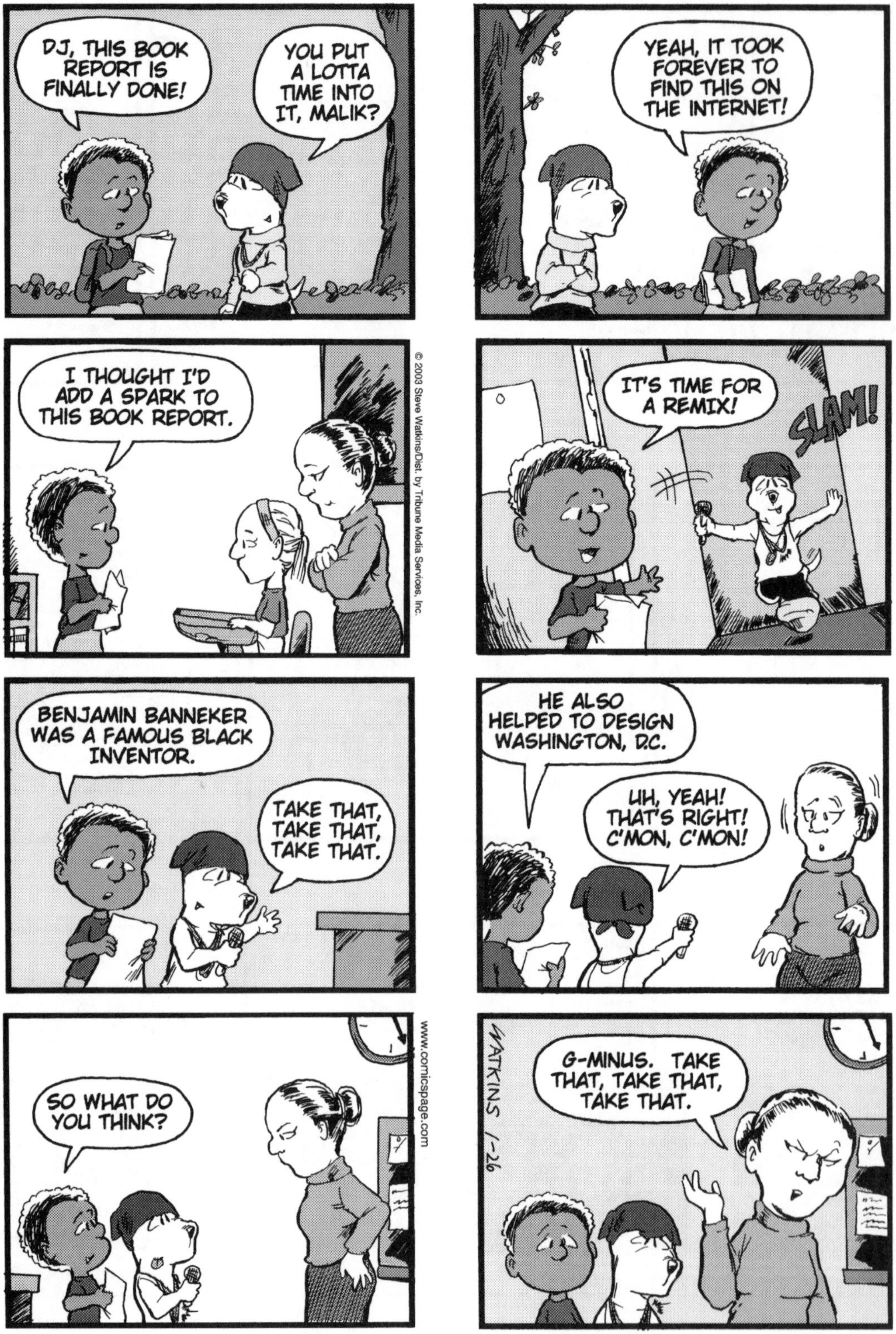

DJ, THIS BOOK REPORT IS FINALLY DONE!
YOU PUT A LOTTA TIME INTO IT, MALIK?
YEAH, IT TOOK FOREVER TO FIND THIS ON THE INTERNET!
I THOUGHT I'D ADD A SPARK TO THIS BOOK REPORT.
© 2003 Steve Watkins/Dist. by Tribune Media Services, Inc.
IT'S TIME FOR A REMIX!
SLAM!
BENJAMIN BANNEKER WAS A FAMOUS BLACK INVENTOR.
TAKE THAT, TAKE THAT, TAKE THAT.
HE ALSO HELPED TO DESIGN WASHINGTON, D.C.
UH, YEAH! THAT'S RIGHT! C'MON, C'MON!
SO WHAT DO YOU THINK?
www.comicspage.com
WATKINS 1-26
G-MINUS. TAKE THAT, TAKE THAT, TAKE THAT.

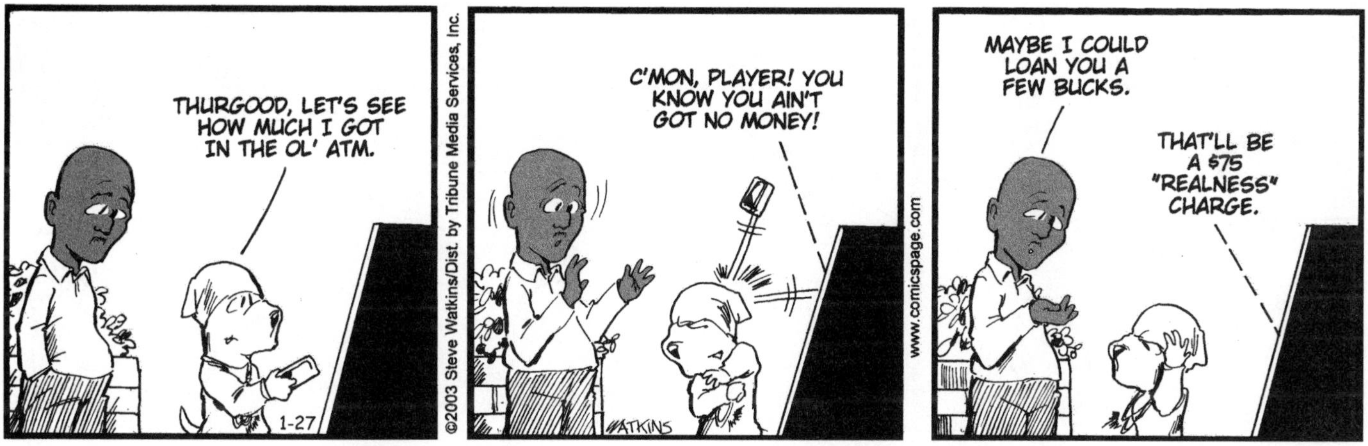
THURGOOD, LET'S SEE HOW MUCH I GOT IN THE OL' ATM.
1-27
©2003 Steve Watkins/Dist. by Tribune Media Services, Inc.
C'MON, PLAYER! YOU KNOW YOU AIN'T GOT NO MONEY!
WATKINS
www.comicspage.com
MAYBE I COULD LOAN YOU A FEW BUCKS.
THAT'LL BE A $75 "REALNESS" CHARGE.

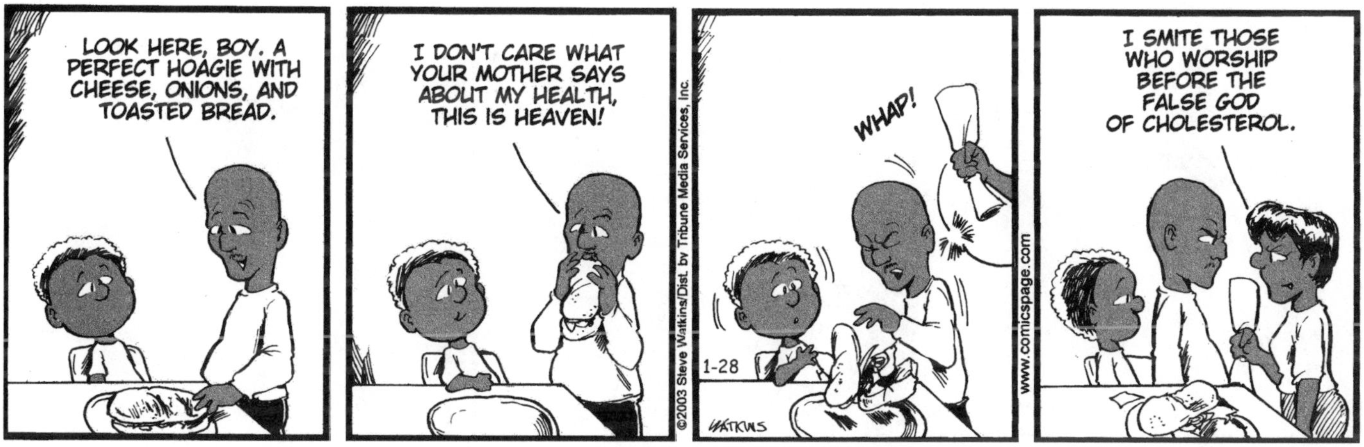
LOOK HERE, BOY. A PERFECT HOAGIE WITH CHEESE, ONIONS, AND TOASTED BREAD.
I DON'T CARE WHAT YOUR MOTHER SAYS ABOUT MY HEALTH, THIS IS HEAVEN!
©2003 Steve Watkins/Dist. by Tribune Media Services, Inc.
WHAP!
1-28
WATKINS
www.comicspage.com
I SMITE THOSE WHO WORSHIP BEFORE THE FALSE GOD OF CHOLESTEROL.

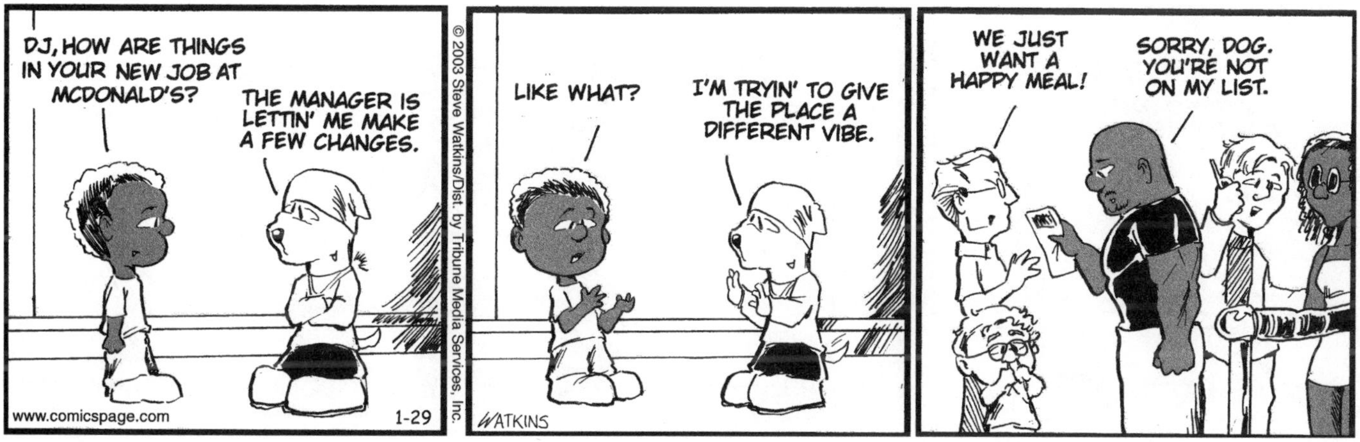
DJ, HOW ARE THINGS IN YOUR NEW JOB AT MCDONALD'S?
THE MANAGER IS LETTIN' ME MAKE A FEW CHANGES.
www.comicspage.com
1-29
© 2003 Steve Watkins/Dist. by Tribune Media Services, Inc.
LIKE WHAT?
I'M TRYIN' TO GIVE THE PLACE A DIFFERENT VIBE.
WATKINS
WE JUST WANT A HAPPY MEAL!
SORRY, DOG. YOU'RE NOT ON MY LIST.

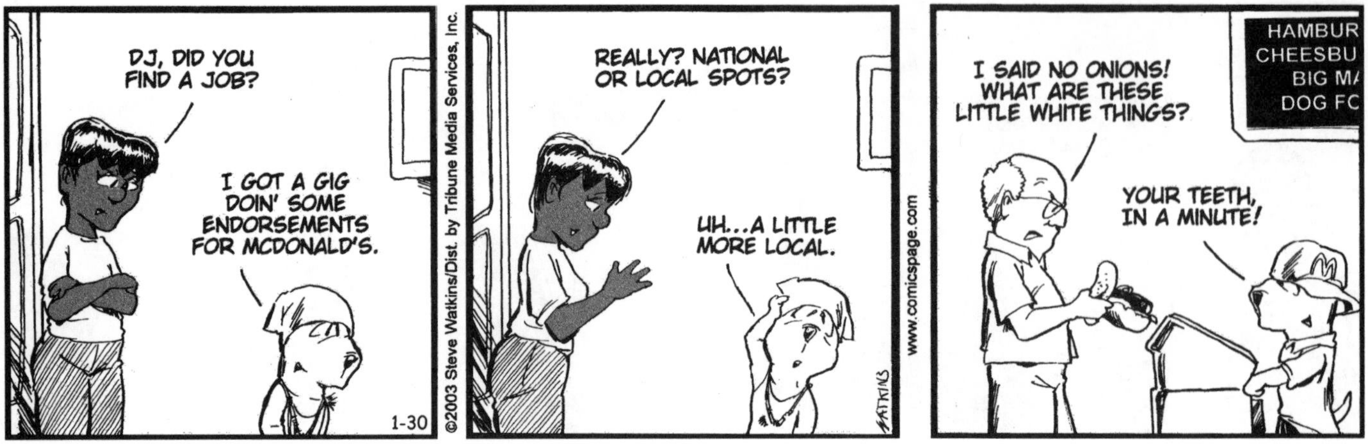
DJ, DID YOU FIND A JOB?
I GOT A GIG DOIN' SOME ENDORSEMENTS FOR MCDONALD'S.
1-30
©2003 Steve Watkins/Dist. by Tribune Media Services, Inc.
REALLY? NATIONAL OR LOCAL SPOTS?
UH...A LITTLE MORE LOCAL.
WATKINS
www.comicspage.com
I SAID NO ONIONS! WHAT ARE THESE LITTLE WHITE THINGS?
YOUR TEETH, IN A MINUTE!

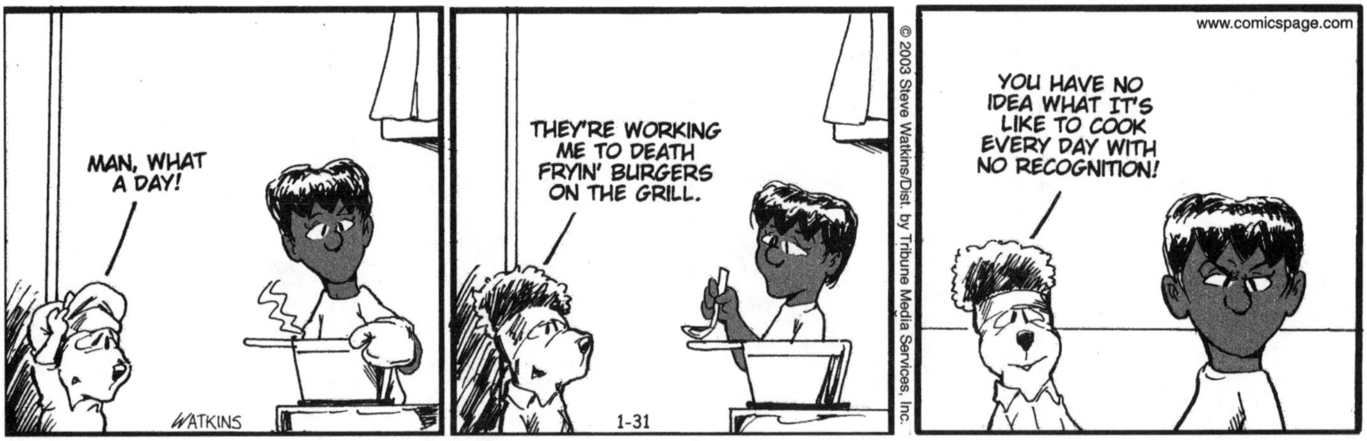
MAN, WHAT A DAY!
WATKINS
THEY'RE WORKING ME TO DEATH FRYIN' BURGERS ON THE GRILL.
1-31
© 2003 Steve Watkins/Dist. by Tribune Media Services, Inc.
www.comicspage.com
YOU HAVE NO IDEA WHAT IT'S LIKE TO COOK EVERY DAY WITH NO RECOGNITION!

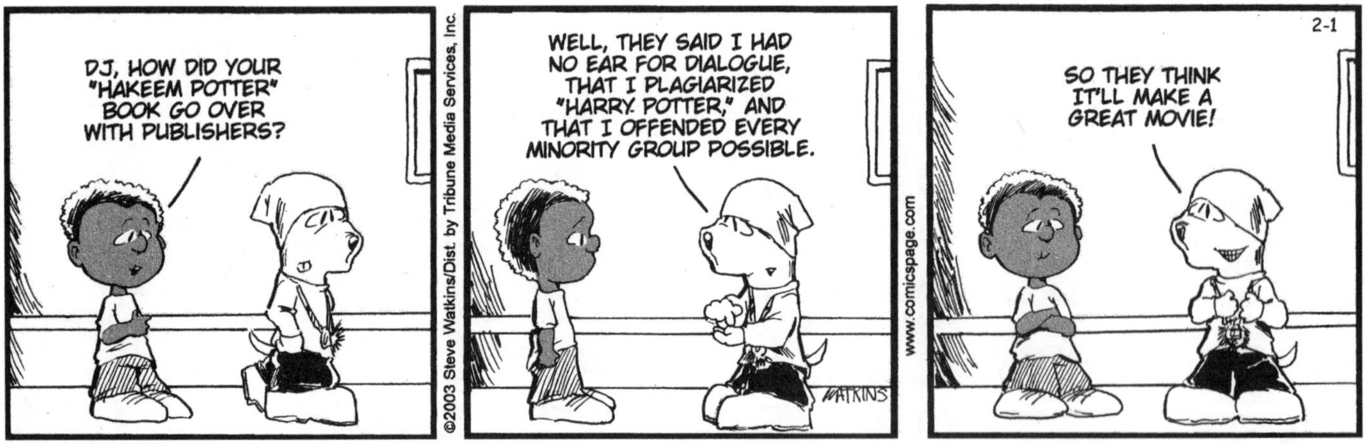
DJ, HOW DID YOUR "HAKEEM POTTER" BOOK GO OVER WITH PUBLISHERS?
©2003 Steve Watkins/Dist. by Tribune Media Services, Inc.
WELL, THEY SAID I HAD NO EAR FOR DIALOGUE, THAT I PLAGIARIZED "HARRY POTTER," AND THAT I OFFENDED EVERY MINORITY GROUP POSSIBLE.
WATKINS
www.comicspage.com
2-1
SO THEY THINK IT'LL MAKE A GREAT MOVIE!

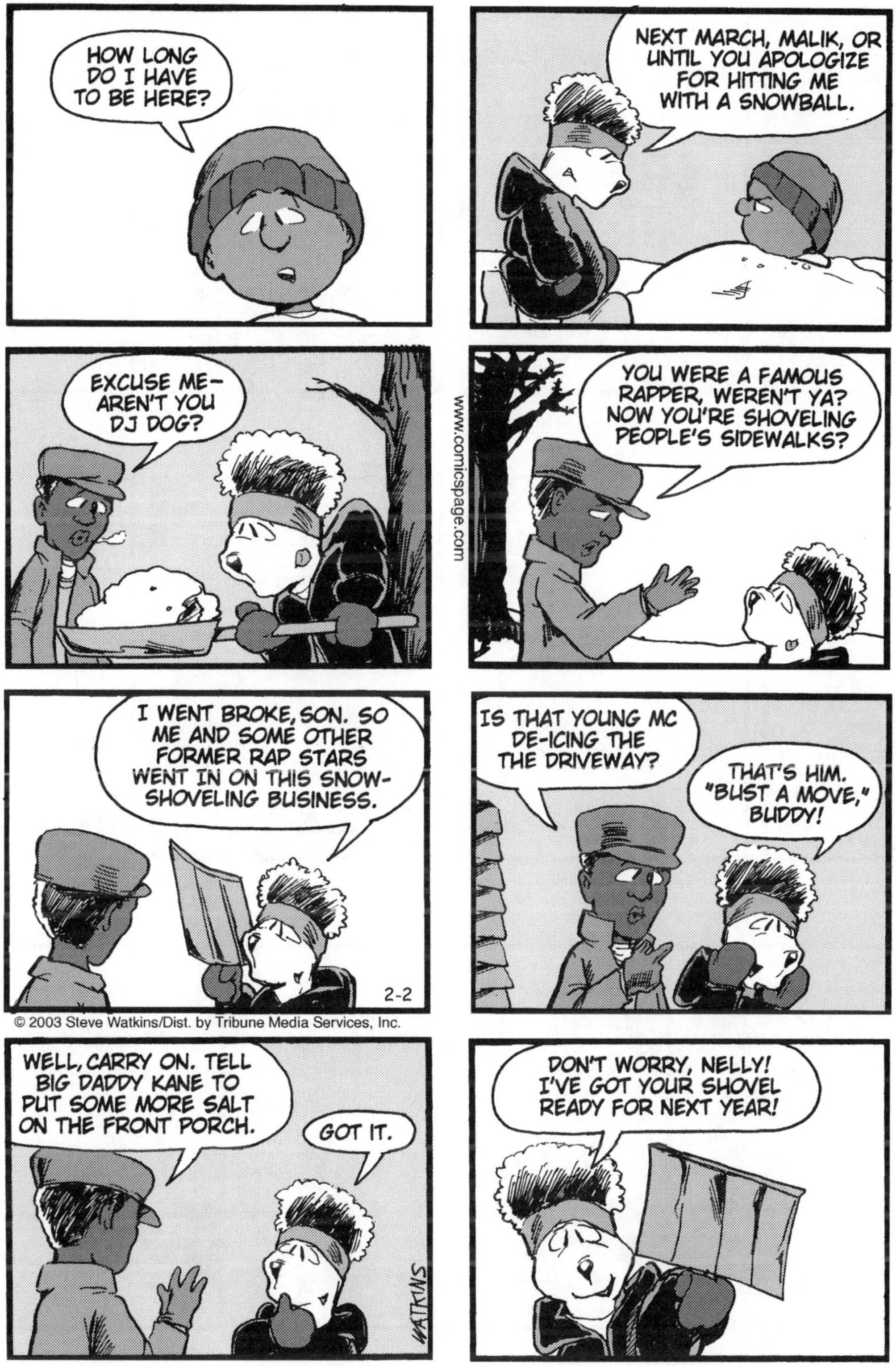
HOW LONG DO I HAVE TO BE HERE?
NEXT MARCH, MALIK, OR UNTIL YOU APOLOGIZE FOR HITTING ME WITH A SNOWBALL.
EXCUSE ME— AREN'T YOU DJ DOG?
YOU WERE A FAMOUS RAPPER, WEREN'T YA? NOW YOU'RE SHOVELING PEOPLE'S SIDEWALKS?
www.comicspage.com
I WENT BROKE, SON. SO ME AND SOME OTHER FORMER RAP STARS WENT IN ON THIS SNOW-SHOVELING BUSINESS.
2-2
IS THAT YOUNG MC DE-ICING THE THE DRIVEWAY?
THAT'S HIM. "BUST A MOVE," BUDDY!
WELL, CARRY ON. TELL BIG DADDY KANE TO PUT SOME MORE SALT ON THE FRONT PORCH.
GOT IT.
WATKINS
DON'T WORRY, NELLY! I'VE GOT YOUR SHOVEL READY FOR NEXT YEAR!

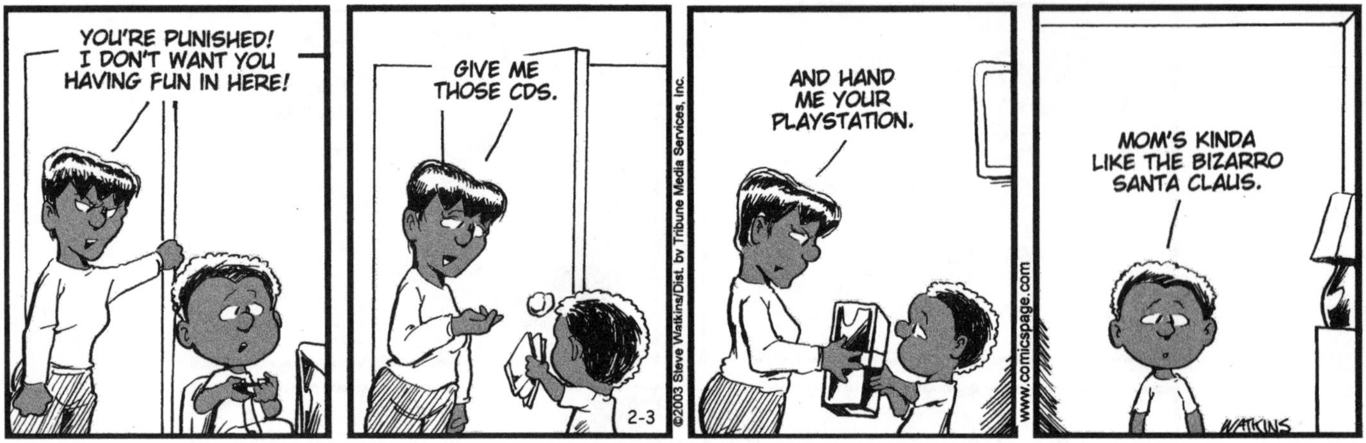
YOU'RE PUNISHED! I DON'T WANT YOU HAVING FUN IN HERE!
GIVE ME THOSE CDS.
2-3
©2003 Steve Watkins/Dist. by Tribune Media Services, Inc.
AND HAND ME YOUR PLAYSTATION.
www.comicspage.com
MOM'S KINDA LIKE THE BIZARRO SANTA CLAUS.
WATKINS

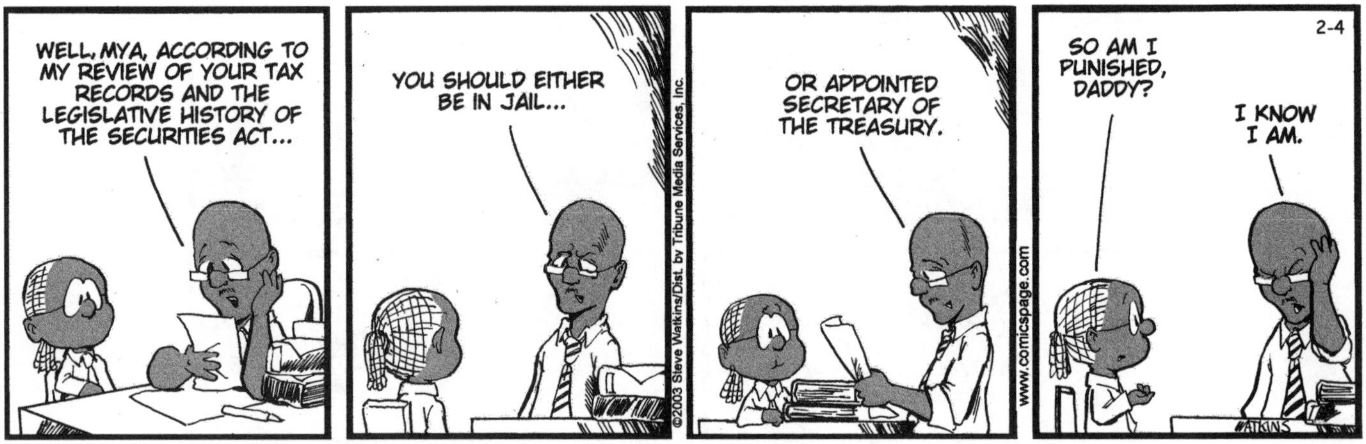
WELL, MYA, ACCORDING TO MY REVIEW OF YOUR TAX RECORDS AND THE LEGISLATIVE HISTORY OF THE SECURITIES ACT...
YOU SHOULD EITHER BE IN JAIL...
©2003 Steve Watkins/Dist. by Tribune Media Services, Inc.
OR APPOINTED SECRETARY OF THE TREASURY.
www.comicspage.com
2-4
SO AM I PUNISHED, DADDY?
I KNOW I AM.
WATKINS

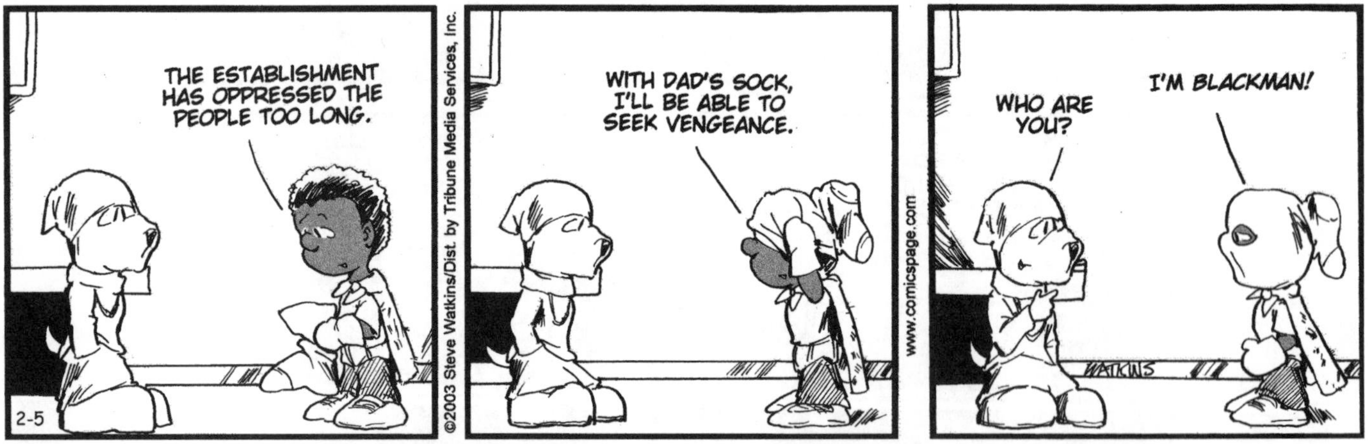
THE ESTABLISHMENT HAS OPPRESSED THE PEOPLE TOO LONG.
2-5
©2003 Steve Watkins/Dist. by Tribune Media Services, Inc.
WITH DAD'S SOCK, I'LL BE ABLE TO SEEK VENGEANCE.
www.comicspage.com
WHO ARE YOU?
I'M *BLACKMAN!*
WATKINS

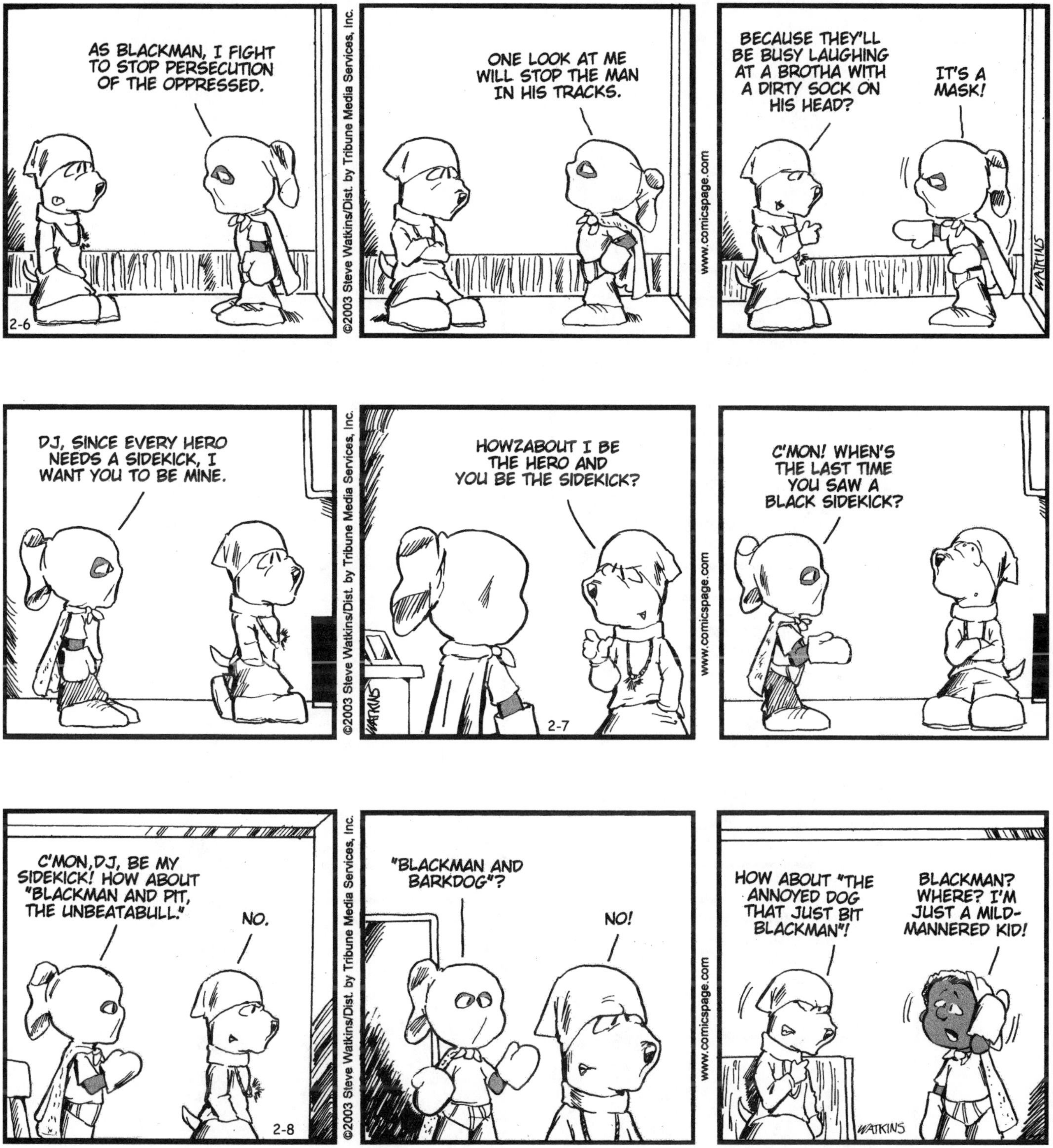

AS BLACKMAN, I FIGHT TO STOP PERSECUTION OF THE OPPRESSED.
2-6
©2003 Steve Watkins/Dist. by Tribune Media Services, Inc.
ONE LOOK AT ME WILL STOP THE MAN IN HIS TRACKS.
www.comicspage.com
BECAUSE THEY'LL BE BUSY LAUGHING AT A BROTHA WITH A DIRTY SOCK ON HIS HEAD?
IT'S A MASK!
WATKINS
DJ, SINCE EVERY HERO NEEDS A SIDEKICK, I WANT YOU TO BE MINE.
©2003 Steve Watkins/Dist. by Tribune Media Services, Inc.
HOWZABOUT I BE THE HERO AND YOU BE THE SIDEKICK?
WATKINS
2-7
www.comicspage.com
C'MON! WHEN'S THE LAST TIME YOU SAW A BLACK SIDEKICK?
C'MON, DJ, BE MY SIDEKICK! HOW ABOUT "BLACKMAN AND PIT, THE UNBEATABULL."
NO.
2-8
©2003 Steve Watkins/Dist. by Tribune Media Services, Inc.
"BLACKMAN AND BARKDOG"?
NO!
www.comicspage.com
HOW ABOUT "THE ANNOYED DOG THAT JUST BIT BLACKMAN"!
BLACKMAN? WHERE? I'M JUST A MILD-MANNERED KID!
WATKINS

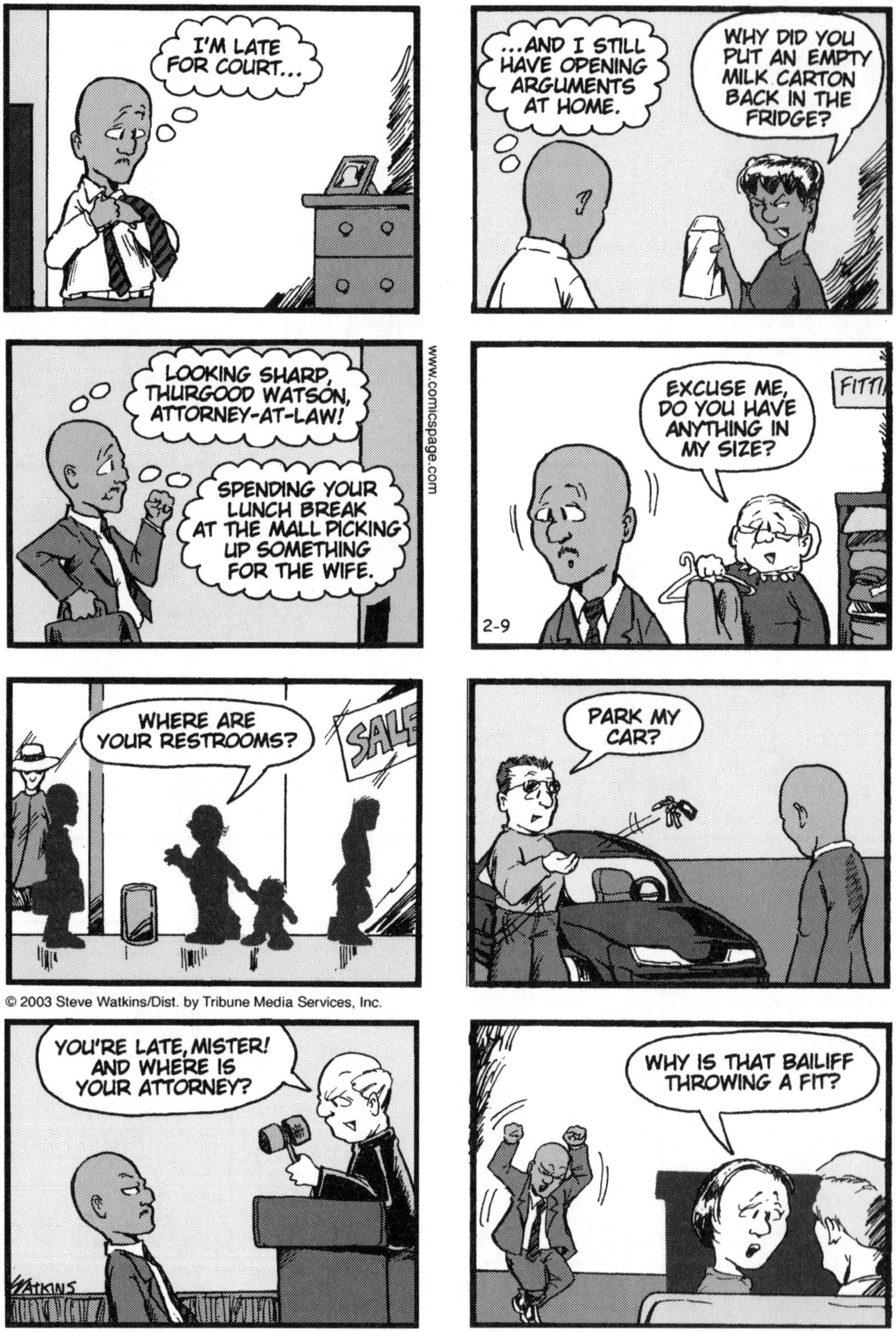
I'M LATE FOR COURT...
...AND I STILL HAVE OPENING ARGUMENTS AT HOME.
WHY DID YOU PUT AN EMPTY MILK CARTON BACK IN THE FRIDGE?
LOOKING SHARP, THURGOOD WATSON, ATTORNEY-AT-LAW!
SPENDING YOUR LUNCH BREAK AT THE MALL PICKING UP SOMETHING FOR THE WIFE.
EXCUSE ME, DO YOU HAVE ANYTHING IN MY SIZE?
2-9
www.comicspage.com
WHERE ARE YOUR RESTROOMS?
PARK MY CAR?
YOU'RE LATE, MISTER! AND WHERE IS YOUR ATTORNEY?
WATKINS
WHY IS THAT BAILIFF THROWING A FIT?

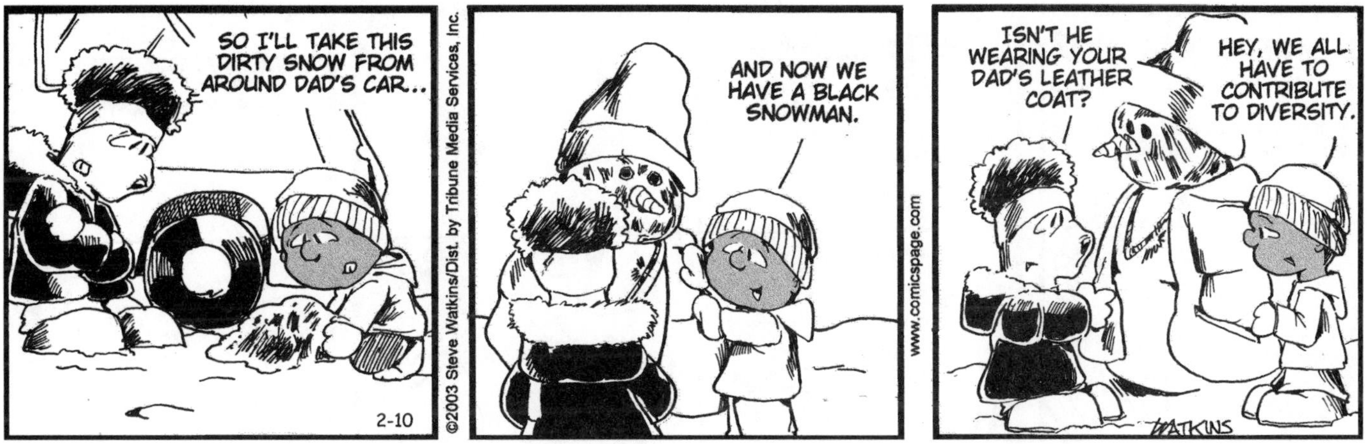
SO I'LL TAKE THIS DIRTY SNOW FROM AROUND DAD'S CAR...
2-10
©2003 Steve Watkins/Dist. by Tribune Media Services, Inc.
AND NOW WE HAVE A BLACK SNOWMAN.
www.comicspage.com
ISN'T HE WEARING YOUR DAD'S LEATHER COAT?
HEY, WE ALL HAVE TO CONTRIBUTE TO DIVERSITY.
WATKINS

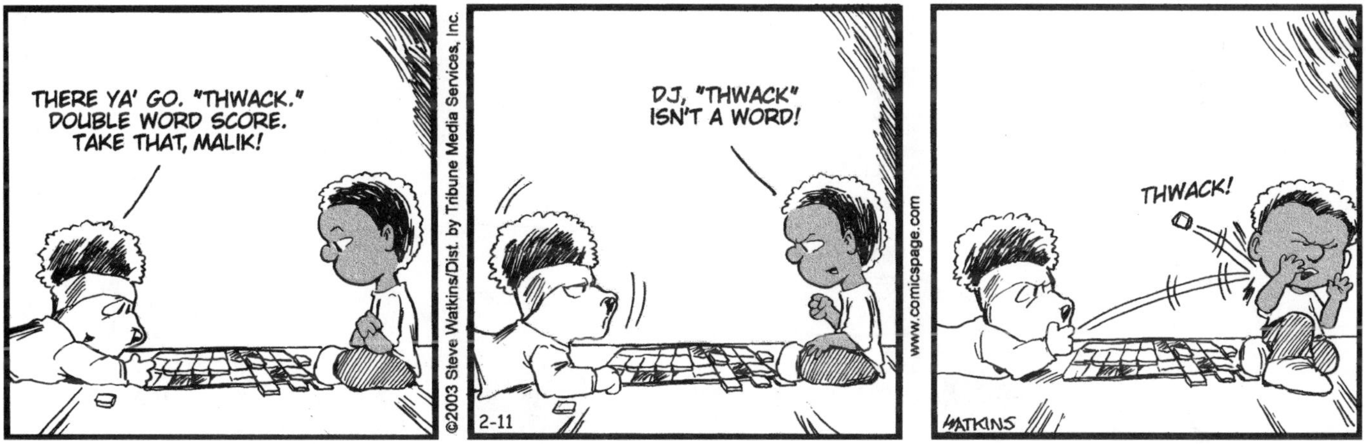
THERE YA' GO. "THWACK." DOUBLE WORD SCORE. TAKE THAT, MALIK!
©2003 Steve Watkins/Dist. by Tribune Media Services, Inc.
DJ, "THWACK" ISN'T A WORD!
2-11
www.comicspage.com
THWACK!
WATKINS

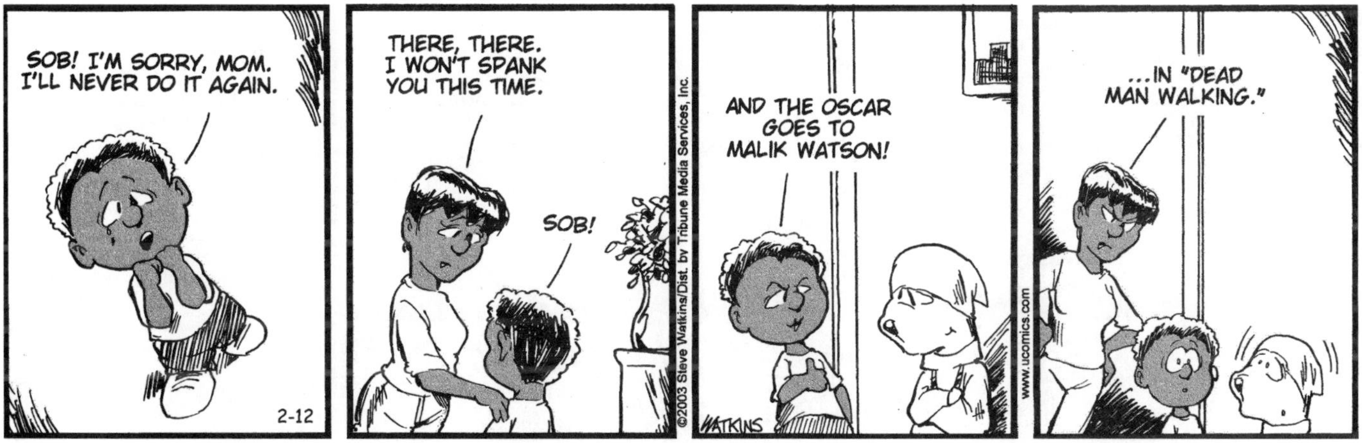
SOB! I'M SORRY, MOM. I'LL NEVER DO IT AGAIN.
2-12
THERE, THERE. I WON'T SPANK YOU THIS TIME.
SOB!
©2003 Steve Watkins/Dist. by Tribune Media Services, Inc.
AND THE OSCAR GOES TO MALIK WATSON!
WATKINS
www.ucomics.com
...IN "DEAD MAN WALKING."

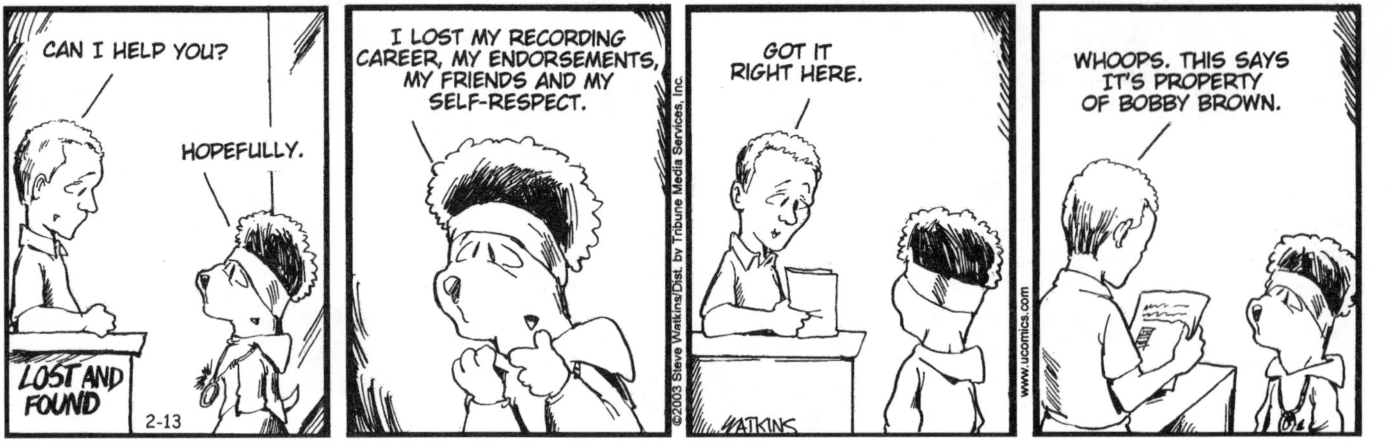
CAN I HELP YOU?
HOPEFULLY.
LOST AND FOUND
2-13
I LOST MY RECORDING CAREER, MY ENDORSEMENTS, MY FRIENDS AND MY SELF-RESPECT.
©2003 Steve Watkins/Dist. by Tribune Media Services, Inc.
GOT IT RIGHT HERE.
WATKINS
www.ucomics.com
WHOOPS. THIS SAYS IT'S PROPERTY OF BOBBY BROWN.

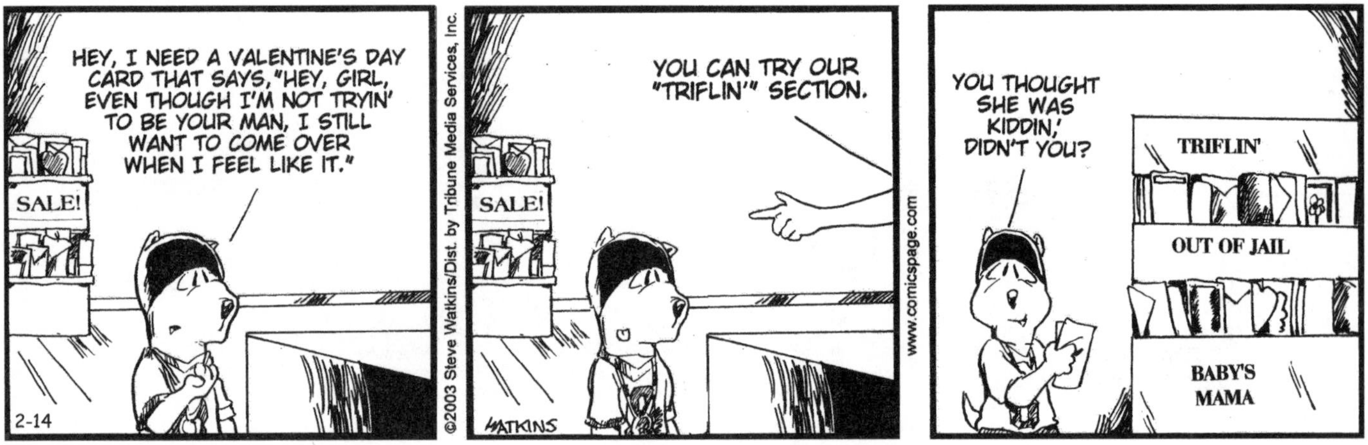
HEY, I NEED A VALENTINE'S DAY CARD THAT SAYS, "HEY, GIRL, EVEN THOUGH I'M NOT TRYIN' TO BE YOUR MAN, I STILL WANT TO COME OVER WHEN I FEEL LIKE IT."
SALE!
2-14
©2003 Steve Watkins/Dist. by Tribune Media Services, Inc.
YOU CAN TRY OUR "TRIFLIN'" SECTION.
SALE!
WATKINS
www.comicspage.com
YOU THOUGHT SHE WAS KIDDIN,' DIDN'T YOU?
TRIFLIN'
OUT OF JAIL
BABY'S MAMA

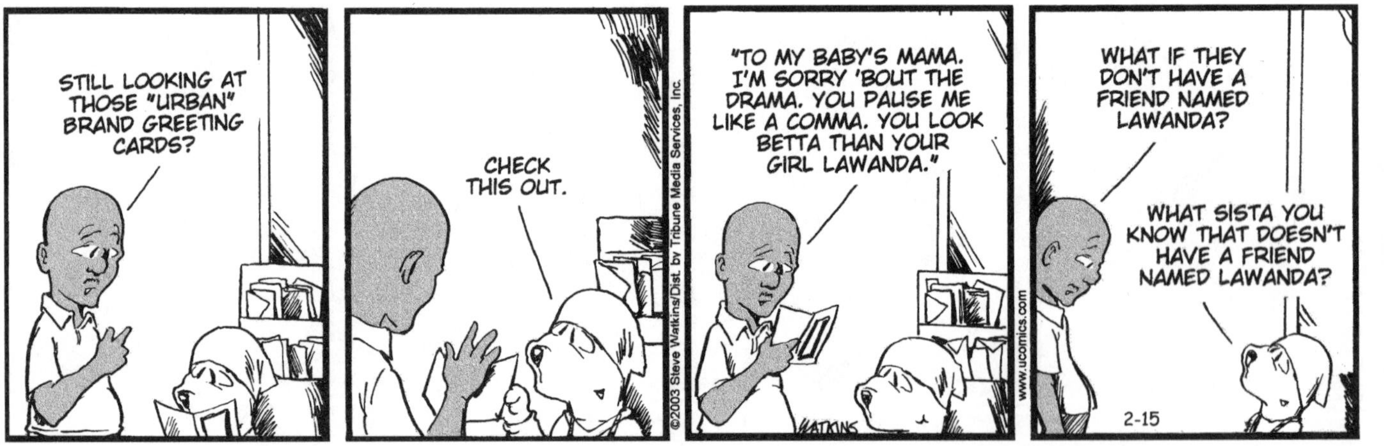
STILL LOOKING AT THOSE "URBAN" BRAND GREETING CARDS?
CHECK THIS OUT.
©2003 Steve Watkins/Dist. by Tribune Media Services, Inc.
"TO MY BABY'S MAMA. I'M SORRY 'BOUT THE DRAMA. YOU PAUSE ME LIKE A COMMA. YOU LOOK BETTA THAN YOUR GIRL LAWANDA."
WATKINS
www.ucomics.com
WHAT IF THEY DON'T HAVE A FRIEND NAMED LAWANDA?
WHAT SISTA YOU KNOW THAT DOESN'T HAVE A FRIEND NAMED LAWANDA?
2-15

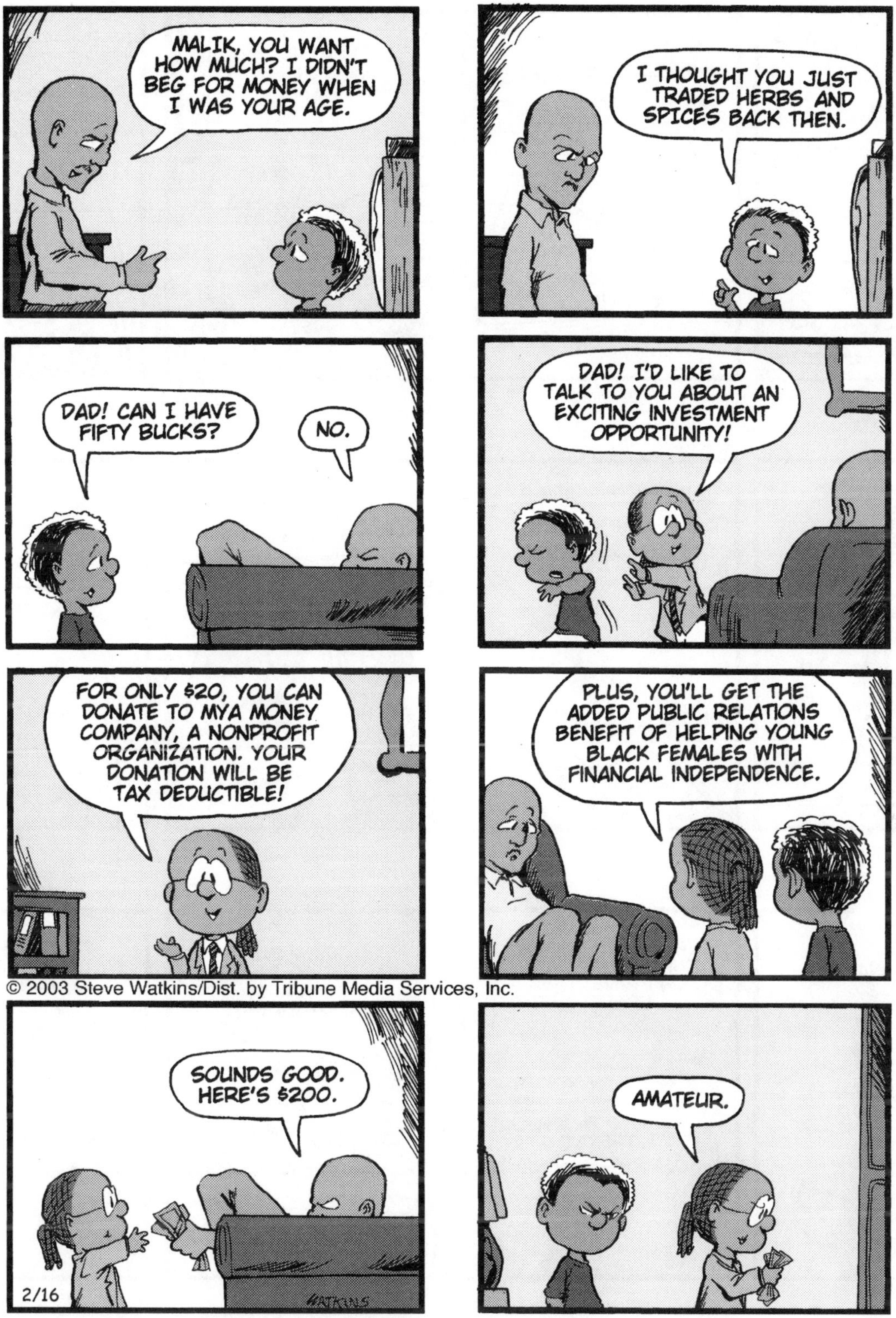
MALIK, YOU WANT HOW MUCH? I DIDN'T BEG FOR MONEY WHEN I WAS YOUR AGE.
I THOUGHT YOU JUST TRADED HERBS AND SPICES BACK THEN.
DAD! CAN I HAVE FIFTY BUCKS?
NO.
DAD! I'D LIKE TO TALK TO YOU ABOUT AN EXCITING INVESTMENT OPPORTUNITY!
FOR ONLY $20, YOU CAN DONATE TO MYA MONEY COMPANY, A NONPROFIT ORGANIZATION. YOUR DONATION WILL BE TAX DEDUCTIBLE!
PLUS, YOU'LL GET THE ADDED PUBLIC RELATIONS BENEFIT OF HELPING YOUNG BLACK FEMALES WITH FINANCIAL INDEPENDENCE.
SOUNDS GOOD. HERE'S $200.
AMATEUR.
2/16

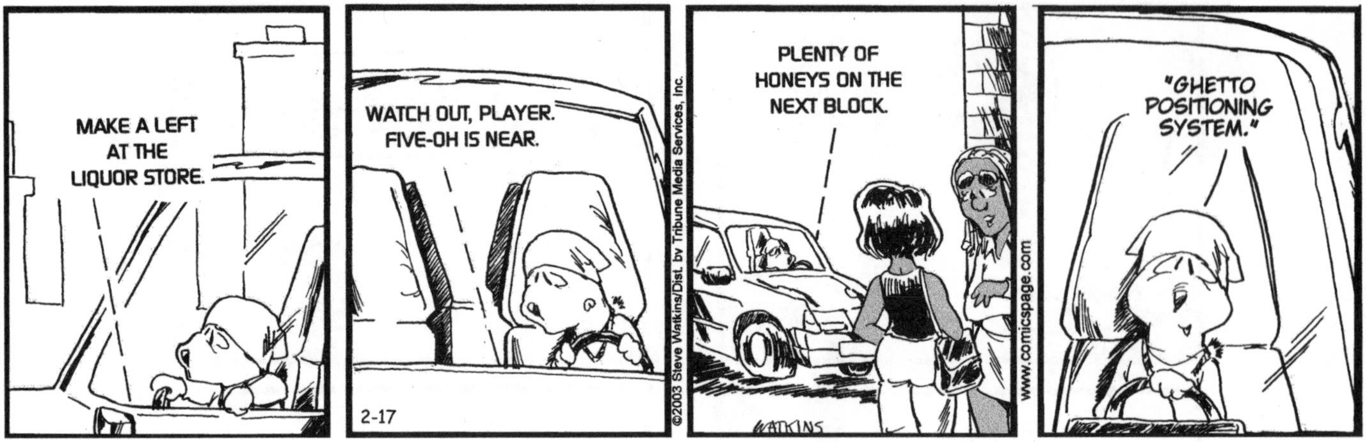

MAKE A LEFT AT THE LIQUOR STORE.
WATCH OUT, PLAYER. FIVE-OH IS NEAR.
2-17
©2003 Steve Watkins/Dist. by Tribune Media Services, Inc.
PLENTY OF HONEYS ON THE NEXT BLOCK.
WATKINS
www.comicspage.com
"GHETTO POSITIONING SYSTEM."

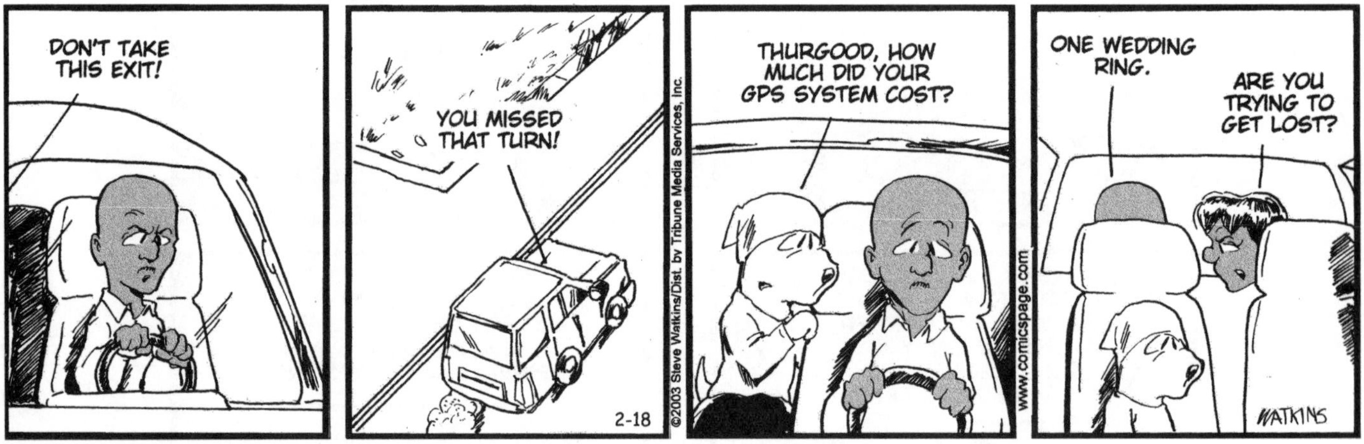

DON'T TAKE THIS EXIT!
YOU MISSED THAT TURN!
2-18
©2003 Steve Watkins/Dist. by Tribune Media Services, Inc.
THURGOOD, HOW MUCH DID YOUR GPS SYSTEM COST?
www.comicspage.com
ONE WEDDING RING.
ARE YOU TRYING TO GET LOST?
WATKINS

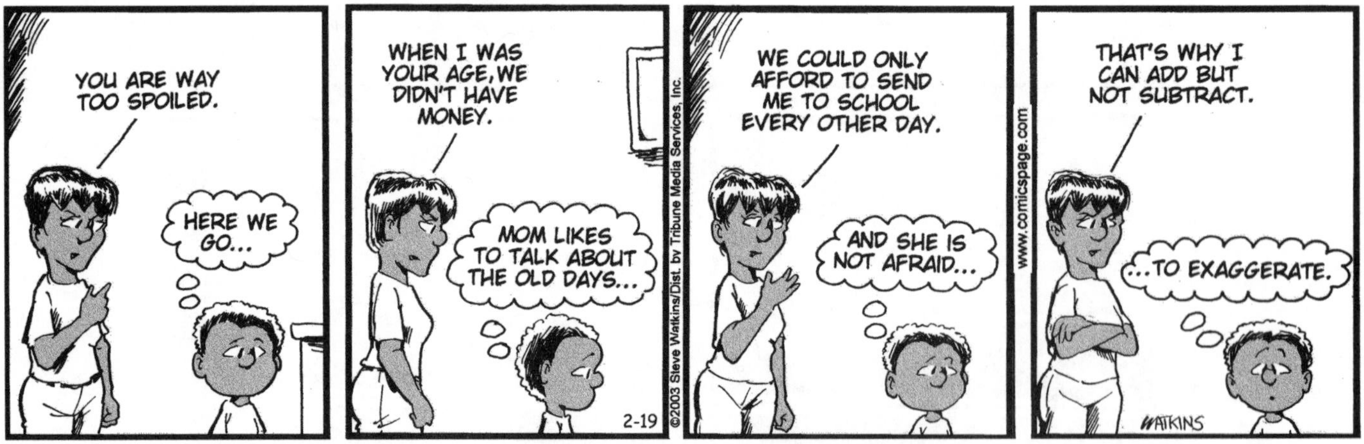

YOU ARE WAY TOO SPOILED.
HERE WE GO...
WHEN I WAS YOUR AGE, WE DIDN'T HAVE MONEY.
MOM LIKES TO TALK ABOUT THE OLD DAYS...
2-19
©2003 Steve Watkins/Dist. by Tribune Media Services, Inc.
WE COULD ONLY AFFORD TO SEND ME TO SCHOOL EVERY OTHER DAY.
AND SHE IS NOT AFRAID...
www.comicspage.com
THAT'S WHY I CAN ADD BUT NOT SUBTRACT.
...TO EXAGGERATE.
WATKINS

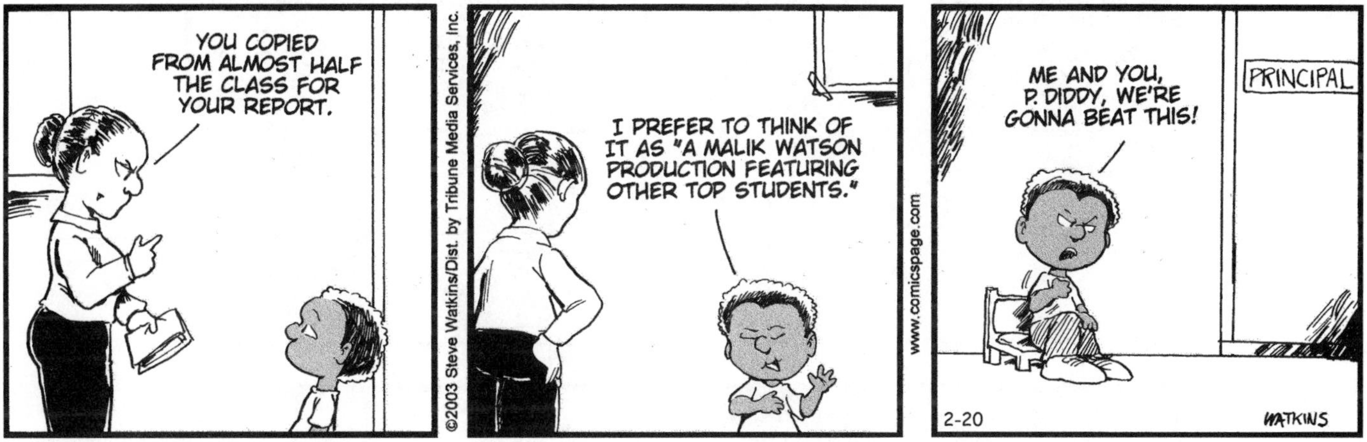
YOU COPIED FROM ALMOST HALF THE CLASS FOR YOUR REPORT.
I PREFER TO THINK OF IT AS "A MALIK WATSON PRODUCTION FEATURING OTHER TOP STUDENTS."
PRINCIPAL
ME AND YOU, P. DIDDY, WE'RE GONNA BEAT THIS!
2-20
WATKINS
©2003 Steve Watkins/Dist. by Tribune Media Services, Inc.
www.comicspage.com

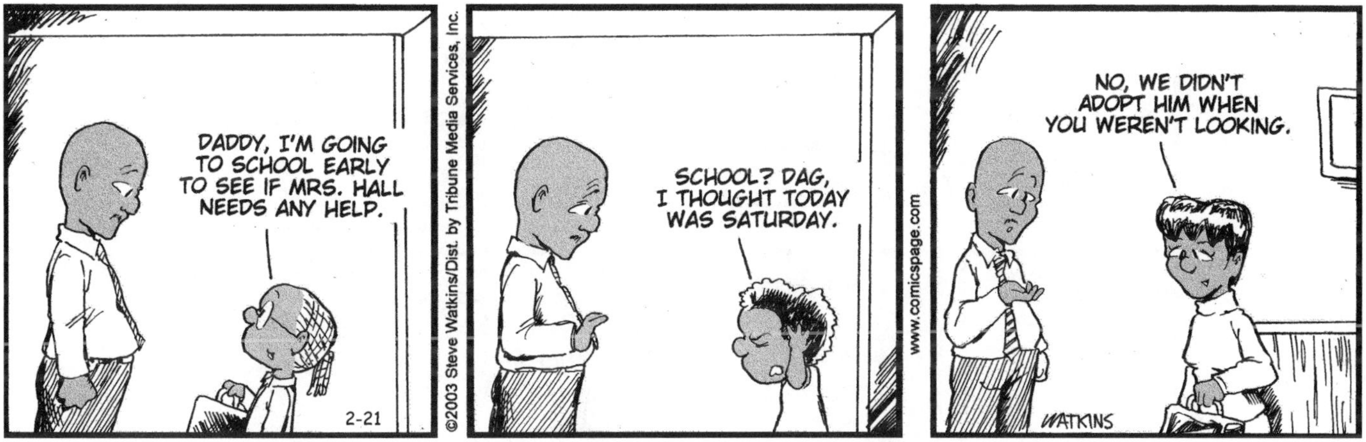
DADDY, I'M GOING TO SCHOOL EARLY TO SEE IF MRS. HALL NEEDS ANY HELP.
2-21
SCHOOL? DAG, I THOUGHT TODAY WAS SATURDAY.
NO, WE DIDN'T ADOPT HIM WHEN YOU WEREN'T LOOKING.
WATKINS
©2003 Steve Watkins/Dist. by Tribune Media Services, Inc.
www.comicspage.com

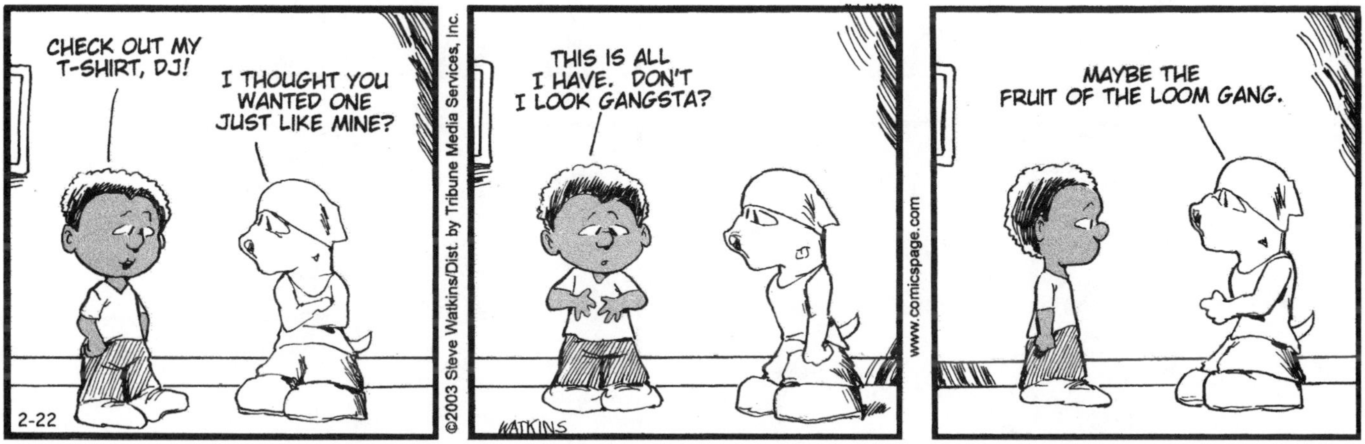
CHECK OUT MY T-SHIRT, DJ!
I THOUGHT YOU WANTED ONE JUST LIKE MINE?
2-22
THIS IS ALL I HAVE. DON'T I LOOK GANGSTA?
WATKINS
MAYBE THE FRUIT OF THE LOOM GANG.
©2003 Steve Watkins/Dist. by Tribune Media Services, Inc.
www.comicspage.com

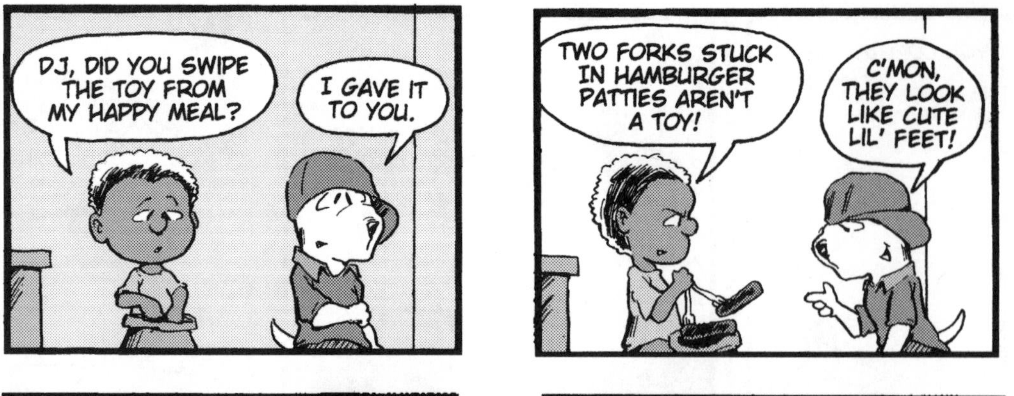
DJ, DID YOU SWIPE THE TOY FROM MY HAPPY MEAL?
I GAVE IT TO YOU.
TWO FORKS STUCK IN HAMBURGER PATTIES AREN'T A TOY!
C'MON, THEY LOOK LIKE CUTE LIL' FEET!

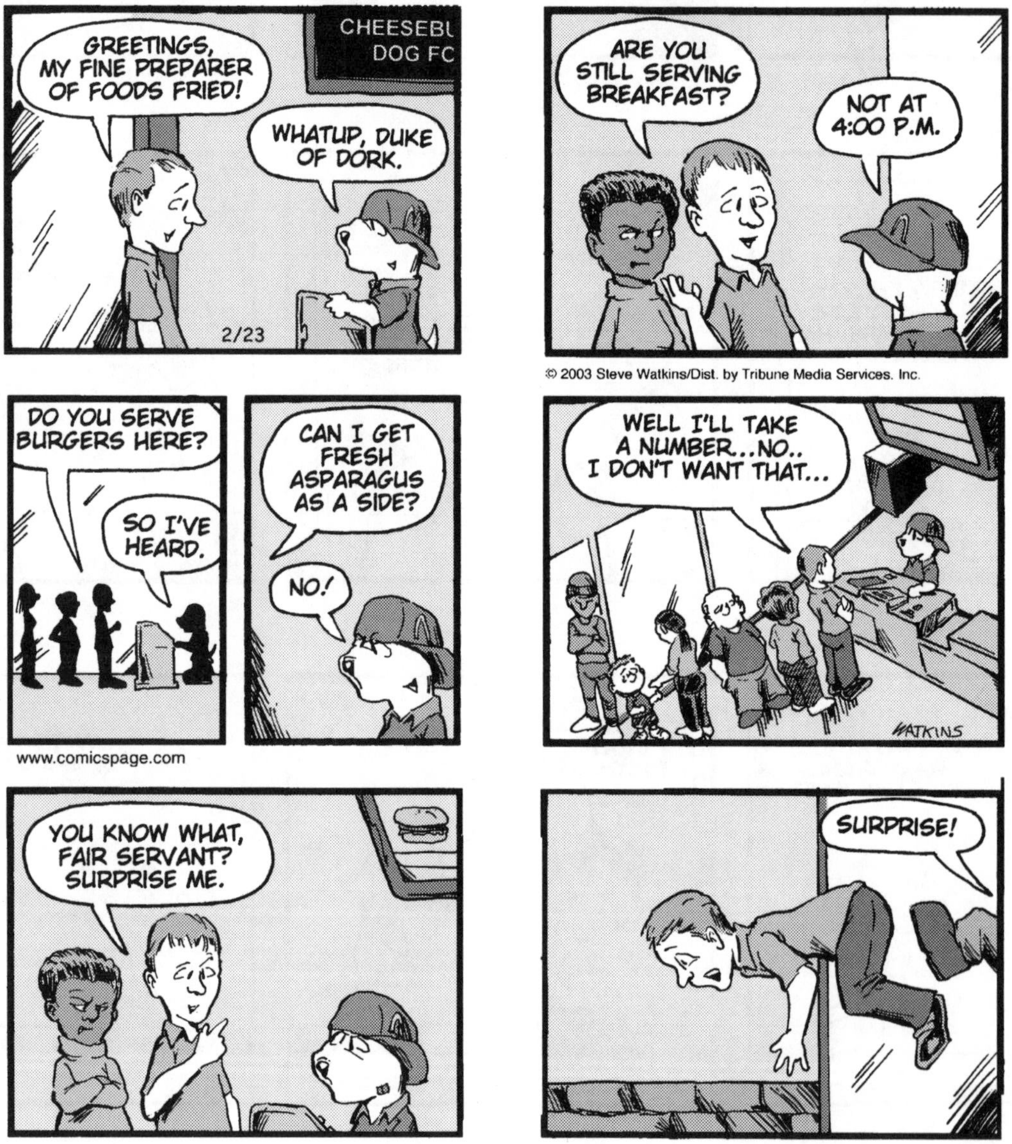
CHEESEBU
DOG FC
GREETINGS, MY FINE PREPARER OF FOODS FRIED!
WHATUP, DUKE OF DORK.
2/23
ARE YOU STILL SERVING BREAKFAST?
NOT AT 4:00 P.M.
© 2003 Steve Watkins/Dist. by Tribune Media Services, Inc.
DO YOU SERVE BURGERS HERE?
SO I'VE HEARD.
CAN I GET FRESH ASPARAGUS AS A SIDE?
NO!
WELL I'LL TAKE A NUMBER...NO.. I DON'T WANT THAT...
WATKINS
www.comicspage.com
YOU KNOW WHAT, FAIR SERVANT? SURPRISE ME.
SURPRISE!

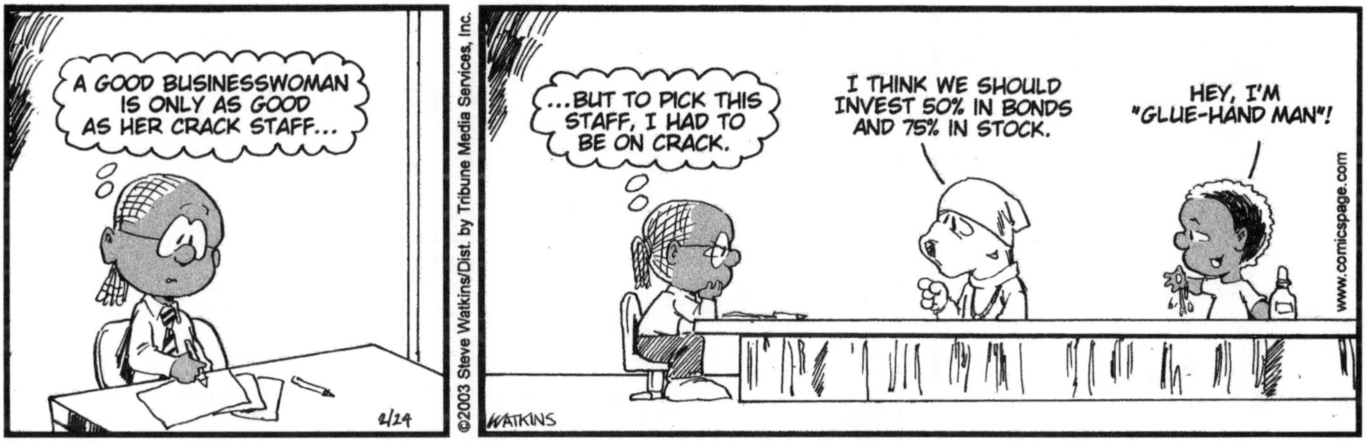
A GOOD BUSINESSWOMAN IS ONLY AS GOOD AS HER CRACK STAFF...
2/24
©2003 Steve Watkins/Dist. by Tribune Media Services, Inc.
...BUT TO PICK THIS STAFF, I HAD TO BE ON CRACK.
I THINK WE SHOULD INVEST 50% IN BONDS AND 75% IN STOCK.
HEY, I'M "GLUE-HAND MAN"!
www.comicspage.com
WATKINS

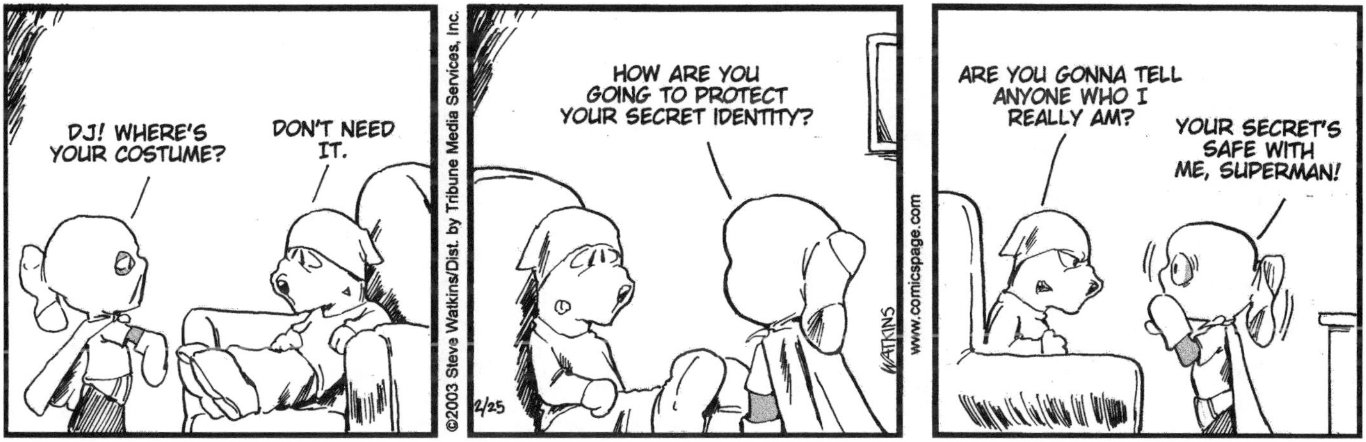
DJ! WHERE'S YOUR COSTUME?
DON'T NEED IT.
©2003 Steve Watkins/Dist. by Tribune Media Services, Inc.
2/25
HOW ARE YOU GOING TO PROTECT YOUR SECRET IDENTITY?
WATKINS
www.comicspage.com
ARE YOU GONNA TELL ANYONE WHO I REALLY AM?
YOUR SECRET'S SAFE WITH ME, SUPERMAN!

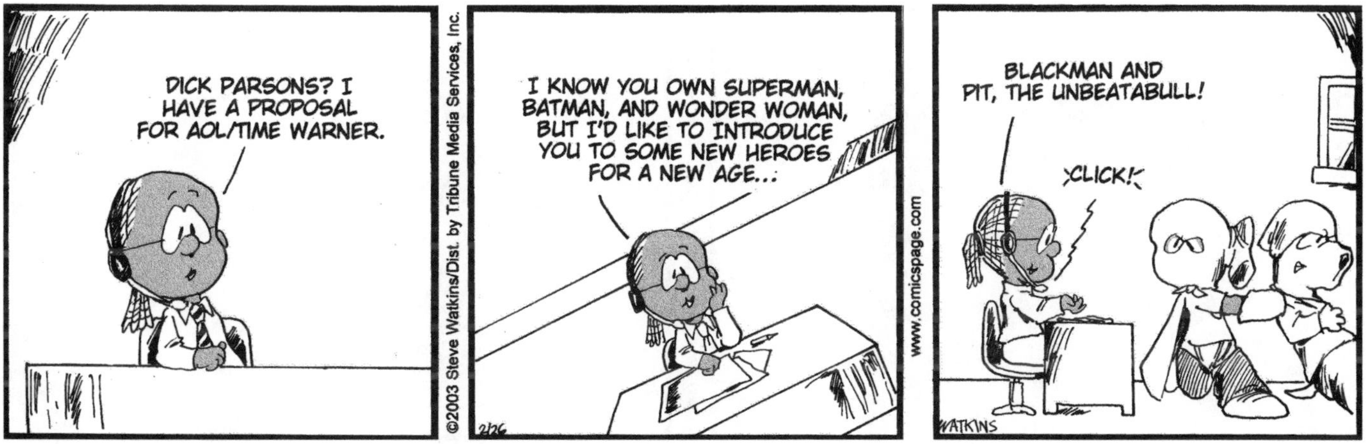
DICK PARSONS? I HAVE A PROPOSAL FOR AOL/TIME WARNER.
©2003 Steve Watkins/Dist. by Tribune Media Services, Inc.
I KNOW YOU OWN SUPERMAN, BATMAN, AND WONDER WOMAN, BUT I'D LIKE TO INTRODUCE YOU TO SOME NEW HEROES FOR A NEW AGE...
2/26
www.comicspage.com
BLACKMAN AND PIT, THE UNBEATABULL!
CLICK!
WATKINS

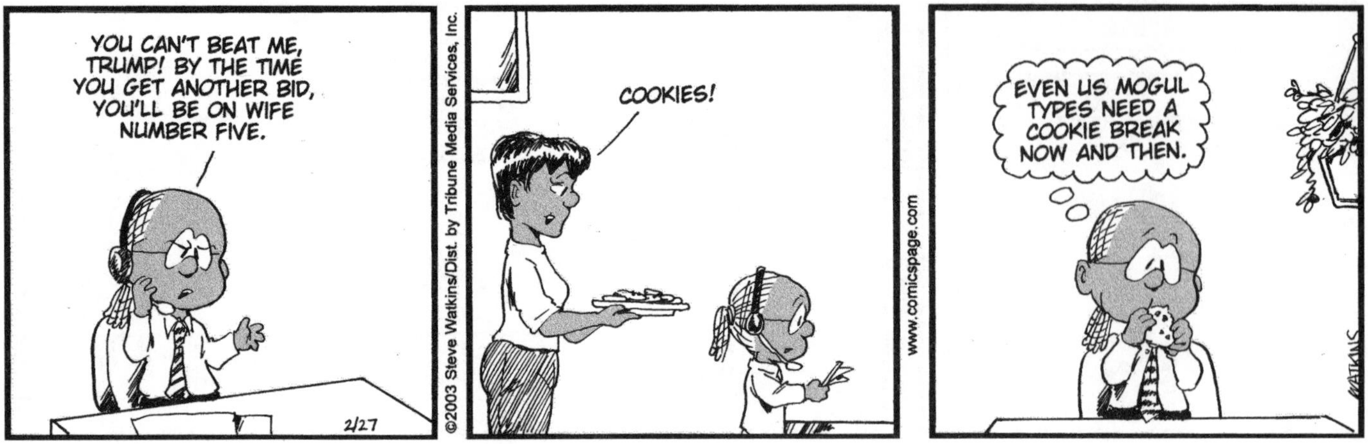
YOU CAN'T BEAT ME, TRUMP! BY THE TIME YOU GET ANOTHER BID, YOU'LL BE ON WIFE NUMBER FIVE.
2/27
©2003 Steve Watkins/Dist. by Tribune Media Services, Inc.
COOKIES!
www.comicspage.com
EVEN US MOGUL TYPES NEED A COOKIE BREAK NOW AND THEN.
WATKINS

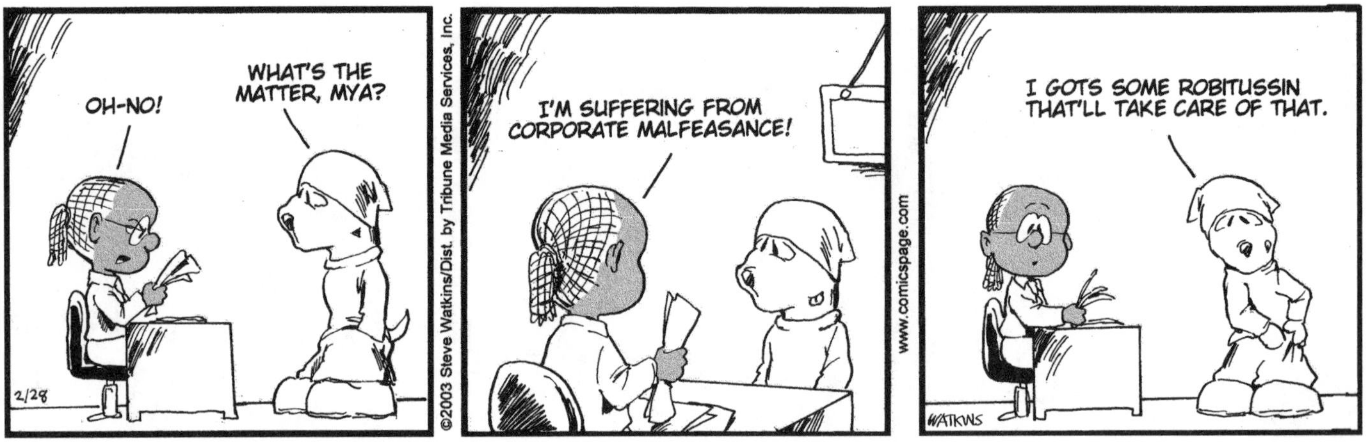
OH-NO!
WHAT'S THE MATTER, MYA?
2/28
©2003 Steve Watkins/Dist. by Tribune Media Services, Inc.
I'M SUFFERING FROM CORPORATE MALFEASANCE!
www.comicspage.com
I GOTS SOME ROBITUSSIN THAT'LL TAKE CARE OF THAT.
WATKINS

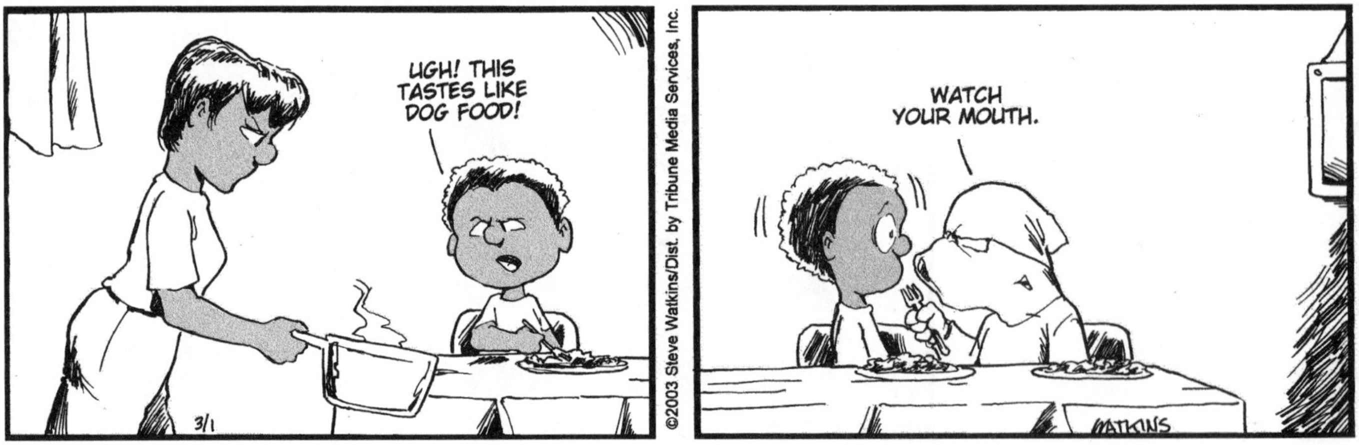
UGH! THIS TASTES LIKE DOG FOOD!
3/1
©2003 Steve Watkins/Dist. by Tribune Media Services, Inc.
WATCH YOUR MOUTH.
WATKINS

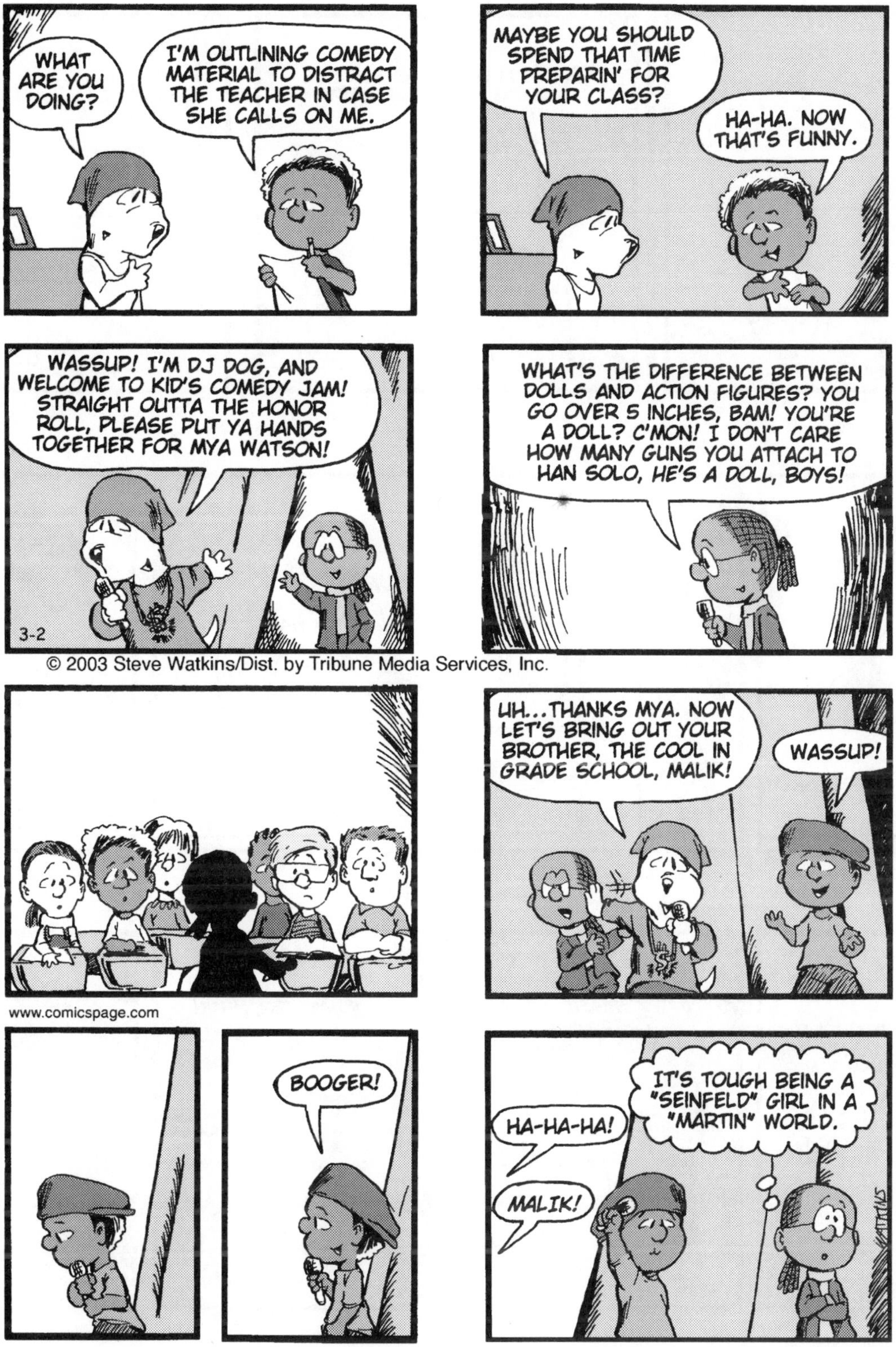
WHAT ARE YOU DOING?
I'M OUTLINING COMEDY MATERIAL TO DISTRACT THE TEACHER IN CASE SHE CALLS ON ME.
MAYBE YOU SHOULD SPEND THAT TIME PREPARIN' FOR YOUR CLASS?
HA-HA. NOW THAT'S FUNNY.
WASSUP! I'M DJ DOG, AND WELCOME TO KID'S COMEDY JAM! STRAIGHT OUTTA THE HONOR ROLL, PLEASE PUT YA HANDS TOGETHER FOR MYA WATSON!
3-2
WHAT'S THE DIFFERENCE BETWEEN DOLLS AND ACTION FIGURES? YOU GO OVER 5 INCHES, BAM! YOU'RE A DOLL? C'MON! I DON'T CARE HOW MANY GUNS YOU ATTACH TO HAN SOLO, HE'S A DOLL, BOYS!
UH...THANKS MYA. NOW LET'S BRING OUT YOUR BROTHER, THE COOL IN GRADE SCHOOL, MALIK!
WASSUP!
BOOGER!
HA-HA-HA!
MALIK!
IT'S TOUGH BEING A "SEINFELD" GIRL IN A "MARTIN" WORLD.

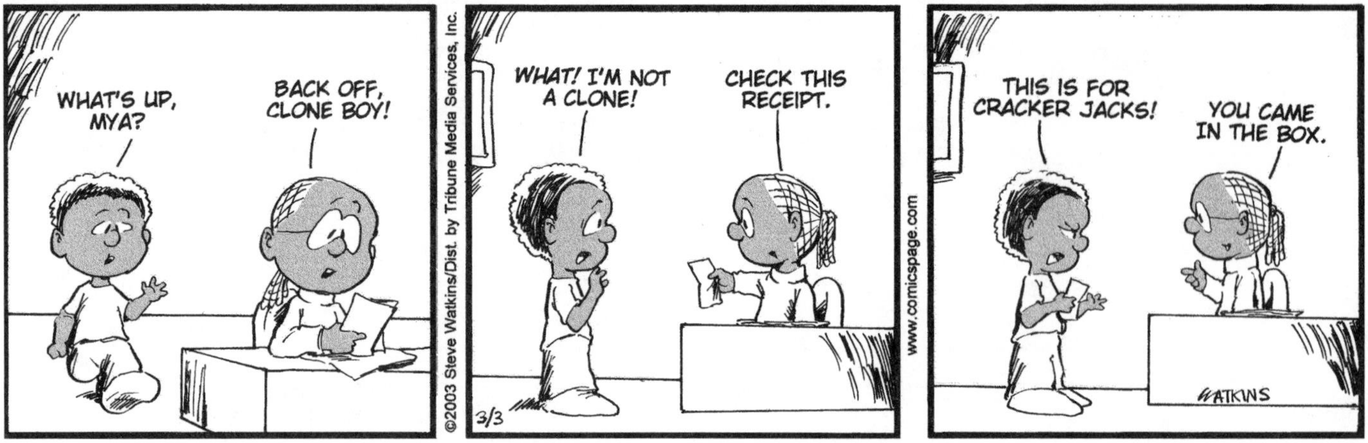
WHAT'S UP, MYA?
BACK OFF, CLONE BOY!
©2003 Steve Watkins/Dist. by Tribune Media Services, Inc.
3/3
WHAT! I'M NOT A CLONE!
CHECK THIS RECEIPT.
www.comicspage.com
THIS IS FOR CRACKER JACKS!
YOU CAME IN THE BOX.
WATKINS

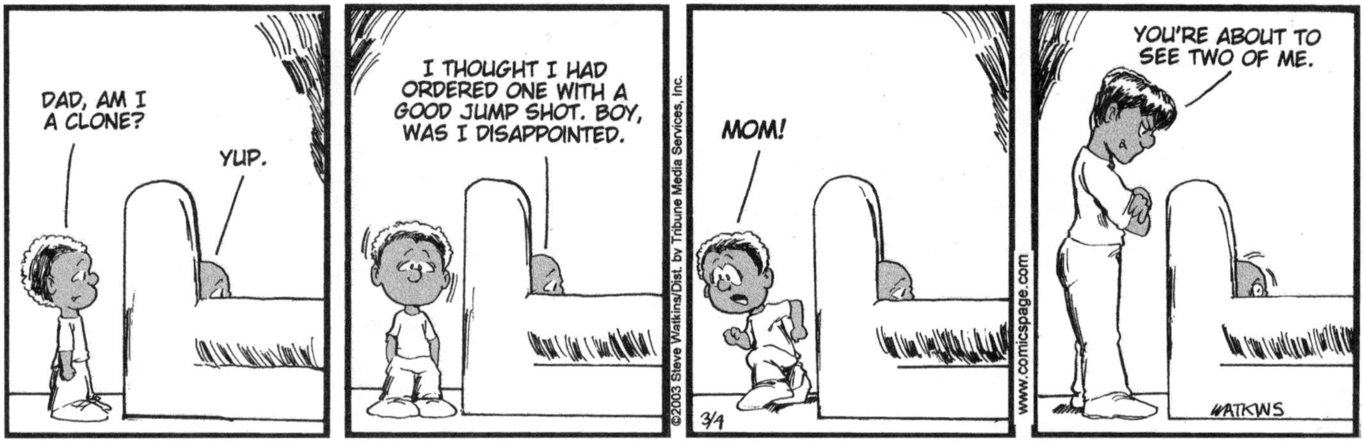
DAD, AM I A CLONE?
YUP.
I THOUGHT I HAD ORDERED ONE WITH A GOOD JUMP SHOT. BOY, WAS I DISAPPOINTED.
©2003 Steve Watkins/Dist. by Tribune Media Services, Inc.
3/4
MOM!
www.comicspage.com
YOU'RE ABOUT TO SEE TWO OF ME.
WATKINS

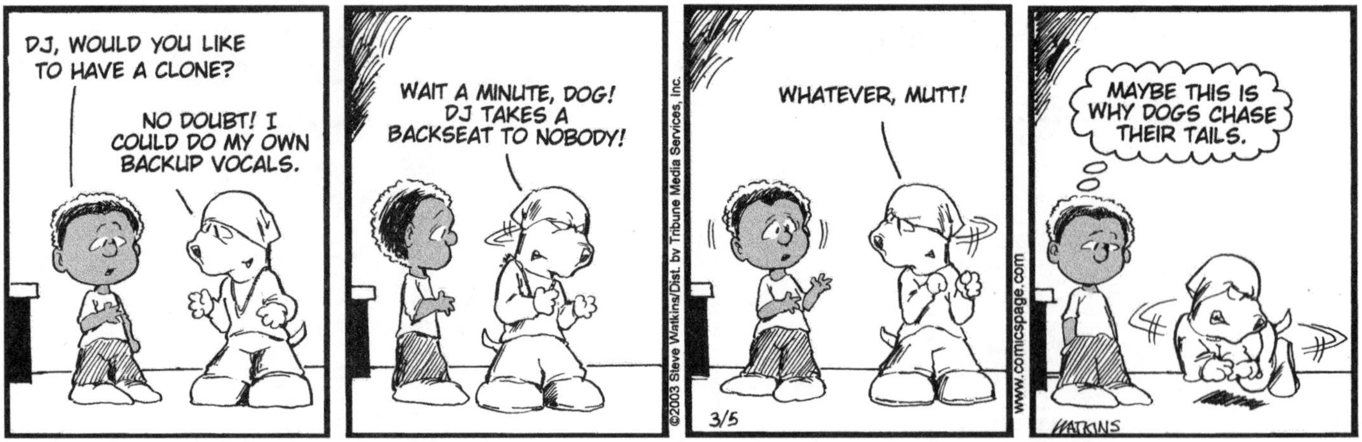
DJ, WOULD YOU LIKE TO HAVE A CLONE?
NO DOUBT! I COULD DO MY OWN BACKUP VOCALS.
WAIT A MINUTE, DOG! DJ TAKES A BACKSEAT TO NOBODY!
©2003 Steve Watkins/Dist. by Tribune Media Services, Inc.
3/5
WHATEVER, MUTT!
www.comicspage.com
MAYBE THIS IS WHY DOGS CHASE THEIR TAILS.
WATKINS

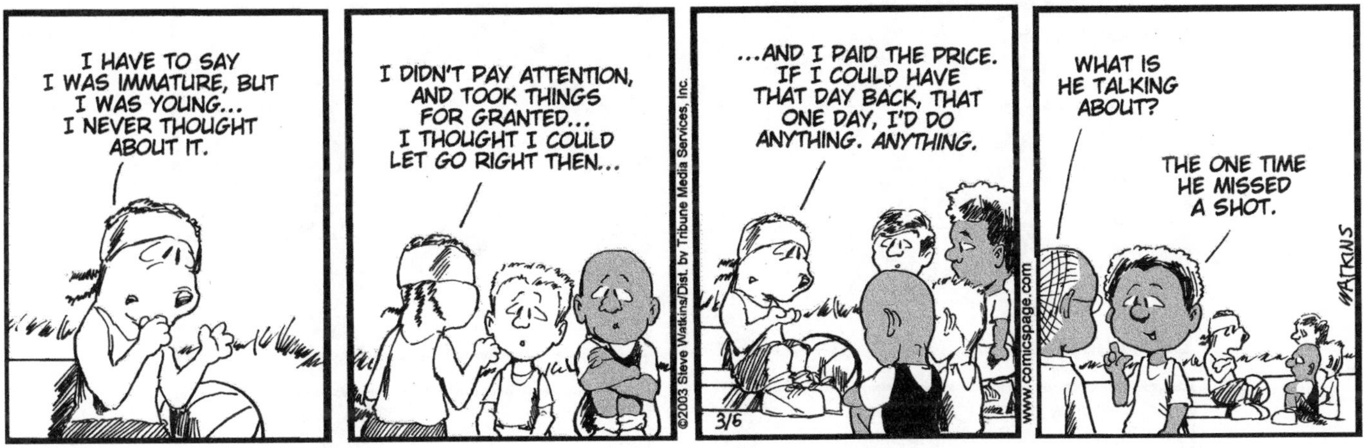
I HAVE TO SAY I WAS IMMATURE, BUT I WAS YOUNG... I NEVER THOUGHT ABOUT IT.
I DIDN'T PAY ATTENTION, AND TOOK THINGS FOR GRANTED... I THOUGHT I COULD LET GO RIGHT THEN...
©2003 Steve Watkins/Dist. by Tribune Media Services, Inc.
...AND I PAID THE PRICE. IF I COULD HAVE THAT DAY BACK, THAT ONE DAY, I'D DO ANYTHING. ANYTHING.
3/6
www.comicspage.com
WHAT IS HE TALKING ABOUT?
THE ONE TIME HE MISSED A SHOT.
WATKINS

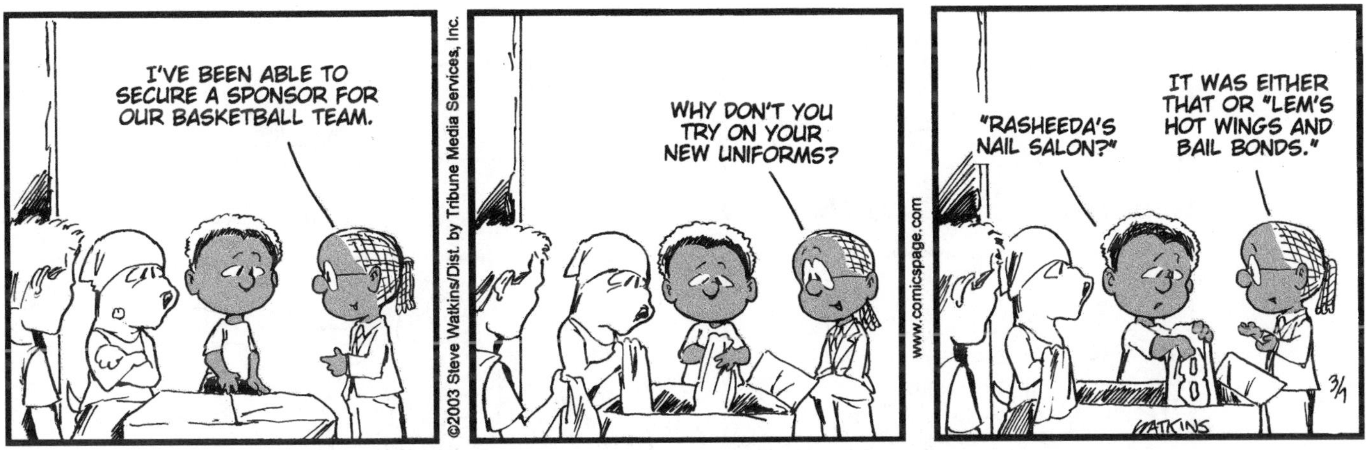
I'VE BEEN ABLE TO SECURE A SPONSOR FOR OUR BASKETBALL TEAM.
©2003 Steve Watkins/Dist. by Tribune Media Services, Inc.
WHY DON'T YOU TRY ON YOUR NEW UNIFORMS?
www.comicspage.com
"RASHEEDA'S NAIL SALON?"
IT WAS EITHER THAT OR "LEM'S HOT WINGS AND BAIL BONDS."
3/7
WATKINS

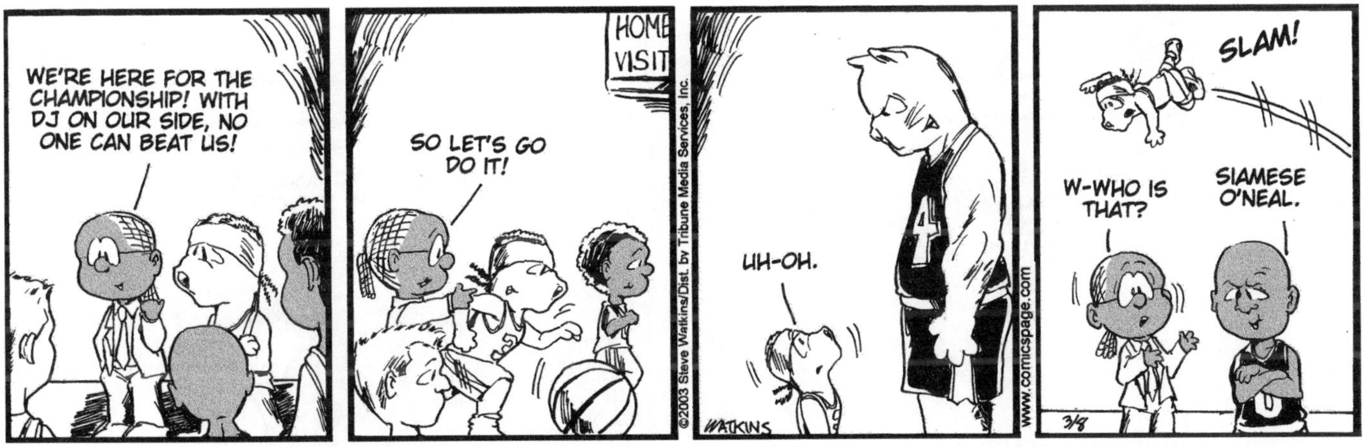
WE'RE HERE FOR THE CHAMPIONSHIP! WITH DJ ON OUR SIDE, NO ONE CAN BEAT US!
HOME
VISIT
SO LET'S GO DO IT!
©2003 Steve Watkins/Dist. by Tribune Media Services, Inc.
UH-OH.
WATKINS
www.comicspage.com
SLAM!
W-WHO IS THAT?
SIAMESE O'NEAL.
3/8

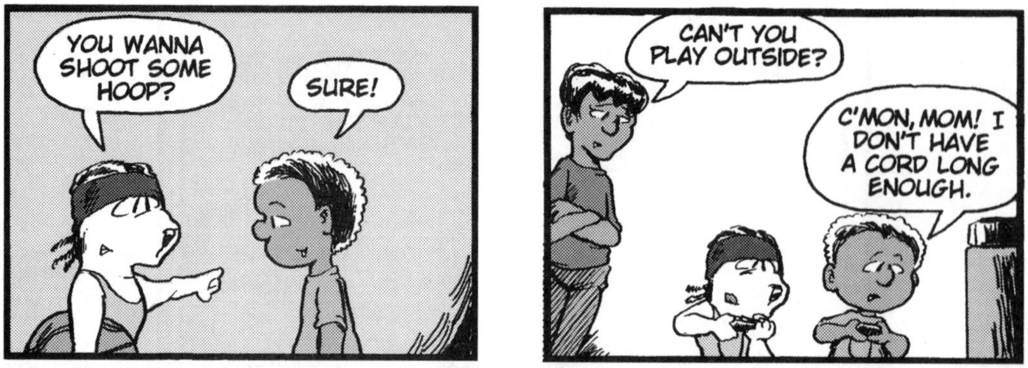
YOU WANNA SHOOT SOME HOOP?
SURE!
CAN'T YOU PLAY OUTSIDE?
C'MON, MOM! I DON'T HAVE A CORD LONG ENOUGH.

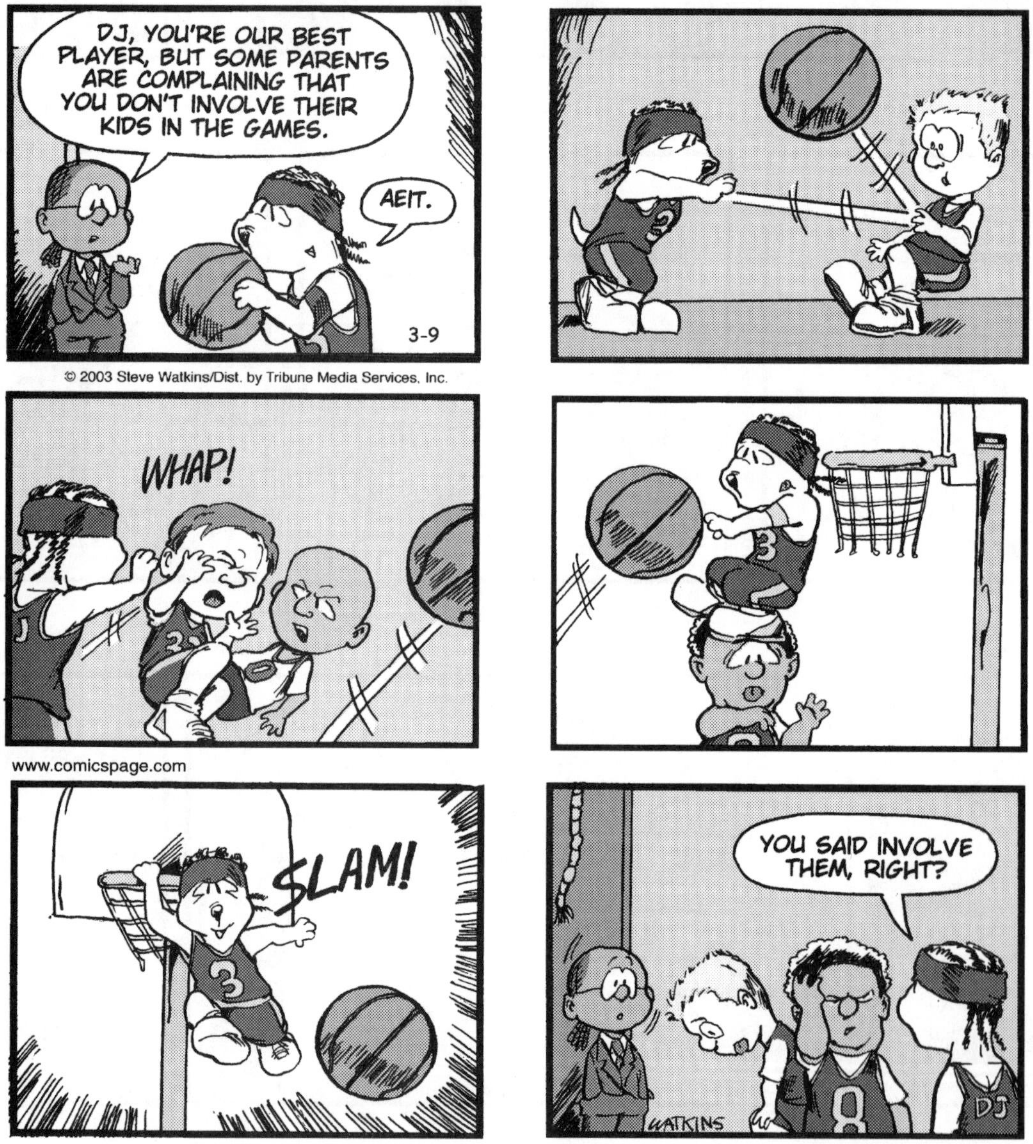
DJ, YOU'RE OUR BEST PLAYER, BUT SOME PARENTS ARE COMPLAINING THAT YOU DON'T INVOLVE THEIR KIDS IN THE GAMES.
AEIT.
3-9
WHAP!
SLAM!
YOU SAID INVOLVE THEM, RIGHT?
WATKINS

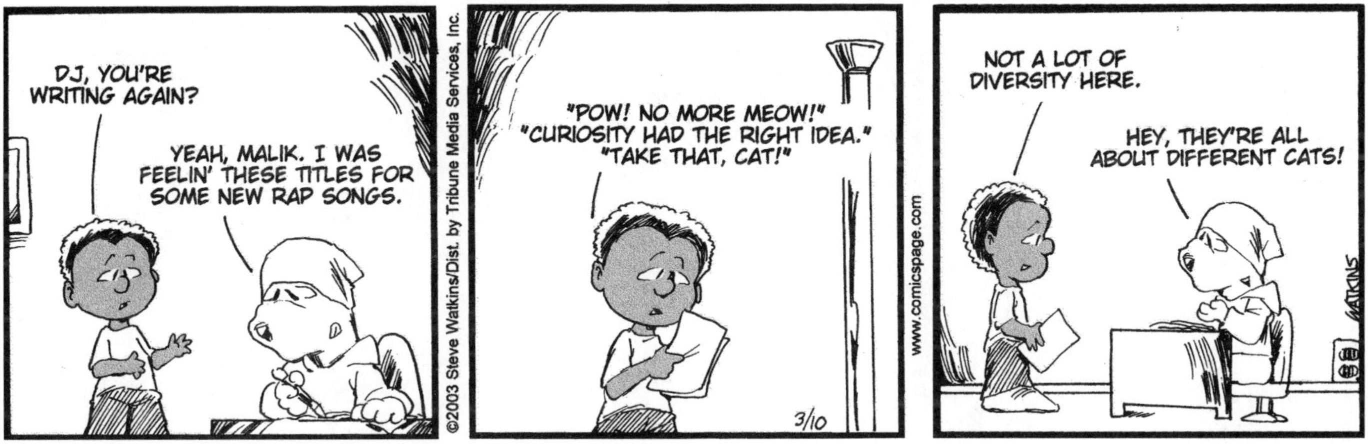
DJ, YOU'RE WRITING AGAIN?
YEAH, MALIK. I WAS FEELIN' THESE TITLES FOR SOME NEW RAP SONGS.
©2003 Steve Watkins/Dist. by Tribune Media Services, Inc.
"POW! NO MORE MEOW!" "CURIOSITY HAD THE RIGHT IDEA." "TAKE THAT, CAT!"
3/10
www.comicspage.com
NOT A LOT OF DIVERSITY HERE.
HEY, THEY'RE ALL ABOUT DIFFERENT CATS!
WATKINS

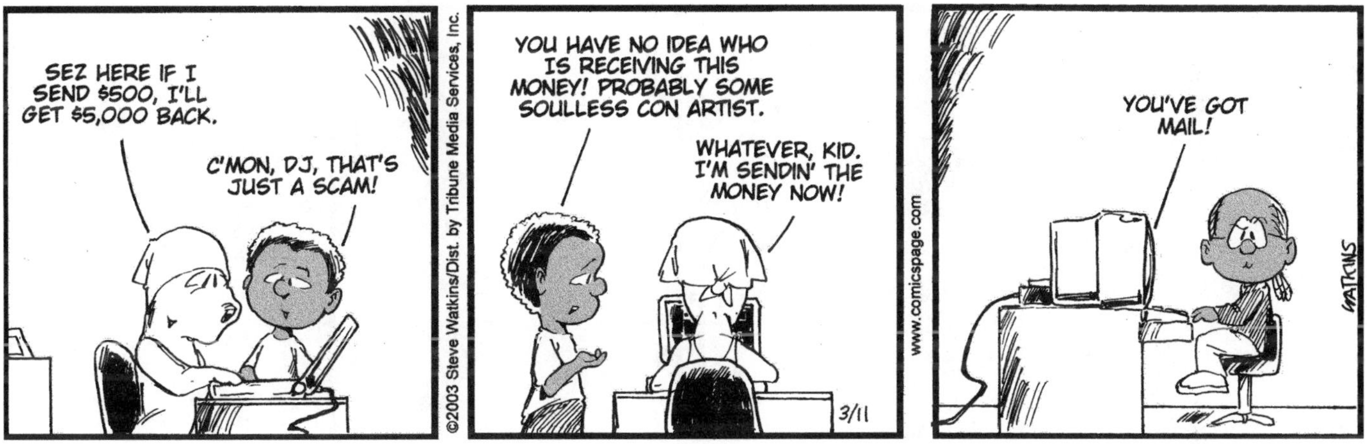
SEZ HERE IF I SEND $500, I'LL GET $5,000 BACK.
C'MON, DJ, THAT'S JUST A SCAM!
©2003 Steve Watkins/Dist. by Tribune Media Services, Inc.
YOU HAVE NO IDEA WHO IS RECEIVING THIS MONEY! PROBABLY SOME SOULLESS CON ARTIST.
WHATEVER, KID. I'M SENDIN' THE MONEY NOW!
3/11
www.comicspage.com
YOU'VE GOT MAIL!
WATKINS

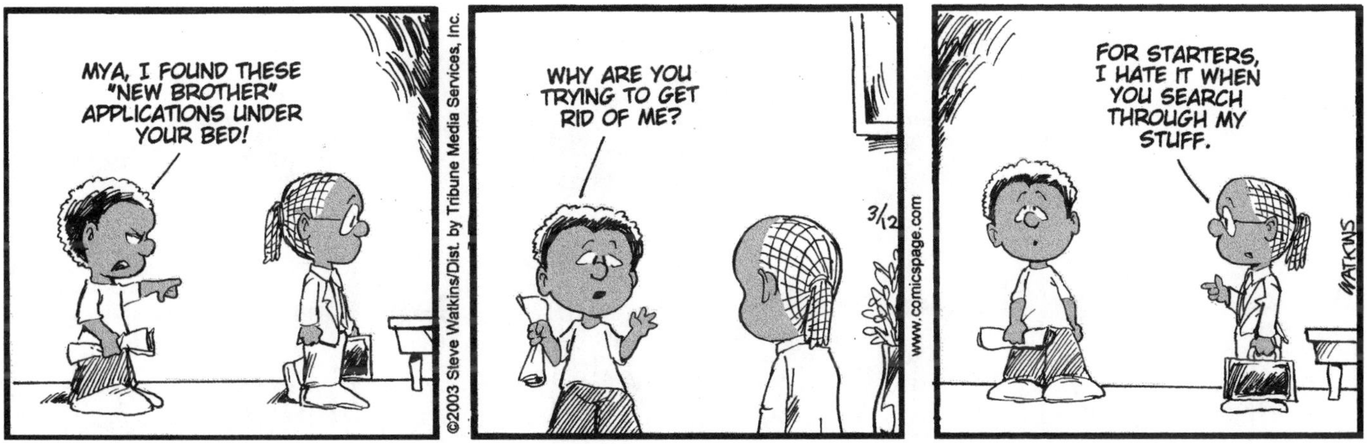
MYA, I FOUND THESE "NEW BROTHER" APPLICATIONS UNDER YOUR BED!
©2003 Steve Watkins/Dist. by Tribune Media Services, Inc.
WHY ARE YOU TRYING TO GET RID OF ME?
3/12
www.comicspage.com
FOR STARTERS, I HATE IT WHEN YOU SEARCH THROUGH MY STUFF.
WATKINS

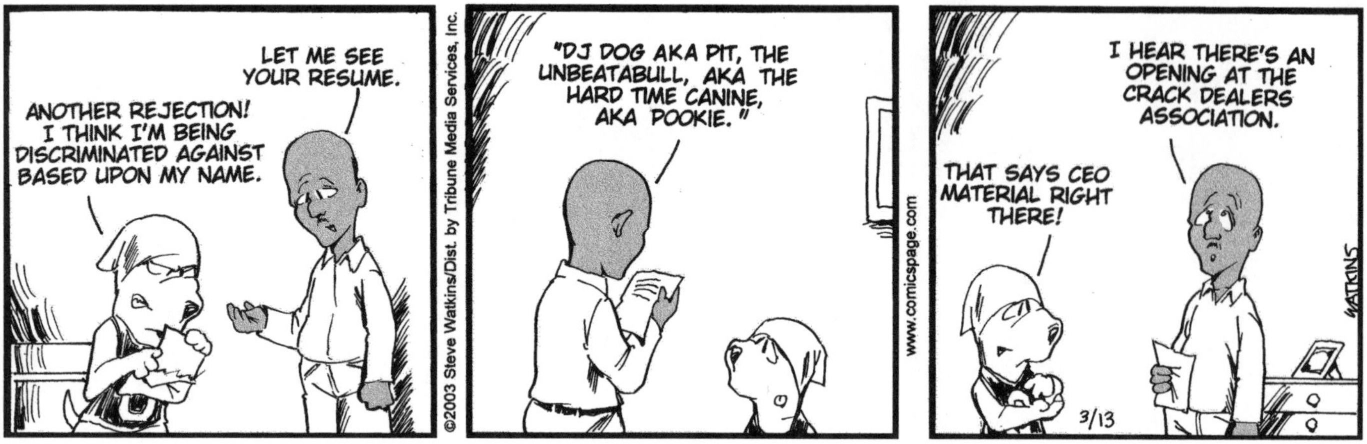
ANOTHER REJECTION! I THINK I'M BEING DISCRIMINATED AGAINST BASED UPON MY NAME.
LET ME SEE YOUR RESUME.
©2003 Steve Watkins/Dist. by Tribune Media Services, Inc.
"DJ DOG AKA PIT, THE UNBEATABULL, AKA THE HARD TIME CANINE, AKA POOKIE."
www.comicspage.com
THAT SAYS CEO MATERIAL RIGHT THERE!
I HEAR THERE'S AN OPENING AT THE CRACK DEALERS ASSOCIATION.
WATKINS
3/13

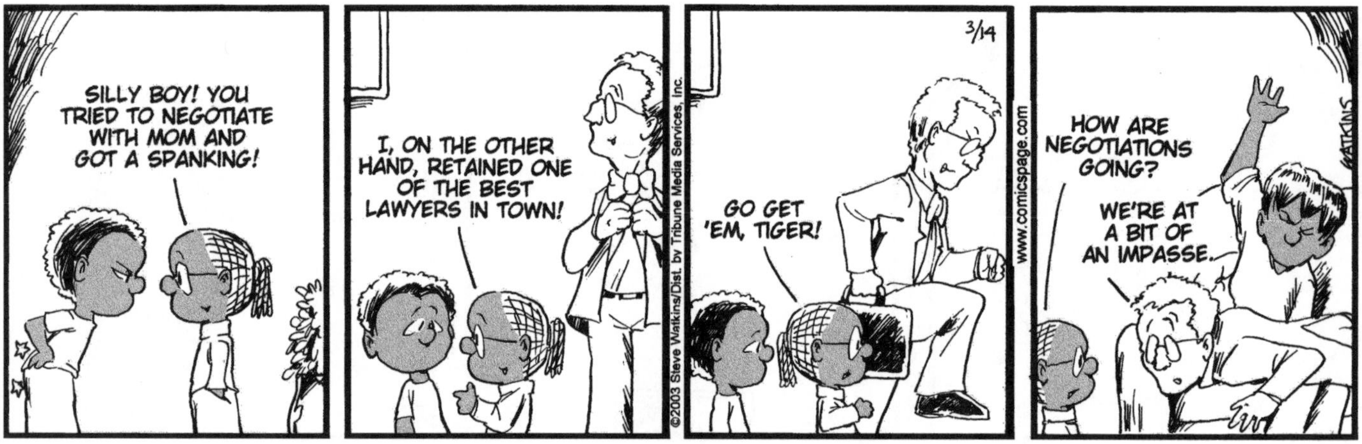
SILLY BOY! YOU TRIED TO NEGOTIATE WITH MOM AND GOT A SPANKING!
I, ON THE OTHER HAND, RETAINED ONE OF THE BEST LAWYERS IN TOWN!
©2003 Steve Watkins/Dist. by Tribune Media Services, Inc.
3/14
GO GET 'EM, TIGER!
www.comicspage.com
HOW ARE NEGOTIATIONS GOING?
WE'RE AT A BIT OF AN IMPASSE.
WATKINS

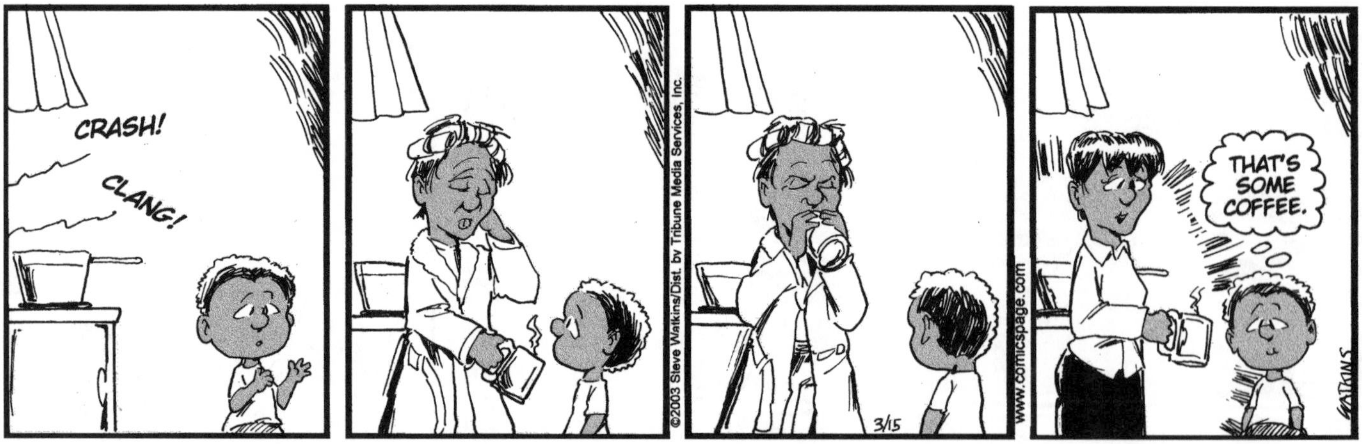
CRASH!
CLANG!
©2003 Steve Watkins/Dist. by Tribune Media Services, Inc.
3/15
www.comicspage.com
THAT'S SOME COFFEE.
WATKINS

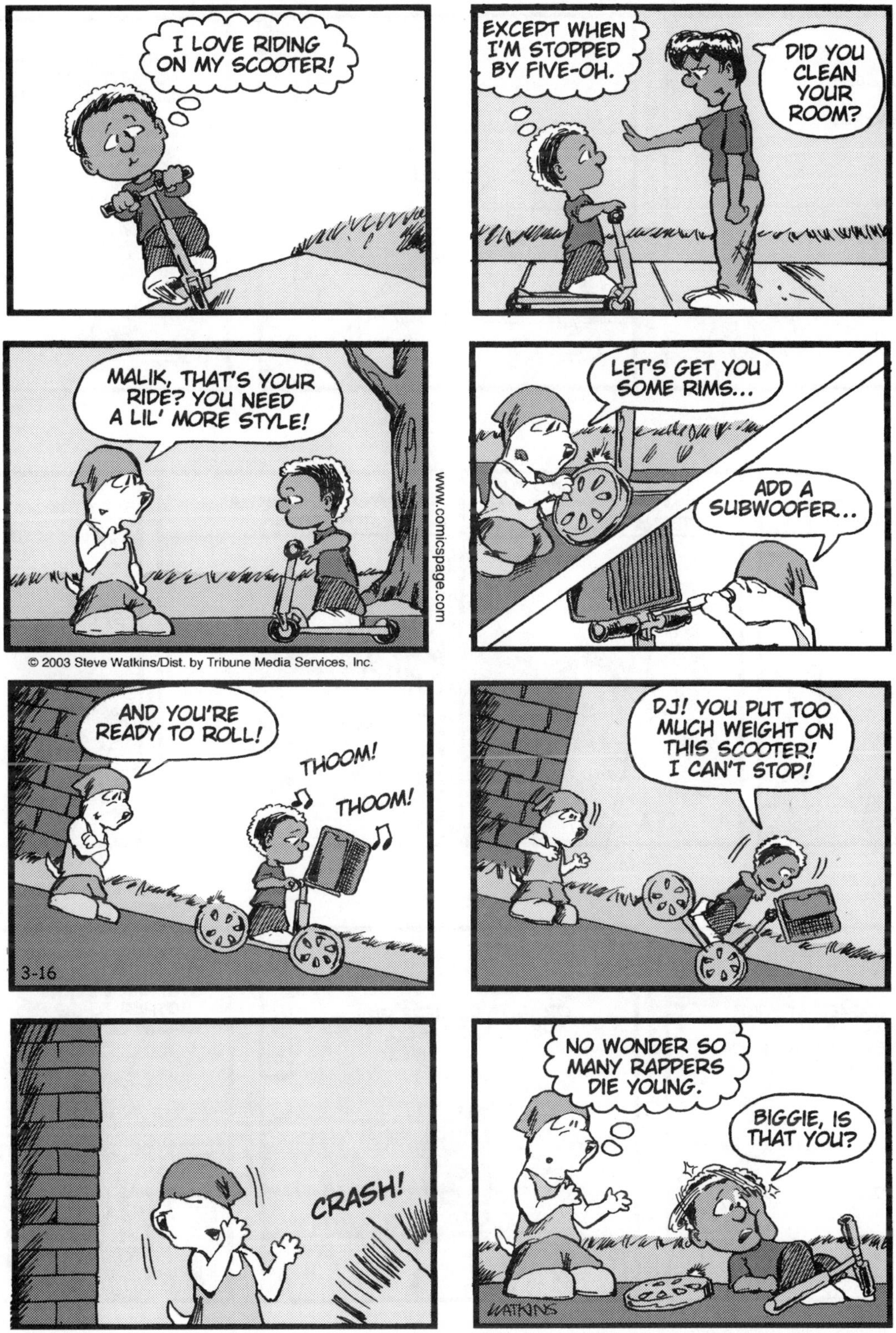
I LOVE RIDING ON MY SCOOTER!
EXCEPT WHEN I'M STOPPED BY FIVE-OH.
DID YOU CLEAN YOUR ROOM?
MALIK, THAT'S YOUR RIDE? YOU NEED A LIL' MORE STYLE!
LET'S GET YOU SOME RIMS...
ADD A SUBWOOFER...
AND YOU'RE READY TO ROLL!
THOOM!
THOOM!
3-16
DJ! YOU PUT TOO MUCH WEIGHT ON THIS SCOOTER! I CAN'T STOP!
CRASH!
NO WONDER SO MANY RAPPERS DIE YOUNG.
BIGGIE, IS THAT YOU?
WATKINS
www.comicspage.com

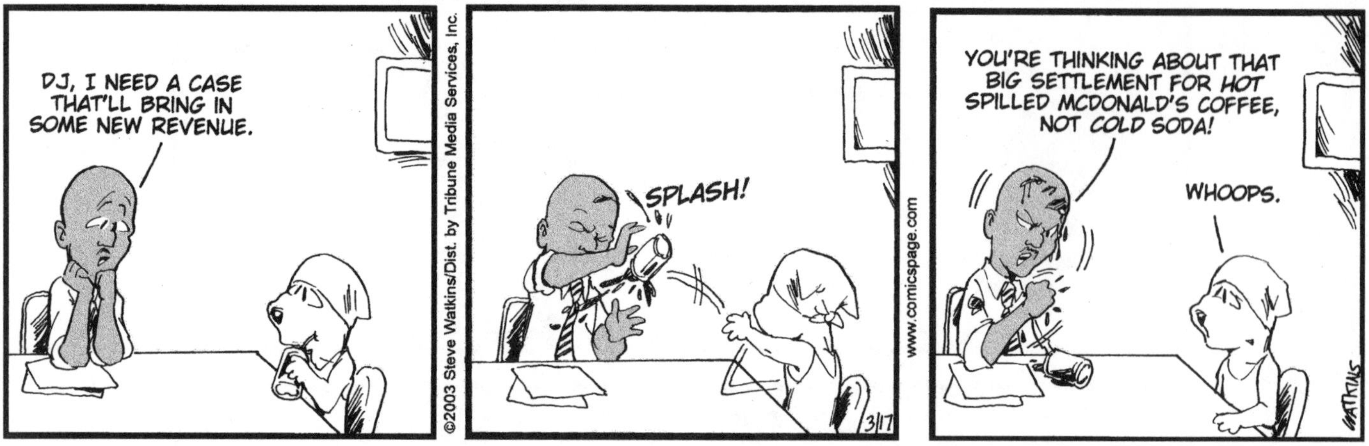
DJ, I NEED A CASE THAT'LL BRING IN SOME NEW REVENUE.
©2003 Steve Watkins/Dist. by Tribune Media Services, Inc.
SPLASH!
www.comicspage.com
3/17
YOU'RE THINKING ABOUT THAT BIG SETTLEMENT FOR HOT SPILLED MCDONALD'S COFFEE, NOT COLD SODA!
WHOOPS.
WATKINS

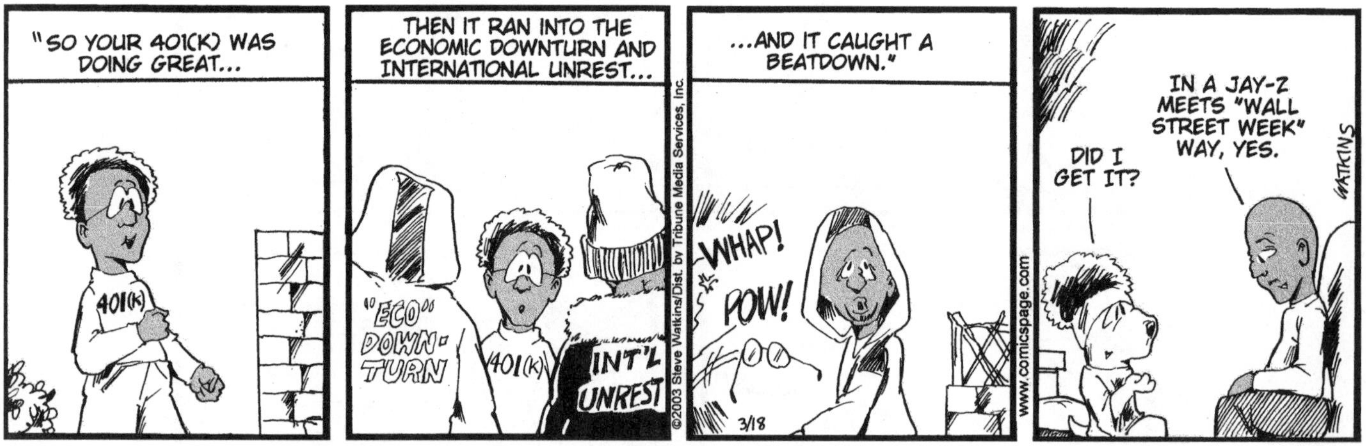
"SO YOUR 401(K) WAS DOING GREAT...
401(K)
THEN IT RAN INTO THE ECONOMIC DOWNTURN AND INTERNATIONAL UNREST...
"ECO" DOWN-TURN
401(K)
INT'L UNREST
©2003 Steve Watkins/Dist. by Tribune Media Services, Inc.
...AND IT CAUGHT A BEATDOWN."
WHAP!
POW!
3/18
www.comicspage.com
DID I GET IT?
IN A JAY-Z MEETS "WALL STREET WEEK" WAY, YES.
WATKINS

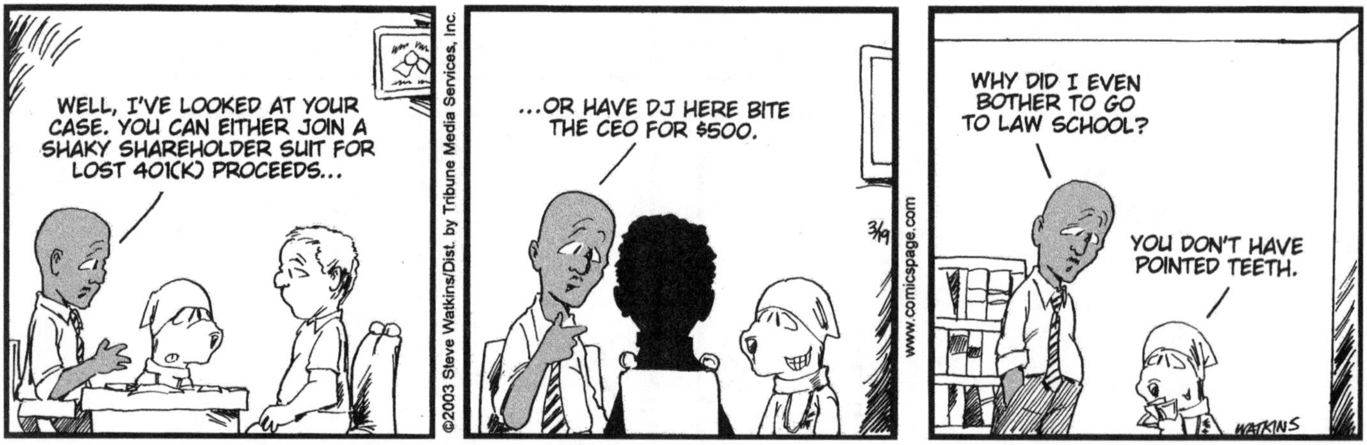
WELL, I'VE LOOKED AT YOUR CASE. YOU CAN EITHER JOIN A SHAKY SHAREHOLDER SUIT FOR LOST 401(K) PROCEEDS...
©2003 Steve Watkins/Dist. by Tribune Media Services, Inc.
...OR HAVE DJ HERE BITE THE CEO FOR $500.
3/19
www.comicspage.com
WHY DID I EVEN BOTHER TO GO TO LAW SCHOOL?
YOU DON'T HAVE POINTED TEETH.
WATKINS

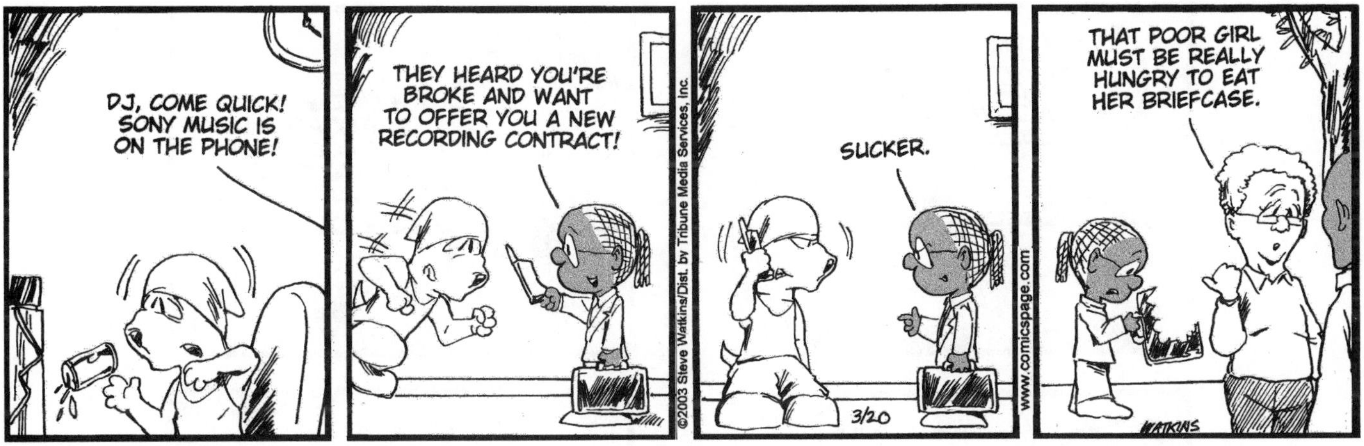
DJ, COME QUICK! SONY MUSIC IS ON THE PHONE!
THEY HEARD YOU'RE BROKE AND WANT TO OFFER YOU A NEW RECORDING CONTRACT!
©2003 Steve Watkins/Dist. by Tribune Media Services, Inc.
SUCKER.
3/20
www.comicspage.com
THAT POOR GIRL MUST BE REALLY HUNGRY TO EAT HER BRIEFCASE.
WATKINS

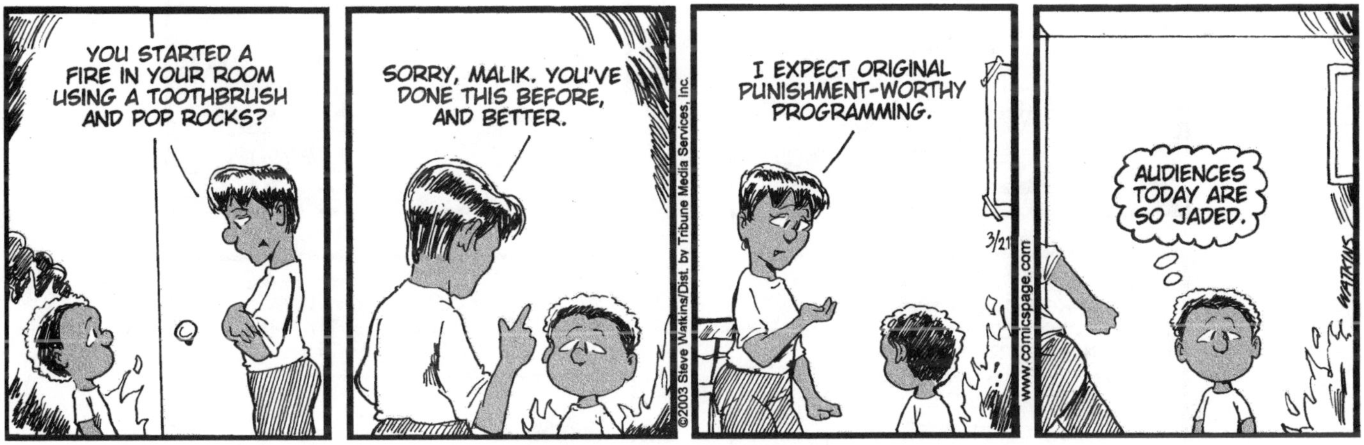
YOU STARTED A FIRE IN YOUR ROOM USING A TOOTHBRUSH AND POP ROCKS?
SORRY, MALIK. YOU'VE DONE THIS BEFORE, AND BETTER.
©2003 Steve Watkins/Dist. by Tribune Media Services, Inc.
I EXPECT ORIGINAL PUNISHMENT-WORTHY PROGRAMMING.
3/21
www.comicspage.com
AUDIENCES TODAY ARE SO JADED.
WATKINS

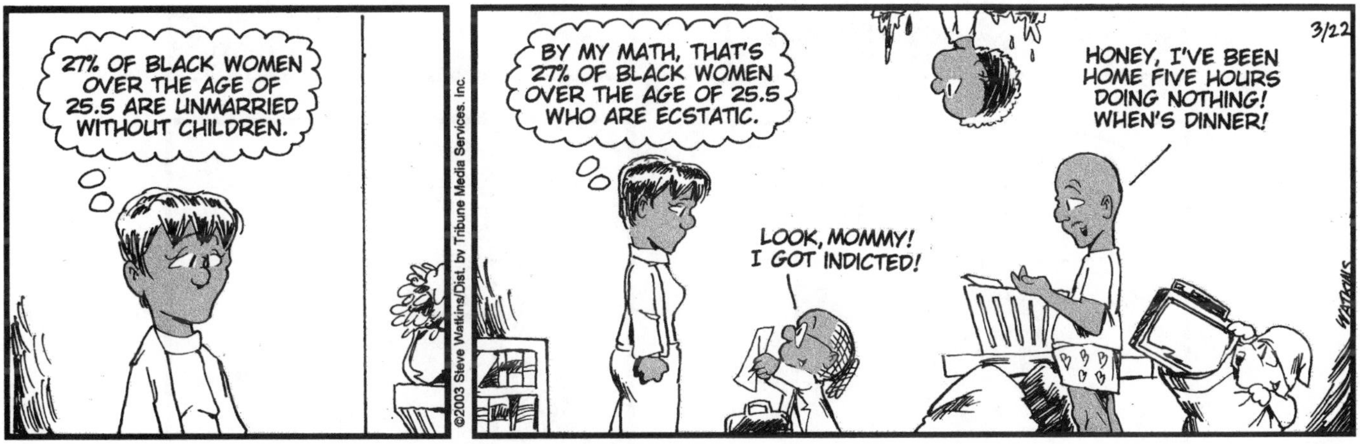
27% OF BLACK WOMEN OVER THE AGE OF 25.5 ARE UNMARRIED WITHOUT CHILDREN.
©2003 Steve Watkins/Dist. by Tribune Media Services, Inc.
BY MY MATH, THAT'S 27% OF BLACK WOMEN OVER THE AGE OF 25.5 WHO ARE ECSTATIC.
3/22
HONEY, I'VE BEEN HOME FIVE HOURS DOING NOTHING! WHEN'S DINNER!
LOOK, MOMMY! I GOT INDICTED!
WATKINS

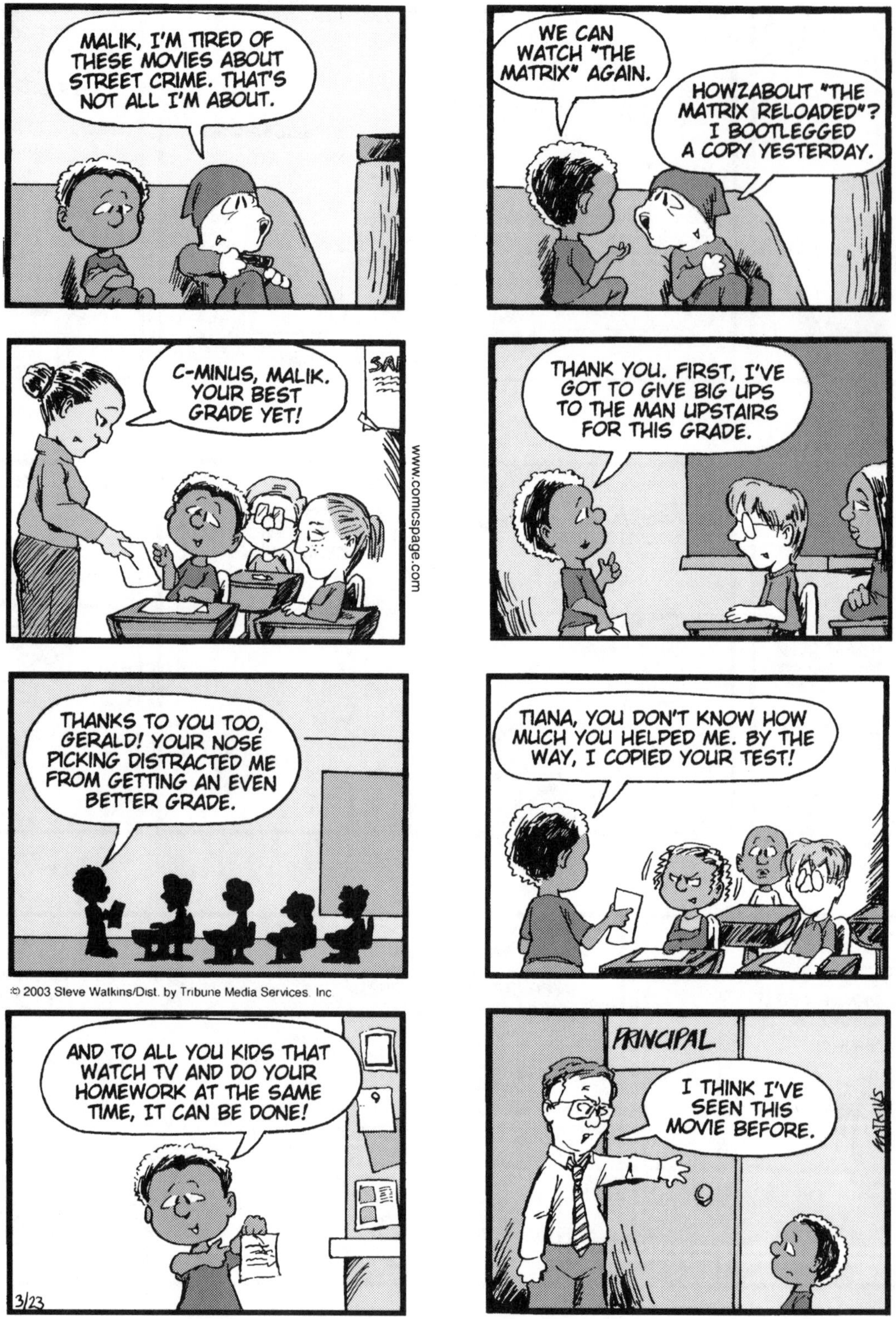
MALIK, I'M TIRED OF THESE MOVIES ABOUT STREET CRIME. THAT'S NOT ALL I'M ABOUT.
WE CAN WATCH "THE MATRIX" AGAIN.
HOWZABOUT "THE MATRIX RELOADED"? I BOOTLEGGED A COPY YESTERDAY.
C-MINUS, MALIK. YOUR BEST GRADE YET!
www.comicspage.com
THANK YOU. FIRST, I'VE GOT TO GIVE BIG UPS TO THE MAN UPSTAIRS FOR THIS GRADE.
THANKS TO YOU TOO, GERALD! YOUR NOSE PICKING DISTRACTED ME FROM GETTING AN EVEN BETTER GRADE.
TIANA, YOU DON'T KNOW HOW MUCH YOU HELPED ME. BY THE WAY, I COPIED YOUR TEST!
©2003 Steve Watkins/Dist. by Tribune Media Services. Inc
AND TO ALL YOU KIDS THAT WATCH TV AND DO YOUR HOMEWORK AT THE SAME TIME, IT CAN BE DONE!
3/23
PRINCIPAL
I THINK I'VE SEEN THIS MOVIE BEFORE.

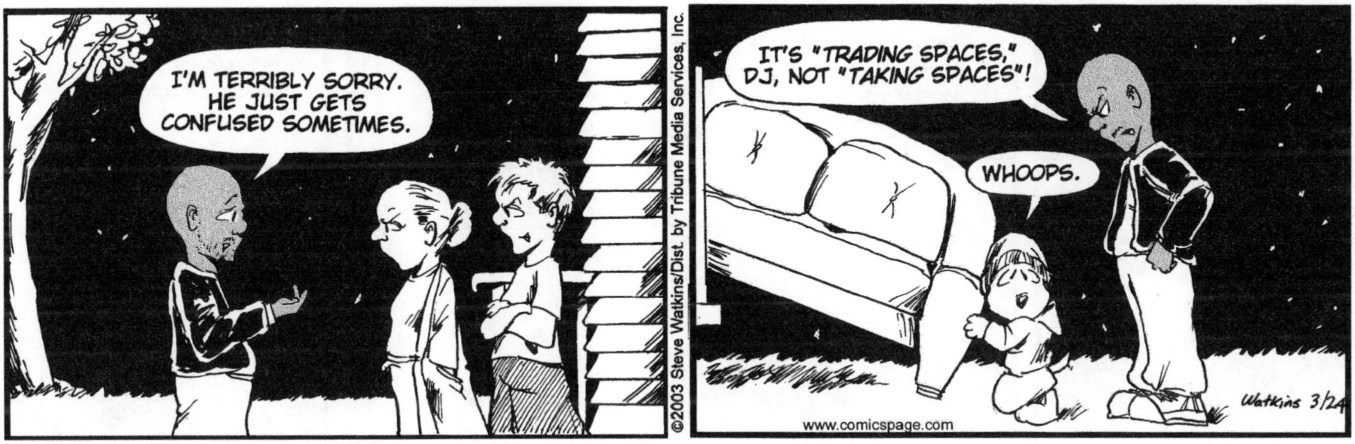

I'M TERRIBLY SORRY. HE JUST GETS CONFUSED SOMETIMES.
©2003 Steve Watkins/Dist. by Tribune Media Services, Inc.
IT'S "TRADING SPACES," DJ, NOT "TAKING SPACES"!
WHOOPS.
Watkins 3/24
www.comicspage.com

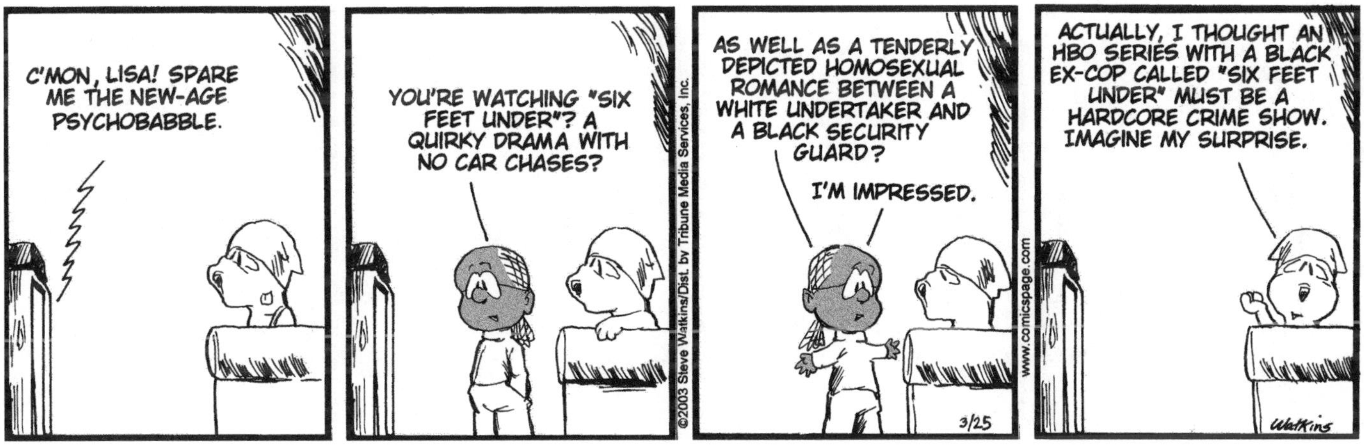

C'MON, LISA! SPARE ME THE NEW-AGE PSYCHOBABBLE.
YOU'RE WATCHING "SIX FEET UNDER"? A QUIRKY DRAMA WITH NO CAR CHASES?
©2003 Steve Watkins/Dist. by Tribune Media Services, Inc.
AS WELL AS A TENDERLY DEPICTED HOMOSEXUAL ROMANCE BETWEEN A WHITE UNDERTAKER AND A BLACK SECURITY GUARD?
I'M IMPRESSED.
3/25
www.comicspage.com
ACTUALLY, I THOUGHT AN HBO SERIES WITH A BLACK EX-COP CALLED "SIX FEET UNDER" MUST BE A HARDCORE CRIME SHOW. IMAGINE MY SURPRISE.
Watkins

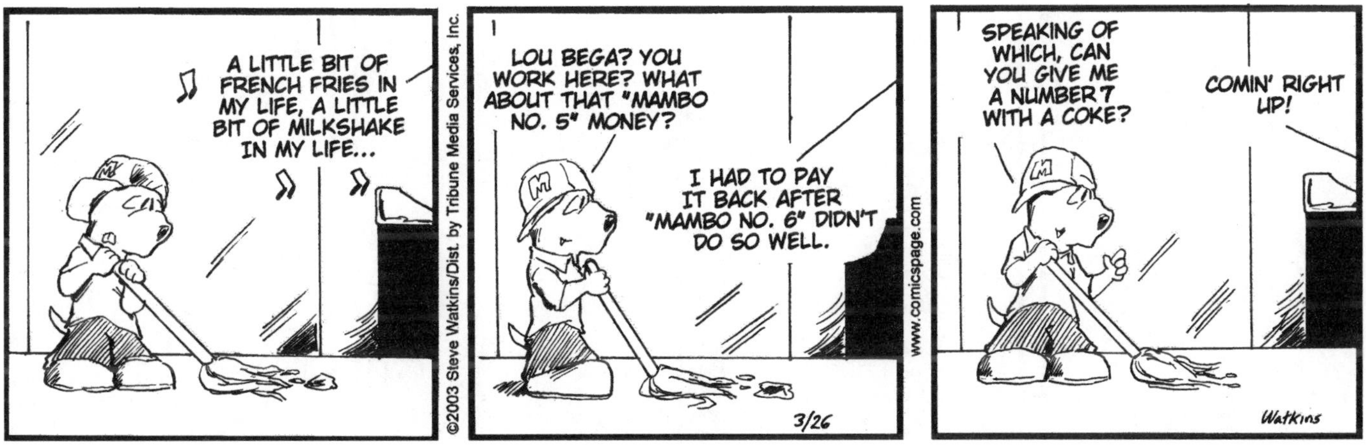

A LITTLE BIT OF FRENCH FRIES IN MY LIFE, A LITTLE BIT OF MILKSHAKE IN MY LIFE...
©2003 Steve Watkins/Dist. by Tribune Media Services, Inc.
LOU BEGA? YOU WORK HERE? WHAT ABOUT THAT "MAMBO NO. 5" MONEY?
I HAD TO PAY IT BACK AFTER "MAMBO NO. 6" DIDN'T DO SO WELL.
3/26
www.comicspage.com
SPEAKING OF WHICH, CAN YOU GIVE ME A NUMBER 7 WITH A COKE?
COMIN' RIGHT UP!
Watkins

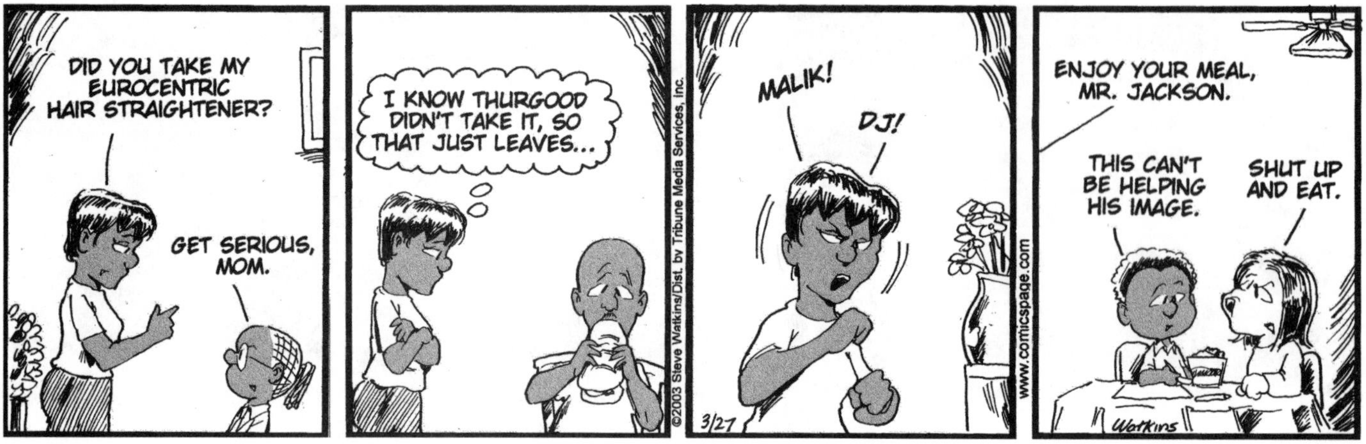
DID YOU TAKE MY EUROCENTRIC HAIR STRAIGHTENER?
GET SERIOUS, MOM.
I KNOW THURGOOD DIDN'T TAKE IT, SO THAT JUST LEAVES...
MALIK!
DJ!
ENJOY YOUR MEAL, MR. JACKSON.
THIS CAN'T BE HELPING HIS IMAGE.
SHUT UP AND EAT.
©2003 Steve Watkins/Dist. by Tribune Media Services, Inc.
www.comicspage.com
3/27
Watkins

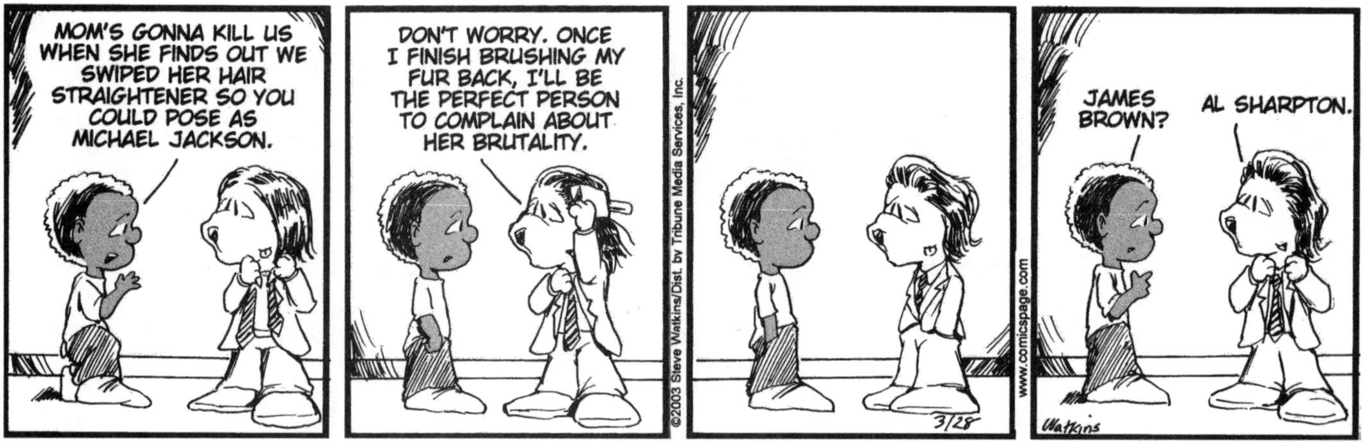
MOM'S GONNA KILL US WHEN SHE FINDS OUT WE SWIPED HER HAIR STRAIGHTENER SO YOU COULD POSE AS MICHAEL JACKSON.
DON'T WORRY. ONCE I FINISH BRUSHING MY FUR BACK, I'LL BE THE PERFECT PERSON TO COMPLAIN ABOUT HER BRUTALITY.
JAMES BROWN?
AL SHARPTON.
©2003 Steve Watkins/Dist. by Tribune Media Services, Inc.
www.comicspage.com
3/28
Watkins

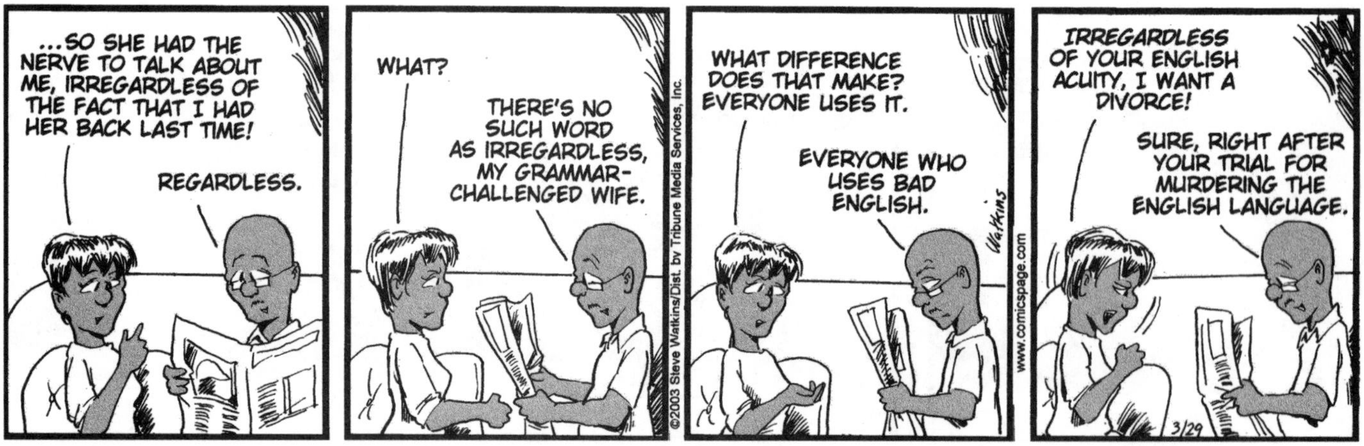
...SO SHE HAD THE NERVE TO TALK ABOUT ME, IRREGARDLESS OF THE FACT THAT I HAD HER BACK LAST TIME!
REGARDLESS.
WHAT?
THERE'S NO SUCH WORD AS IRREGARDLESS, MY GRAMMAR-CHALLENGED WIFE.
WHAT DIFFERENCE DOES THAT MAKE? EVERYONE USES IT.
EVERYONE WHO USES BAD ENGLISH.
IRREGARDLESS OF YOUR ENGLISH ACUITY, I WANT A DIVORCE!
SURE, RIGHT AFTER YOUR TRIAL FOR MURDERING THE ENGLISH LANGUAGE.
©2003 Steve Watkins/Dist. by Tribune Media Services, Inc.
www.comicspage.com
Watkins
3/29

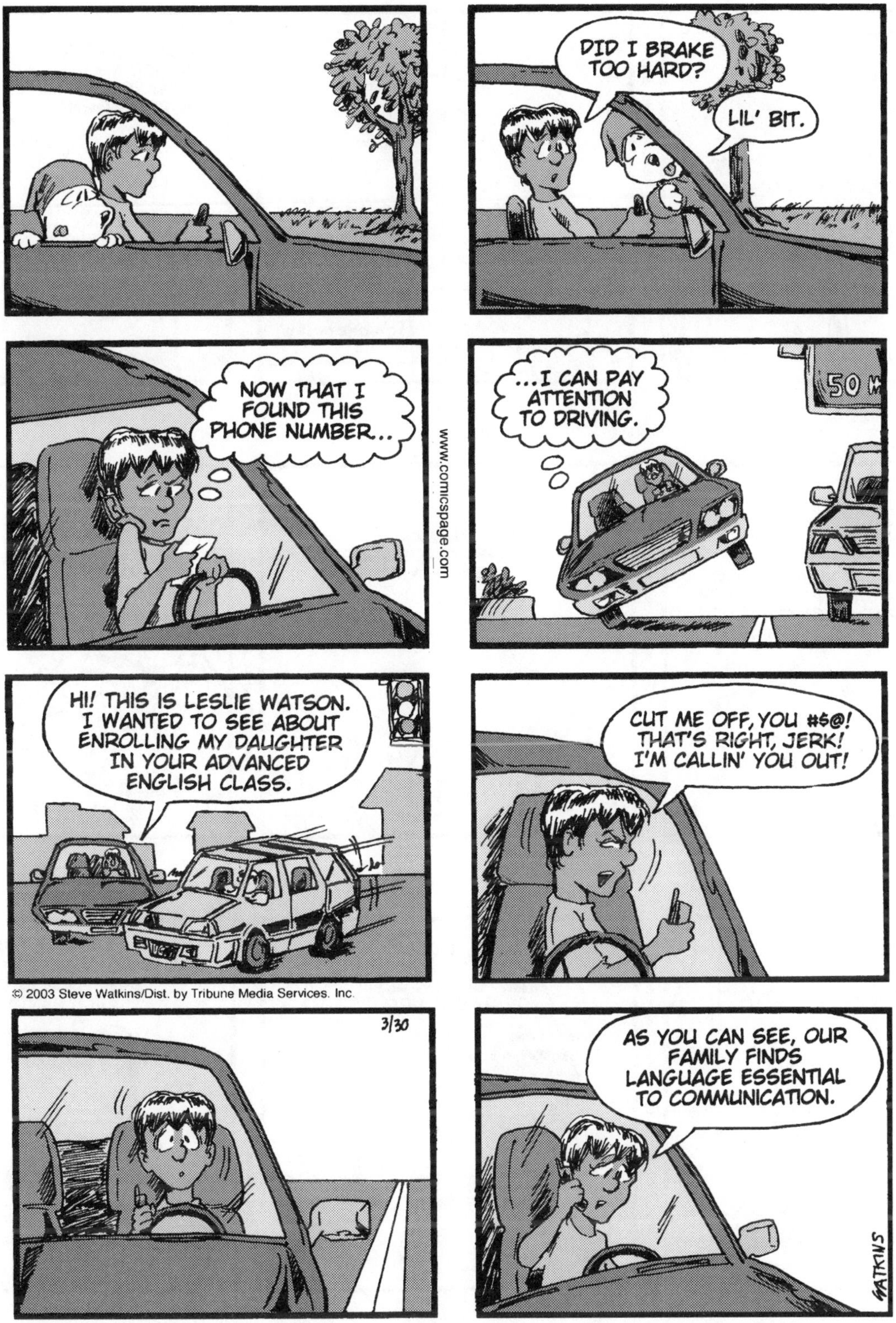
DID I BRAKE TOO HARD?
LIL' BIT.
NOW THAT I FOUND THIS PHONE NUMBER...
...I CAN PAY ATTENTION TO DRIVING.
HI! THIS IS LESLIE WATSON. I WANTED TO SEE ABOUT ENROLLING MY DAUGHTER IN YOUR ADVANCED ENGLISH CLASS.
CUT ME OFF, YOU #$@! THAT'S RIGHT, JERK! I'M CALLIN' YOU OUT!
3/30
AS YOU CAN SEE, OUR FAMILY FINDS LANGUAGE ESSENTIAL TO COMMUNICATION.
WATKINS
www.comicspage.com

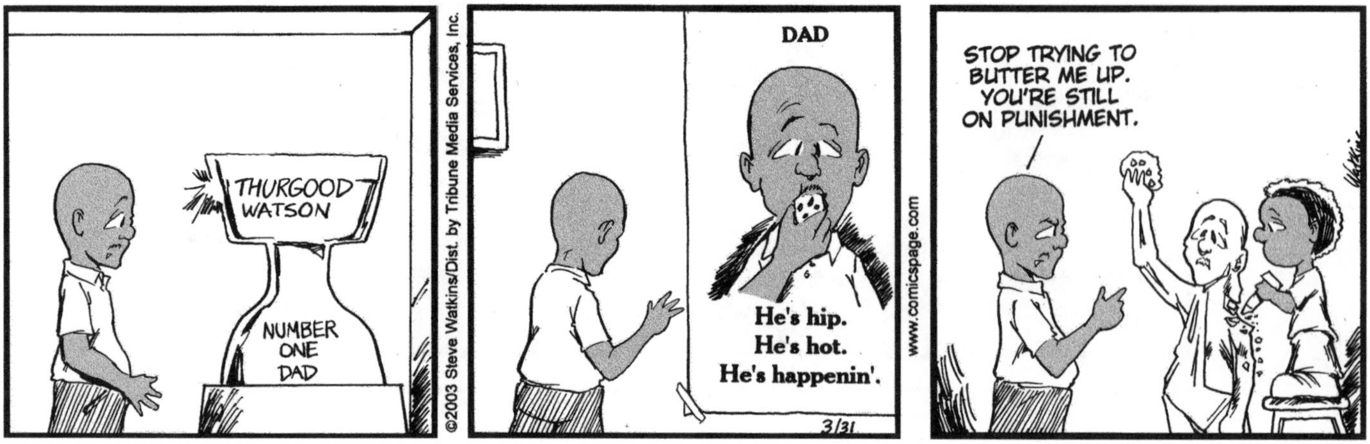
THURGOOD WATSON
NUMBER ONE DAD
©2003 Steve Watkins/Dist. by Tribune Media Services, Inc.
DAD
He's hip.
He's hot.
He's happenin'.
3/31
www.comicspage.com
STOP TRYING TO BUTTER ME UP. YOU'RE STILL ON PUNISHMENT.

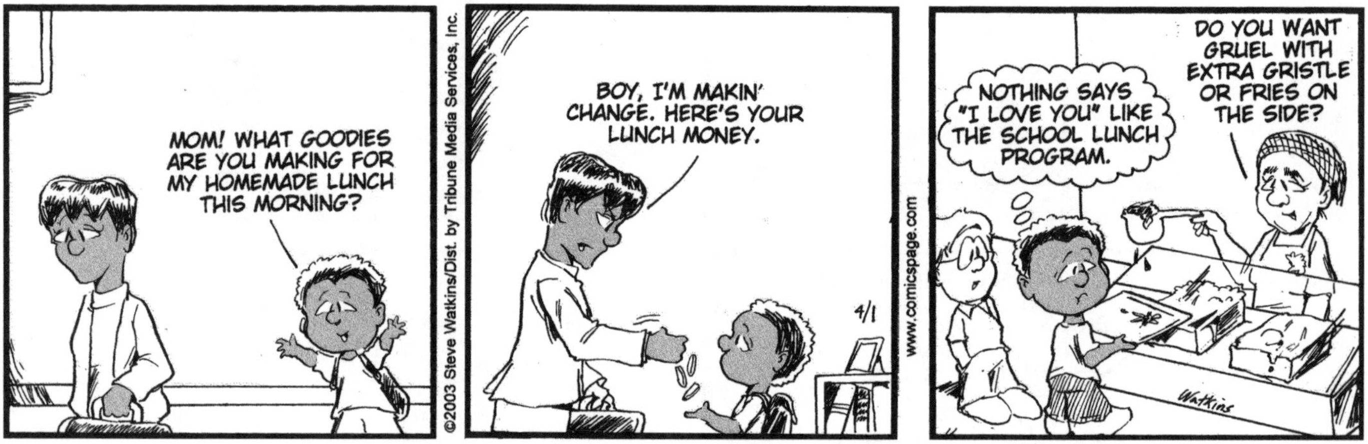
MOM! WHAT GOODIES ARE YOU MAKING FOR MY HOMEMADE LUNCH THIS MORNING?
©2003 Steve Watkins/Dist. by Tribune Media Services, Inc.
BOY, I'M MAKIN' CHANGE. HERE'S YOUR LUNCH MONEY.
4/1
www.comicspage.com
NOTHING SAYS "I LOVE YOU" LIKE THE SCHOOL LUNCH PROGRAM.
DO YOU WANT GRUEL WITH EXTRA GRISTLE OR FRIES ON THE SIDE?
Watkins

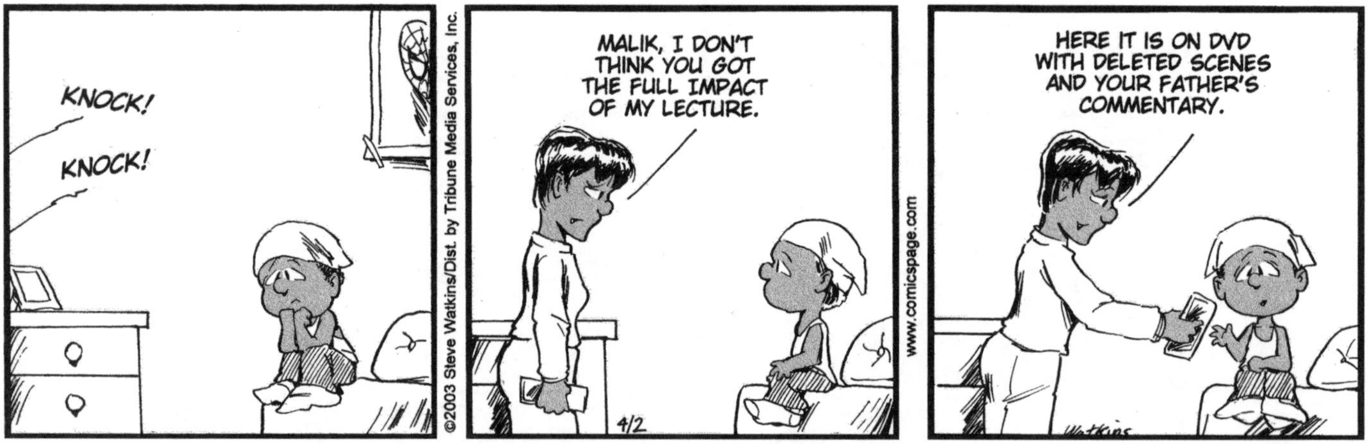
KNOCK!
KNOCK!
©2003 Steve Watkins/Dist. by Tribune Media Services, Inc.
MALIK, I DON'T THINK YOU GOT THE FULL IMPACT OF MY LECTURE.
4/2
www.comicspage.com
HERE IT IS ON DVD WITH DELETED SCENES AND YOUR FATHER'S COMMENTARY.

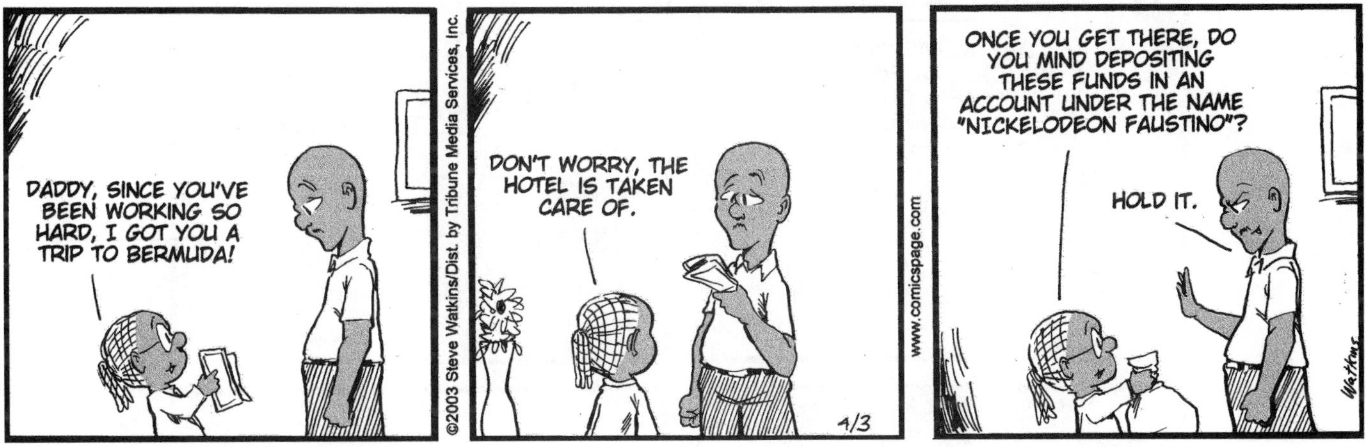
DADDY, SINCE YOU'VE BEEN WORKING SO HARD, I GOT YOU A TRIP TO BERMUDA!
©2003 Steve Watkins/Dist. by Tribune Media Services, Inc.
DON'T WORRY, THE HOTEL IS TAKEN CARE OF.
4/3
www.comicspage.com
ONCE YOU GET THERE, DO YOU MIND DEPOSITING THESE FUNDS IN AN ACCOUNT UNDER THE NAME "NICKELODEON FAUSTINO"?
HOLD IT.

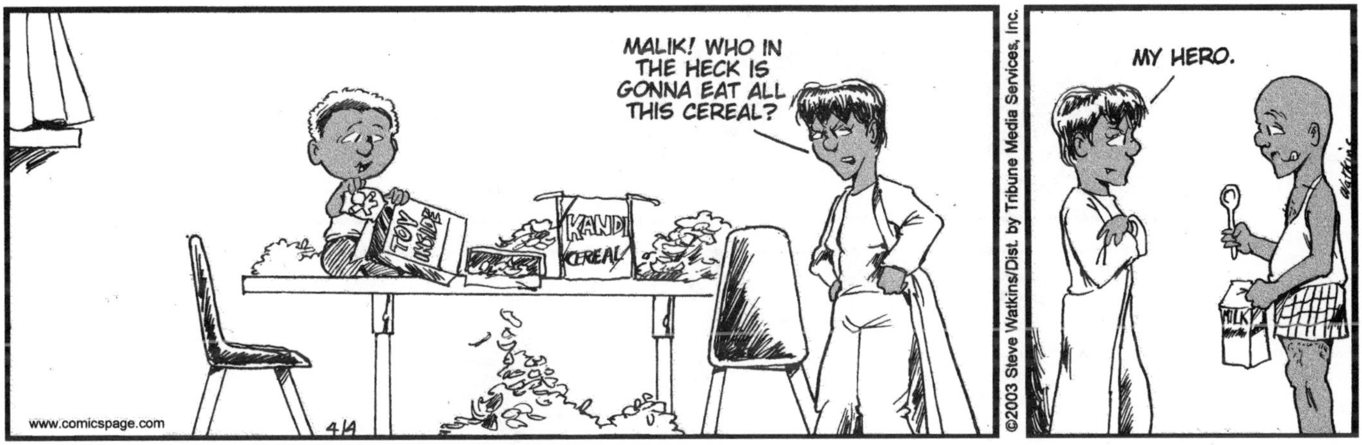
TOY INSIDE
KANDI CEREAL
MALIK! WHO IN THE HECK IS GONNA EAT ALL THIS CEREAL?
www.comicspage.com
4/4
©2003 Steve Watkins/Dist. by Tribune Media Services, Inc.
MY HERO.
MILK

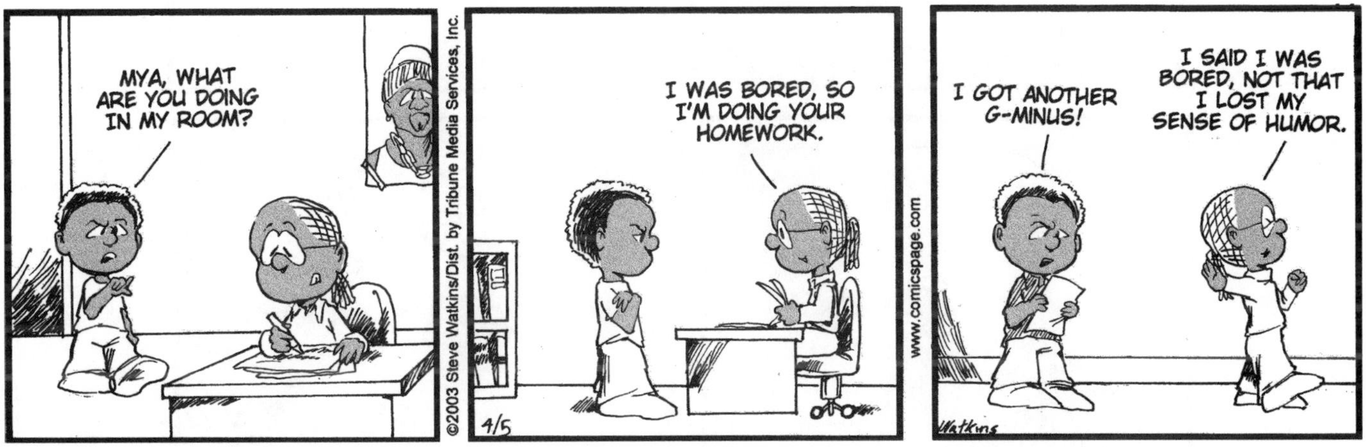
MYA, WHAT ARE YOU DOING IN MY ROOM?
©2003 Steve Watkins/Dist. by Tribune Media Services, Inc.
I WAS BORED, SO I'M DOING YOUR HOMEWORK.
4/5
www.comicspage.com
I GOT ANOTHER G-MINUS!
I SAID I WAS BORED, NOT THAT I LOST MY SENSE OF HUMOR.

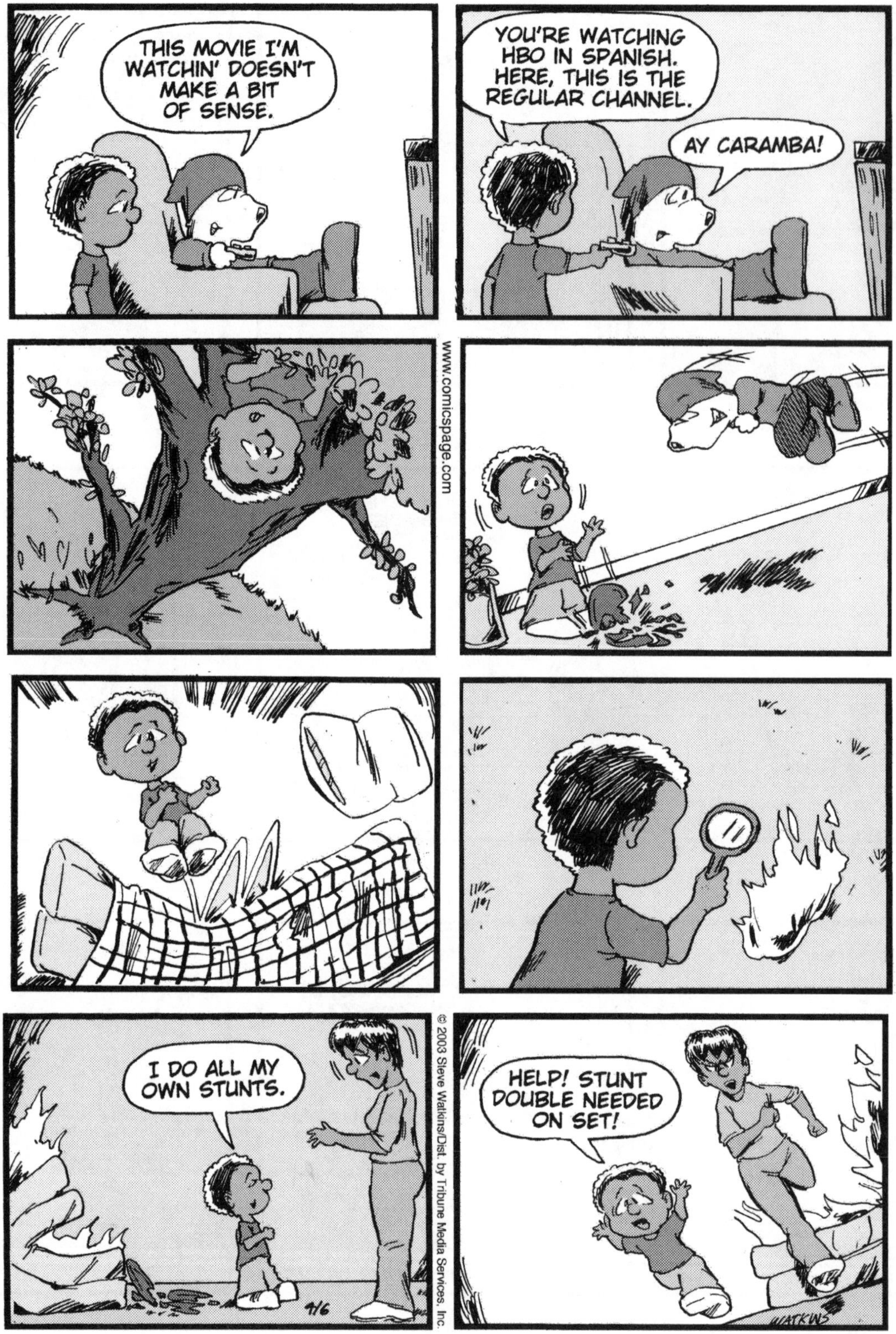
THIS MOVIE I'M WATCHIN' DOESN'T MAKE A BIT OF SENSE.
YOU'RE WATCHING HBO IN SPANISH. HERE, THIS IS THE REGULAR CHANNEL.
AY CARAMBA!
www.comicspage.com
I DO ALL MY OWN STUNTS.
4/6
HELP! STUNT DOUBLE NEEDED ON SET!
WATKINS
© 2003 Steve Watkins/Dist. by Tribune Media Services, Inc.

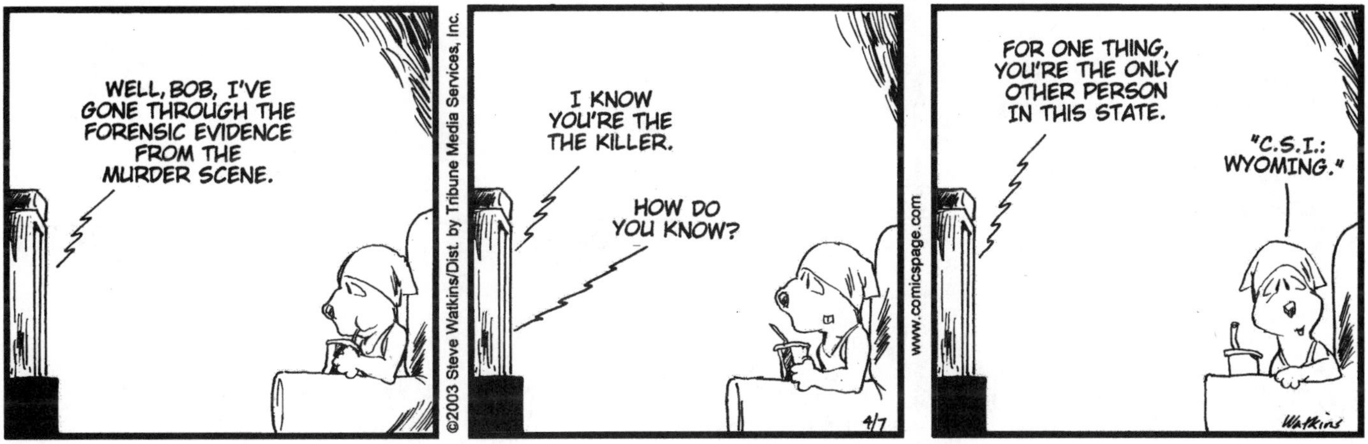
WELL, BOB, I'VE GONE THROUGH THE FORENSIC EVIDENCE FROM THE MURDER SCENE.
©2003 Steve Watkins/Dist. by Tribune Media Services, Inc.
I KNOW YOU'RE THE THE KILLER.
HOW DO YOU KNOW?
www.comicspage.com
4/7
FOR ONE THING, YOU'RE THE ONLY OTHER PERSON IN THIS STATE.
"C.S.I.: WYOMING."
Watkins

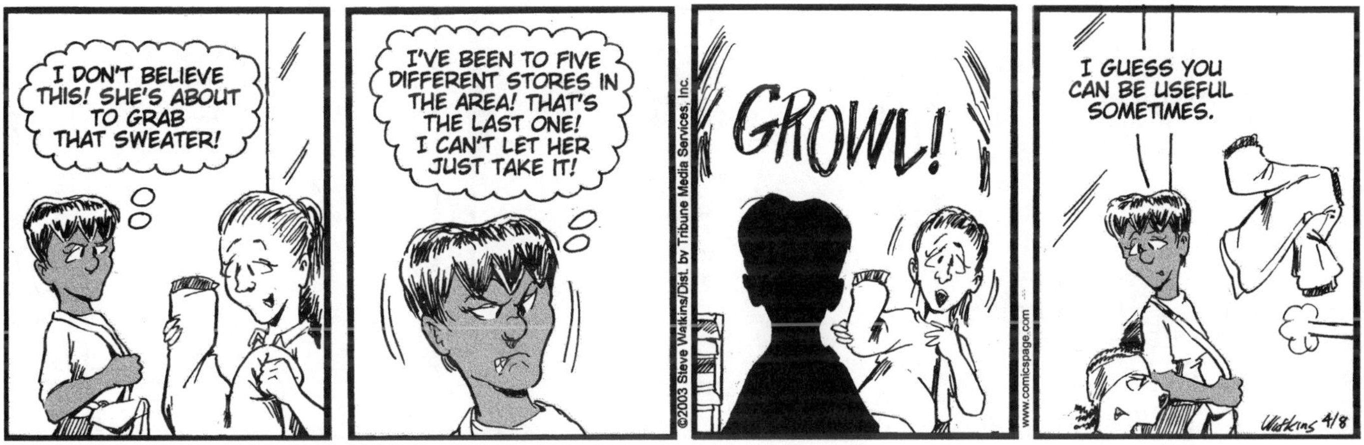
I DON'T BELIEVE THIS! SHE'S ABOUT TO GRAB THAT SWEATER!
I'VE BEEN TO FIVE DIFFERENT STORES IN THE AREA! THAT'S THE LAST ONE! I CAN'T LET HER JUST TAKE IT!
©2003 Steve Watkins/Dist. by Tribune Media Services, Inc.
GROWL!
www.comicspage.com
I GUESS YOU CAN BE USEFUL SOMETIMES.
Watkins 4/8

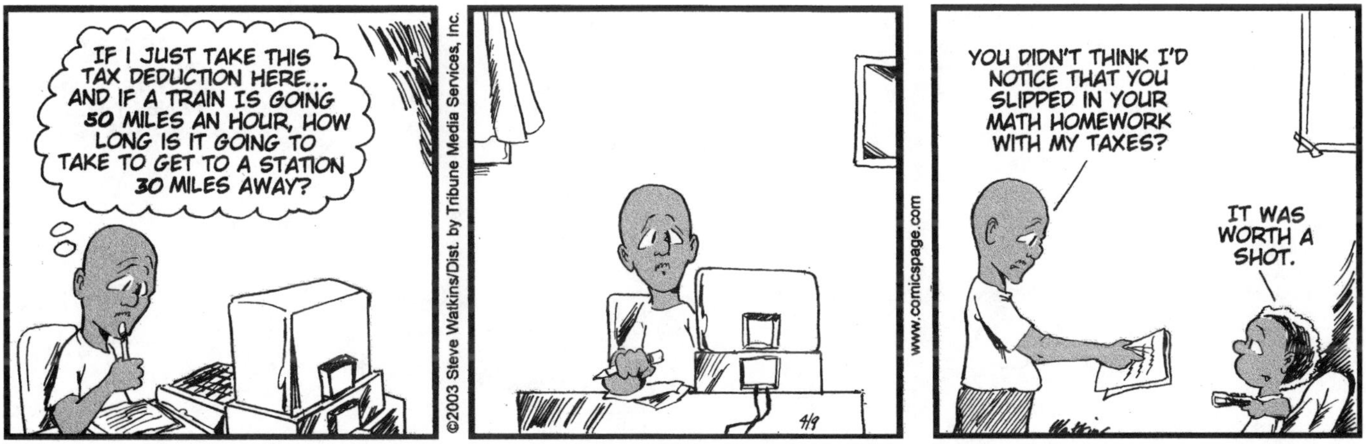
IF I JUST TAKE THIS TAX DEDUCTION HERE... AND IF A TRAIN IS GOING 50 MILES AN HOUR, HOW LONG IS IT GOING TO TAKE TO GET TO A STATION 30 MILES AWAY?
©2003 Steve Watkins/Dist. by Tribune Media Services, Inc.
4/9
www.comicspage.com
YOU DIDN'T THINK I'D NOTICE THAT YOU SLIPPED IN YOUR MATH HOMEWORK WITH MY TAXES?
IT WAS WORTH A SHOT.

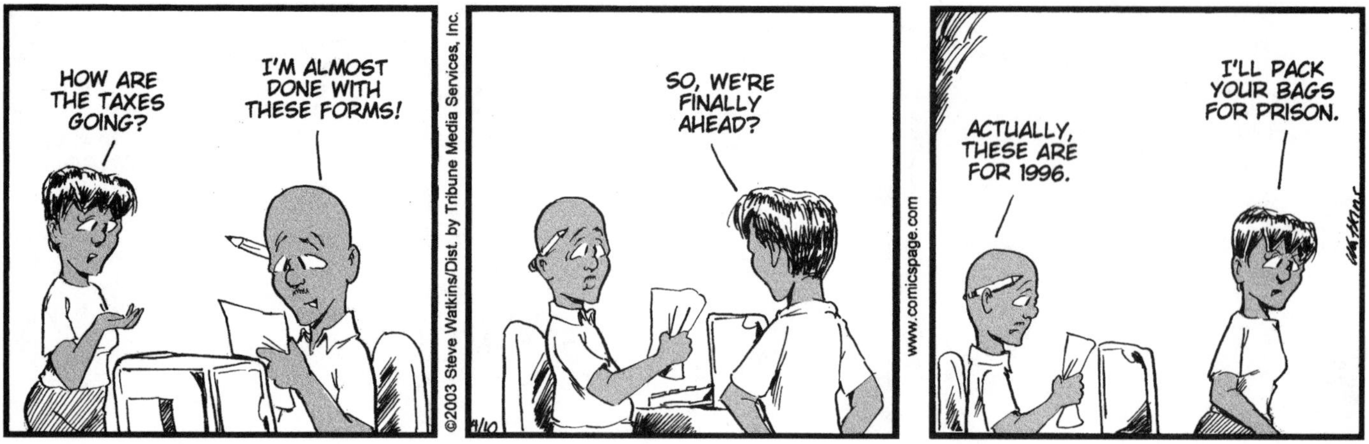
HOW ARE THE TAXES GOING?
I'M ALMOST DONE WITH THESE FORMS!
©2003 Steve Watkins/Dist. by Tribune Media Services, Inc.
SO, WE'RE FINALLY AHEAD?
4/10
www.comicspage.com
ACTUALLY, THESE ARE FOR 1996.
I'LL PACK YOUR BAGS FOR PRISON.
Watkins

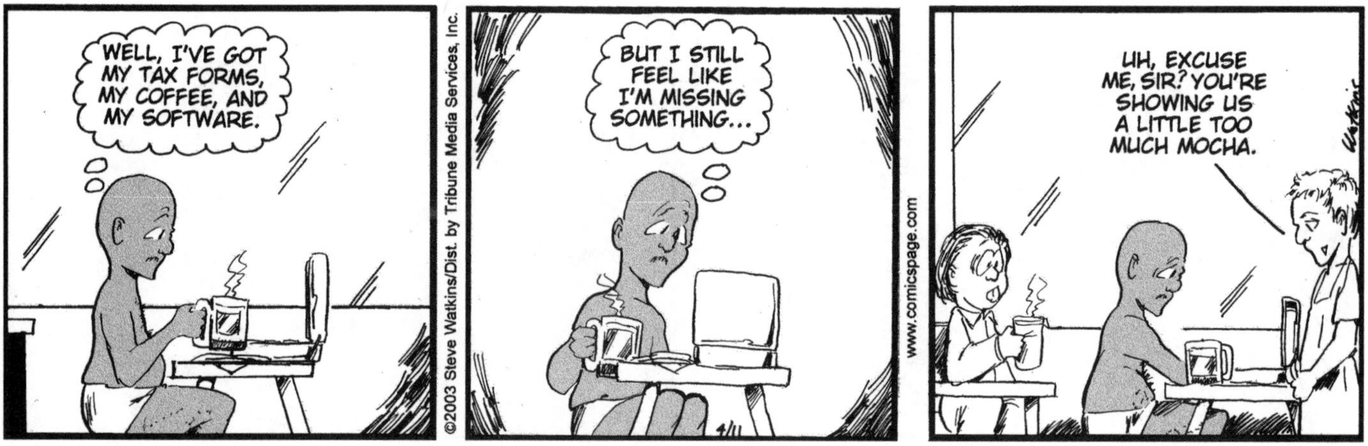
WELL, I'VE GOT MY TAX FORMS, MY COFFEE, AND MY SOFTWARE.
©2003 Steve Watkins/Dist. by Tribune Media Services, Inc.
BUT I STILL FEEL LIKE I'M MISSING SOMETHING...
4/11
www.comicspage.com
UH, EXCUSE ME, SIR? YOU'RE SHOWING US A LITTLE TOO MUCH MOCHA.
Watkins

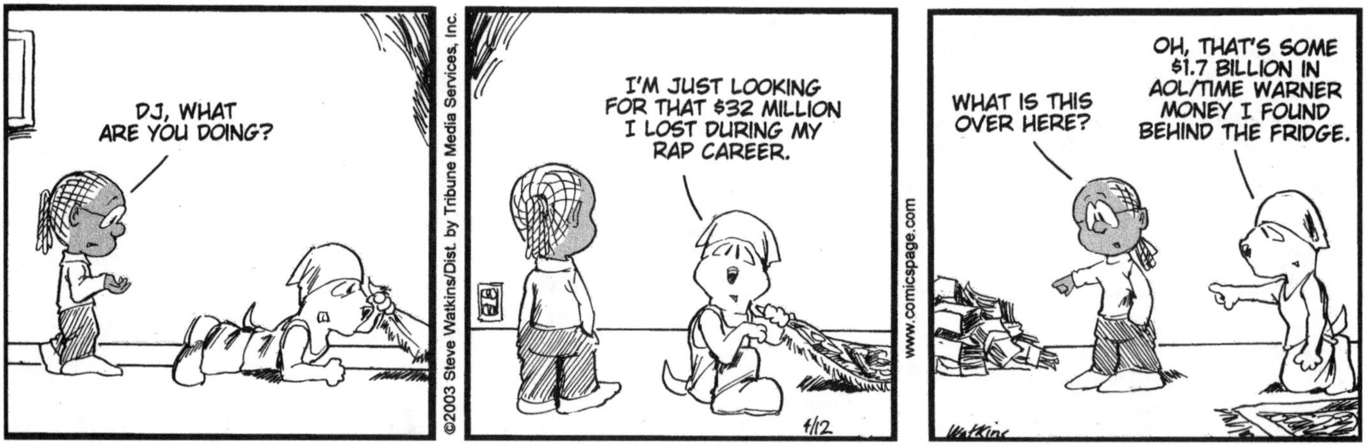
DJ, WHAT ARE YOU DOING?
©2003 Steve Watkins/Dist. by Tribune Media Services, Inc.
I'M JUST LOOKING FOR THAT $32 MILLION I LOST DURING MY RAP CAREER.
4/12
www.comicspage.com
WHAT IS THIS OVER HERE?
OH, THAT'S SOME $1.7 BILLION IN AOL/TIME WARNER MONEY I FOUND BEHIND THE FRIDGE.
Watkins

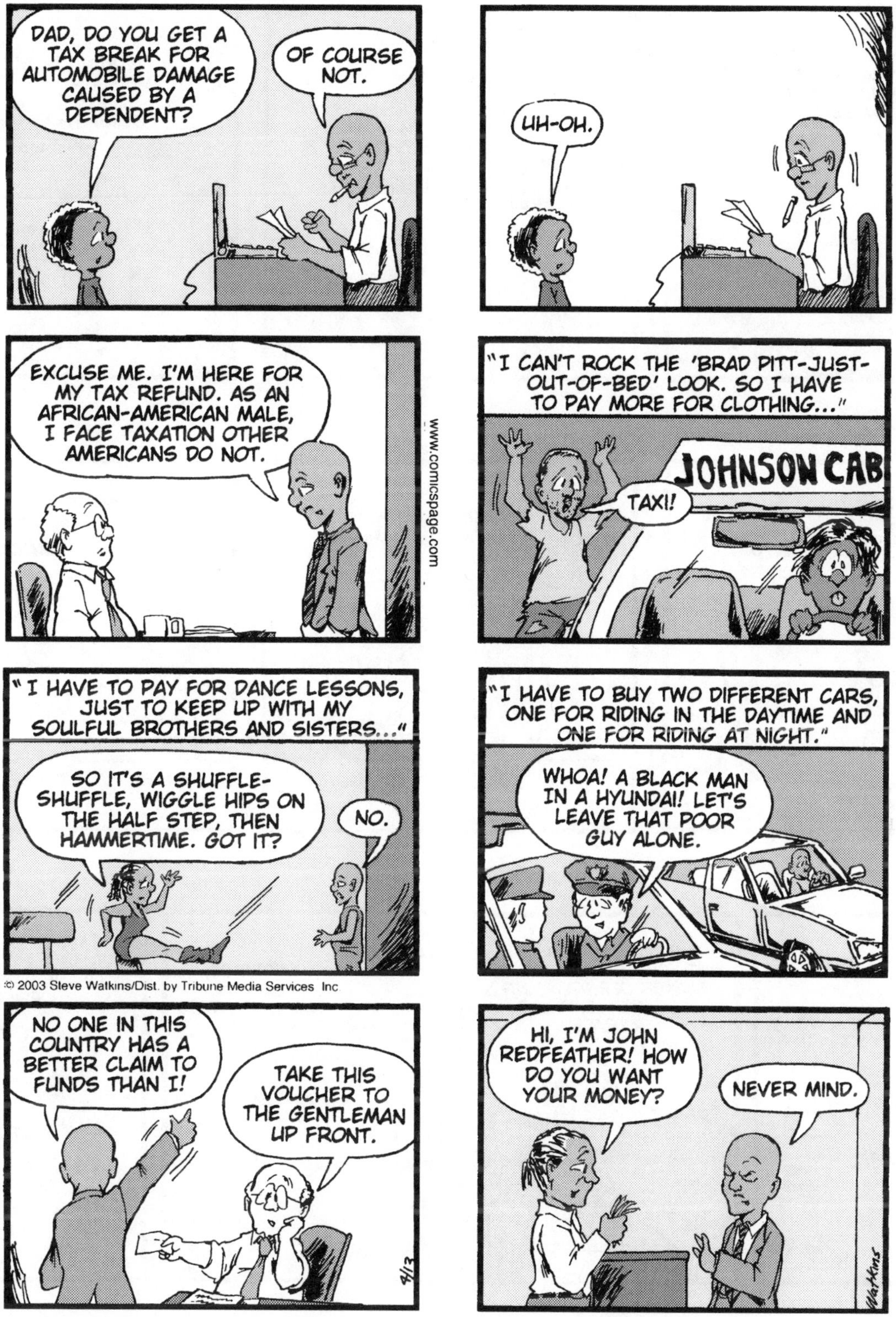
DAD, DO YOU GET A TAX BREAK FOR AUTOMOBILE DAMAGE CAUSED BY A DEPENDENT?
OF COURSE NOT.
UH-OH.
EXCUSE ME. I'M HERE FOR MY TAX REFUND. AS AN AFRICAN-AMERICAN MALE, I FACE TAXATION OTHER AMERICANS DO NOT.
"I CAN'T ROCK THE 'BRAD PITT-JUST-OUT-OF-BED' LOOK. SO I HAVE TO PAY MORE FOR CLOTHING..."
JOHNSON CAB
TAXI!
"I HAVE TO PAY FOR DANCE LESSONS, JUST TO KEEP UP WITH MY SOULFUL BROTHERS AND SISTERS..."
SO IT'S A SHUFFLE-SHUFFLE, WIGGLE HIPS ON THE HALF STEP, THEN HAMMERTIME. GOT IT?
NO.
"I HAVE TO BUY TWO DIFFERENT CARS, ONE FOR RIDING IN THE DAYTIME AND ONE FOR RIDING AT NIGHT."
WHOA! A BLACK MAN IN A HYUNDAI! LET'S LEAVE THAT POOR GUY ALONE.
NO ONE IN THIS COUNTRY HAS A BETTER CLAIM TO FUNDS THAN I!
TAKE THIS VOUCHER TO THE GENTLEMAN UP FRONT.
9/13
HI, I'M JOHN REDFEATHER! HOW DO YOU WANT YOUR MONEY?
NEVER MIND.
Watkins

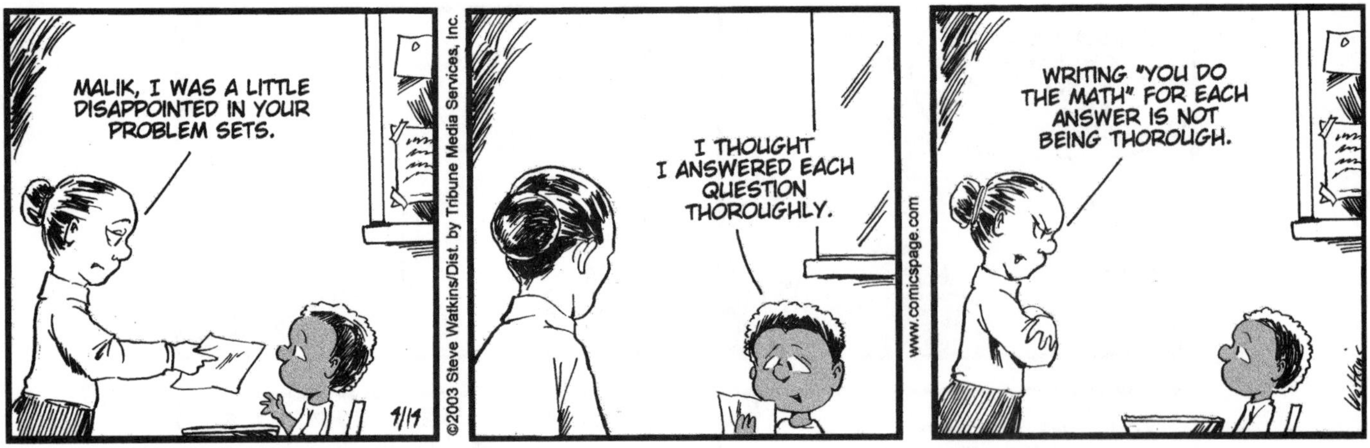
MALIK, I WAS A LITTLE DISAPPOINTED IN YOUR PROBLEM SETS.
I THOUGHT I ANSWERED EACH QUESTION THOROUGHLY.
WRITING "YOU DO THE MATH" FOR EACH ANSWER IS NOT BEING THOROUGH.
©2003 Steve Watkins/Dist. by Tribune Media Services, Inc.
www.comicspage.com

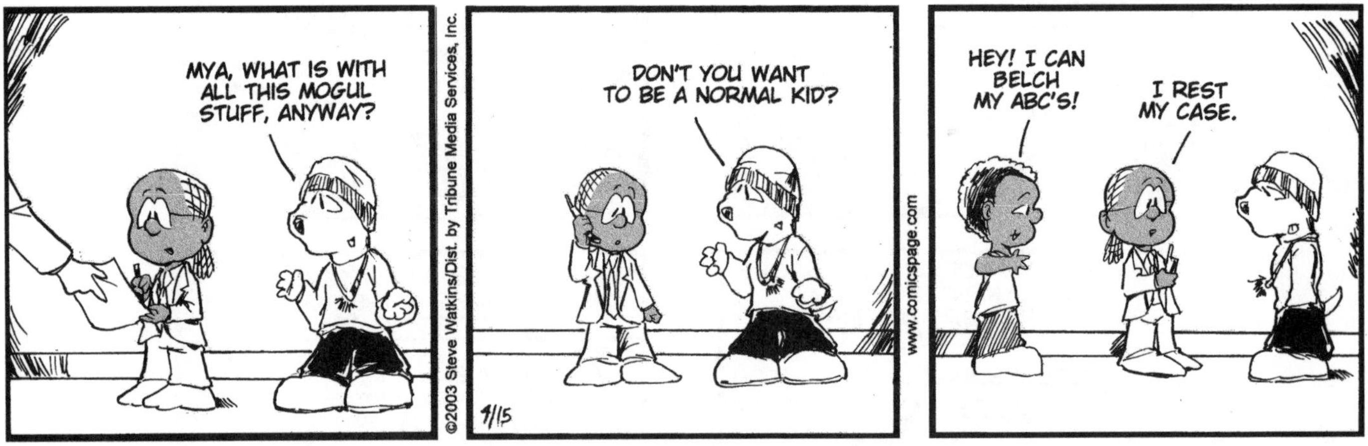
MYA, WHAT IS WITH ALL THIS MOGUL STUFF, ANYWAY?
DON'T YOU WANT TO BE A NORMAL KID?
HEY! I CAN BELCH MY ABC'S!
I REST MY CASE.
©2003 Steve Watkins/Dist. by Tribune Media Services, Inc.
www.comicspage.com

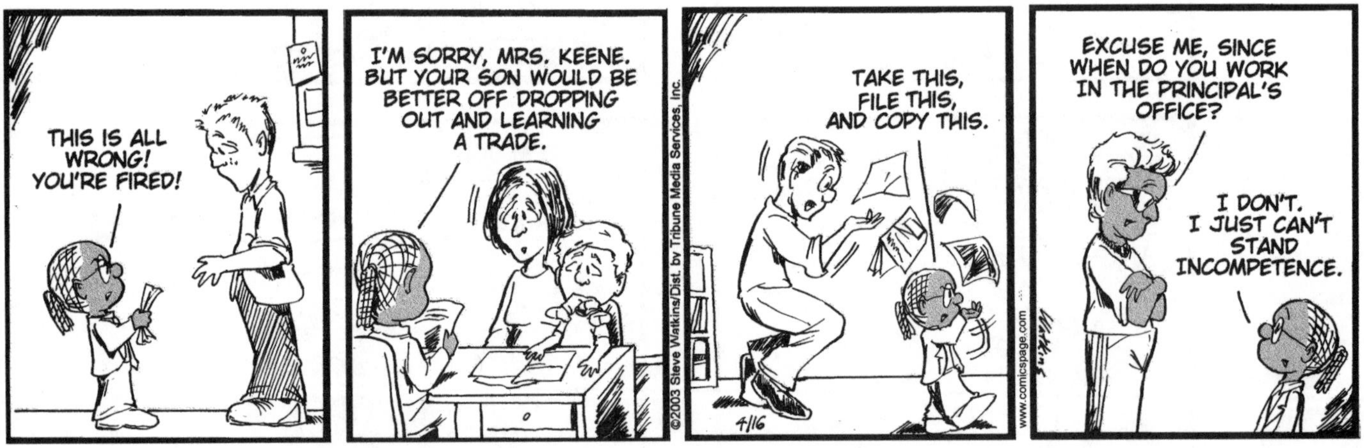
THIS IS ALL WRONG! YOU'RE FIRED!
I'M SORRY, MRS. KEENE. BUT YOUR SON WOULD BE BETTER OFF DROPPING OUT AND LEARNING A TRADE.
TAKE THIS, FILE THIS, AND COPY THIS.
EXCUSE ME, SINCE WHEN DO YOU WORK IN THE PRINCIPAL'S OFFICE?
I DON'T. I JUST CAN'T STAND INCOMPETENCE.
©2003 Steve Watkins/Dist. by Tribune Media Services, Inc.
www.comicspage.com

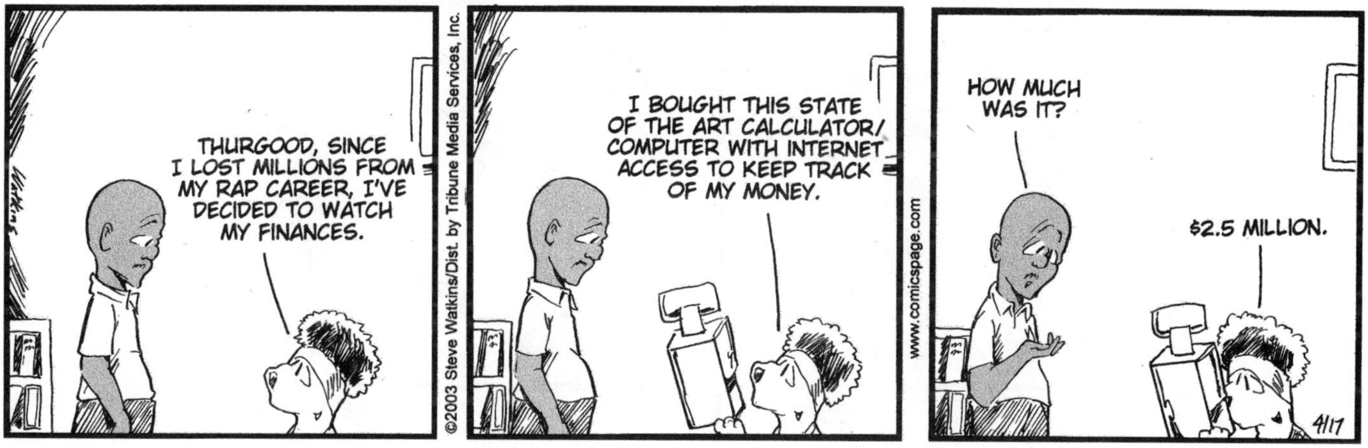
THURGOOD, SINCE I LOST MILLIONS FROM MY RAP CAREER, I'VE DECIDED TO WATCH MY FINANCES.
I BOUGHT THIS STATE OF THE ART CALCULATOR/ COMPUTER WITH INTERNET ACCESS TO KEEP TRACK OF MY MONEY.
HOW MUCH WAS IT?
$2.5 MILLION.
4/17

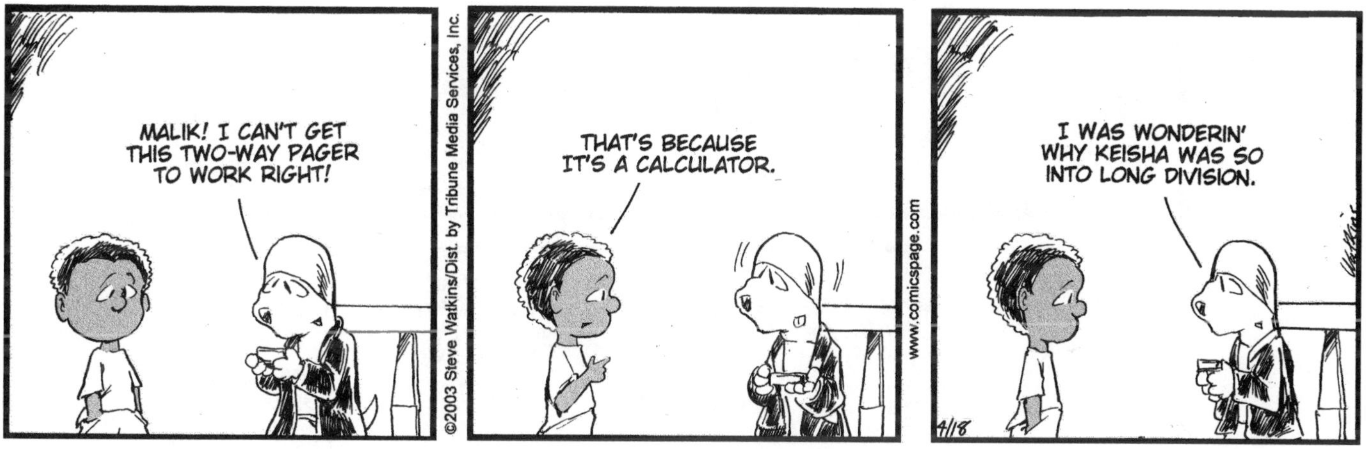
MALIK! I CAN'T GET THIS TWO-WAY PAGER TO WORK RIGHT!
THAT'S BECAUSE IT'S A CALCULATOR.
I WAS WONDERIN' WHY KEISHA WAS SO INTO LONG DIVISION.
4/18

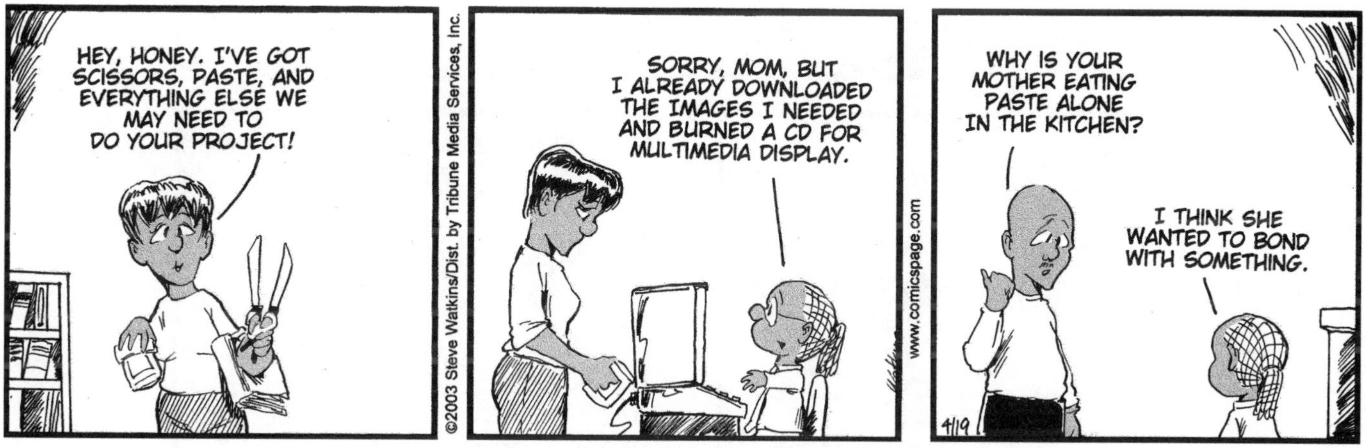
HEY, HONEY. I'VE GOT SCISSORS, PASTE, AND EVERYTHING ELSE WE MAY NEED TO DO YOUR PROJECT!
SORRY, MOM, BUT I ALREADY DOWNLOADED THE IMAGES I NEEDED AND BURNED A CD FOR MULTIMEDIA DISPLAY.
WHY IS YOUR MOTHER EATING PASTE ALONE IN THE KITCHEN?
I THINK SHE WANTED TO BOND WITH SOMETHING.
4/19

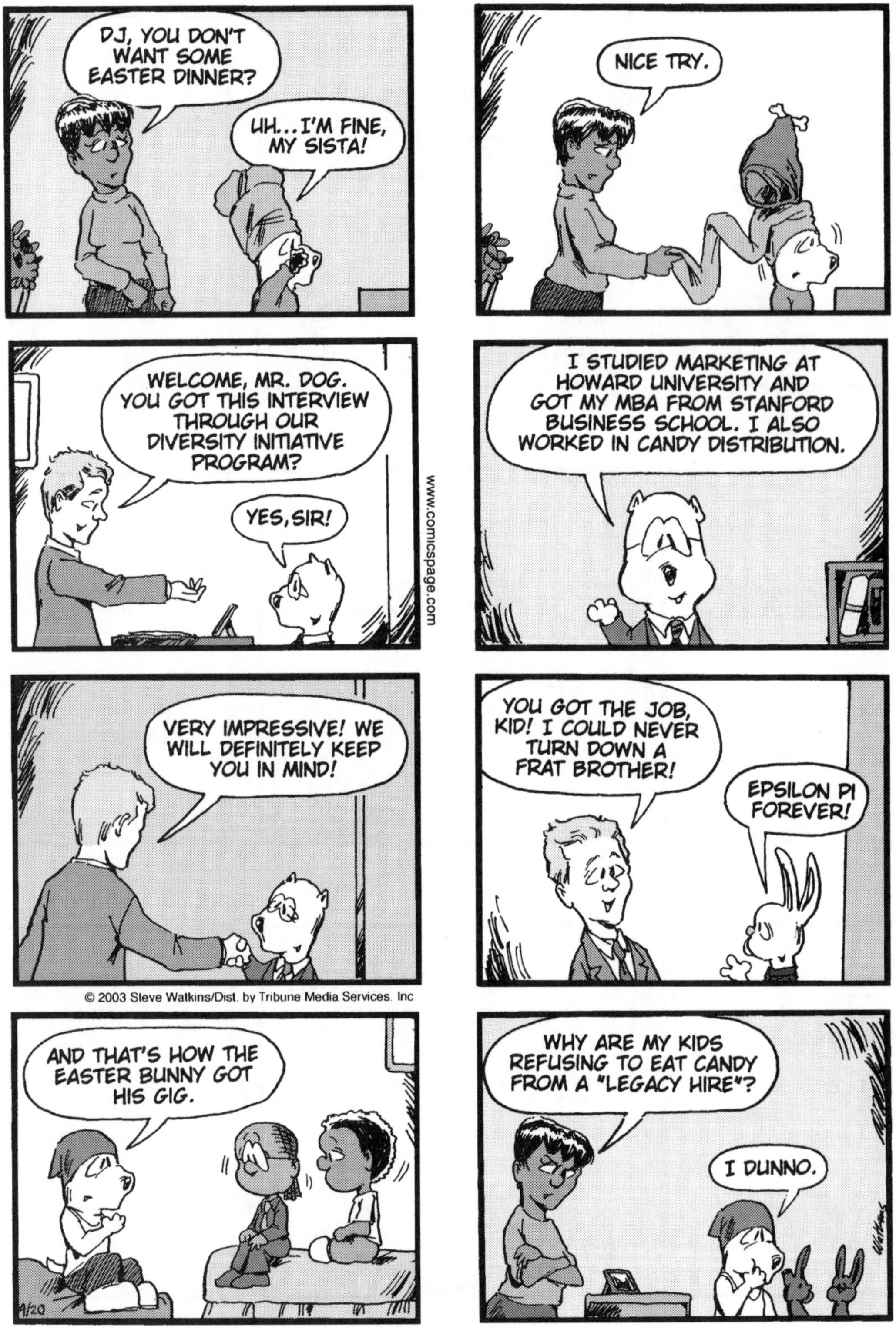
DJ, YOU DON'T WANT SOME EASTER DINNER?
UH... I'M FINE, MY SISTA!
NICE TRY.
WELCOME, MR. DOG. YOU GOT THIS INTERVIEW THROUGH OUR DIVERSITY INITIATIVE PROGRAM?
YES, SIR!
I STUDIED MARKETING AT HOWARD UNIVERSITY AND GOT MY MBA FROM STANFORD BUSINESS SCHOOL. I ALSO WORKED IN CANDY DISTRIBUTION.
VERY IMPRESSIVE! WE WILL DEFINITELY KEEP YOU IN MIND!
YOU GOT THE JOB, KID! I COULD NEVER TURN DOWN A FRAT BROTHER!
EPSILON PI FOREVER!
AND THAT'S HOW THE EASTER BUNNY GOT HIS GIG.
WHY ARE MY KIDS REFUSING TO EAT CANDY FROM A "LEGACY HIRE"?
I DUNNO.
www.comicspage.com
4/20

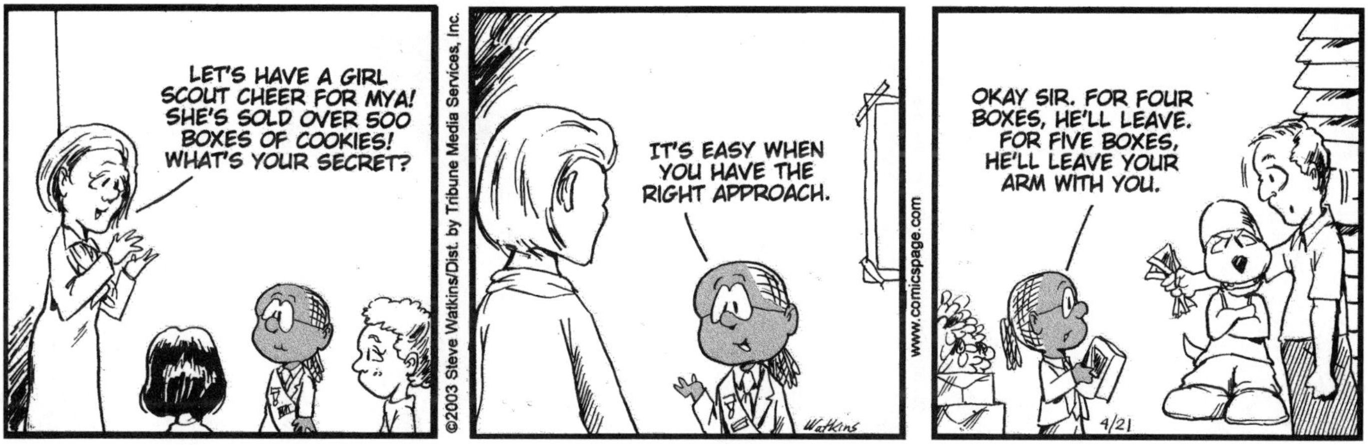
LET'S HAVE A GIRL SCOUT CHEER FOR MYA! SHE'S SOLD OVER 500 BOXES OF COOKIES! WHAT'S YOUR SECRET?
©2003 Steve Watkins/Dist. by Tribune Media Services, Inc.
IT'S EASY WHEN YOU HAVE THE RIGHT APPROACH.
Watkins
www.comicspage.com
OKAY SIR. FOR FOUR BOXES, HE'LL LEAVE. FOR FIVE BOXES, HE'LL LEAVE YOUR ARM WITH YOU.
4/21

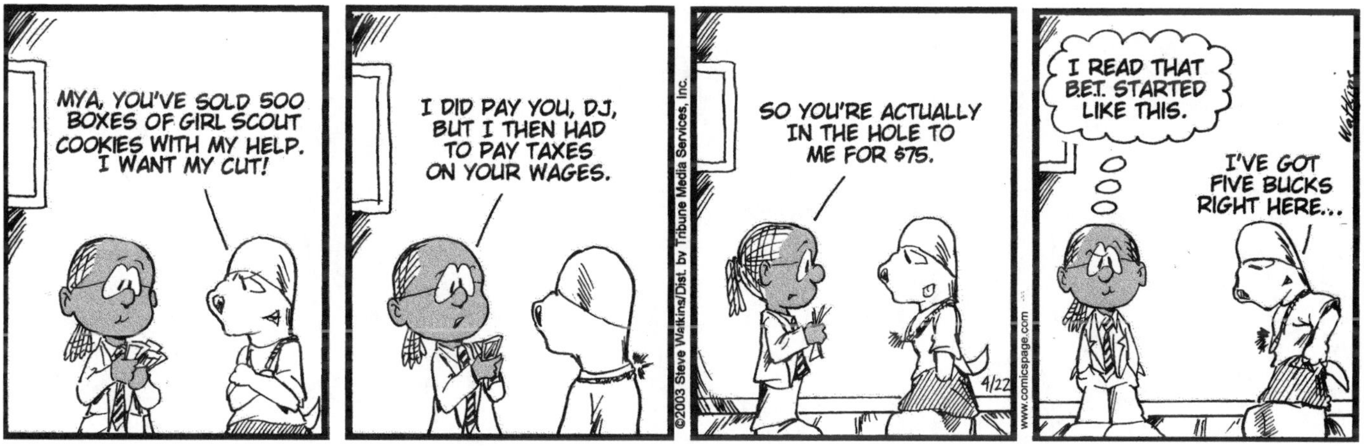
MYA, YOU'VE SOLD 500 BOXES OF GIRL SCOUT COOKIES WITH MY HELP. I WANT MY CUT!
I DID PAY YOU, DJ, BUT I THEN HAD TO PAY TAXES ON YOUR WAGES.
©2003 Steve Watkins/Dist. by Tribune Media Services, Inc.
SO YOU'RE ACTUALLY IN THE HOLE TO ME FOR $75.
4/22
www.comicspage.com
I READ THAT B.E.T. STARTED LIKE THIS.
I'VE GOT FIVE BUCKS RIGHT HERE...
Watkins

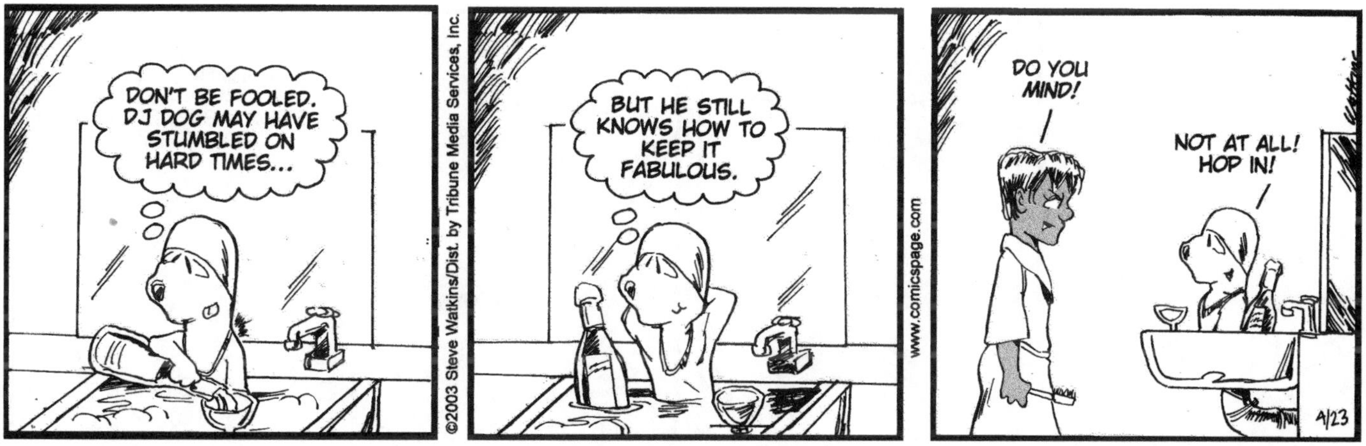
DON'T BE FOOLED. DJ DOG MAY HAVE STUMBLED ON HARD TIMES...
©2003 Steve Watkins/Dist. by Tribune Media Services, Inc.
BUT HE STILL KNOWS HOW TO KEEP IT FABULOUS.
www.comicspage.com
DO YOU MIND!
NOT AT ALL! HOP IN!
4/23

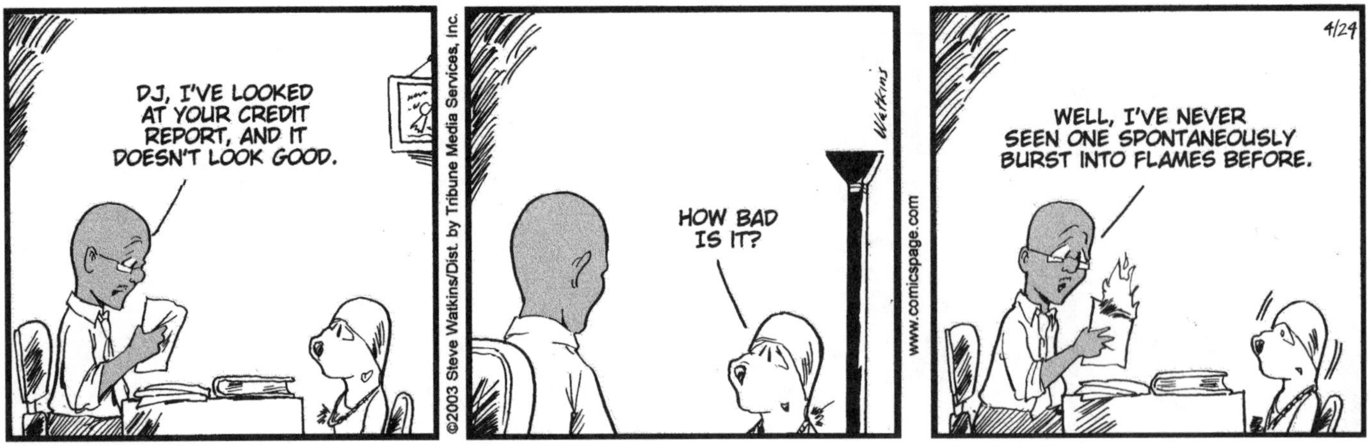
4/24
DJ, I'VE LOOKED AT YOUR CREDIT REPORT, AND IT DOESN'T LOOK GOOD.
HOW BAD IS IT?
WELL, I'VE NEVER SEEN ONE SPONTANEOUSLY BURST INTO FLAMES BEFORE.
©2003 Steve Watkins/Dist. by Tribune Media Services, Inc.
www.comicspage.com
Watkins

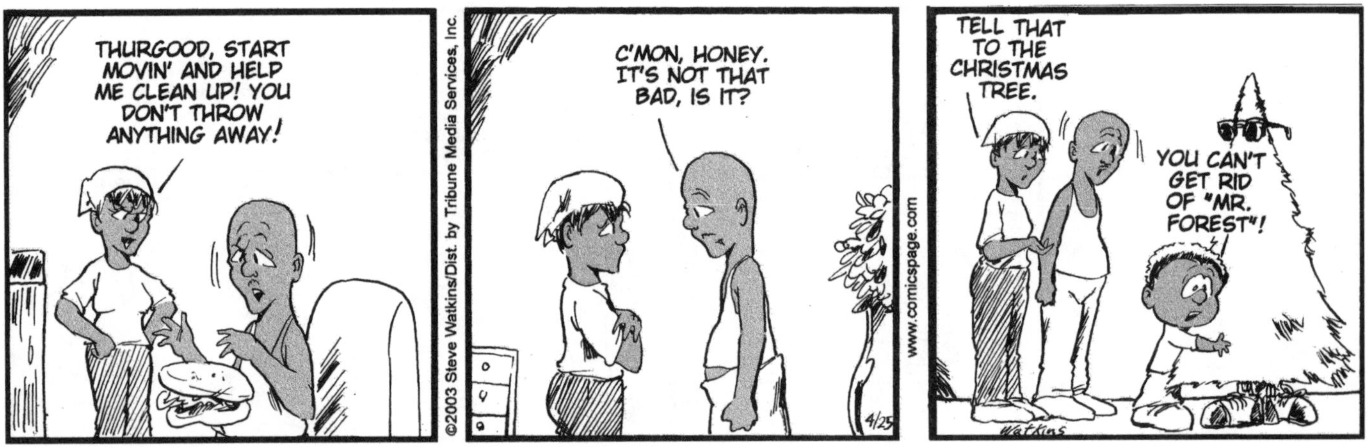
4/25
THURGOOD, START MOVIN' AND HELP ME CLEAN UP! YOU DON'T THROW ANYTHING AWAY!
C'MON, HONEY. IT'S NOT THAT BAD, IS IT?
TELL THAT TO THE CHRISTMAS TREE.
YOU CAN'T GET RID OF "MR. FOREST"!
©2003 Steve Watkins/Dist. by Tribune Media Services, Inc.
www.comicspage.com
Watkins

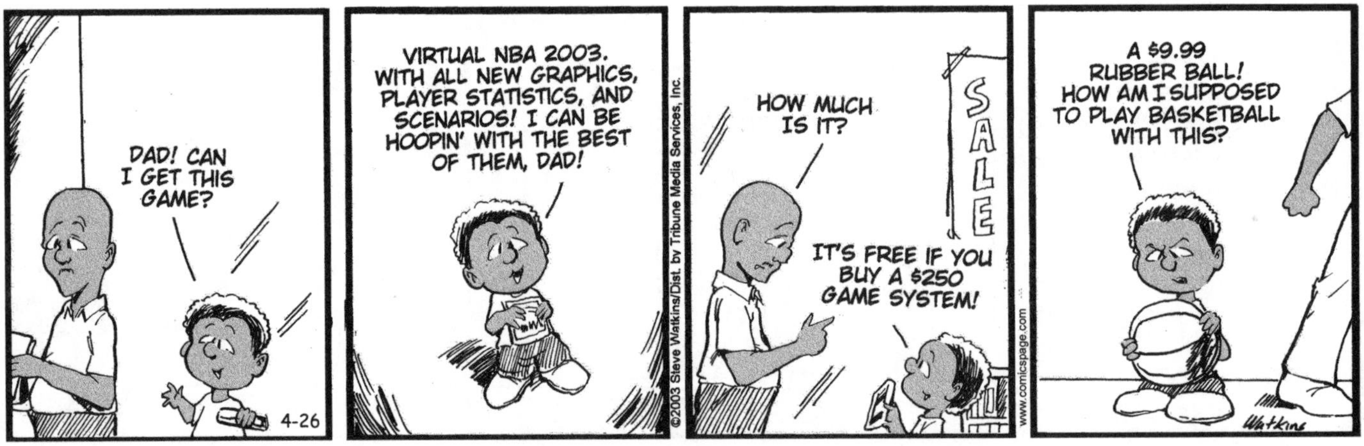
4-26
DAD! CAN I GET THIS GAME?
VIRTUAL NBA 2003. WITH ALL NEW GRAPHICS, PLAYER STATISTICS, AND SCENARIOS! I CAN BE HOOPIN' WITH THE BEST OF THEM, DAD!
HOW MUCH IS IT?
SALE
IT'S FREE IF YOU BUY A $250 GAME SYSTEM!
A $9.99 RUBBER BALL! HOW AM I SUPPOSED TO PLAY BASKETBALL WITH THIS?
©2003 Steve Watkins/Dist. by Tribune Media Services, Inc.
www.comicspage.com
Watkins

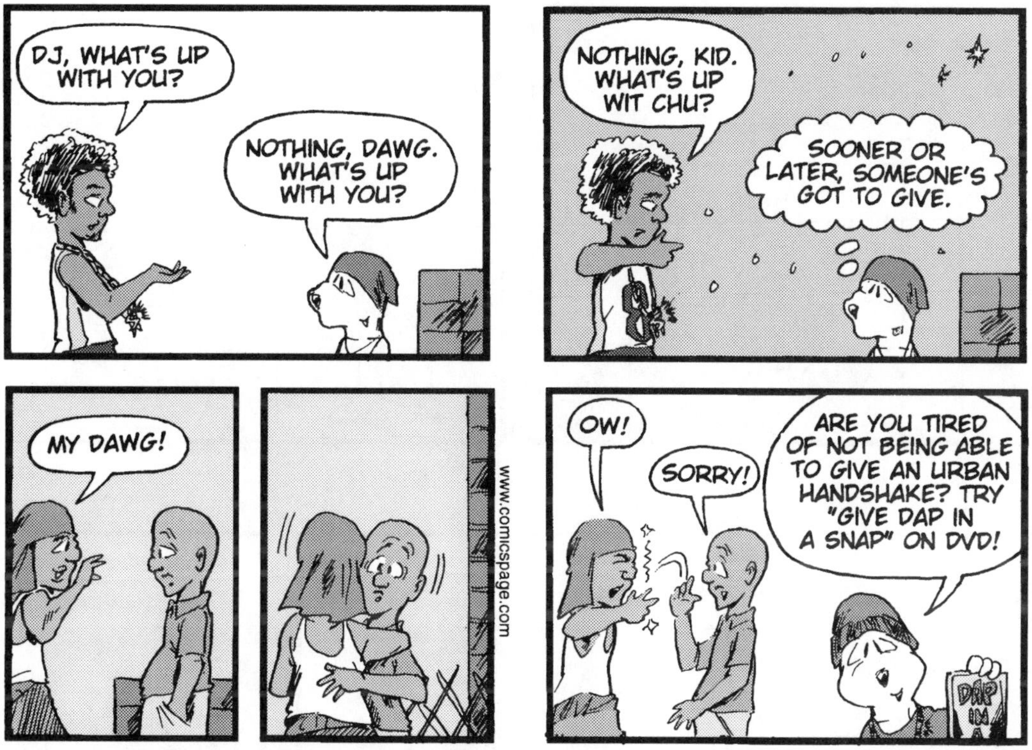

DJ, WHAT'S UP WITH YOU?
NOTHING, DAWG. WHAT'S UP WITH YOU?
NOTHING, KID. WHAT'S UP WIT CHU?
SOONER OR LATER, SOMEONE'S GOT TO GIVE.
MY DAWG!
www.comicspage.com
OW!
SORRY!
ARE YOU TIRED OF NOT BEING ABLE TO GIVE AN URBAN HANDSHAKE? TRY "GIVE DAP IN A SNAP" ON DVD!

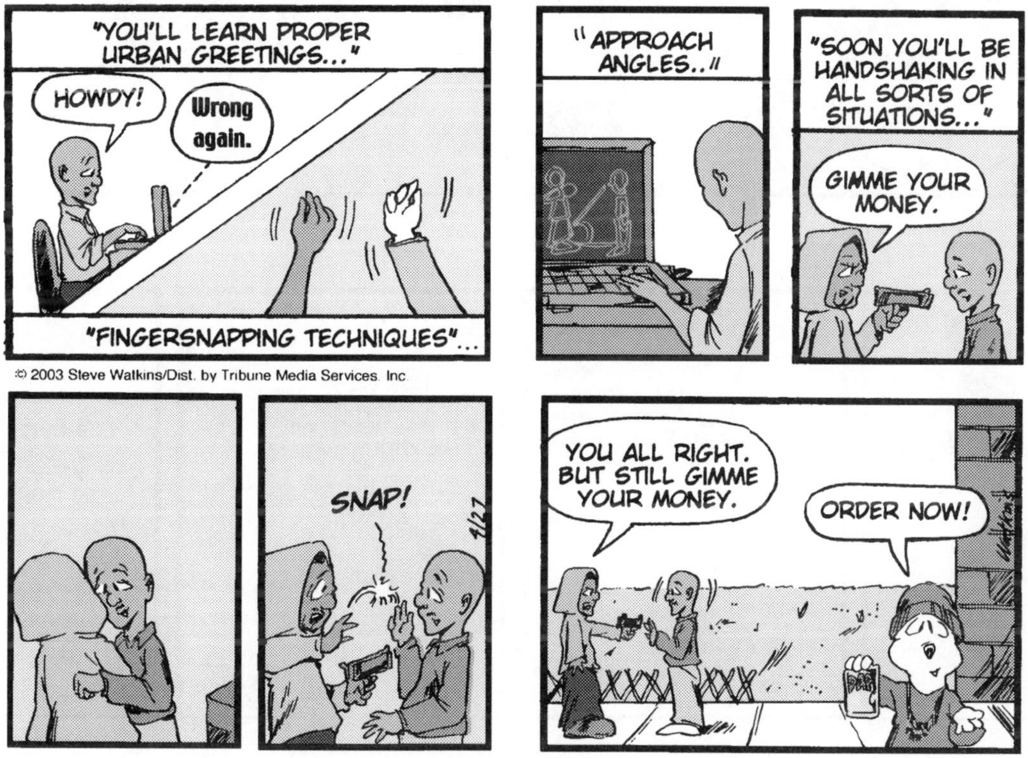

"YOU'LL LEARN PROPER URBAN GREETINGS..."
HOWDY!
Wrong again.
"FINGERSNAPPING TECHNIQUES"...
"APPROACH ANGLES..."
"SOON YOU'LL BE HANDSHAKING IN ALL SORTS OF SITUATIONS..."
GIMME YOUR MONEY.
SNAP!
YOU ALL RIGHT. BUT STILL GIMME YOUR MONEY.
ORDER NOW!

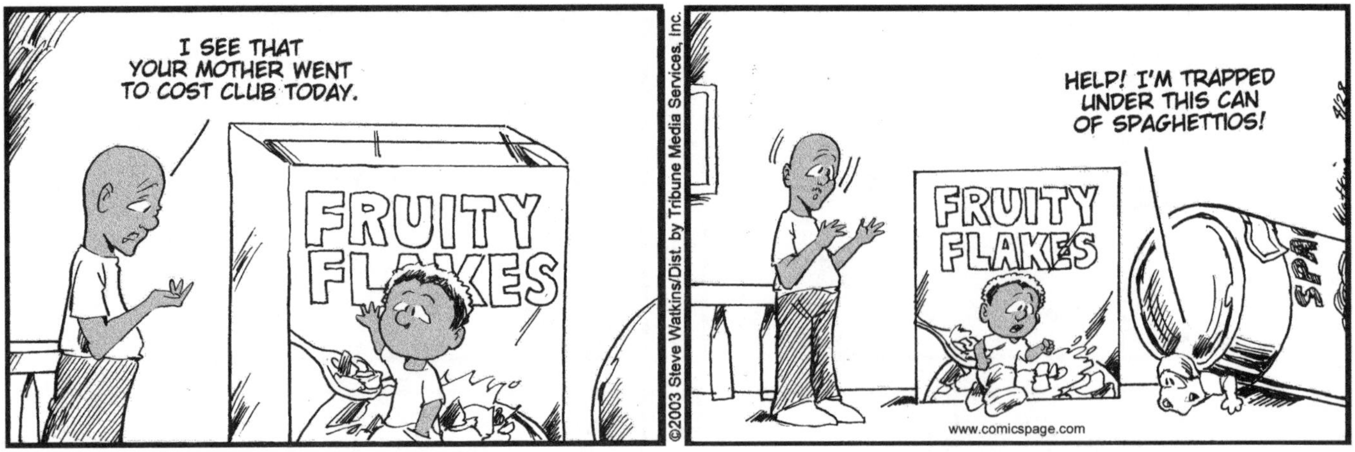
I SEE THAT YOUR MOTHER WENT TO COST CLUB TODAY.
FRUITY FLAKES
©2003 Steve Watkins/Dist. by Tribune Media Services, Inc.
HELP! I'M TRAPPED UNDER THIS CAN OF SPAGHETTIOS!
FRUITY FLAKES
www.comicspage.com

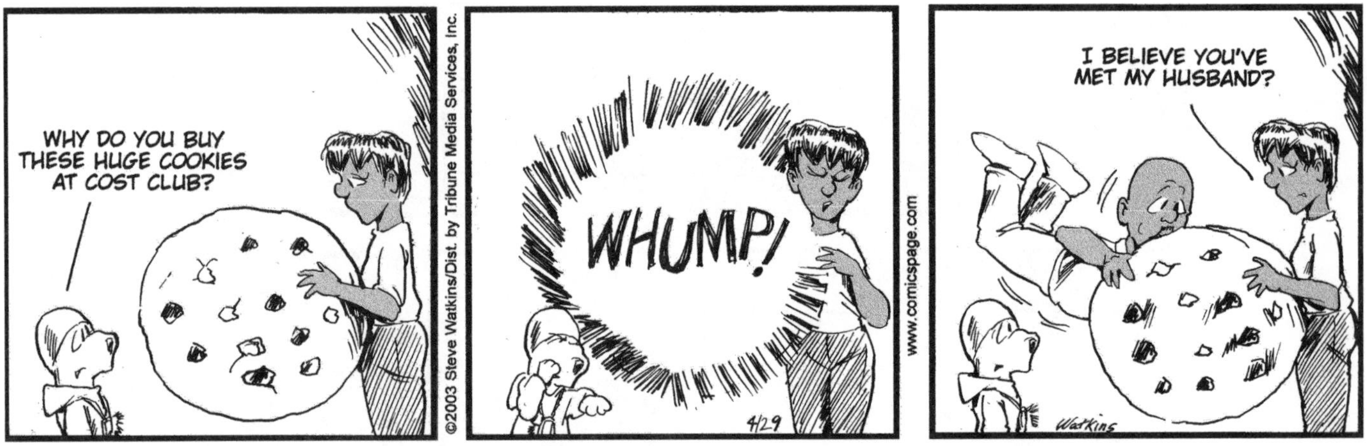
WHY DO YOU BUY THESE HUGE COOKIES AT COST CLUB?
©2003 Steve Watkins/Dist. by Tribune Media Services, Inc.
WHUMP!
4/29
www.comicspage.com
I BELIEVE YOU'VE MET MY HUSBAND?

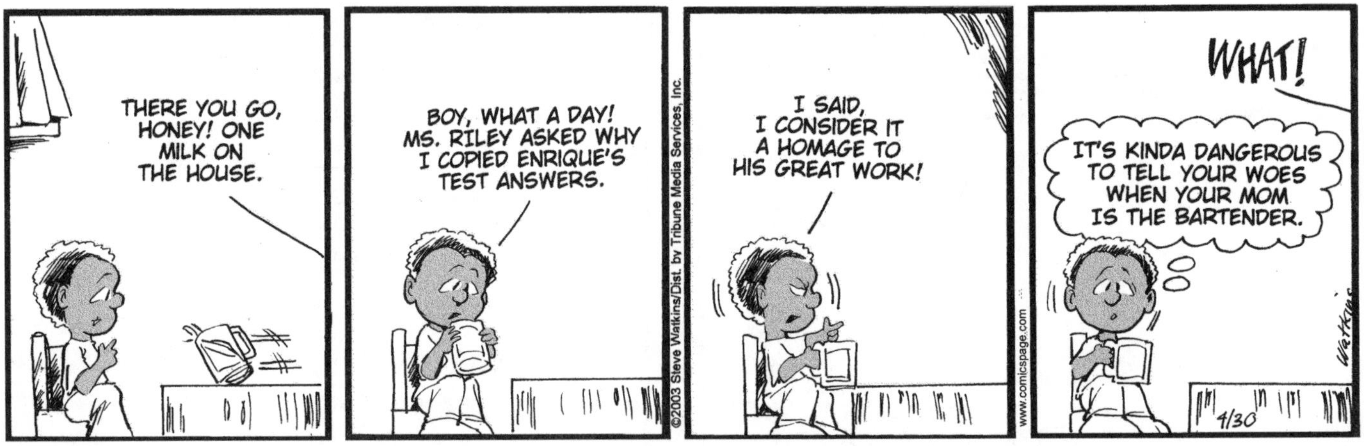
THERE YOU GO, HONEY! ONE MILK ON THE HOUSE.
BOY, WHAT A DAY! MS. RILEY ASKED WHY I COPIED ENRIQUE'S TEST ANSWERS.
©2003 Steve Watkins/Dist. by Tribune Media Services, Inc.
I SAID, I CONSIDER IT A HOMAGE TO HIS GREAT WORK!
www.comicspage.com
WHAT!
IT'S KINDA DANGEROUS TO TELL YOUR WOES WHEN YOUR MOM IS THE BARTENDER.
4/30

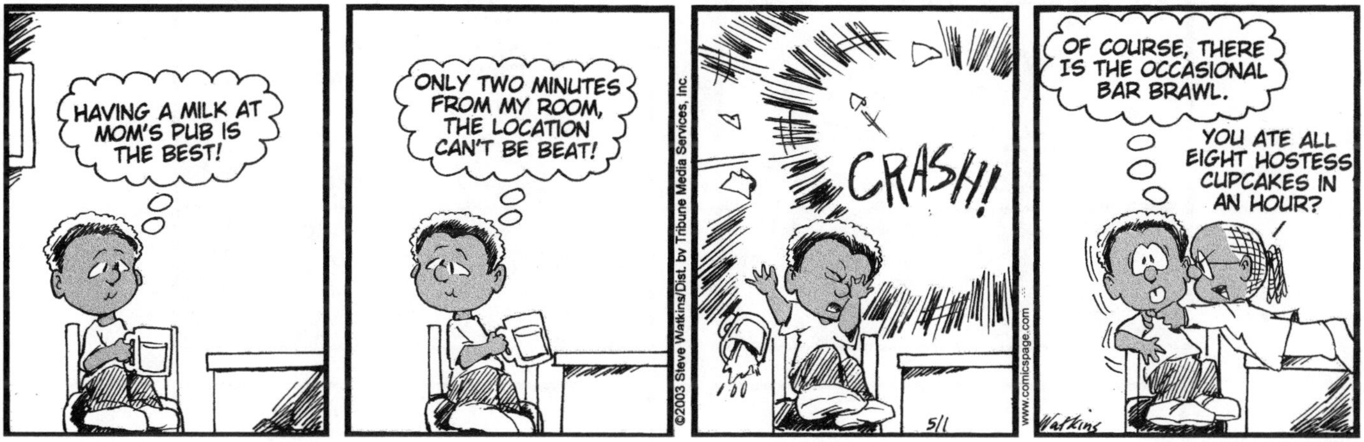
HAVING A MILK AT MOM'S PUB IS THE BEST!
ONLY TWO MINUTES FROM MY ROOM, THE LOCATION CAN'T BE BEAT!
©2003 Steve Watkins/Dist. by Tribune Media Services, Inc.
CRASH!
5/1
www.comicspage.com
OF COURSE, THERE IS THE OCCASIONAL BAR BRAWL.
YOU ATE ALL EIGHT HOSTESS CUPCAKES IN AN HOUR?
Watkins

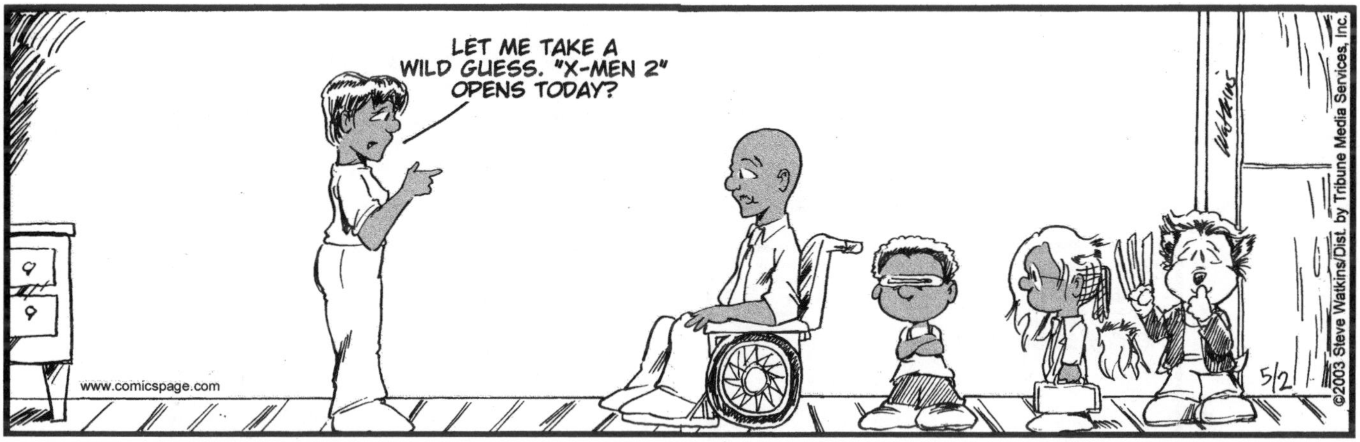
LET ME TAKE A WILD GUESS. "X-MEN 2" OPENS TODAY?
Watkins
www.comicspage.com
5/2
©2003 Steve Watkins/Dist. by Tribune Media Services, Inc.

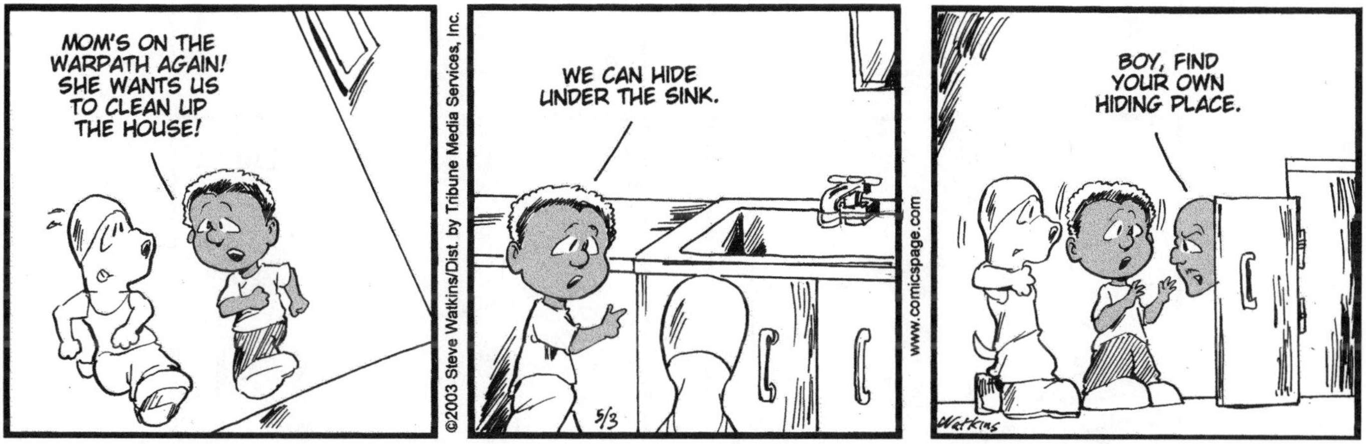
MOM'S ON THE WARPATH AGAIN! SHE WANTS US TO CLEAN UP THE HOUSE!
©2003 Steve Watkins/Dist. by Tribune Media Services, Inc.
WE CAN HIDE UNDER THE SINK.
5/3
www.comicspage.com
BOY, FIND YOUR OWN HIDING PLACE.
Watkins

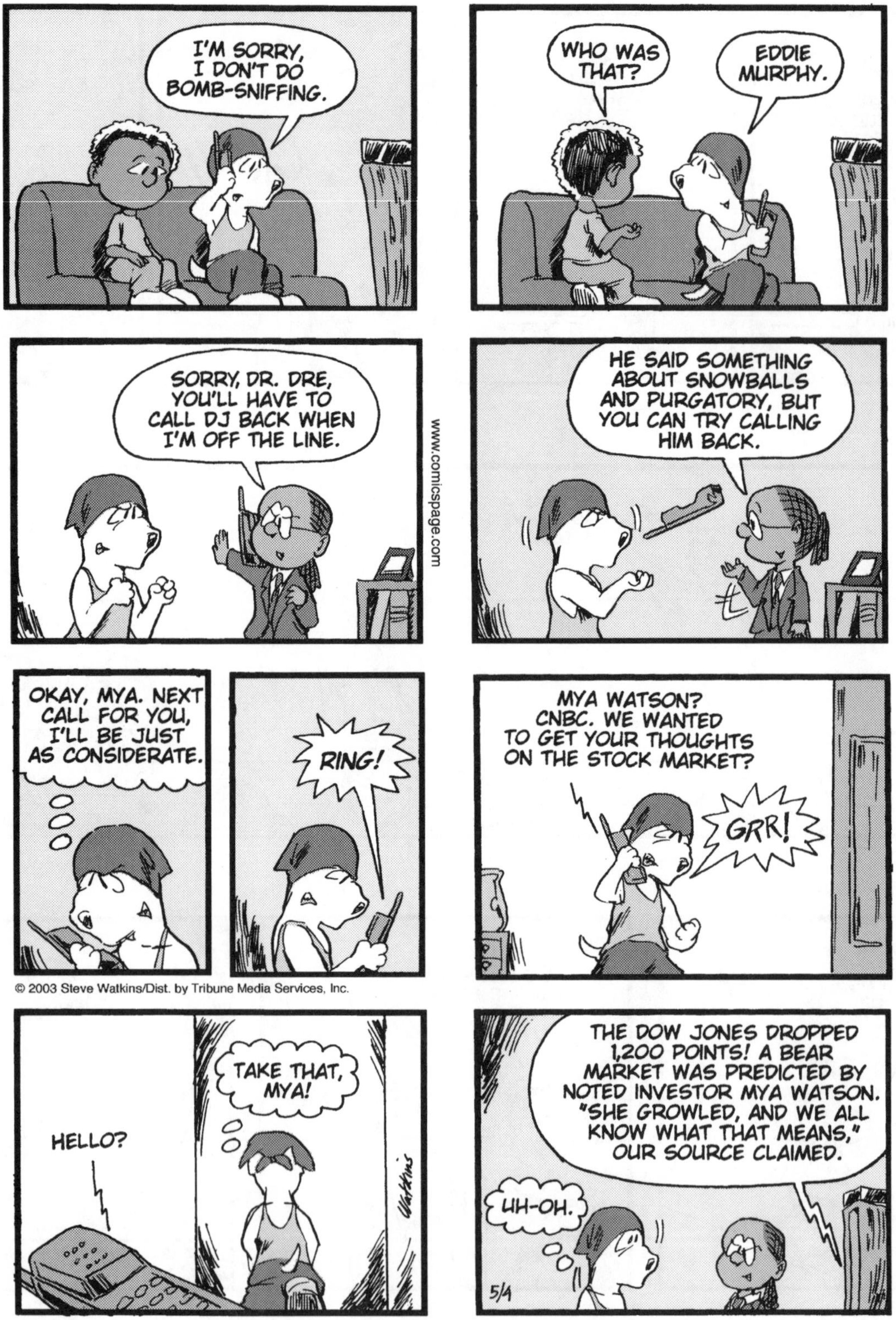
I'M SORRY, I DON'T DO BOMB-SNIFFING.
WHO WAS THAT?
EDDIE MURPHY.
SORRY, DR. DRE, YOU'LL HAVE TO CALL DJ BACK WHEN I'M OFF THE LINE.
www.comicspage.com
HE SAID SOMETHING ABOUT SNOWBALLS AND PURGATORY, BUT YOU CAN TRY CALLING HIM BACK.
OKAY, MYA. NEXT CALL FOR YOU, I'LL BE JUST AS CONSIDERATE.
RING!
MYA WATSON? CNBC. WE WANTED TO GET YOUR THOUGHTS ON THE STOCK MARKET?
GRR!
HELLO?
TAKE THAT, MYA!
Watkins
THE DOW JONES DROPPED 1,200 POINTS! A BEAR MARKET WAS PREDICTED BY NOTED INVESTOR MYA WATSON. "SHE GROWLED, AND WE ALL KNOW WHAT THAT MEANS," OUR SOURCE CLAIMED.
UH-OH.
5/4

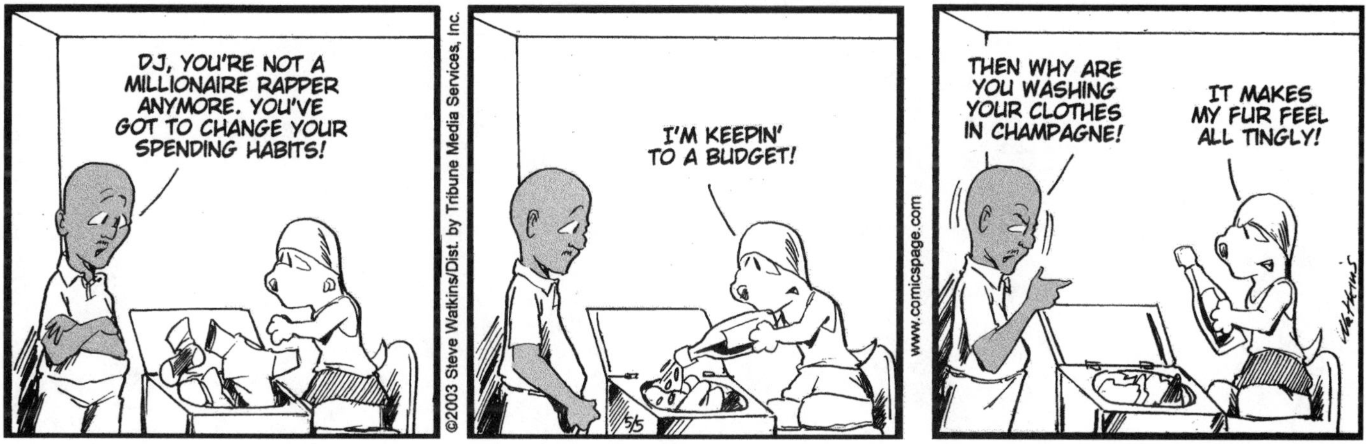
DJ, YOU'RE NOT A MILLIONAIRE RAPPER ANYMORE. YOU'VE GOT TO CHANGE YOUR SPENDING HABITS!
I'M KEEPIN' TO A BUDGET!
5/5
©2003 Steve Watkins/Dist. by Tribune Media Services, Inc.
THEN WHY ARE YOU WASHING YOUR CLOTHES IN CHAMPAGNE!
IT MAKES MY FUR FEEL ALL TINGLY!
www.comicspage.com
WATKINS

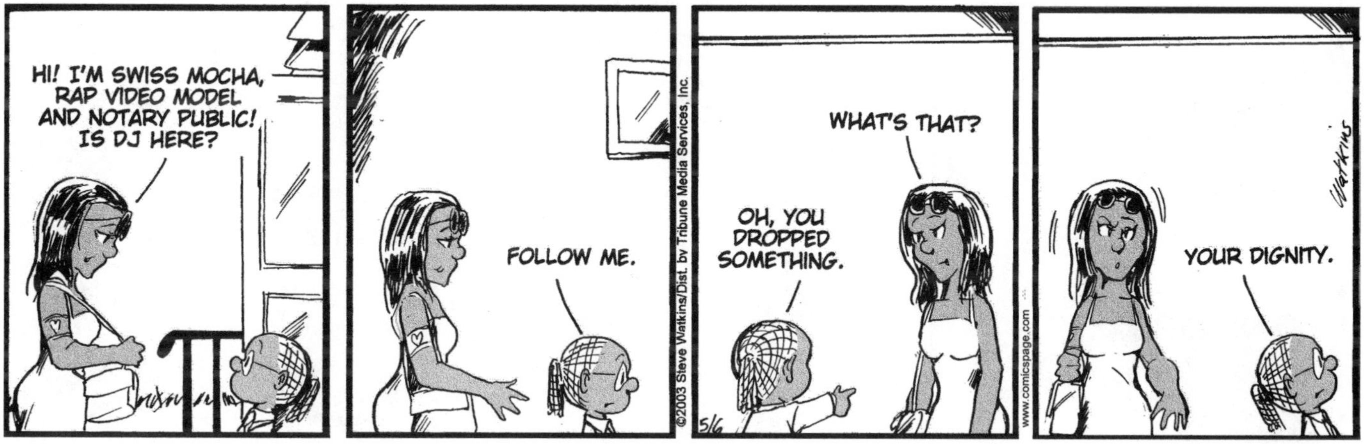
HI! I'M SWISS MOCHA, RAP VIDEO MODEL AND NOTARY PUBLIC! IS DJ HERE?
FOLLOW ME.
©2003 Steve Watkins/Dist. by Tribune Media Services, Inc.
OH, YOU DROPPED SOMETHING.
WHAT'S THAT?
5/6
www.comicspage.com
YOUR DIGNITY.
WATKINS

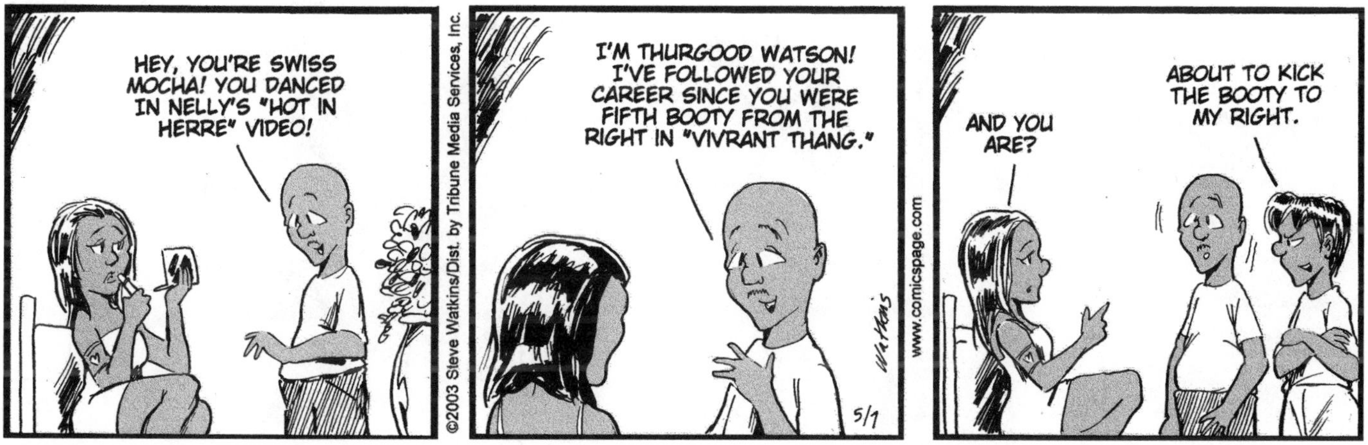
HEY, YOU'RE SWISS MOCHA! YOU DANCED IN NELLY'S "HOT IN HERRE" VIDEO!
©2003 Steve Watkins/Dist. by Tribune Media Services, Inc.
I'M THURGOOD WATSON! I'VE FOLLOWED YOUR CAREER SINCE YOU WERE FIFTH BOOTY FROM THE RIGHT IN "VIVRANT THANG."
WATKINS
5/1
www.comicspage.com
AND YOU ARE?
ABOUT TO KICK THE BOOTY TO MY RIGHT.

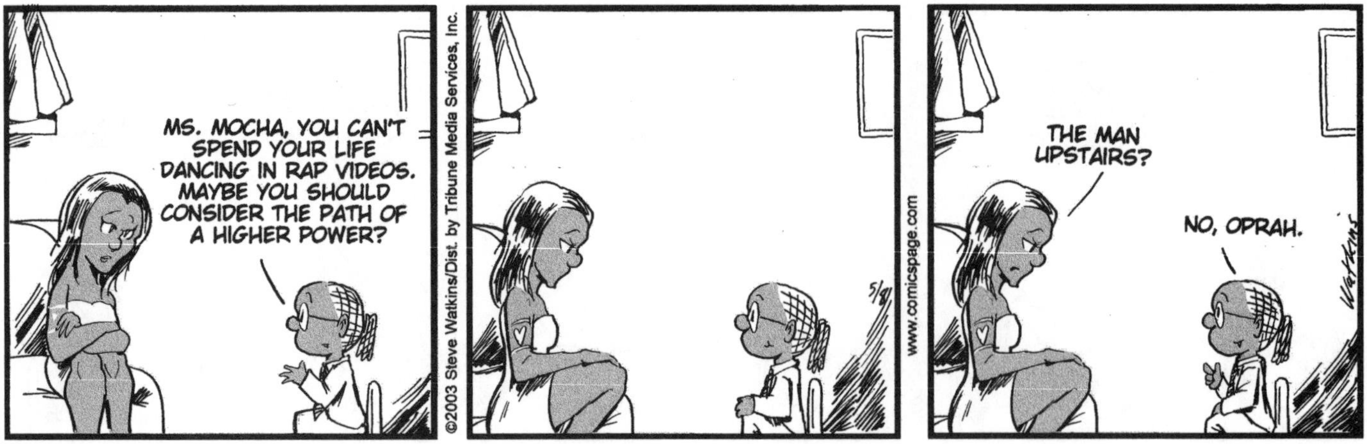
MS. MOCHA, YOU CAN'T SPEND YOUR LIFE DANCING IN RAP VIDEOS. MAYBE YOU SHOULD CONSIDER THE PATH OF A HIGHER POWER?
©2003 Steve Watkins/Dist. by Tribune Media Services, Inc.
www.comicspage.com
THE MAN UPSTAIRS?
NO, OPRAH.

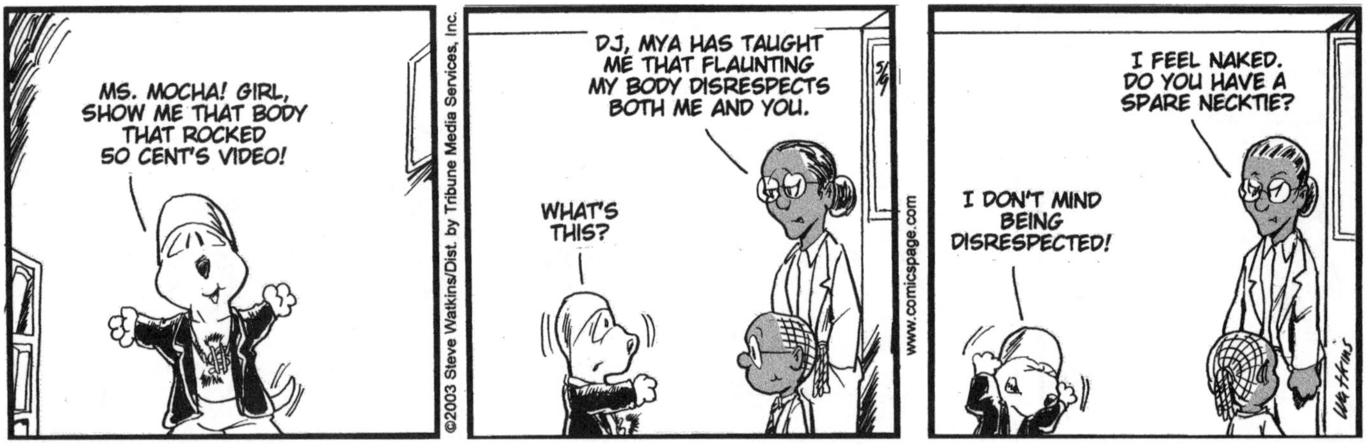
MS. MOCHA! GIRL, SHOW ME THAT BODY THAT ROCKED 50 CENT'S VIDEO!
©2003 Steve Watkins/Dist. by Tribune Media Services, Inc.
DJ, MYA HAS TAUGHT ME THAT FLAUNTING MY BODY DISRESPECTS BOTH ME AND YOU.
WHAT'S THIS?
www.comicspage.com
I FEEL NAKED. DO YOU HAVE A SPARE NECKTIE?
I DON'T MIND BEING DISRESPECTED!

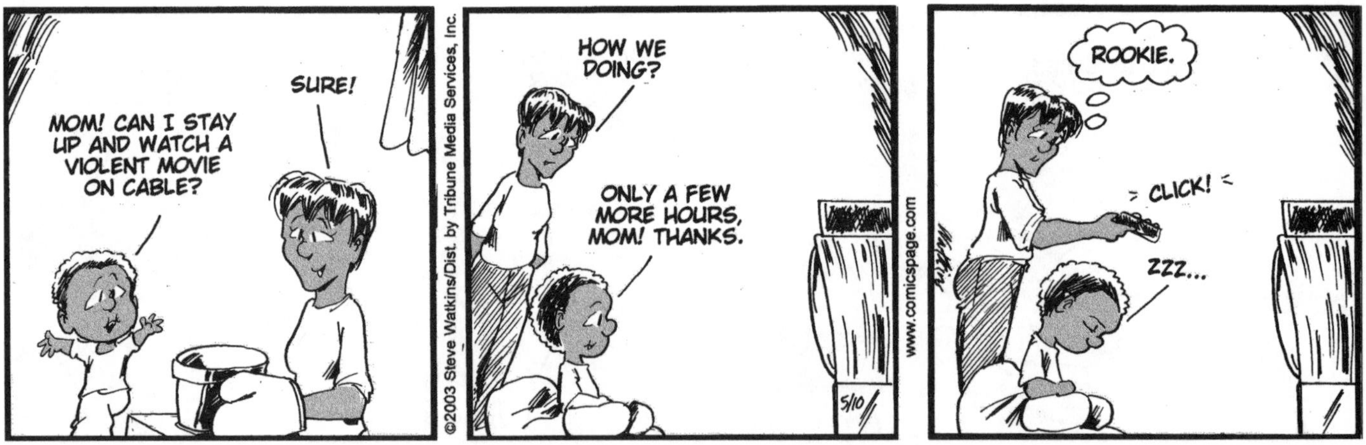
MOM! CAN I STAY UP AND WATCH A VIOLENT MOVIE ON CABLE?
SURE!
©2003 Steve Watkins/Dist. by Tribune Media Services, Inc.
HOW WE DOING?
ONLY A FEW MORE HOURS, MOM! THANKS.
www.comicspage.com
ROOKIE.
CLICK!
ZZZ...

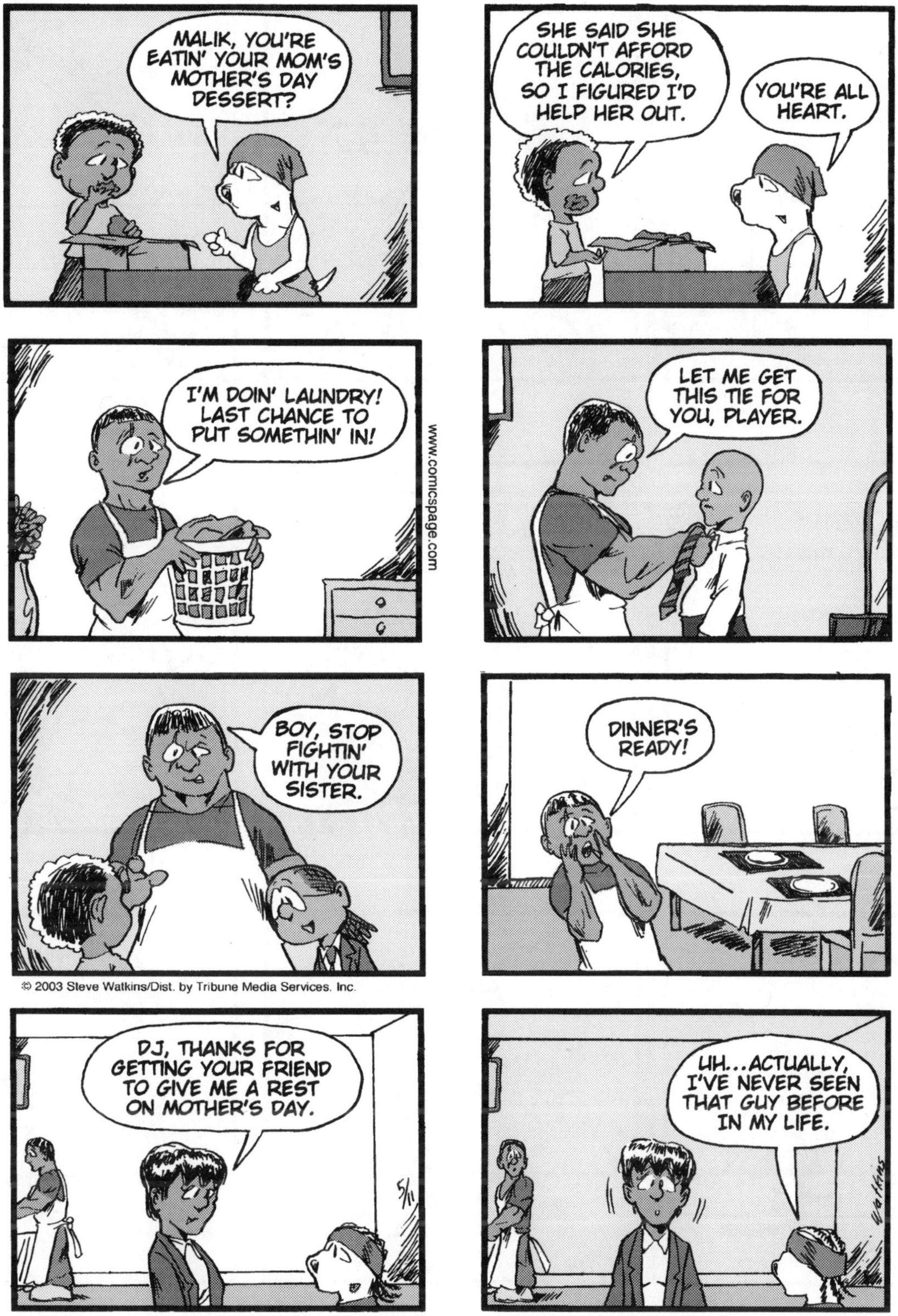
MALIK, YOU'RE EATIN' YOUR MOM'S MOTHER'S DAY DESSERT?
SHE SAID SHE COULDN'T AFFORD THE CALORIES, SO I FIGURED I'D HELP HER OUT.
YOU'RE ALL HEART.
I'M DOIN' LAUNDRY! LAST CHANCE TO PUT SOMETHIN' IN!
www.comicspage.com
LET ME GET THIS TIE FOR YOU, PLAYER.
BOY, STOP FIGHTIN' WITH YOUR SISTER.
DINNER'S READY!
DJ, THANKS FOR GETTING YOUR FRIEND TO GIVE ME A REST ON MOTHER'S DAY.
5/11
UH...ACTUALLY, I'VE NEVER SEEN THAT GUY BEFORE IN MY LIFE.

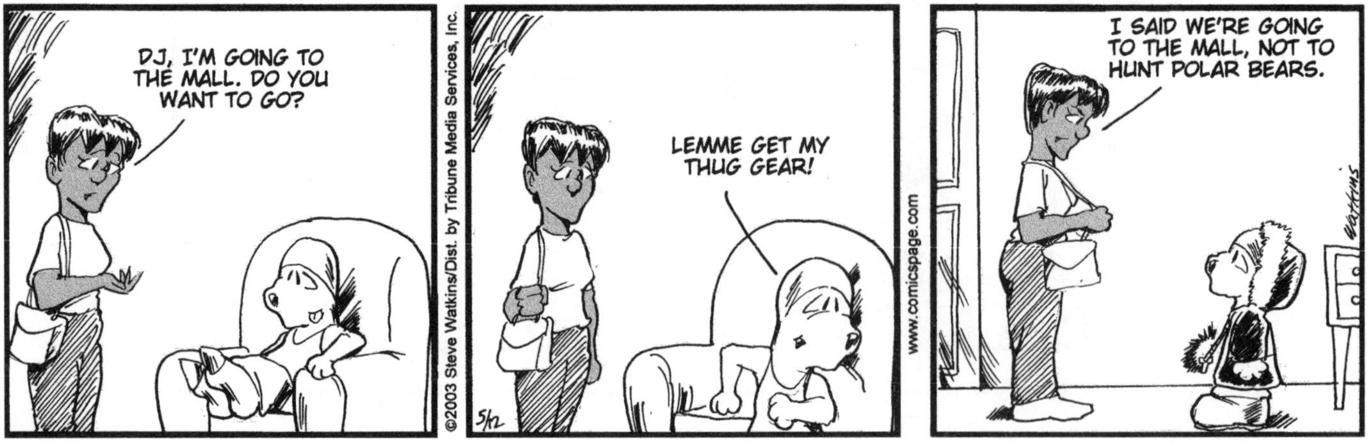
DJ, I'M GOING TO THE MALL. DO YOU WANT TO GO?
LEMME GET MY THUG GEAR!
I SAID WE'RE GOING TO THE MALL, NOT TO HUNT POLAR BEARS.
5/12
WATKINS

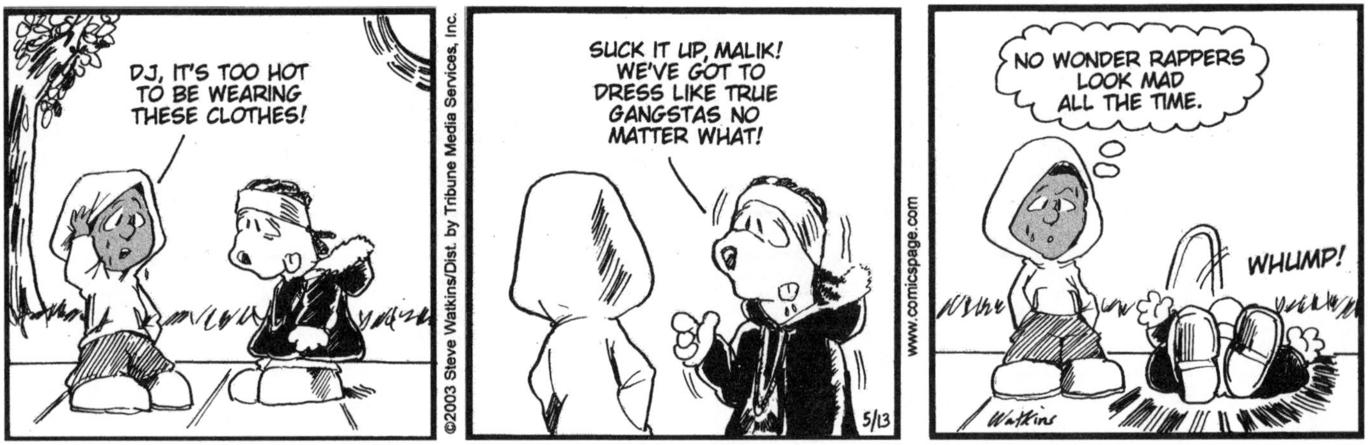
DJ, IT'S TOO HOT TO BE WEARING THESE CLOTHES!
SUCK IT UP, MALIK! WE'VE GOT TO DRESS LIKE TRUE GANGSTAS NO MATTER WHAT!
5/13
NO WONDER RAPPERS LOOK MAD ALL THE TIME.
WHUMP!
Watkins

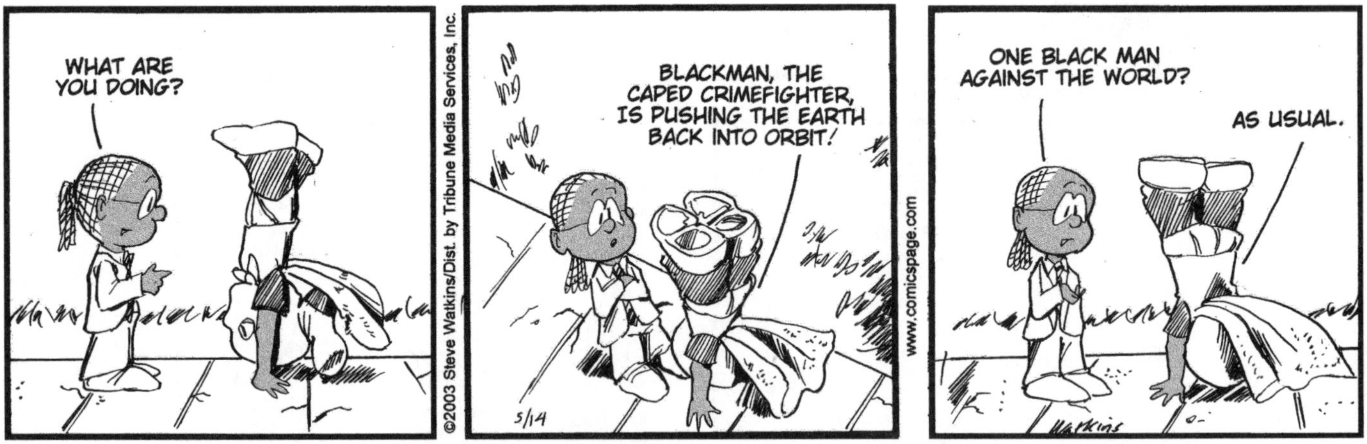
WHAT ARE YOU DOING?
BLACKMAN, THE CAPED CRIMEFIGHTER, IS PUSHING THE EARTH BACK INTO ORBIT!
5/14
ONE BLACK MAN AGAINST THE WORLD?
AS USUAL.
Watkins

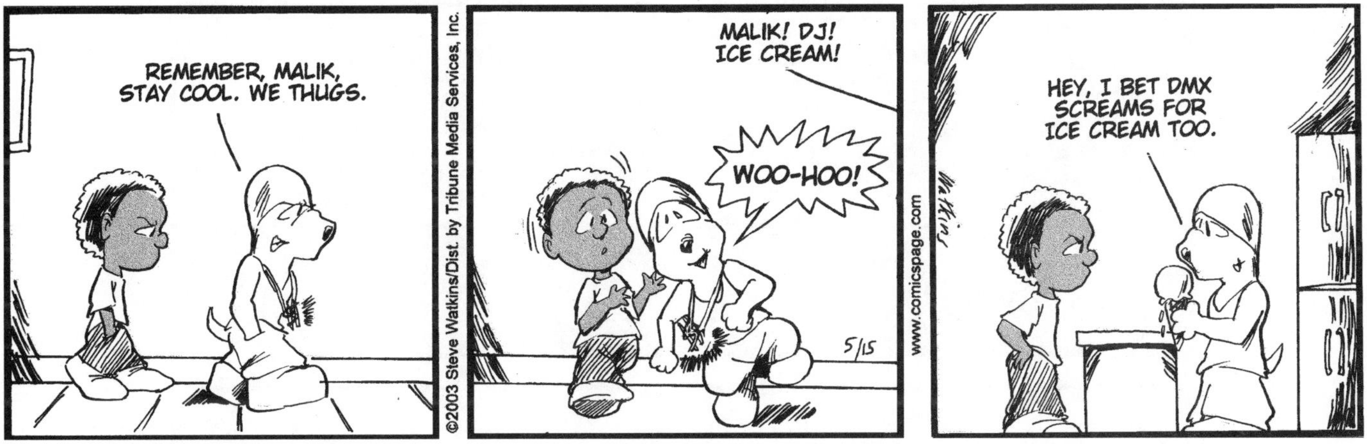
REMEMBER, MALIK, STAY COOL. WE THUGS.
©2003 Steve Watkins/Dist. by Tribune Media Services, Inc.
MALIK! DJ! ICE CREAM!
WOO-HOO!
5/15
www.comicspage.com
Watkins
HEY, I BET DMX SCREAMS FOR ICE CREAM TOO.

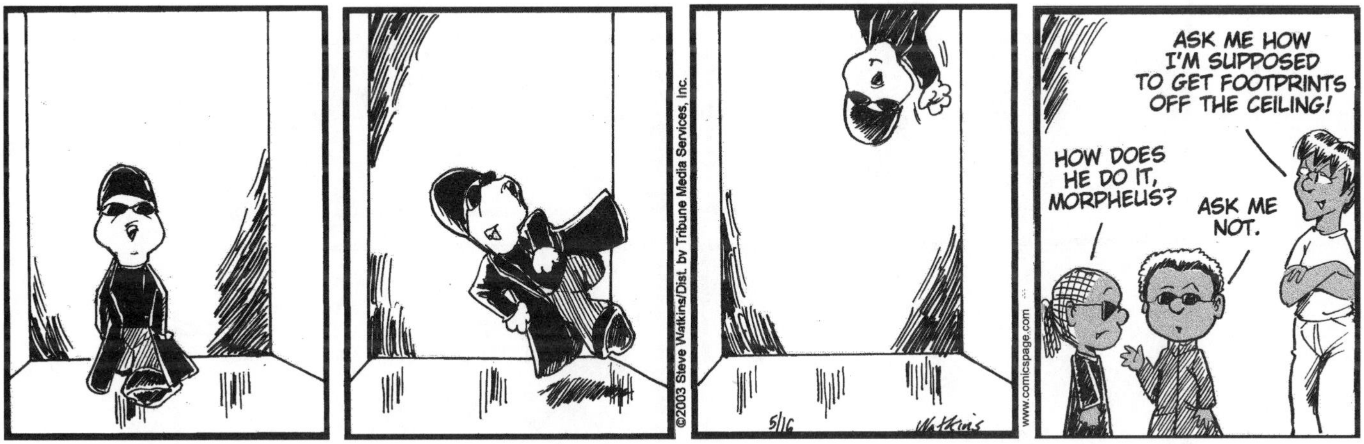
©2003 Steve Watkins/Dist. by Tribune Media Services, Inc.
5/16
Watkins
www.comicspage.com
ASK ME HOW I'M SUPPOSED TO GET FOOTPRINTS OFF THE CEILING!
HOW DOES HE DO IT, MORPHEUS?
ASK ME NOT.

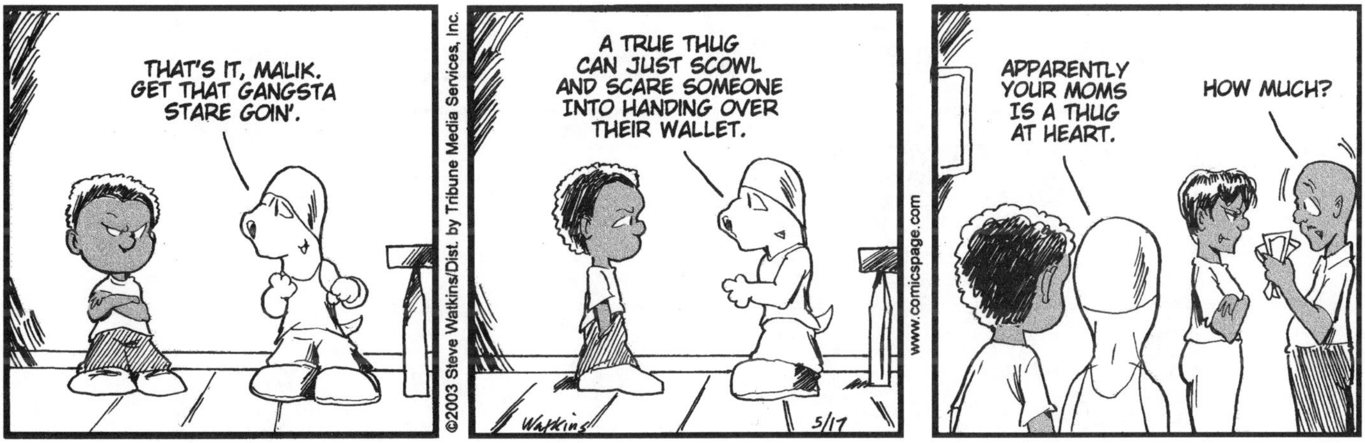
THAT'S IT, MALIK. GET THAT GANGSTA STARE GOIN'.
©2003 Steve Watkins/Dist. by Tribune Media Services, Inc.
A TRUE THUG CAN JUST SCOWL AND SCARE SOMEONE INTO HANDING OVER THEIR WALLET.
Watkins
5/17
www.comicspage.com
APPARENTLY YOUR MOMS IS A THUG AT HEART.
HOW MUCH?

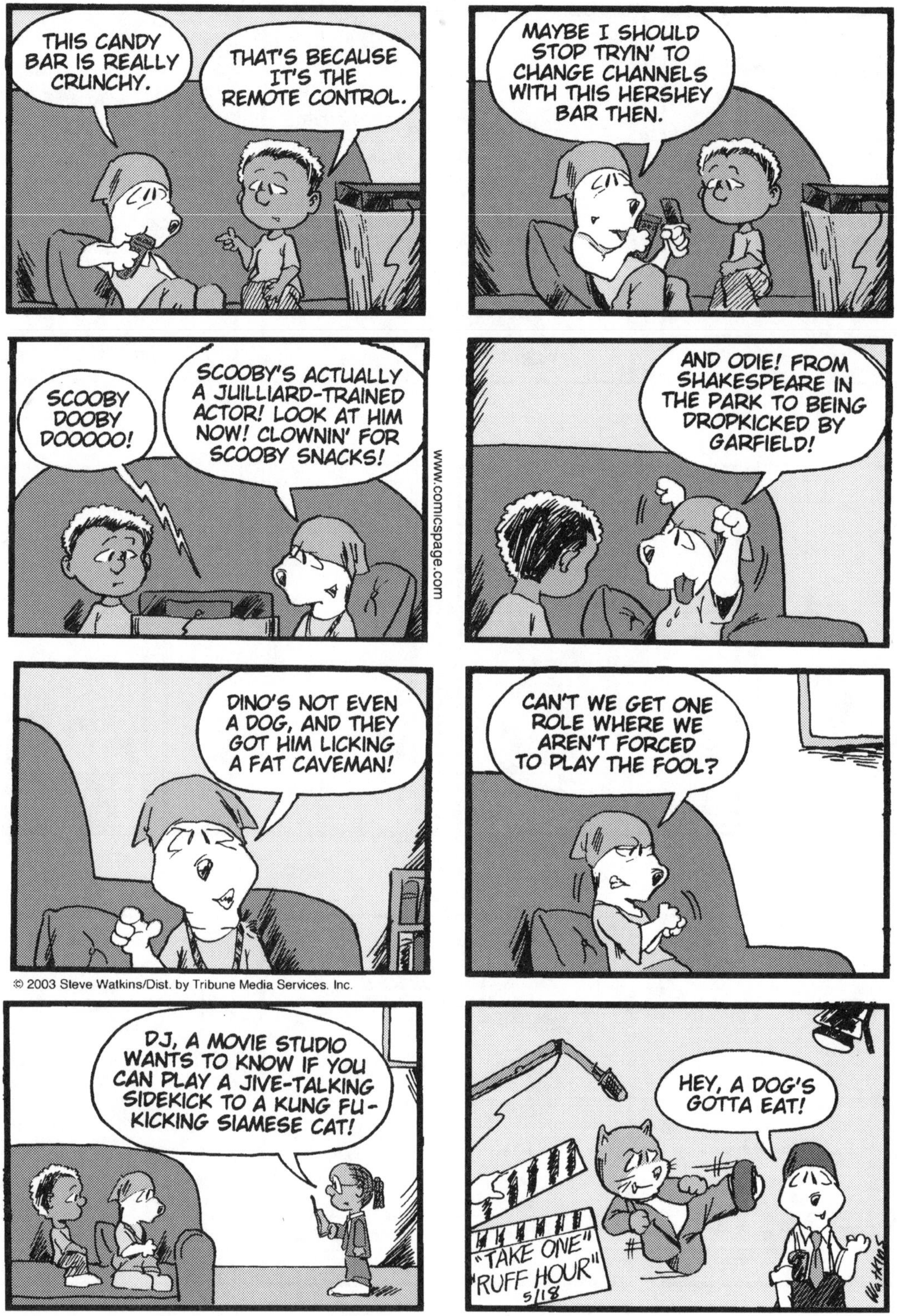
THIS CANDY BAR IS REALLY CRUNCHY.
THAT'S BECAUSE IT'S THE REMOTE CONTROL.
MAYBE I SHOULD STOP TRYIN' TO CHANGE CHANNELS WITH THIS HERSHEY BAR THEN.
SCOOBY DOOBY DOOOOOO!
SCOOBY'S ACTUALLY A JUILLIARD-TRAINED ACTOR! LOOK AT HIM NOW! CLOWNIN' FOR SCOOBY SNACKS!
AND ODIE! FROM SHAKESPEARE IN THE PARK TO BEING DROPKICKED BY GARFIELD!
DINO'S NOT EVEN A DOG, AND THEY GOT HIM LICKING A FAT CAVEMAN!
CAN'T WE GET ONE ROLE WHERE WE AREN'T FORCED TO PLAY THE FOOL?
DJ, A MOVIE STUDIO WANTS TO KNOW IF YOU CAN PLAY A JIVE-TALKING SIDEKICK TO A KUNG FU-KICKING SIAMESE CAT!
HEY, A DOG'S GOTTA EAT!
"TAKE ONE" "RUFF HOUR" 5/18
Watkins
www.comicspage.com

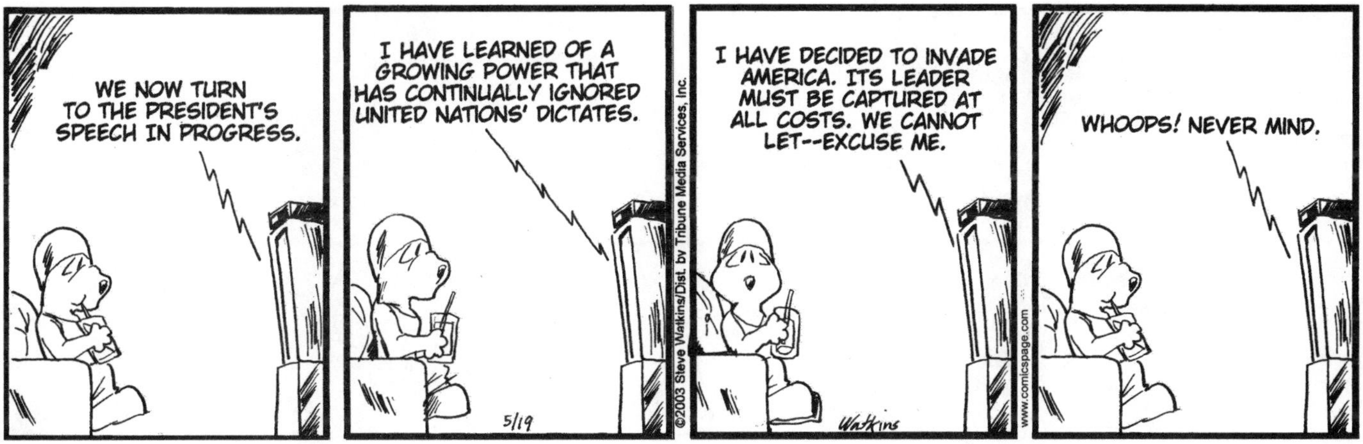
WE NOW TURN TO THE PRESIDENT'S SPEECH IN PROGRESS.
I HAVE LEARNED OF A GROWING POWER THAT HAS CONTINUALLY IGNORED UNITED NATIONS' DICTATES.
5/19
©2003 Steve Watkins/Dist. by Tribune Media Services, Inc.
I HAVE DECIDED TO INVADE AMERICA. ITS LEADER MUST BE CAPTURED AT ALL COSTS. WE CANNOT LET--EXCUSE ME.
Watkins
www.comicspage.com
WHOOPS! NEVER MIND.

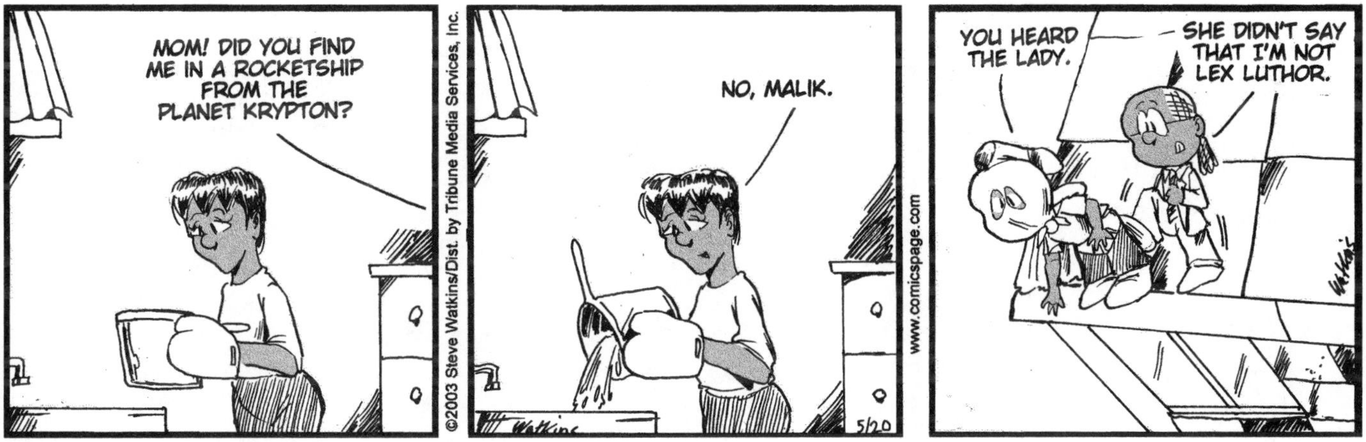
MOM! DID YOU FIND ME IN A ROCKETSHIP FROM THE PLANET KRYPTON?
©2003 Steve Watkins/Dist. by Tribune Media Services, Inc.
NO, MALIK.
5/20
www.comicspage.com
YOU HEARD THE LADY.
SHE DIDN'T SAY THAT I'M NOT LEX LUTHOR.

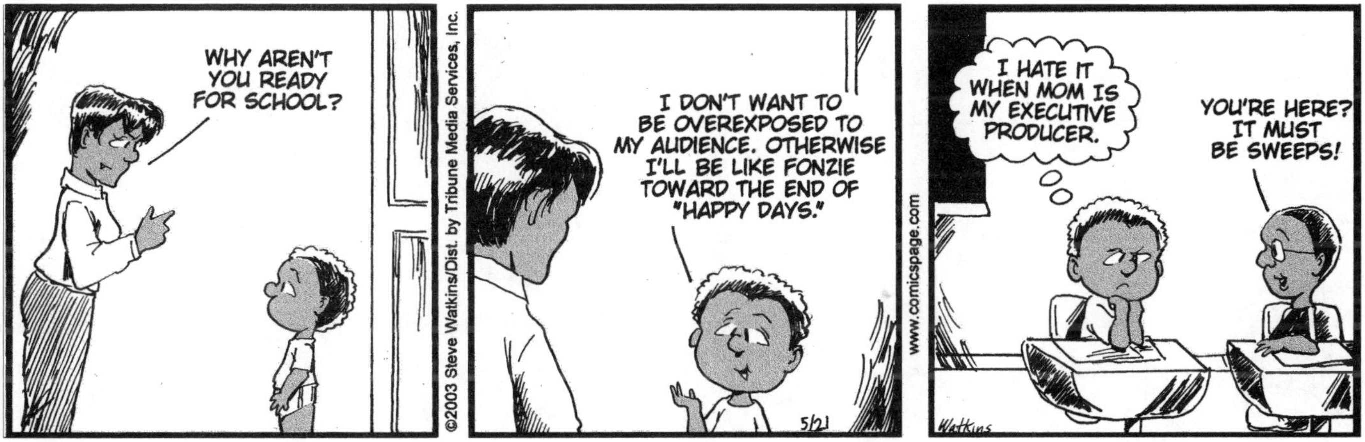
WHY AREN'T YOU READY FOR SCHOOL?
©2003 Steve Watkins/Dist. by Tribune Media Services, Inc.
I DON'T WANT TO BE OVEREXPOSED TO MY AUDIENCE. OTHERWISE I'LL BE LIKE FONZIE TOWARD THE END OF "HAPPY DAYS."
5/21
www.comicspage.com
I HATE IT WHEN MOM IS MY EXECUTIVE PRODUCER.
YOU'RE HERE? IT MUST BE SWEEPS!
Watkins

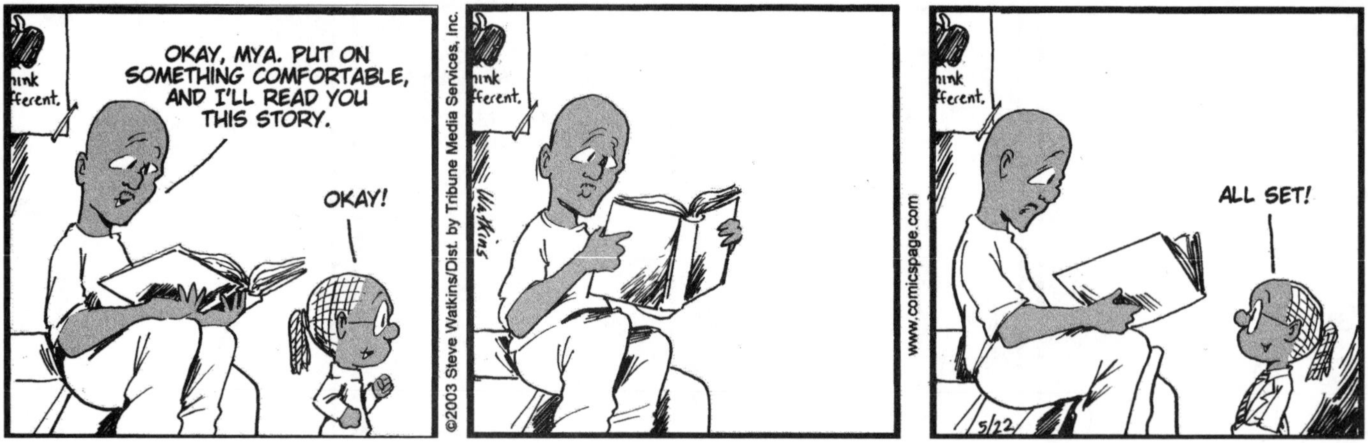
OKAY, MYA. PUT ON SOMETHING COMFORTABLE, AND I'LL READ YOU THIS STORY.
OKAY!
Watkins
ALL SET!
5/22
©2003 Steve Watkins/Dist. by Tribune Media Services, Inc.
www.comicspage.com

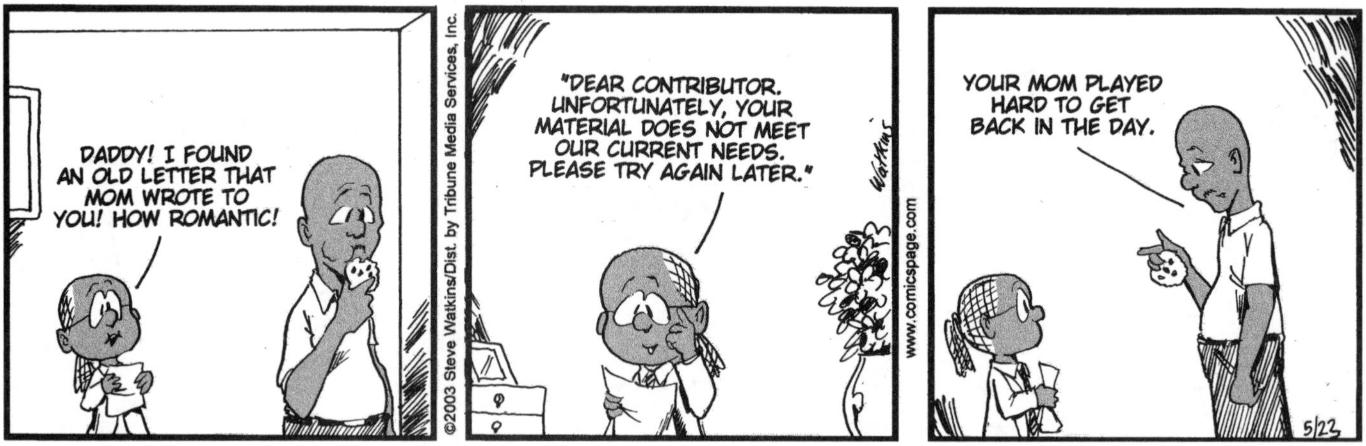
DADDY! I FOUND AN OLD LETTER THAT MOM WROTE TO YOU! HOW ROMANTIC!
"DEAR CONTRIBUTOR. UNFORTUNATELY, YOUR MATERIAL DOES NOT MEET OUR CURRENT NEEDS. PLEASE TRY AGAIN LATER."
Watkins
YOUR MOM PLAYED HARD TO GET BACK IN THE DAY.
5/23
©2003 Steve Watkins/Dist. by Tribune Media Services, Inc.
www.comicspage.com

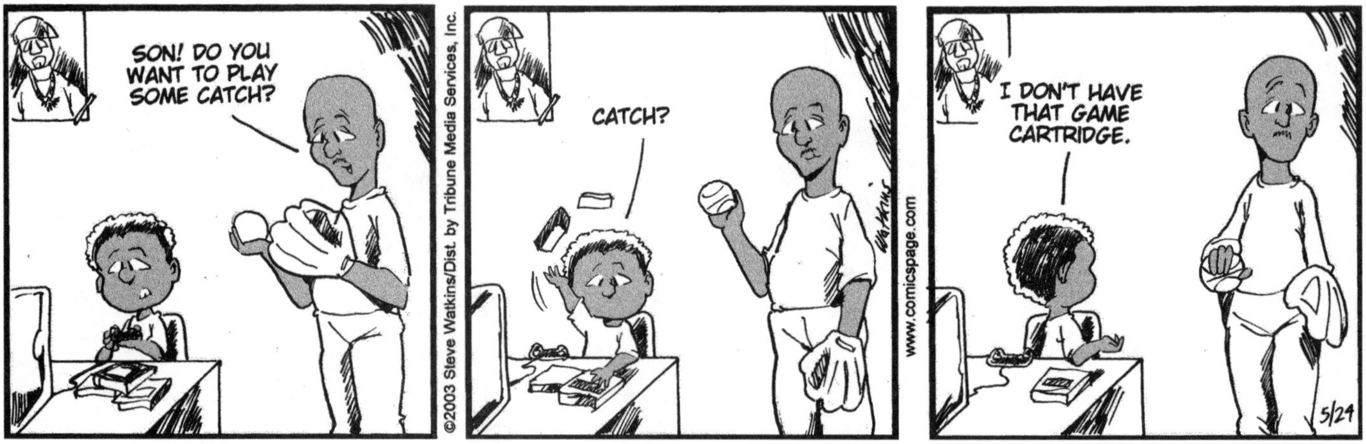
SON! DO YOU WANT TO PLAY SOME CATCH?
CATCH?
Watkins
I DON'T HAVE THAT GAME CARTRIDGE.
5/24
©2003 Steve Watkins/Dist. by Tribune Media Services, Inc.
www.comicspage.com

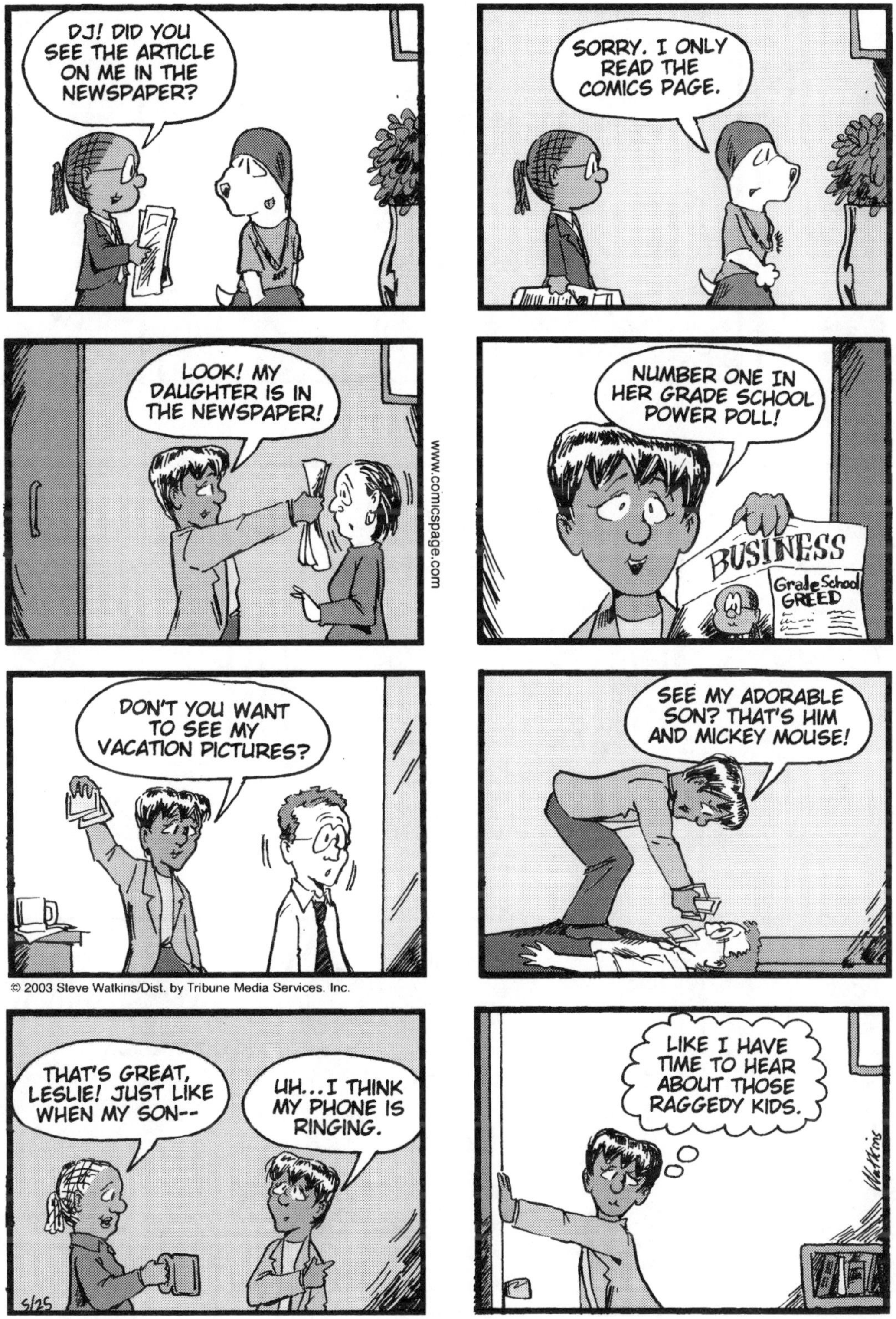
DJ! DID YOU SEE THE ARTICLE ON ME IN THE NEWSPAPER?
SORRY. I ONLY READ THE COMICS PAGE.
LOOK! MY DAUGHTER IS IN THE NEWSPAPER!
NUMBER ONE IN HER GRADE SCHOOL POWER POLL!
BUSINESS
Grade School GREED
DON'T YOU WANT TO SEE MY VACATION PICTURES?
SEE MY ADORABLE SON? THAT'S HIM AND MICKEY MOUSE!
THAT'S GREAT, LESLIE! JUST LIKE WHEN MY SON--
UH...I THINK MY PHONE IS RINGING.
LIKE I HAVE TIME TO HEAR ABOUT THOSE RAGGEDY KIDS.
www.comicspage.com
5/25
Watkins

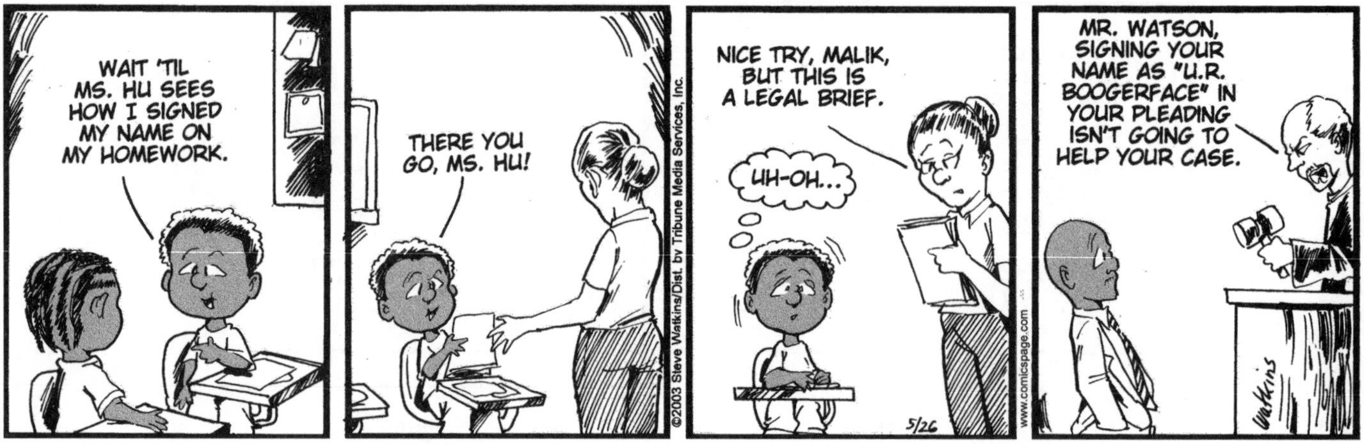
WAIT 'TIL MS. HU SEES HOW I SIGNED MY NAME ON MY HOMEWORK.
THERE YOU GO, MS. HU!
©2003 Steve Watkins/Dist. by Tribune Media Services, Inc.
NICE TRY, MALIK, BUT THIS IS A LEGAL BRIEF.
UH-OH...
5/26
www.comicspage.com
MR. WATSON, SIGNING YOUR NAME AS "U.R. BOOGERFACE" IN YOUR PLEADING ISN'T GOING TO HELP YOUR CASE.
Watkins

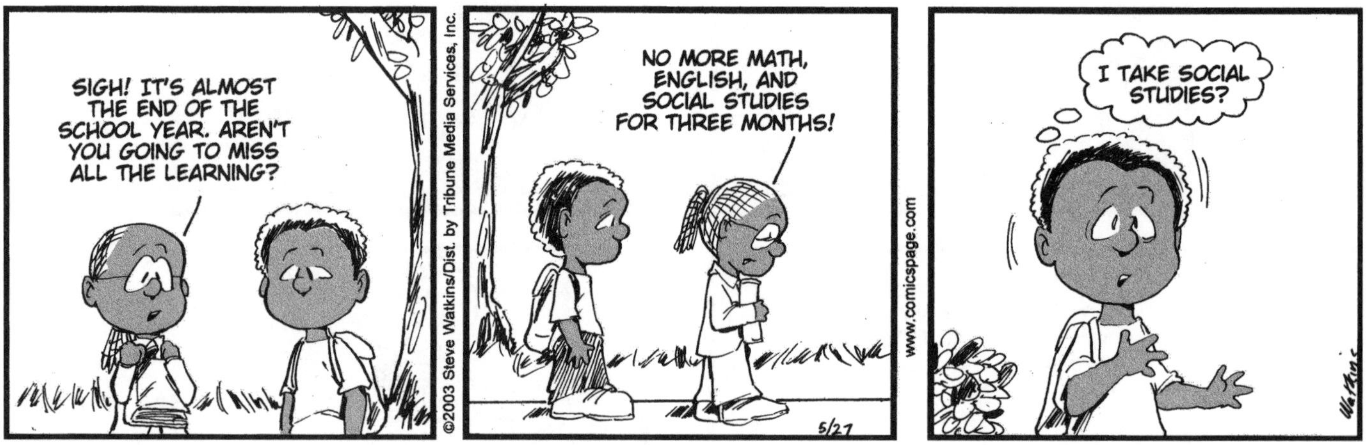
SIGH! IT'S ALMOST THE END OF THE SCHOOL YEAR. AREN'T YOU GOING TO MISS ALL THE LEARNING?
©2003 Steve Watkins/Dist. by Tribune Media Services, Inc.
NO MORE MATH, ENGLISH, AND SOCIAL STUDIES FOR THREE MONTHS!
5/27
www.comicspage.com
I TAKE SOCIAL STUDIES?
Watkins

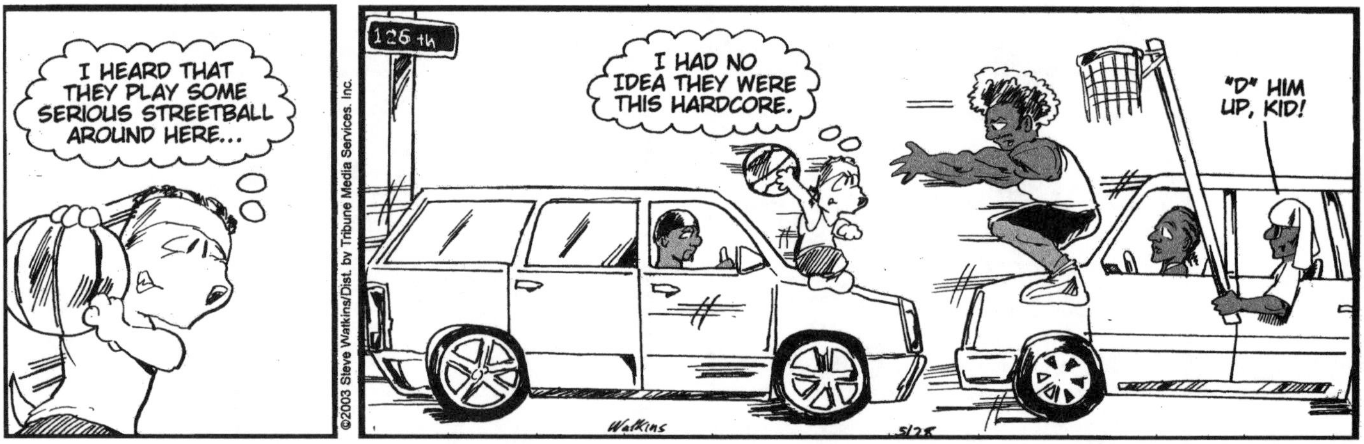
I HEARD THAT THEY PLAY SOME SERIOUS STREETBALL AROUND HERE...
©2003 Steve Watkins/Dist. by Tribune Media Services, Inc.
125 th
I HAD NO IDEA THEY WERE THIS HARDCORE.
"D" HIM UP, KID!
Watkins
5/28

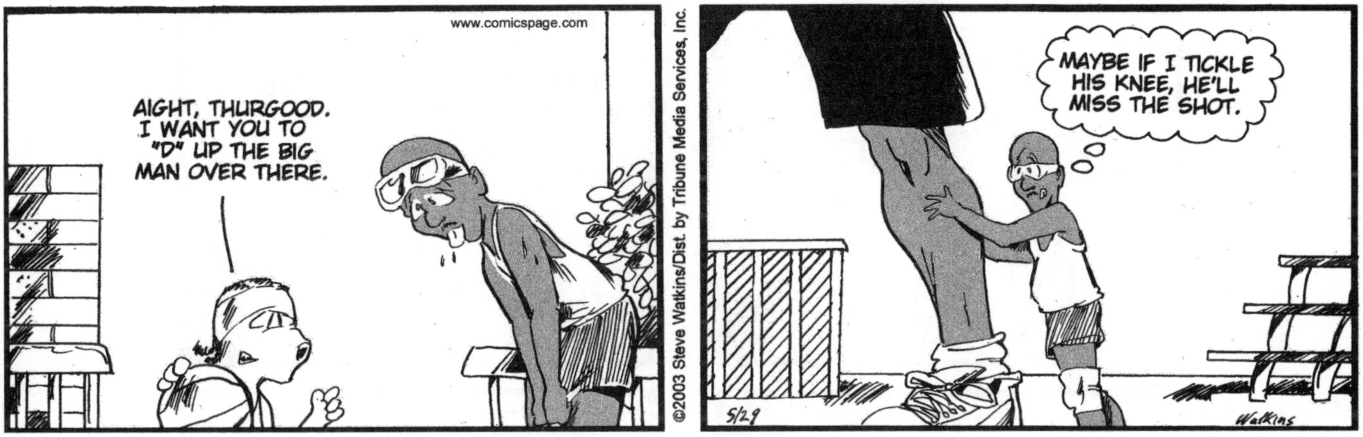
www.comicspage.com
AIGHT, THURGOOD. I WANT YOU TO "D" UP THE BIG MAN OVER THERE.
©2003 Steve Watkins/Dist. by Tribune Media Services, Inc.
MAYBE IF I TICKLE HIS KNEE, HE'LL MISS THE SHOT.
5/29
Watkins

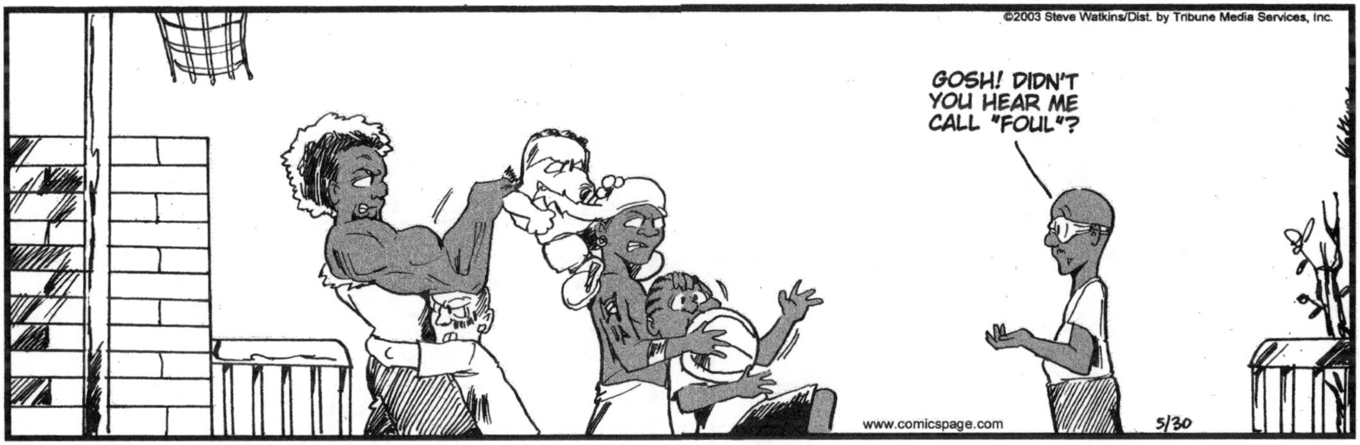
©2003 Steve Watkins/Dist. by Tribune Media Services, Inc.
GOSH! DIDN'T YOU HEAR ME CALL "FOUL"?
www.comicspage.com
5/30

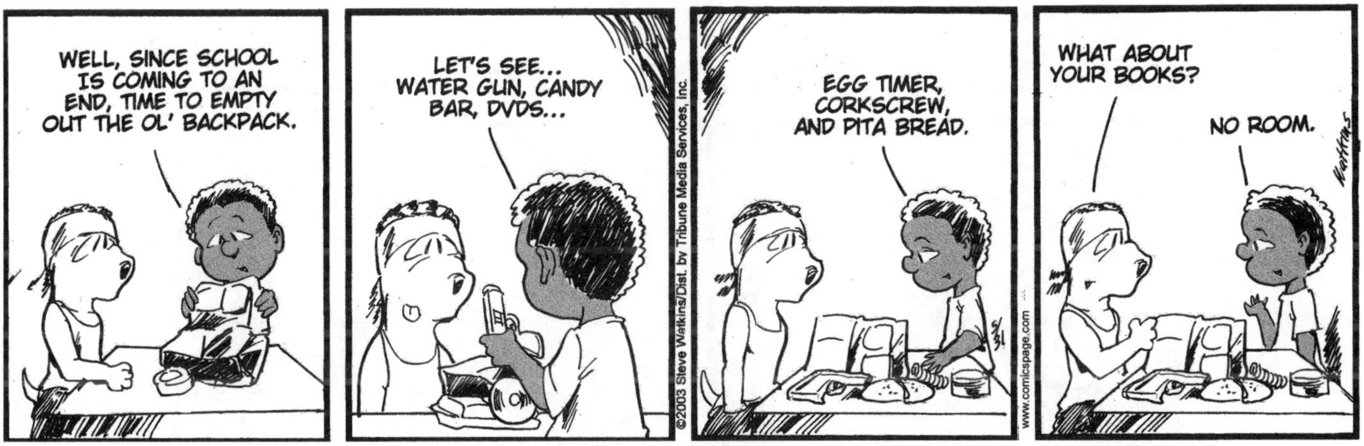
WELL, SINCE SCHOOL IS COMING TO AN END, TIME TO EMPTY OUT THE OL' BACKPACK.
LET'S SEE... WATER GUN, CANDY BAR, DVDS...
©2003 Steve Watkins/Dist. by Tribune Media Services, Inc.
EGG TIMER, CORKSCREW, AND PITA BREAD.
5/31
www.comicspage.com
WHAT ABOUT YOUR BOOKS?
NO ROOM.
Watkins

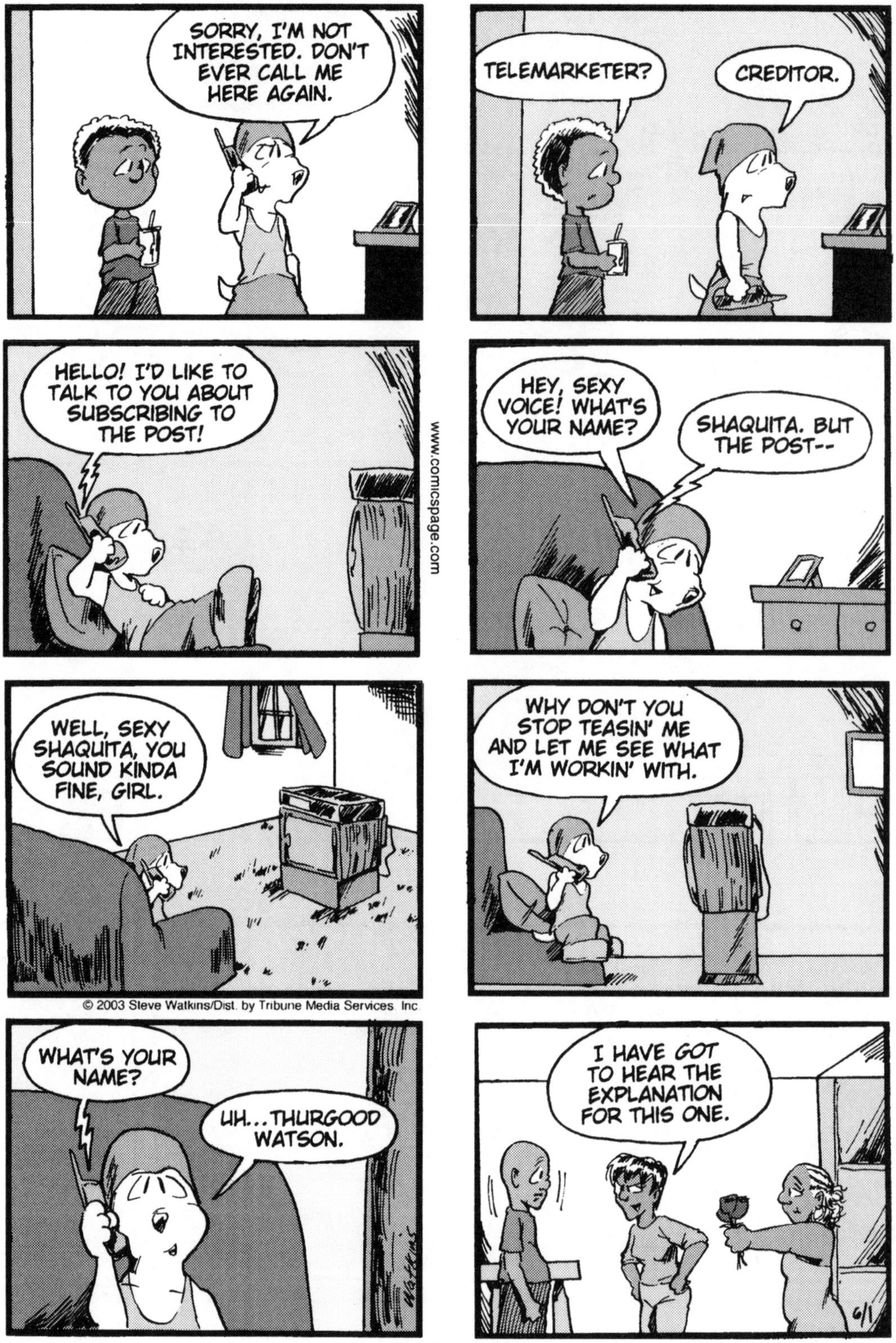
SORRY, I'M NOT INTERESTED. DON'T EVER CALL ME HERE AGAIN.
TELEMARKETER?
CREDITOR.
HELLO! I'D LIKE TO TALK TO YOU ABOUT SUBSCRIBING TO THE POST!
HEY, SEXY VOICE! WHAT'S YOUR NAME?
SHAQUITA. BUT THE POST--
WELL, SEXY SHAQUITA, YOU SOUND KINDA FINE, GIRL.
WHY DON'T YOU STOP TEASIN' ME AND LET ME SEE WHAT I'M WORKIN' WITH.
WHAT'S YOUR NAME?
UH...THURGOOD WATSON.
I HAVE GOT TO HEAR THE EXPLANATION FOR THIS ONE.

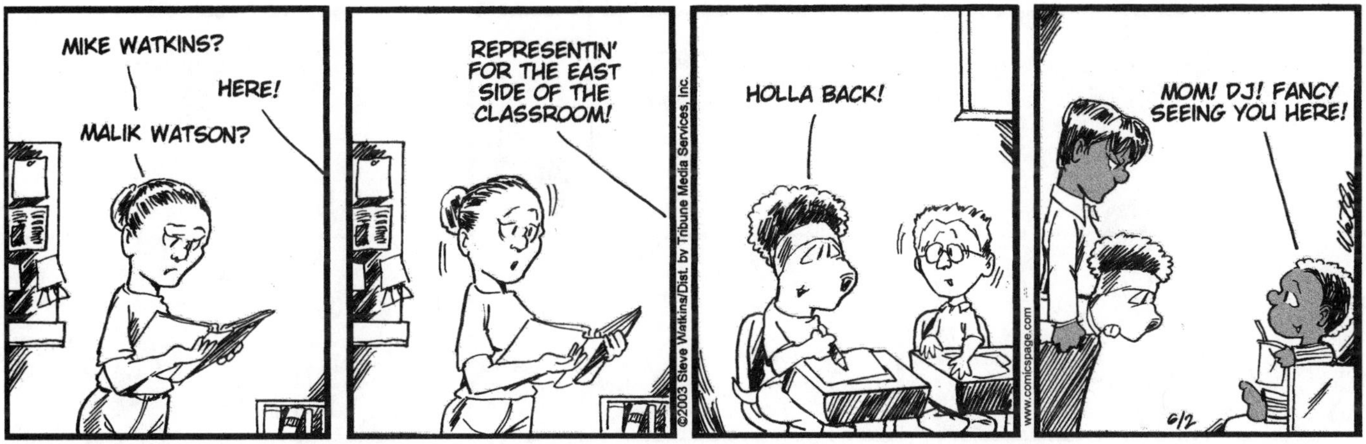
MIKE WATKINS?
HERE!
MALIK WATSON?
REPRESENTIN' FOR THE EAST SIDE OF THE CLASSROOM!
©2003 Steve Watkins/Dist. by Tribune Media Services, Inc.
HOLLA BACK!
www.comicspage.com
MOM! DJ! FANCY SEEING YOU HERE!
6/2

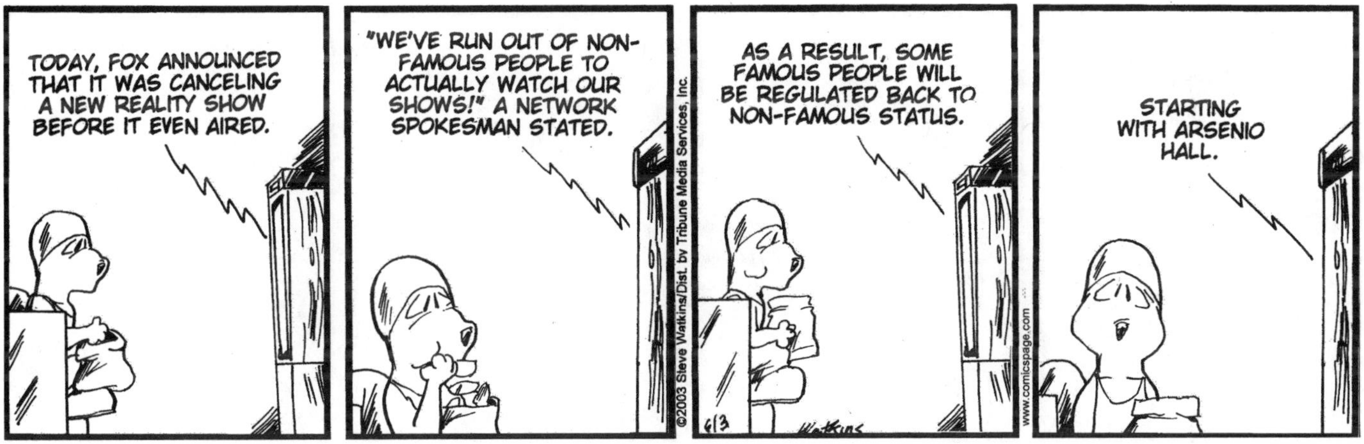
TODAY, FOX ANNOUNCED THAT IT WAS CANCELING A NEW REALITY SHOW BEFORE IT EVEN AIRED.
"WE'VE RUN OUT OF NON-FAMOUS PEOPLE TO ACTUALLY WATCH OUR SHOWS!" A NETWORK SPOKESMAN STATED.
©2003 Steve Watkins/Dist. by Tribune Media Services, Inc.
AS A RESULT, SOME FAMOUS PEOPLE WILL BE REGULATED BACK TO NON-FAMOUS STATUS.
6/3
www.comicspage.com
STARTING WITH ARSENIO HALL.

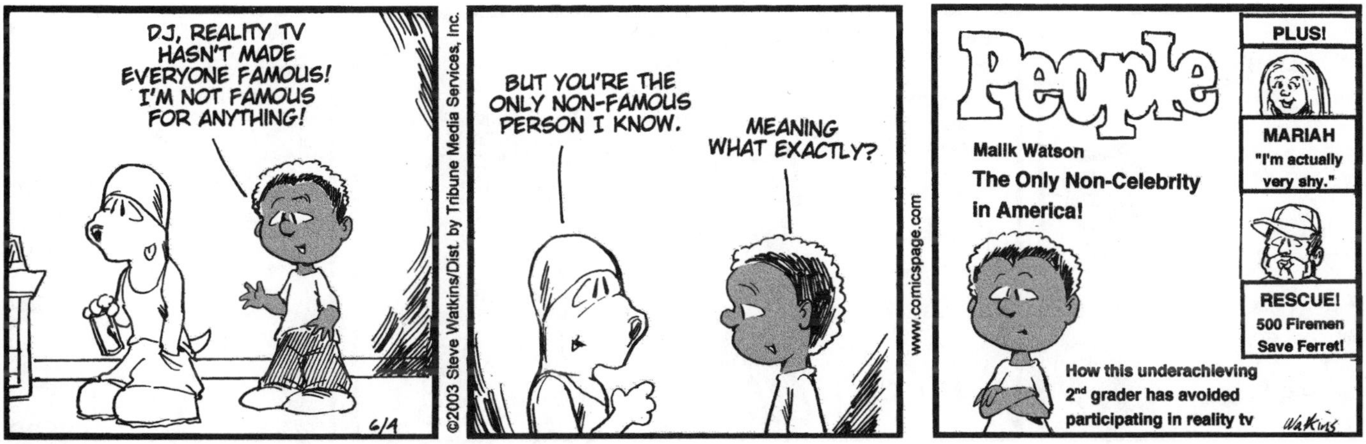
DJ, REALITY TV HASN'T MADE EVERYONE FAMOUS! I'M NOT FAMOUS FOR ANYTHING!
6/4
©2003 Steve Watkins/Dist. by Tribune Media Services, Inc.
BUT YOU'RE THE ONLY NON-FAMOUS PERSON I KNOW.
MEANING WHAT EXACTLY?
www.comicspage.com
People
PLUS!
MARIAH
"I'm actually very shy."
RESCUE!
500 Firemen Save Ferret!
Malik Watson
The Only Non-Celebrity in America!
How this underachieving 2nd grader has avoided participating in reality tv

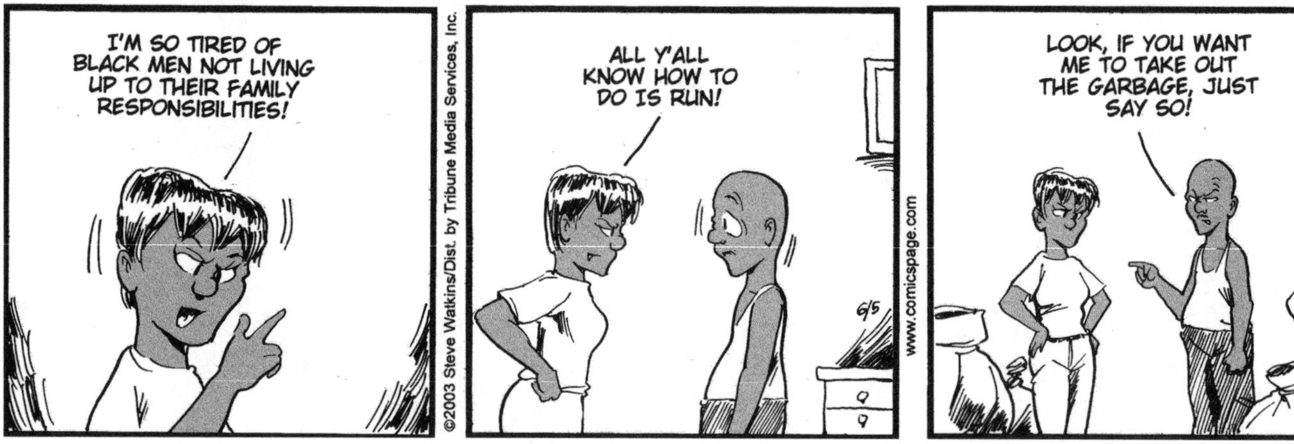
I'M SO TIRED OF BLACK MEN NOT LIVING UP TO THEIR FAMILY RESPONSIBILITIES!
©2003 Steve Watkins/Dist. by Tribune Media Services, Inc.
ALL Y'ALL KNOW HOW TO DO IS RUN!
6/5
www.comicspage.com
LOOK, IF YOU WANT ME TO TAKE OUT THE GARBAGE, JUST SAY SO!
Watkins

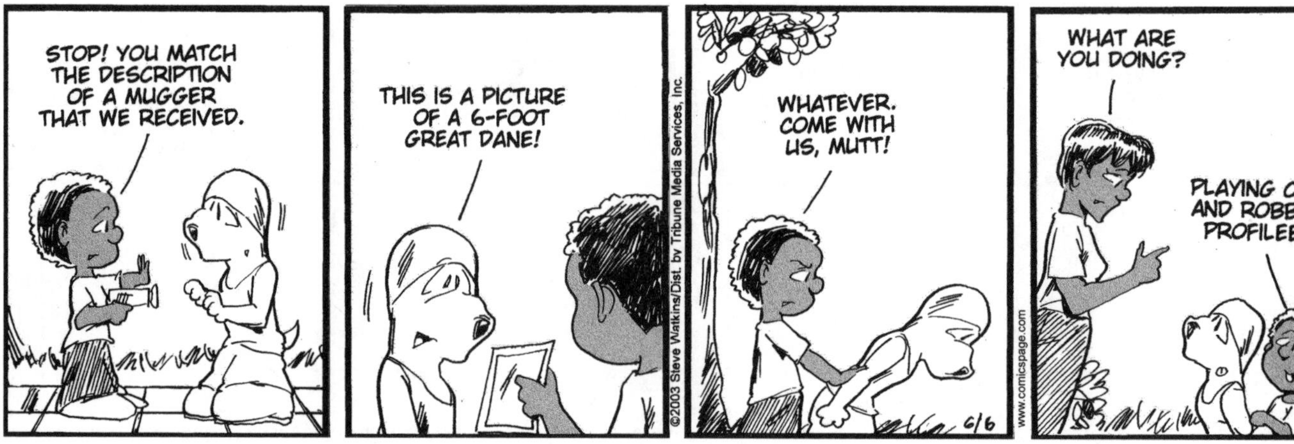
STOP! YOU MATCH THE DESCRIPTION OF A MUGGER THAT WE RECEIVED.
THIS IS A PICTURE OF A 6-FOOT GREAT DANE!
©2003 Steve Watkins/Dist. by Tribune Media Services, Inc.
WHATEVER. COME WITH US, MUTT!
6/6
www.comicspage.com
WHAT ARE YOU DOING?
Watkins
PLAYING COPS AND ROBBER-PROFILEES!

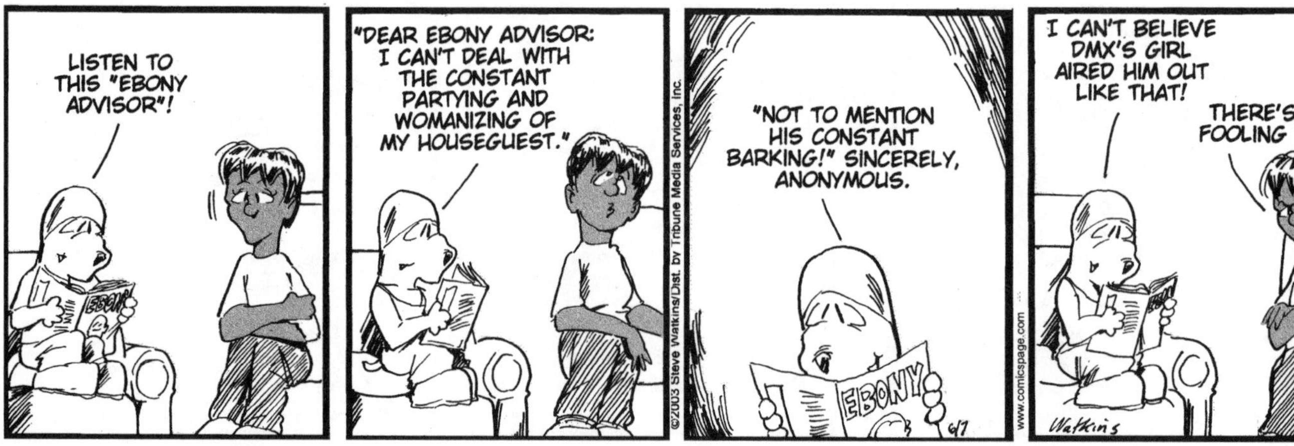
LISTEN TO THIS "EBONY ADVISOR"!
EBONY
"DEAR EBONY ADVISOR: I CAN'T DEAL WITH THE CONSTANT PARTYING AND WOMANIZING OF MY HOUSEGUEST."
©2003 Steve Watkins/Dist. by Tribune Media Services, Inc.
"NOT TO MENTION HIS CONSTANT BARKING!" SINCERELY, ANONYMOUS.
EBONY
6/7
www.comicspage.com
I CAN'T BELIEVE DMX'S GIRL AIRED HIM OUT LIKE THAT!
THERE'S NO FOOLING YOU.
Watkins

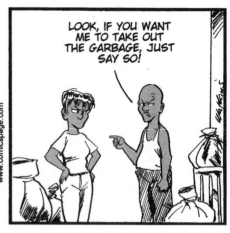

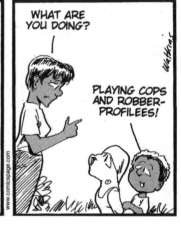

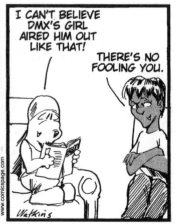

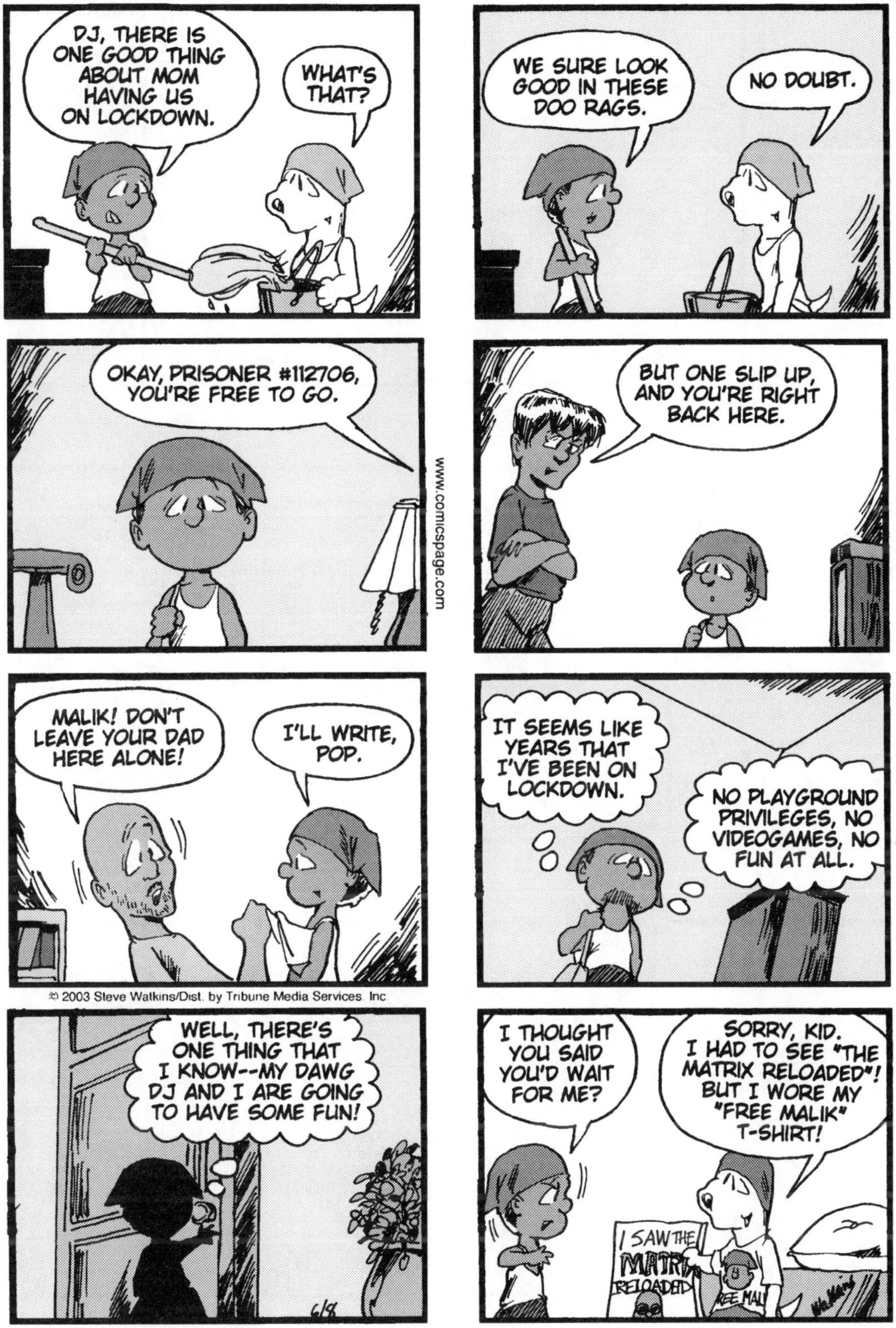
DJ, THERE IS ONE GOOD THING ABOUT MOM HAVING US ON LOCKDOWN.
WHAT'S THAT?
WE SURE LOOK GOOD IN THESE DOO RAGS.
NO DOUBT.
OKAY, PRISONER #112706, YOU'RE FREE TO GO.
BUT ONE SLIP UP, AND YOU'RE RIGHT BACK HERE.
MALIK! DON'T LEAVE YOUR DAD HERE ALONE!
I'LL WRITE, POP.
IT SEEMS LIKE YEARS THAT I'VE BEEN ON LOCKDOWN.
NO PLAYGROUND PRIVILEGES, NO VIDEOGAMES, NO FUN AT ALL.
WELL, THERE'S ONE THING THAT I KNOW--MY DAWG DJ AND I ARE GOING TO HAVE SOME FUN!
I THOUGHT YOU SAID YOU'D WAIT FOR ME?
SORRY, KID. I HAD TO SEE "THE MATRIX RELOADED"! BUT I WORE MY "FREE MALIK" T-SHIRT!
I SAW THE MATRIX RELOADED

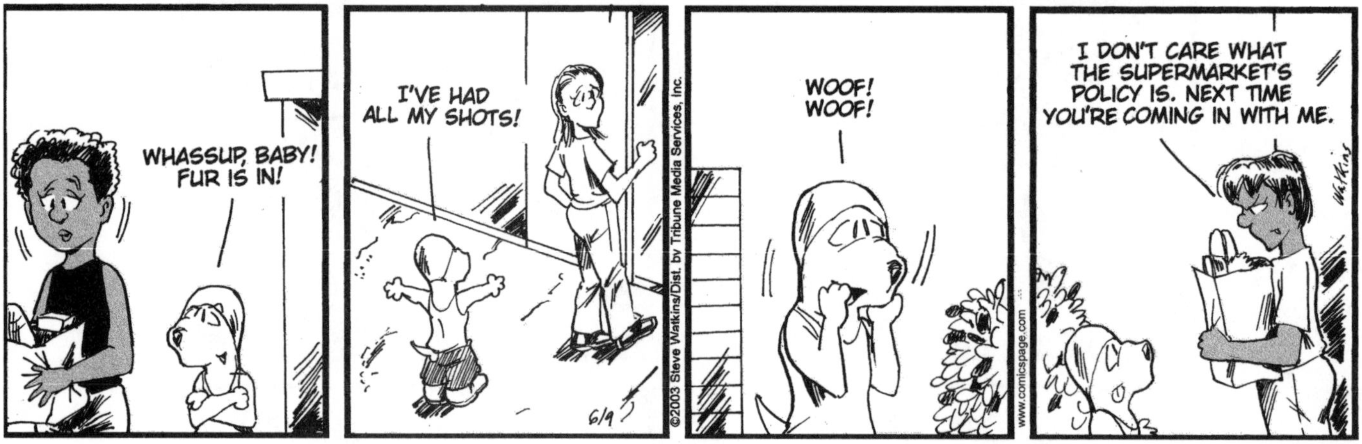
WHASSUP, BABY! FUR IS IN!
I'VE HAD ALL MY SHOTS!
6/9
©2003 Steve Watkins/Dist. by Tribune Media Services, Inc.
WOOF! WOOF!
www.comicspage.com
I DON'T CARE WHAT THE SUPERMARKET'S POLICY IS. NEXT TIME YOU'RE COMING IN WITH ME.
Watkins

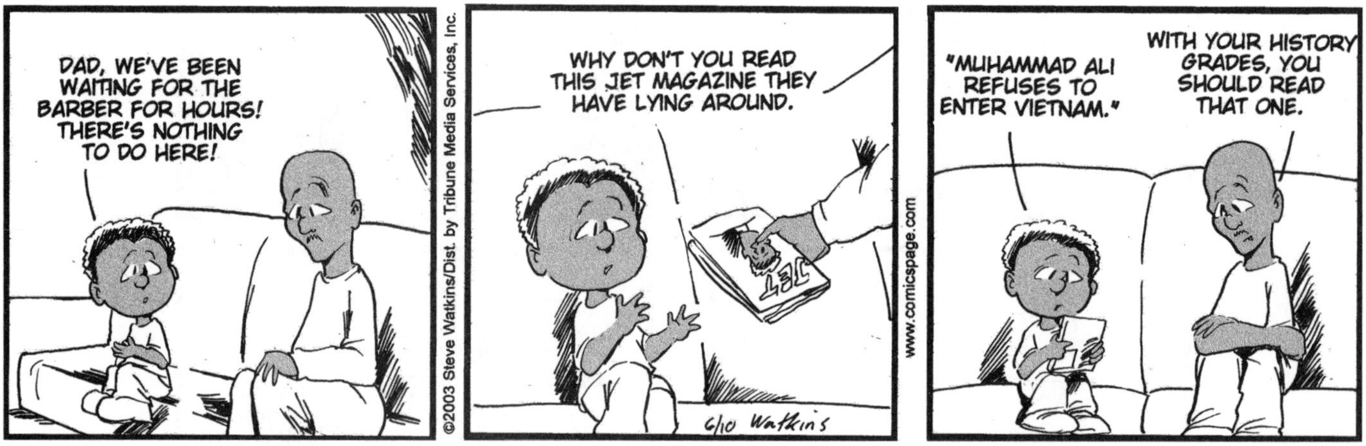
DAD, WE'VE BEEN WAITING FOR THE BARBER FOR HOURS! THERE'S NOTHING TO DO HERE!
©2003 Steve Watkins/Dist. by Tribune Media Services, Inc.
WHY DON'T YOU READ THIS JET MAGAZINE THEY HAVE LYING AROUND.
JET
6/10 Watkins
www.comicspage.com
"MUHAMMAD ALI REFUSES TO ENTER VIETNAM."
WITH YOUR HISTORY GRADES, YOU SHOULD READ THAT ONE.

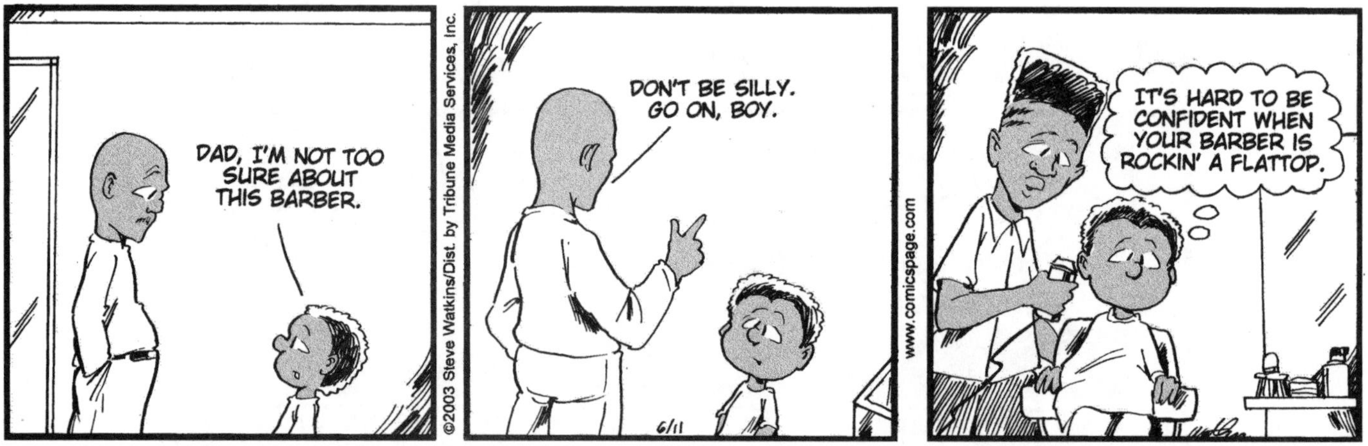
DAD, I'M NOT TOO SURE ABOUT THIS BARBER.
©2003 Steve Watkins/Dist. by Tribune Media Services, Inc.
DON'T BE SILLY. GO ON, BOY.
6/11
www.comicspage.com
IT'S HARD TO BE CONFIDENT WHEN YOUR BARBER IS ROCKIN' A FLATTOP.

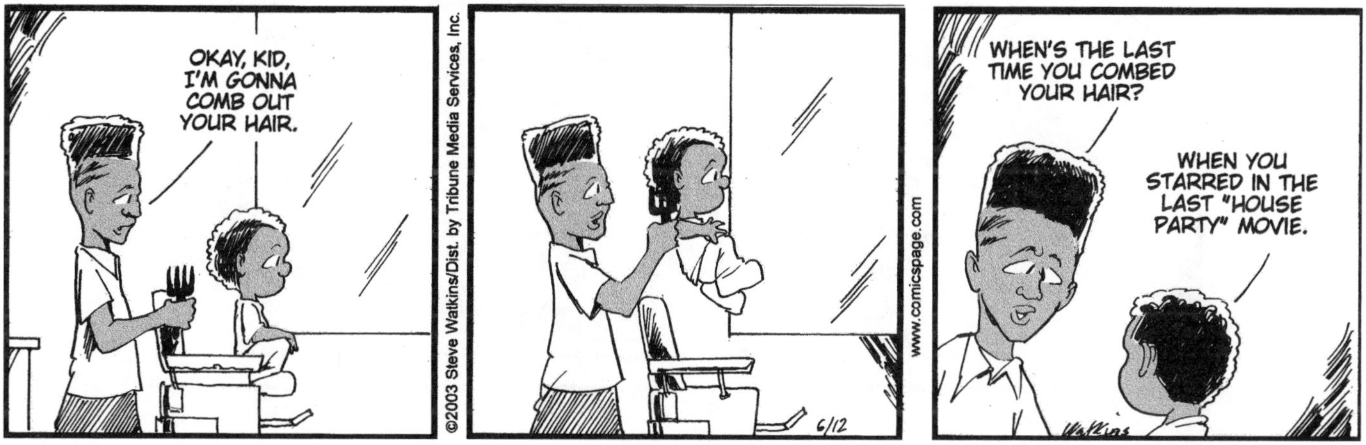
OKAY, KID, I'M GONNA COMB OUT YOUR HAIR.
WHEN'S THE LAST TIME YOU COMBED YOUR HAIR?
WHEN YOU STARRED IN THE LAST "HOUSE PARTY" MOVIE.
6/12
WATKINS

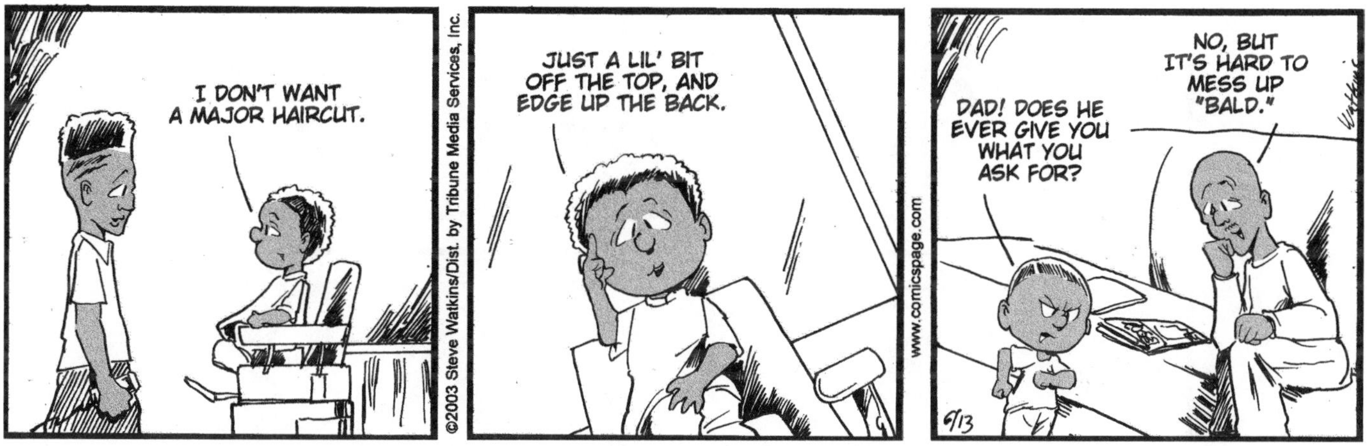
I DON'T WANT A MAJOR HAIRCUT.
JUST A LIL' BIT OFF THE TOP, AND EDGE UP THE BACK.
DAD! DOES HE EVER GIVE YOU WHAT YOU ASK FOR?
NO, BUT IT'S HARD TO MESS UP "BALD."
6/13

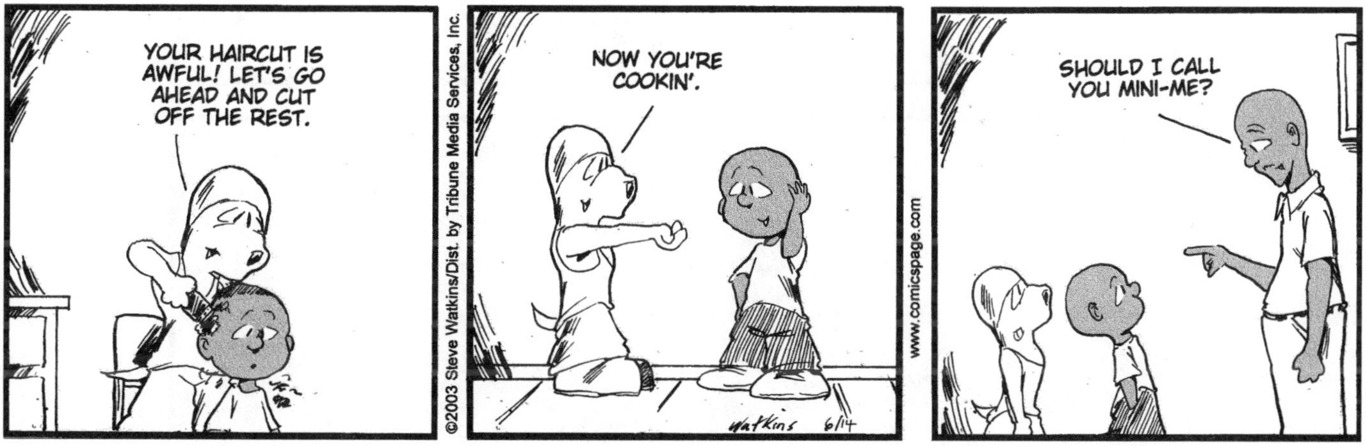
YOUR HAIRCUT IS AWFUL! LET'S GO AHEAD AND CUT OFF THE REST.
NOW YOU'RE COOKIN'.
SHOULD I CALL YOU MINI-ME?
WATKINS 6/14

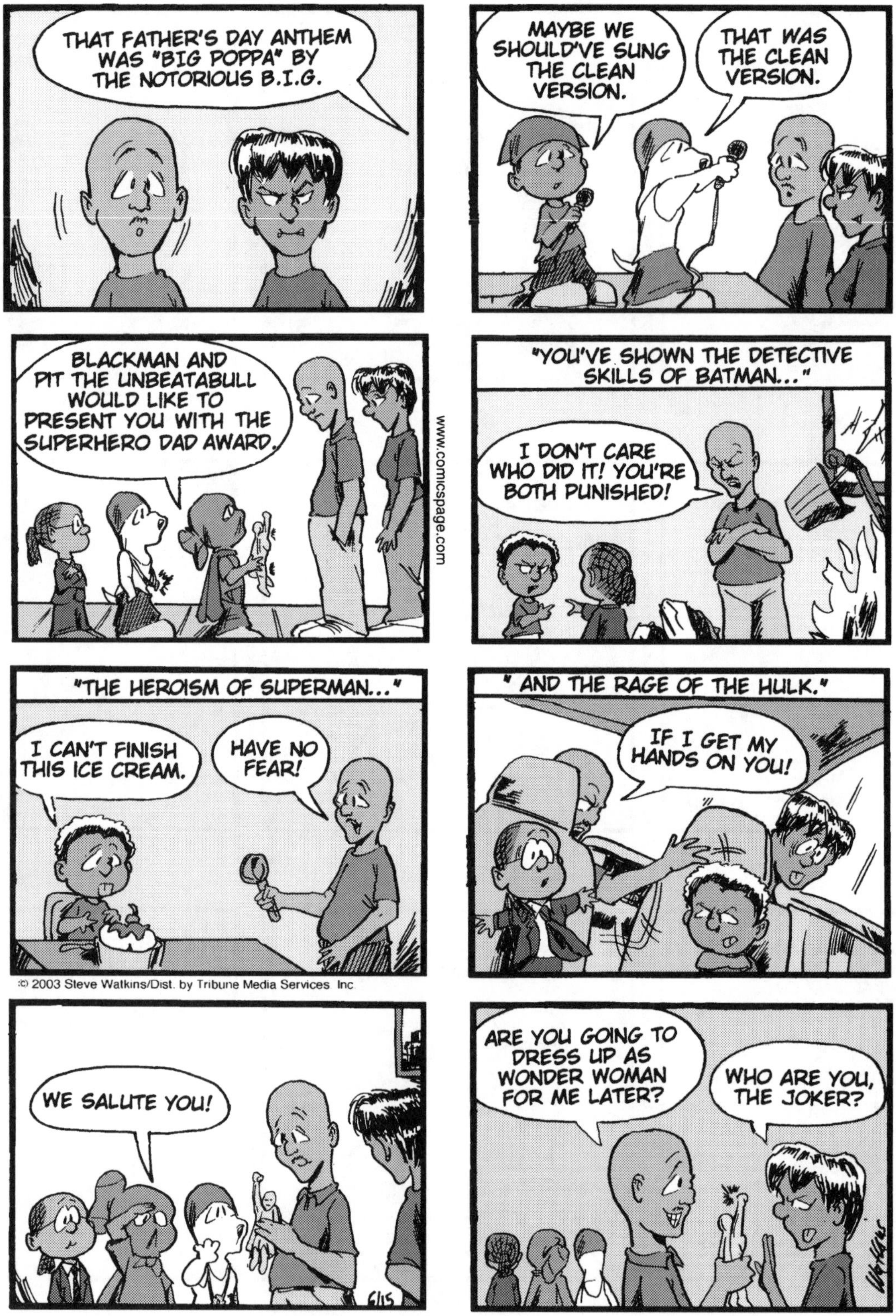
THAT FATHER'S DAY ANTHEM WAS "BIG POPPA" BY THE NOTORIOUS B.I.G.
MAYBE WE SHOULD'VE SUNG THE CLEAN VERSION.
THAT WAS THE CLEAN VERSION.
BLACKMAN AND PIT THE UNBEATABULL WOULD LIKE TO PRESENT YOU WITH THE SUPERHERO DAD AWARD.
www.comicspage.com
"YOU'VE SHOWN THE DETECTIVE SKILLS OF BATMAN..."
I DON'T CARE WHO DID IT! YOU'RE BOTH PUNISHED!
"THE HEROISM OF SUPERMAN..."
I CAN'T FINISH THIS ICE CREAM.
HAVE NO FEAR!
" AND THE RAGE OF THE HULK."
IF I GET MY HANDS ON YOU!
(c) 2003 Steve Watkins/Dist. by Tribune Media Services Inc.
WE SALUTE YOU!
6/15
ARE YOU GOING TO DRESS UP AS WONDER WOMAN FOR ME LATER?
WHO ARE YOU, THE JOKER?

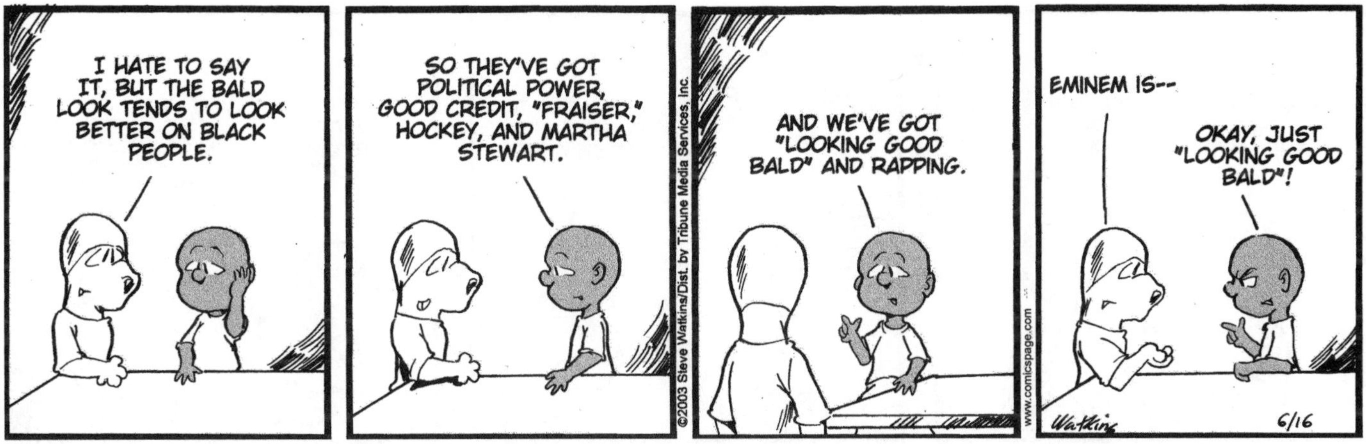
I HATE TO SAY IT, BUT THE BALD LOOK TENDS TO LOOK BETTER ON BLACK PEOPLE.
SO THEY'VE GOT POLITICAL POWER, GOOD CREDIT, "FRAISER," HOCKEY, AND MARTHA STEWART.
©2003 Steve Watkins/Dist. by Tribune Media Services, Inc.
AND WE'VE GOT "LOOKING GOOD BALD" AND RAPPING.
www.comicspage.com
EMINEM IS--
OKAY, JUST "LOOKING GOOD BALD"!
Watkins
6/16

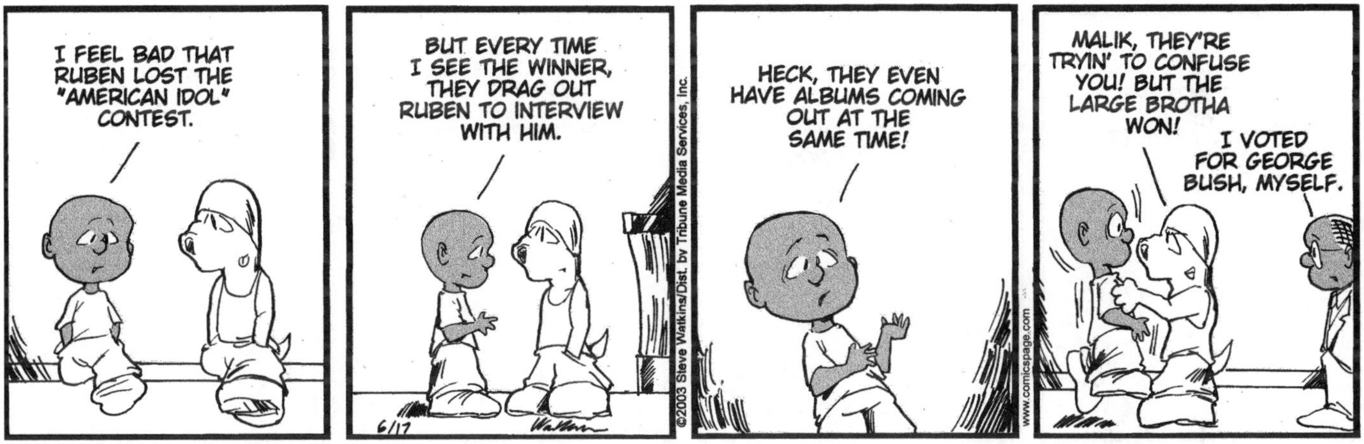
I FEEL BAD THAT RUBEN LOST THE "AMERICAN IDOL" CONTEST.
BUT EVERY TIME I SEE THE WINNER, THEY DRAG OUT RUBEN TO INTERVIEW WITH HIM.
6/17
©2003 Steve Watkins/Dist. by Tribune Media Services, Inc.
HECK, THEY EVEN HAVE ALBUMS COMING OUT AT THE SAME TIME!
www.comicspage.com
MALIK, THEY'RE TRYIN' TO CONFUSE YOU! BUT THE LARGE BROTHA WON!
I VOTED FOR GEORGE BUSH, MYSELF.

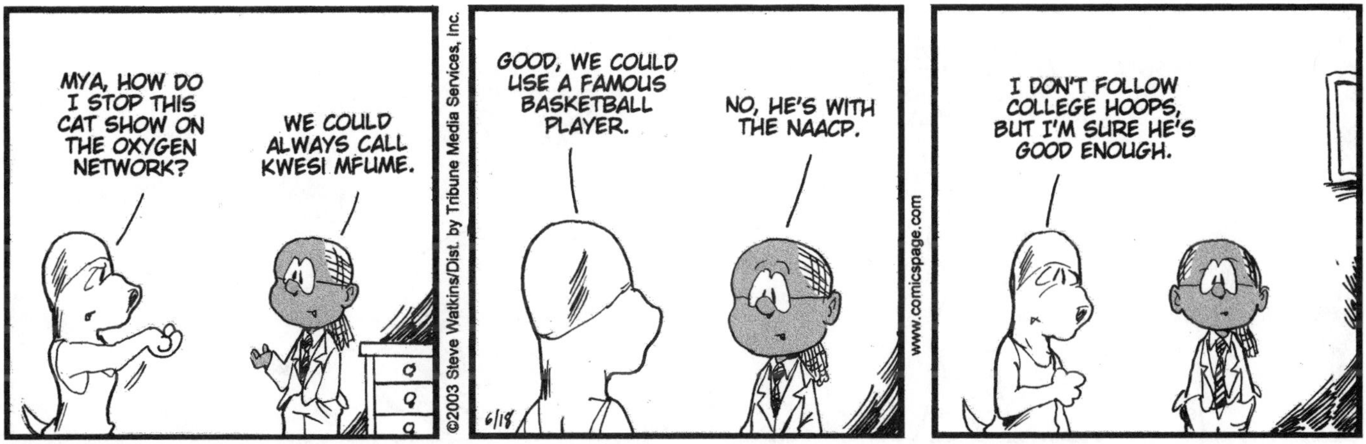
MYA, HOW DO I STOP THIS CAT SHOW ON THE OXYGEN NETWORK?
WE COULD ALWAYS CALL KWESI MFUME.
©2003 Steve Watkins/Dist. by Tribune Media Services, Inc.
GOOD, WE COULD USE A FAMOUS BASKETBALL PLAYER.
NO, HE'S WITH THE NAACP.
6/18
www.comicspage.com
I DON'T FOLLOW COLLEGE HOOPS, BUT I'M SURE HE'S GOOD ENOUGH.

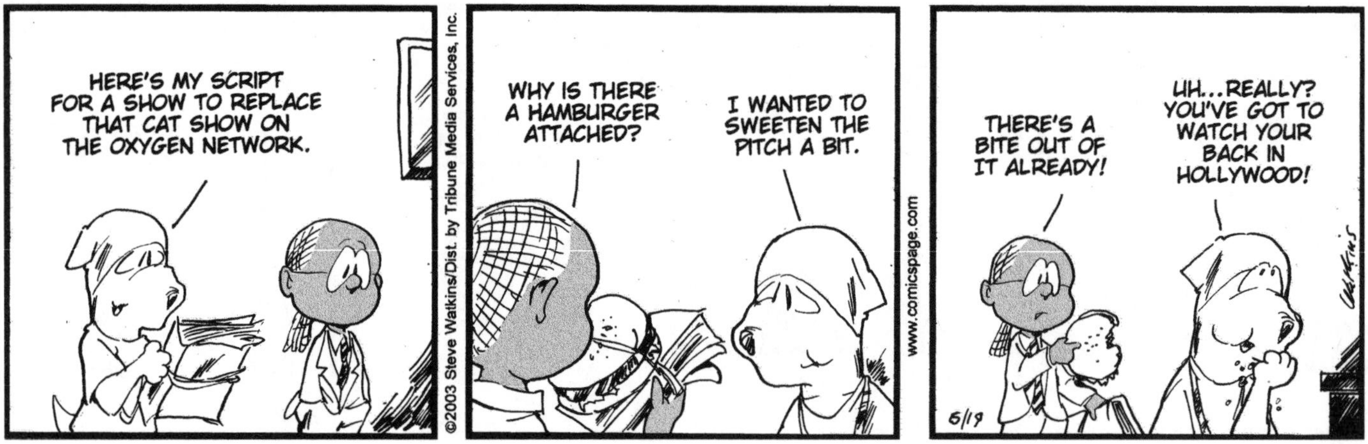
HERE'S MY SCRIPT FOR A SHOW TO REPLACE THAT CAT SHOW ON THE OXYGEN NETWORK.
©2003 Steve Watkins/Dist. by Tribune Media Services, Inc.
WHY IS THERE A HAMBURGER ATTACHED?
I WANTED TO SWEETEN THE PITCH A BIT.
www.comicspage.com
THERE'S A BITE OUT OF IT ALREADY!
UH...REALLY? YOU'VE GOT TO WATCH YOUR BACK IN HOLLYWOOD!
6/19

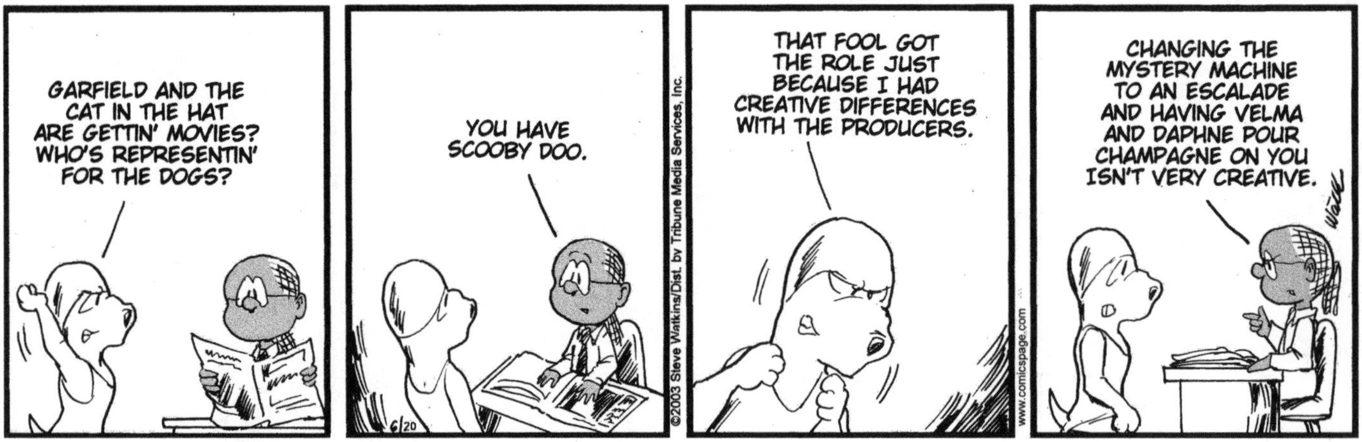
GARFIELD AND THE CAT IN THE HAT ARE GETTIN' MOVIES? WHO'S REPRESENTIN' FOR THE DOGS?
YOU HAVE SCOOBY DOO.
6/20
©2003 Steve Watkins/Dist. by Tribune Media Services, Inc.
THAT FOOL GOT THE ROLE JUST BECAUSE I HAD CREATIVE DIFFERENCES WITH THE PRODUCERS.
www.comicspage.com
CHANGING THE MYSTERY MACHINE TO AN ESCALADE AND HAVING VELMA AND DAPHNE POUR CHAMPAGNE ON YOU ISN'T VERY CREATIVE.

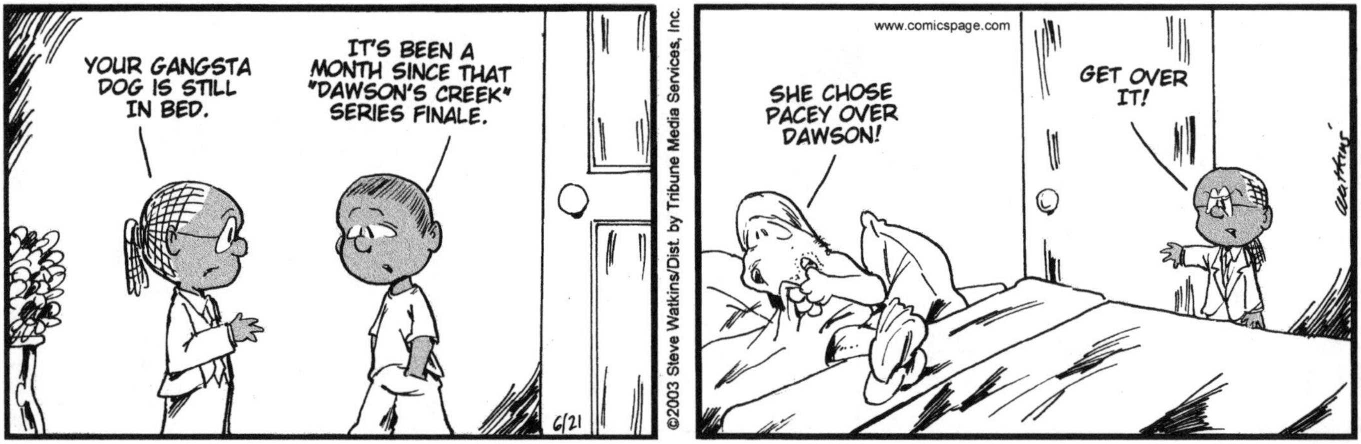
YOUR GANGSTA DOG IS STILL IN BED.
IT'S BEEN A MONTH SINCE THAT "DAWSON'S CREEK" SERIES FINALE.
6/21
©2003 Steve Watkins/Dist. by Tribune Media Services, Inc.
www.comicspage.com
SHE CHOSE PACEY OVER DAWSON!
GET OVER IT!

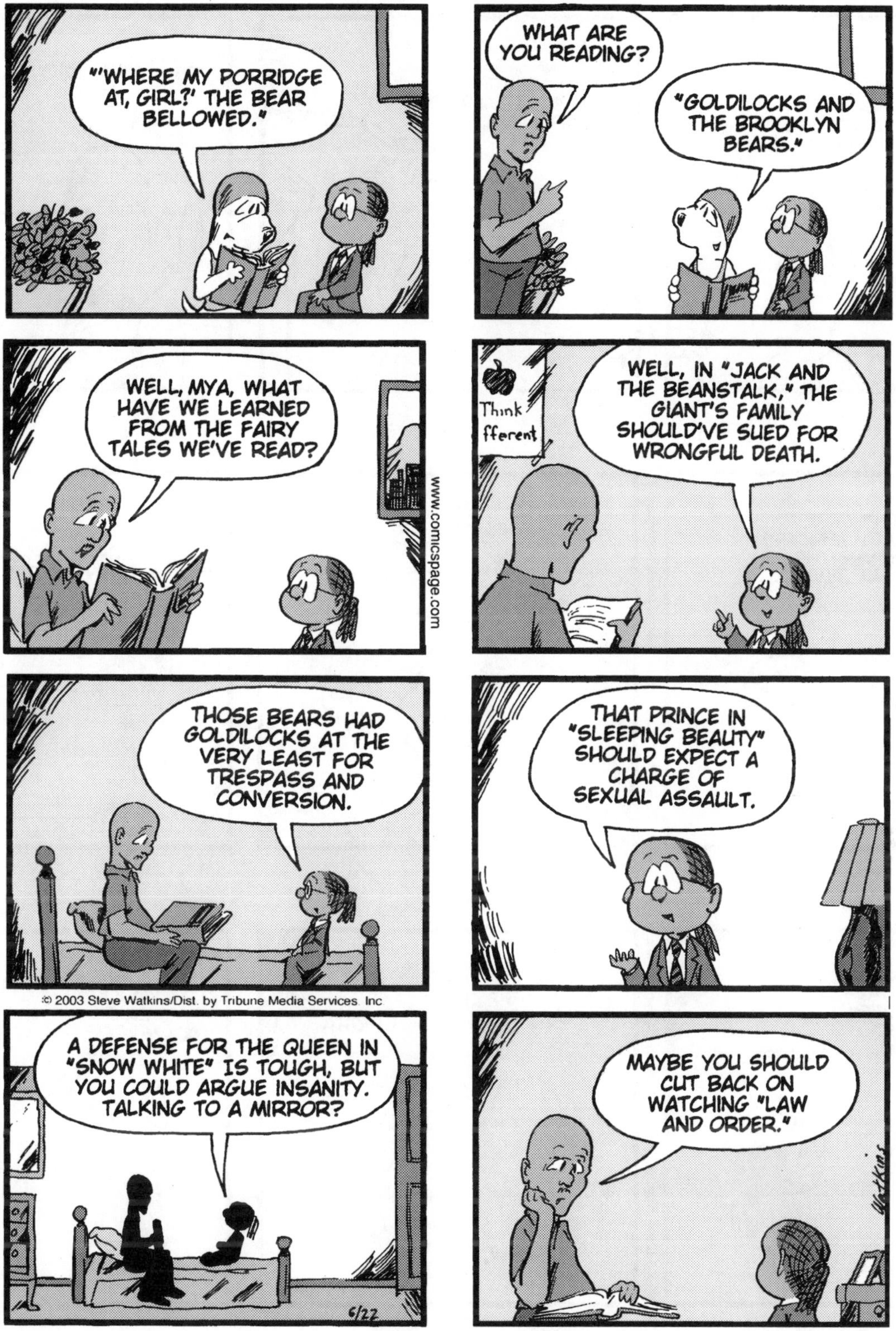
"'WHERE MY PORRIDGE AT, GIRL?' THE BEAR BELLOWED."
WHAT ARE YOU READING?
"GOLDILOCKS AND THE BROOKLYN BEARS."
WELL, MYA, WHAT HAVE WE LEARNED FROM THE FAIRY TALES WE'VE READ?
www.comicspage.com
Think
fferent
WELL, IN "JACK AND THE BEANSTALK," THE GIANT'S FAMILY SHOULD'VE SUED FOR WRONGFUL DEATH.
THOSE BEARS HAD GOLDILOCKS AT THE VERY LEAST FOR TRESPASS AND CONVERSION.
THAT PRINCE IN "SLEEPING BEAUTY" SHOULD EXPECT A CHARGE OF SEXUAL ASSAULT.
© 2003 Steve Watkins/Dist. by Tribune Media Services, Inc.
A DEFENSE FOR THE QUEEN IN "SNOW WHITE" IS TOUGH, BUT YOU COULD ARGUE INSANITY. TALKING TO A MIRROR?
6/22
MAYBE YOU SHOULD CUT BACK ON WATCHING "LAW AND ORDER."
Watkins

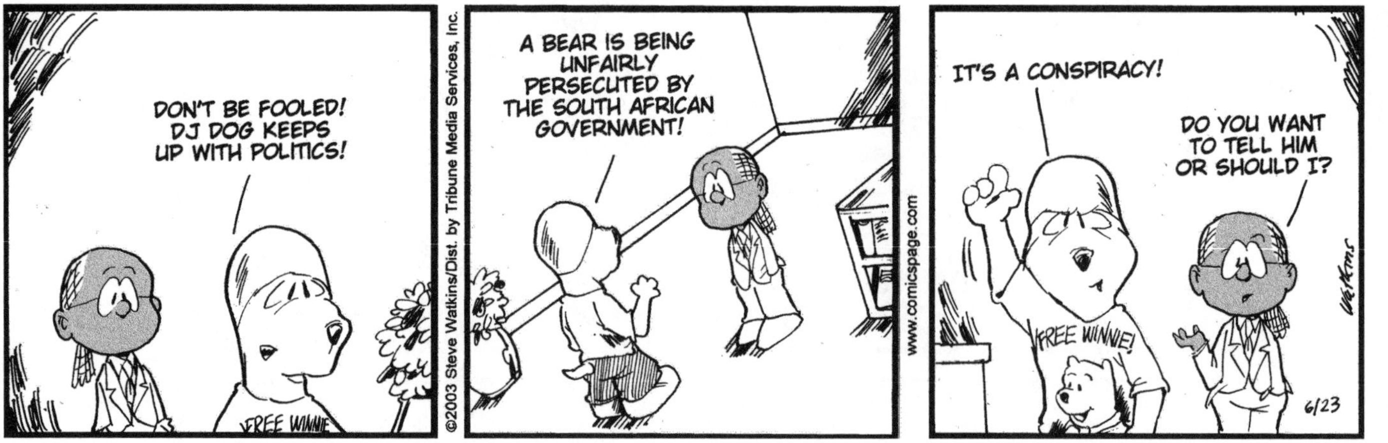
DON'T BE FOOLED! DJ DOG KEEPS UP WITH POLITICS!
FREE WINNIE
©2003 Steve Watkins/Dist. by Tribune Media Services, Inc.
A BEAR IS BEING UNFAIRLY PERSECUTED BY THE SOUTH AFRICAN GOVERNMENT!
www.comicspage.com
IT'S A CONSPIRACY!
DO YOU WANT TO TELL HIM OR SHOULD I?
FREE WINNIE!
6/23

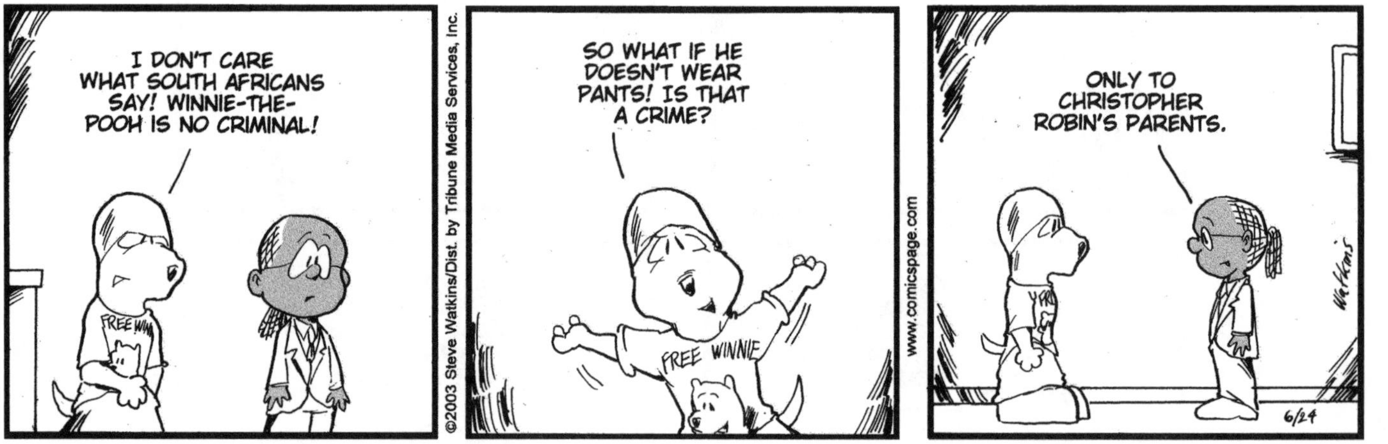
I DON'T CARE WHAT SOUTH AFRICANS SAY! WINNIE-THE-POOH IS NO CRIMINAL!
©2003 Steve Watkins/Dist. by Tribune Media Services, Inc.
SO WHAT IF HE DOESN'T WEAR PANTS! IS THAT A CRIME?
FREE WINNIE
www.comicspage.com
ONLY TO CHRISTOPHER ROBIN'S PARENTS.
6/24

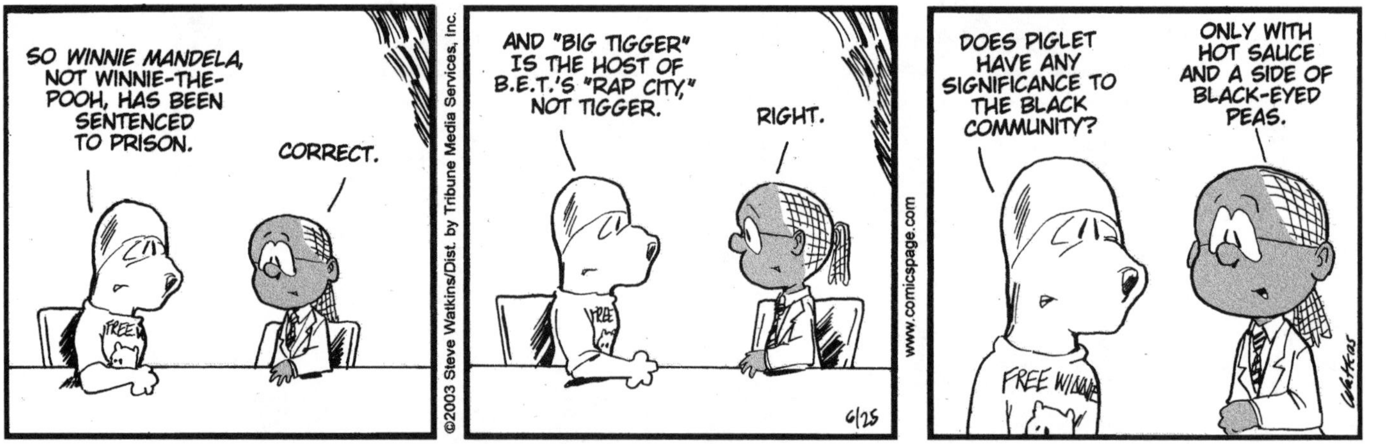
SO *WINNIE MANDELA*, NOT WINNIE-THE-POOH, HAS BEEN SENTENCED TO PRISON.
CORRECT.
©2003 Steve Watkins/Dist. by Tribune Media Services, Inc.
AND "BIG TIGGER" IS THE HOST OF B.E.T.'S "RAP CITY," NOT TIGGER.
RIGHT.
6/25
www.comicspage.com
DOES PIGLET HAVE ANY SIGNIFICANCE TO THE BLACK COMMUNITY?
ONLY WITH HOT SAUCE AND A SIDE OF BLACK-EYED PEAS.
FREE WINNIE

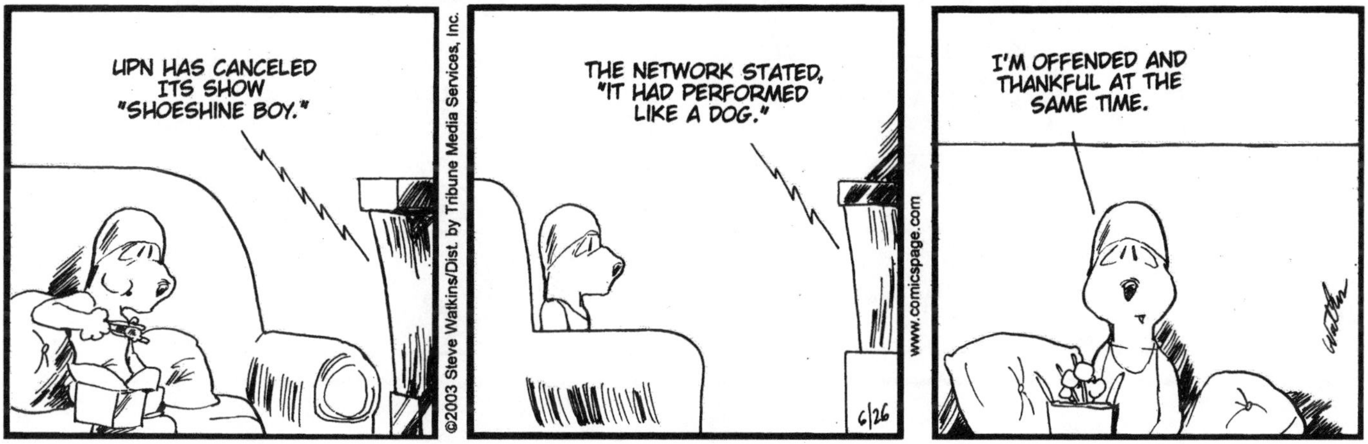
UPN HAS CANCELED ITS SHOW "SHOESHINE BOY."
©2003 Steve Watkins/Dist. by Tribune Media Services, Inc.
THE NETWORK STATED, "IT HAD PERFORMED LIKE A DOG."
6/26
www.comicspage.com
I'M OFFENDED AND THANKFUL AT THE SAME TIME.

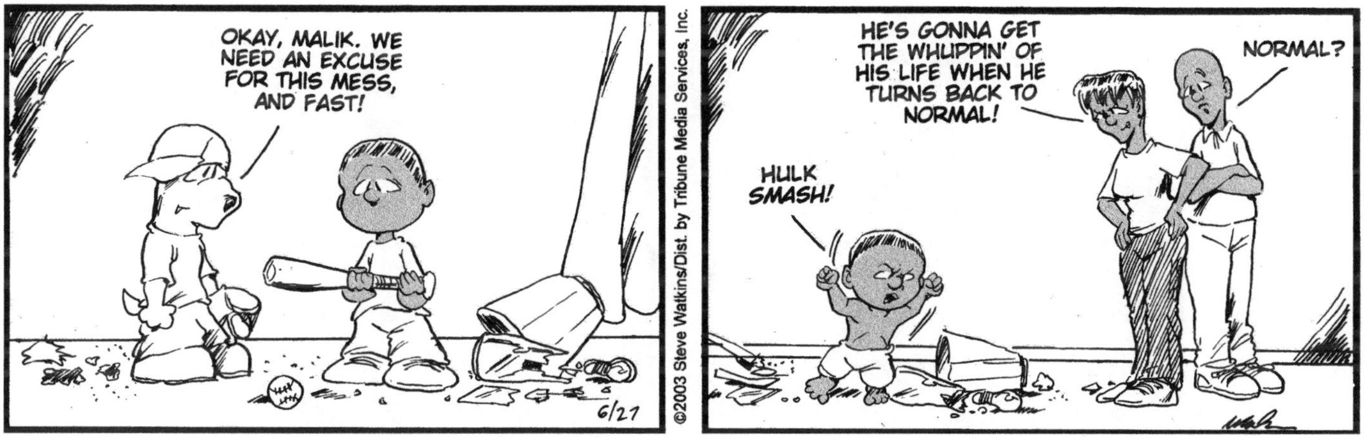
OKAY, MALIK. WE NEED AN EXCUSE FOR THIS MESS, AND FAST!
6/27
©2003 Steve Watkins/Dist. by Tribune Media Services, Inc.
HULK SMASH!
HE'S GONNA GET THE WHUPPIN' OF HIS LIFE WHEN HE TURNS BACK TO NORMAL!
NORMAL?

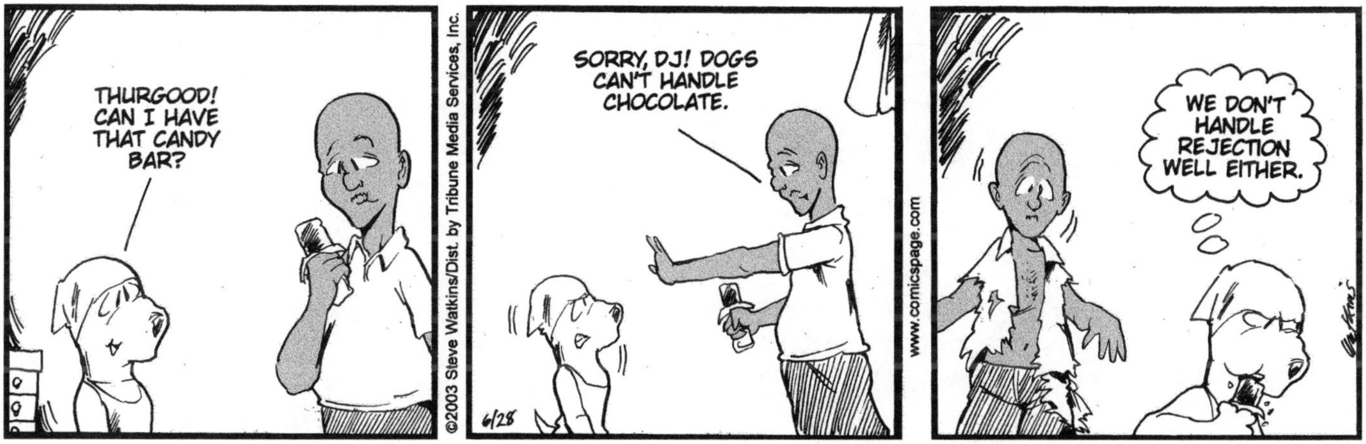
THURGOOD! CAN I HAVE THAT CANDY BAR?
©2003 Steve Watkins/Dist. by Tribune Media Services, Inc.
SORRY, DJ! DOGS CAN'T HANDLE CHOCOLATE.
6/28
www.comicspage.com
WE DON'T HANDLE REJECTION WELL EITHER.

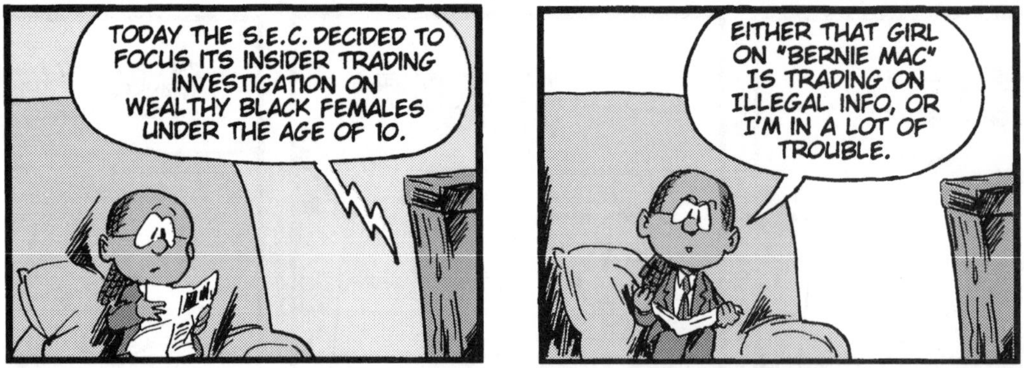
TODAY THE S.E.C. DECIDED TO FOCUS ITS INSIDER TRADING INVESTIGATION ON WEALTHY BLACK FEMALES UNDER THE AGE OF 10.
EITHER THAT GIRL ON "BERNIE MAC" IS TRADING ON ILLEGAL INFO, OR I'M IN A LOT OF TROUBLE.

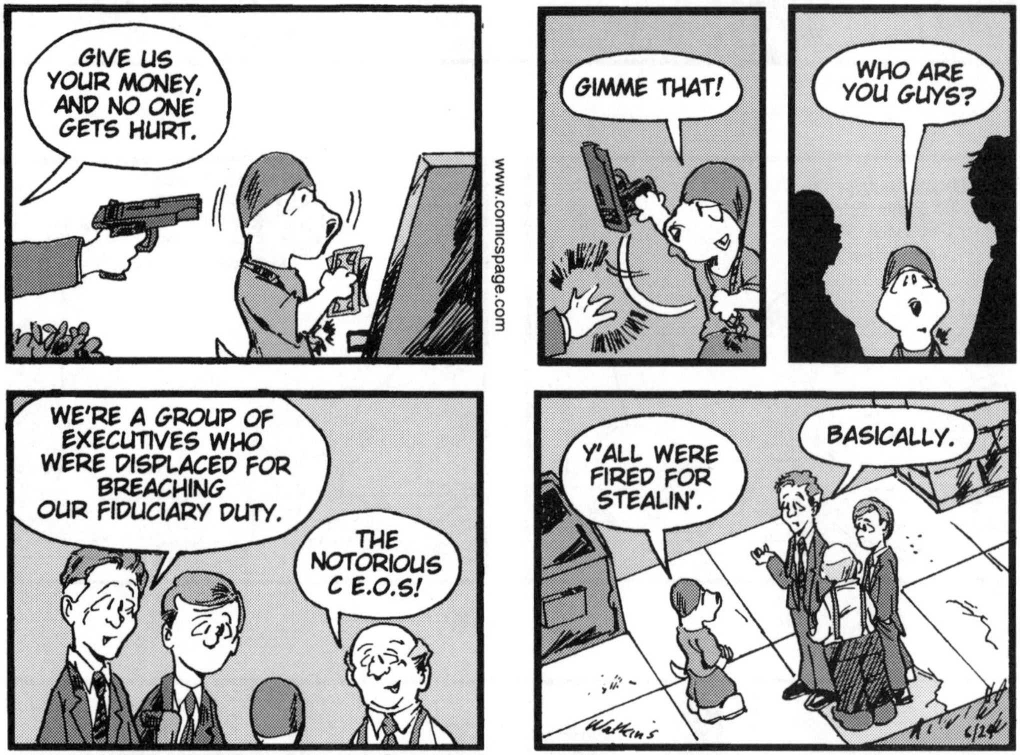
GIVE US YOUR MONEY, AND NO ONE GETS HURT.
GIMME THAT!
WHO ARE YOU GUYS?
WE'RE A GROUP OF EXECUTIVES WHO WERE DISPLACED FOR BREACHING OUR FIDUCIARY DUTY.
THE NOTORIOUS C E.O.S!
Y'ALL WERE FIRED FOR STEALIN'.
BASICALLY.
Watkins
6/24

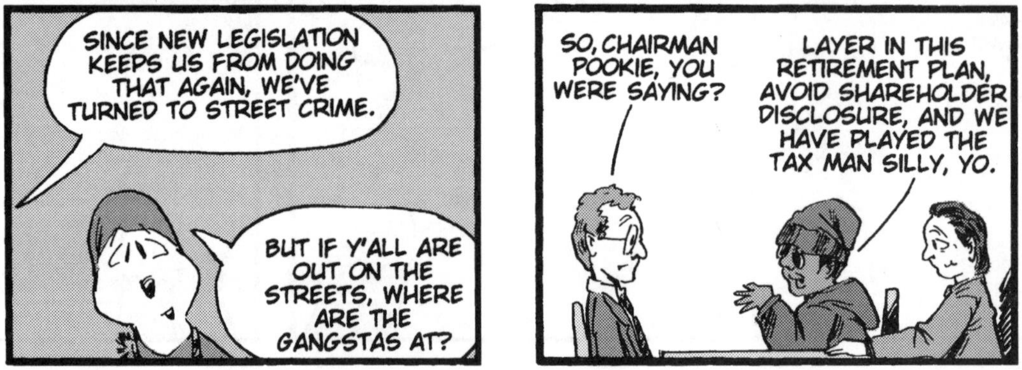
SINCE NEW LEGISLATION KEEPS US FROM DOING THAT AGAIN, WE'VE TURNED TO STREET CRIME.
BUT IF Y'ALL ARE OUT ON THE STREETS, WHERE ARE THE GANGSTAS AT?
SO, CHAIRMAN POOKIE, YOU WERE SAYING?
LAYER IN THIS RETIREMENT PLAN, AVOID SHAREHOLDER DISCLOSURE, AND WE HAVE PLAYED THE TAX MAN SILLY, YO.

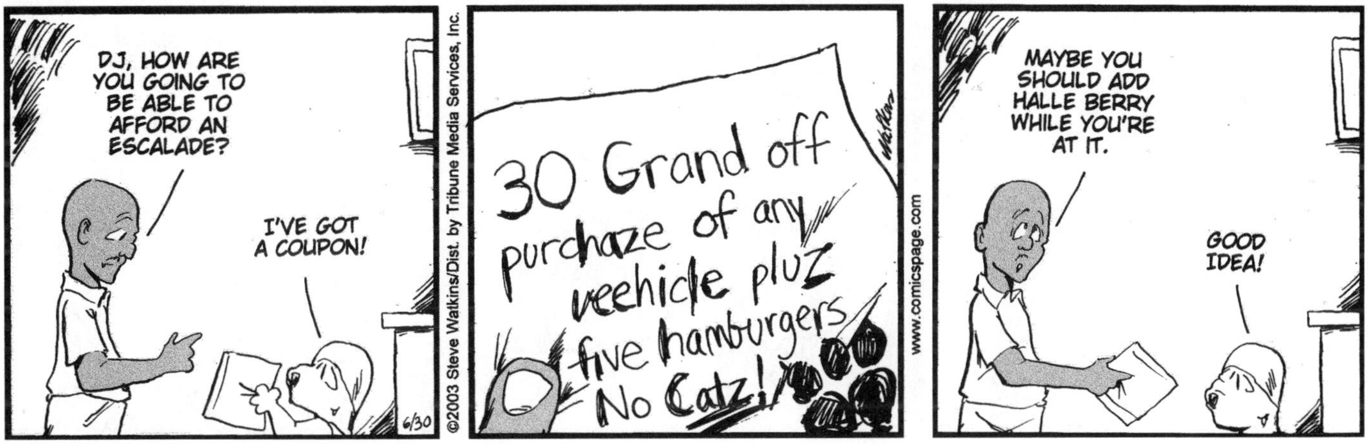
DJ, HOW ARE YOU GOING TO BE ABLE TO AFFORD AN ESCALADE?
I'VE GOT A COUPON!
6/30
30 Grand off purchaze of any veehicle pluZ five hamburgers No Catz!
MAYBE YOU SHOULD ADD HALLE BERRY WHILE YOU'RE AT IT.
GOOD IDEA!

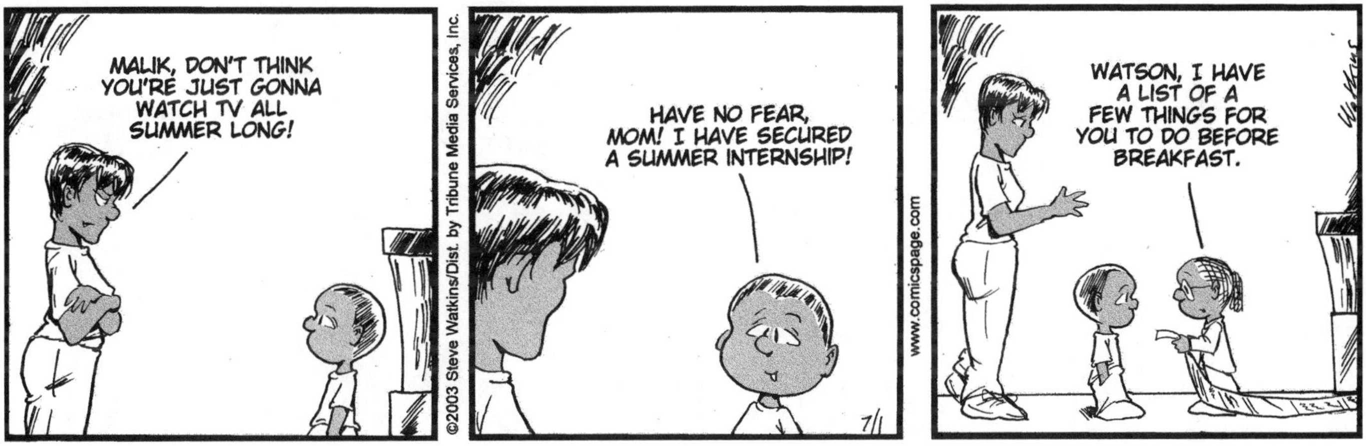
MALIK, DON'T THINK YOU'RE JUST GONNA WATCH TV ALL SUMMER LONG!
HAVE NO FEAR, MOM! I HAVE SECURED A SUMMER INTERNSHIP!
7/1
WATSON, I HAVE A LIST OF A FEW THINGS FOR YOU TO DO BEFORE BREAKFAST.

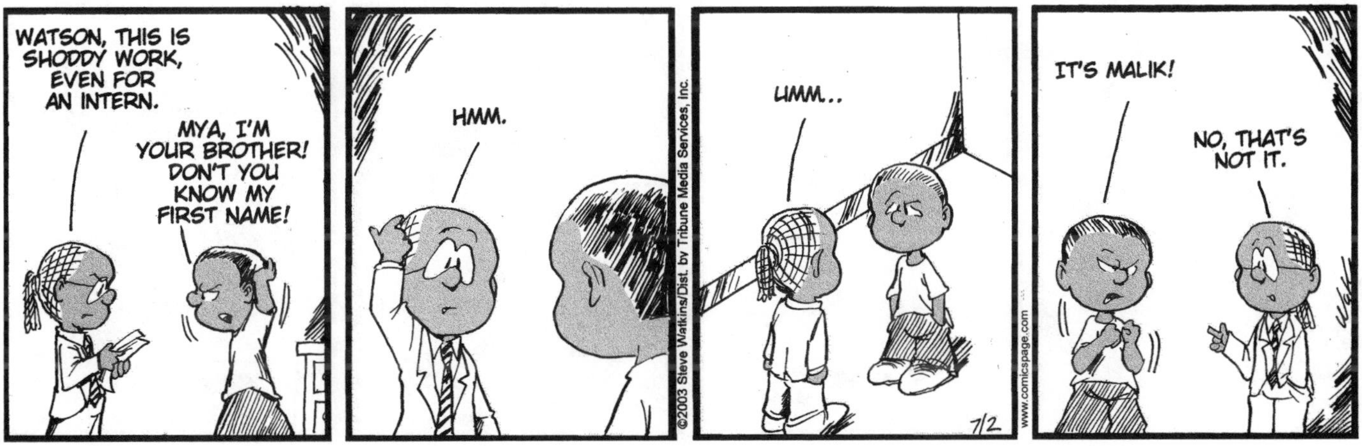
WATSON, THIS IS SHODDY WORK, EVEN FOR AN INTERN.
MYA, I'M YOUR BROTHER! DON'T YOU KNOW MY FIRST NAME!
HMM.
UMM...
7/2
IT'S MALIK!
NO, THAT'S NOT IT.

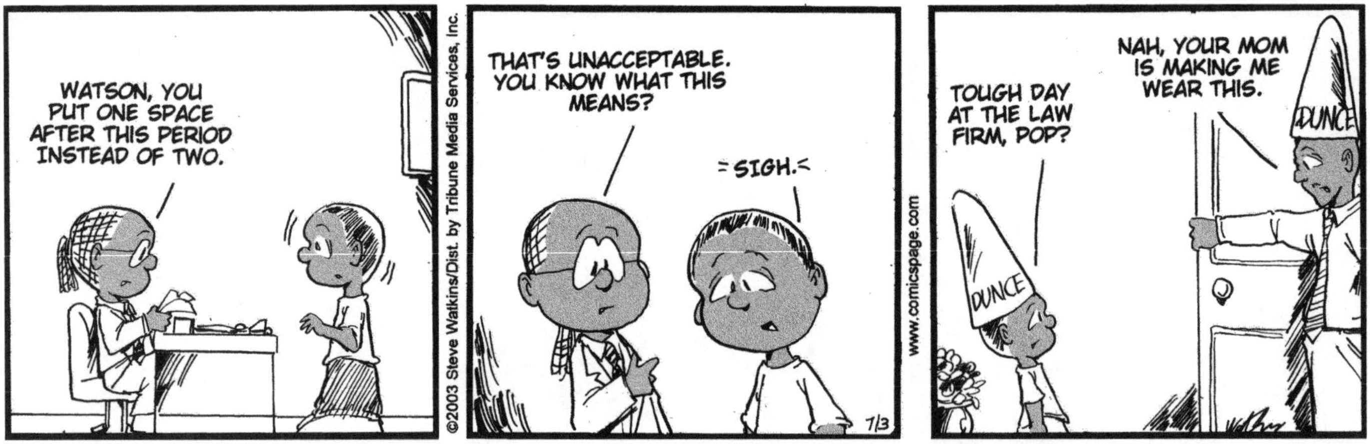
WATSON, YOU PUT ONE SPACE AFTER THIS PERIOD INSTEAD OF TWO.
©2003 Steve Watkins/Dist. by Tribune Media Services, Inc.
THAT'S UNACCEPTABLE. YOU KNOW WHAT THIS MEANS?
=SIGH.=
7/3
www.comicspage.com
TOUGH DAY AT THE LAW FIRM, POP?
NAH, YOUR MOM IS MAKING ME WEAR THIS.
DUNCE
DUNCE

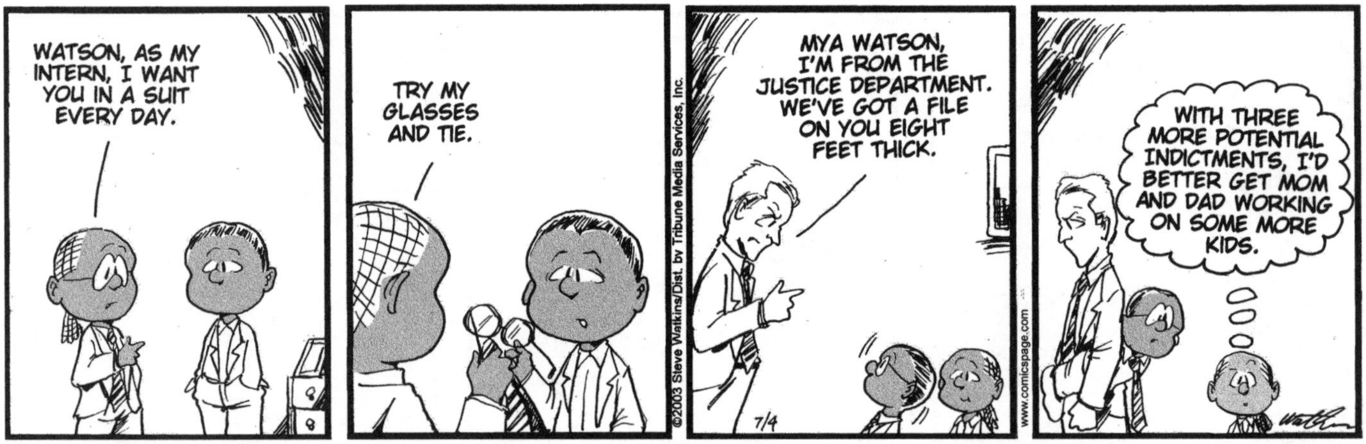
WATSON, AS MY INTERN, I WANT YOU IN A SUIT EVERY DAY.
TRY MY GLASSES AND TIE.
©2003 Steve Watkins/Dist. by Tribune Media Services, Inc.
MYA WATSON, I'M FROM THE JUSTICE DEPARTMENT. WE'VE GOT A FILE ON YOU EIGHT FEET THICK.
7/4
www.comicspage.com
WITH THREE MORE POTENTIAL INDICTMENTS, I'D BETTER GET MOM AND DAD WORKING ON SOME MORE KIDS.

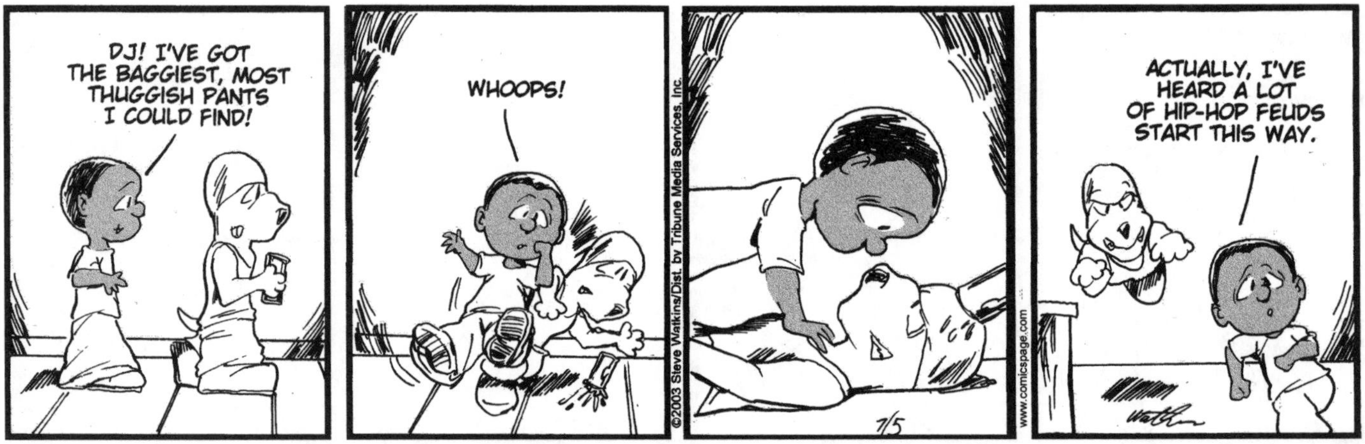
DJ! I'VE GOT THE BAGGIEST, MOST THUGGISH PANTS I COULD FIND!
WHOOPS!
©2003 Steve Watkins/Dist. by Tribune Media Services, Inc.
7/5
www.comicspage.com
ACTUALLY, I'VE HEARD A LOT OF HIP-HOP FEUDS START THIS WAY.

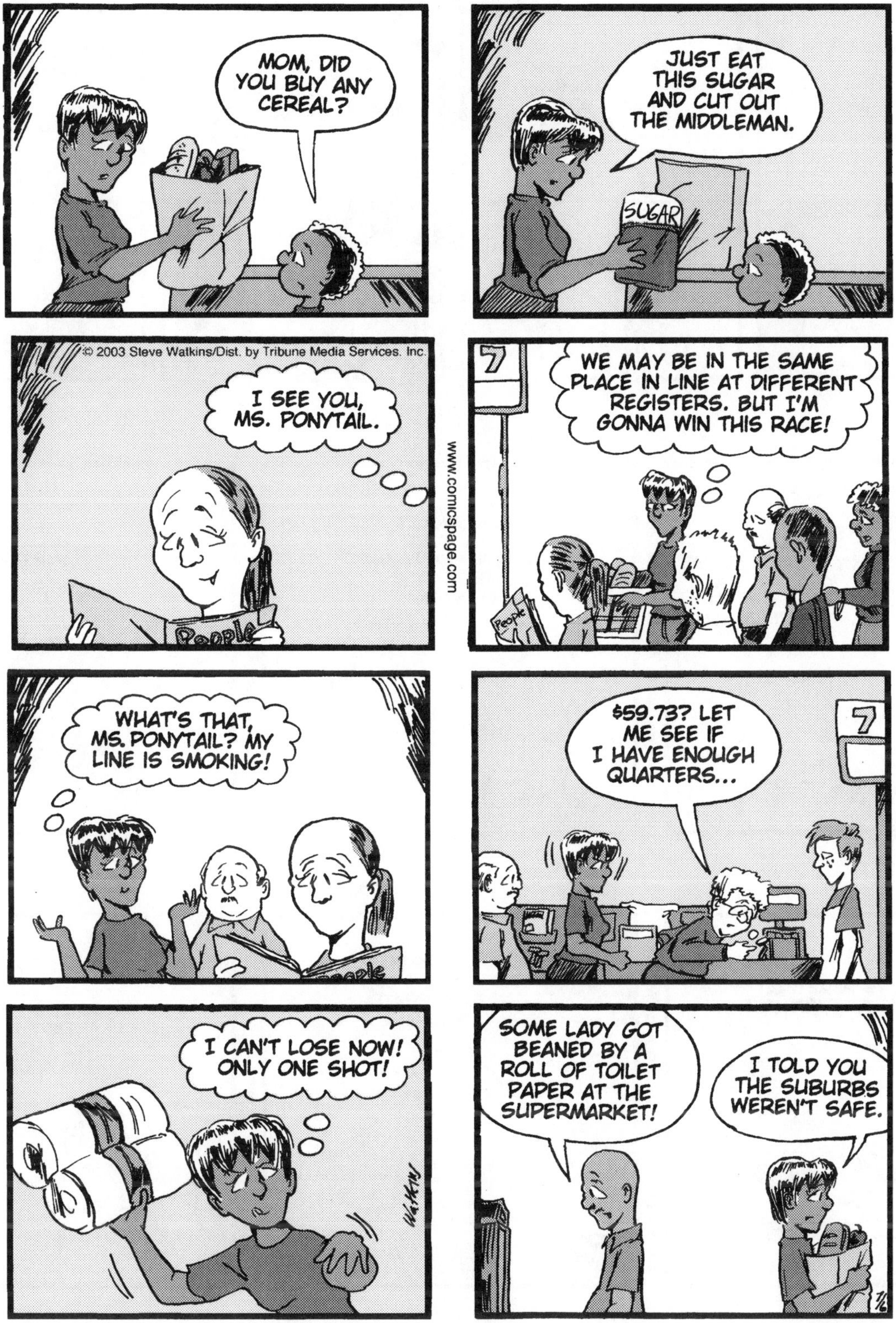
MOM, DID YOU BUY ANY CEREAL?
JUST EAT THIS SUGAR AND CUT OUT THE MIDDLEMAN.
SUGAR
© 2003 Steve Watkins/Dist. by Tribune Media Services. Inc.
I SEE YOU, MS. PONYTAIL.
People
7
WE MAY BE IN THE SAME PLACE IN LINE AT DIFFERENT REGISTERS. BUT I'M GONNA WIN THIS RACE!
www.comicspage.com
WHAT'S THAT, MS. PONYTAIL? MY LINE IS SMOKING!
$59.73? LET ME SEE IF I HAVE ENOUGH QUARTERS...
I CAN'T LOSE NOW! ONLY ONE SHOT!
SOME LADY GOT BEANED BY A ROLL OF TOILET PAPER AT THE SUPERMARKET!
I TOLD YOU THE SUBURBS WEREN'T SAFE.

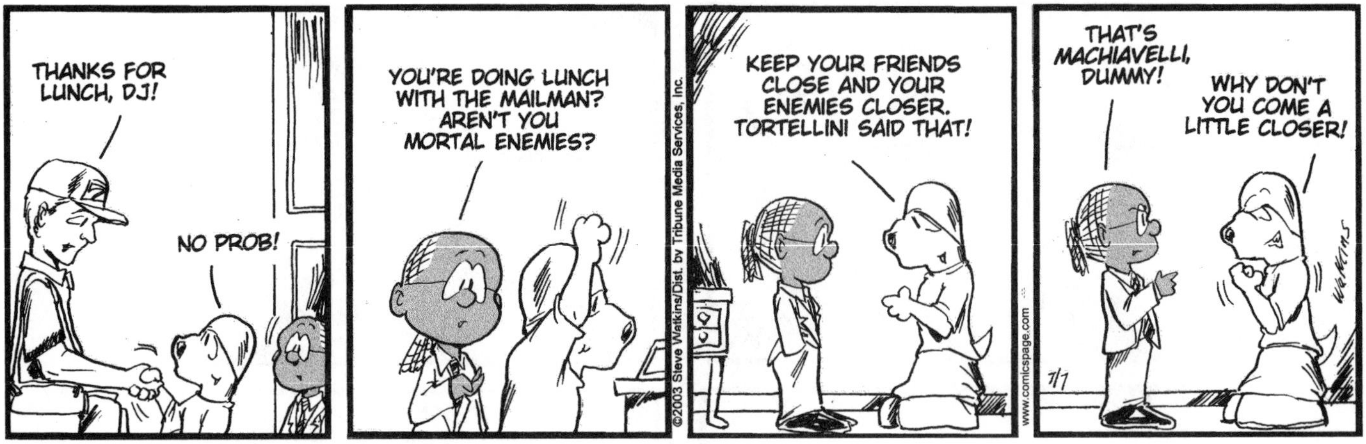
THANKS FOR LUNCH, DJ!
NO PROB!
YOU'RE DOING LUNCH WITH THE MAILMAN? AREN'T YOU MORTAL ENEMIES?
©2003 Steve Watkins/Dist. by Tribune Media Services, Inc.
KEEP YOUR FRIENDS CLOSE AND YOUR ENEMIES CLOSER. TORTELLINI SAID THAT!
www.comicspage.com
7/7
THAT'S MACHIAVELLI, DUMMY!
WHY DON'T YOU COME A LITTLE CLOSER!

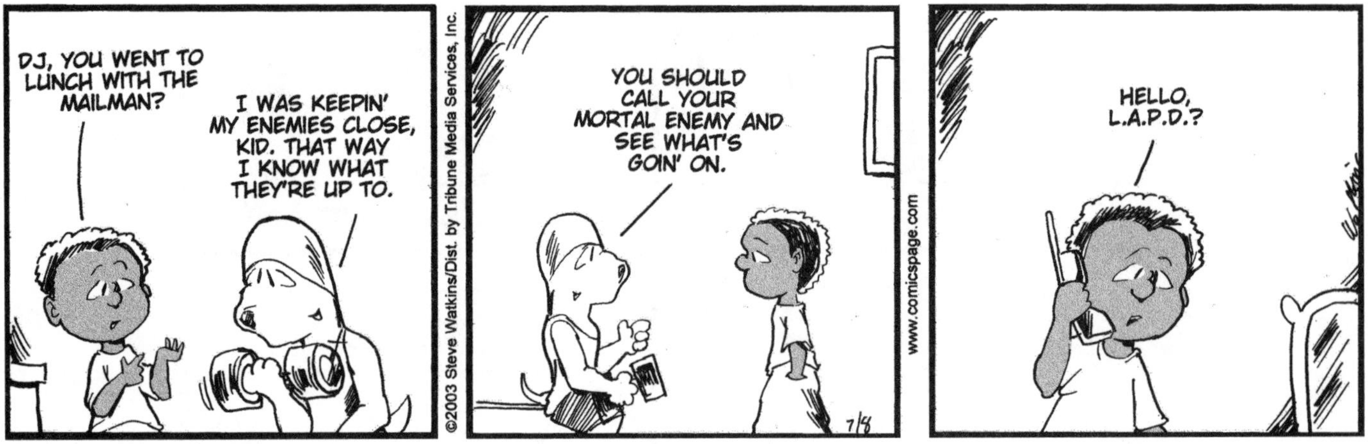
DJ, YOU WENT TO LUNCH WITH THE MAILMAN?
I WAS KEEPIN' MY ENEMIES CLOSE, KID. THAT WAY I KNOW WHAT THEY'RE UP TO.
©2003 Steve Watkins/Dist. by Tribune Media Services, Inc.
YOU SHOULD CALL YOUR MORTAL ENEMY AND SEE WHAT'S GOIN' ON.
7/8
www.comicspage.com
HELLO, L.A.P.D.?

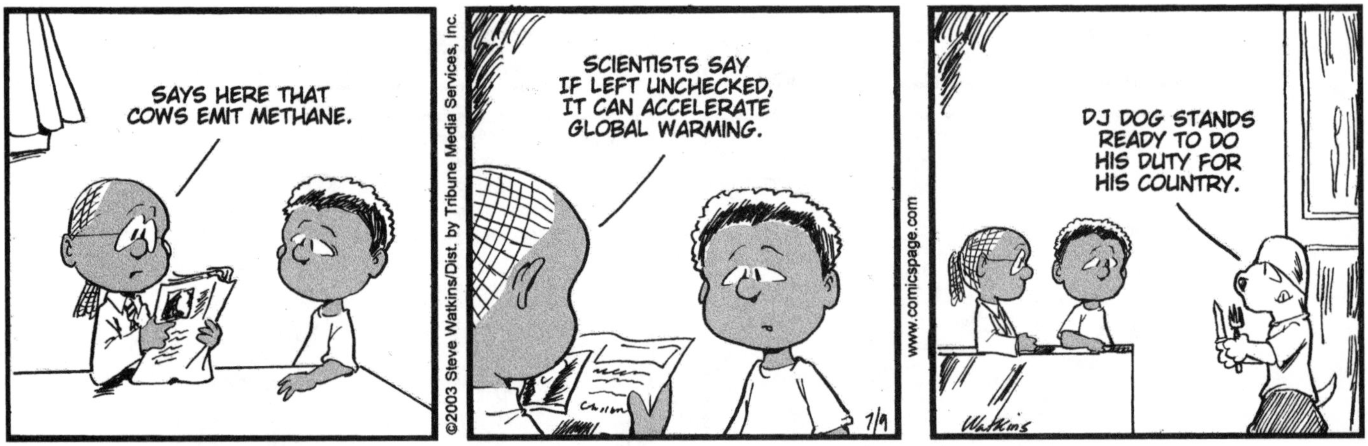
SAYS HERE THAT COWS EMIT METHANE.
©2003 Steve Watkins/Dist. by Tribune Media Services, Inc.
SCIENTISTS SAY IF LEFT UNCHECKED, IT CAN ACCELERATE GLOBAL WARMING.
7/9
www.comicspage.com
DJ DOG STANDS READY TO DO HIS DUTY FOR HIS COUNTRY.
Watkins

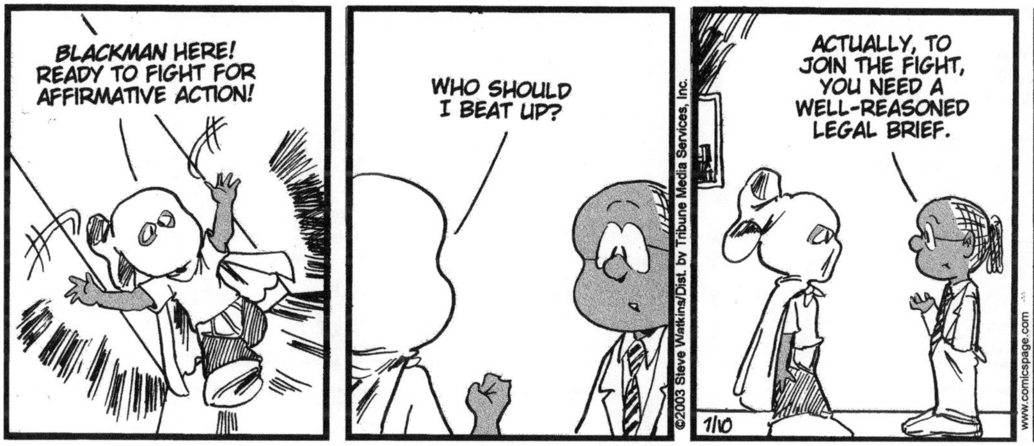
BLACKMAN HERE! READY TO FIGHT FOR AFFIRMATIVE ACTION!
WHO SHOULD I BEAT UP?
©2003 Steve Watkins/Dist. by Tribune Media Services, Inc.
ACTUALLY, TO JOIN THE FIGHT, YOU NEED A WELL-REASONED LEGAL BRIEF.
7/10
www.comicspage.com
BLACKMAN AND HIS ARCH FOE, BASIC GRAMMAR, TANGLE AGAIN!
Watkins

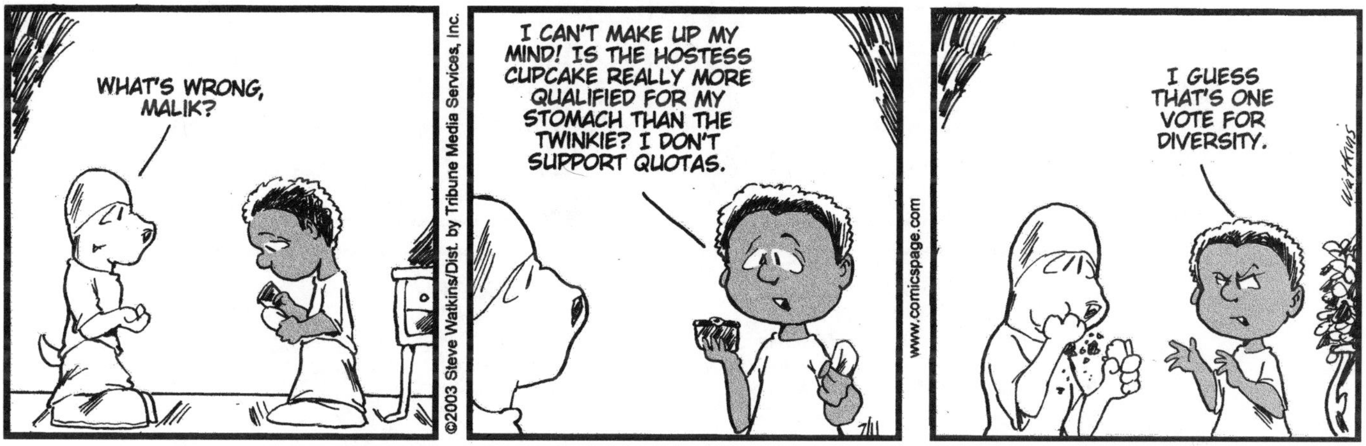
WHAT'S WRONG, MALIK?
©2003 Steve Watkins/Dist. by Tribune Media Services, Inc.
I CAN'T MAKE UP MY MIND! IS THE HOSTESS CUPCAKE REALLY MORE QUALIFIED FOR MY STOMACH THAN THE TWINKIE? I DON'T SUPPORT QUOTAS.
7/11
www.comicspage.com
I GUESS THAT'S ONE VOTE FOR DIVERSITY.
Watkins

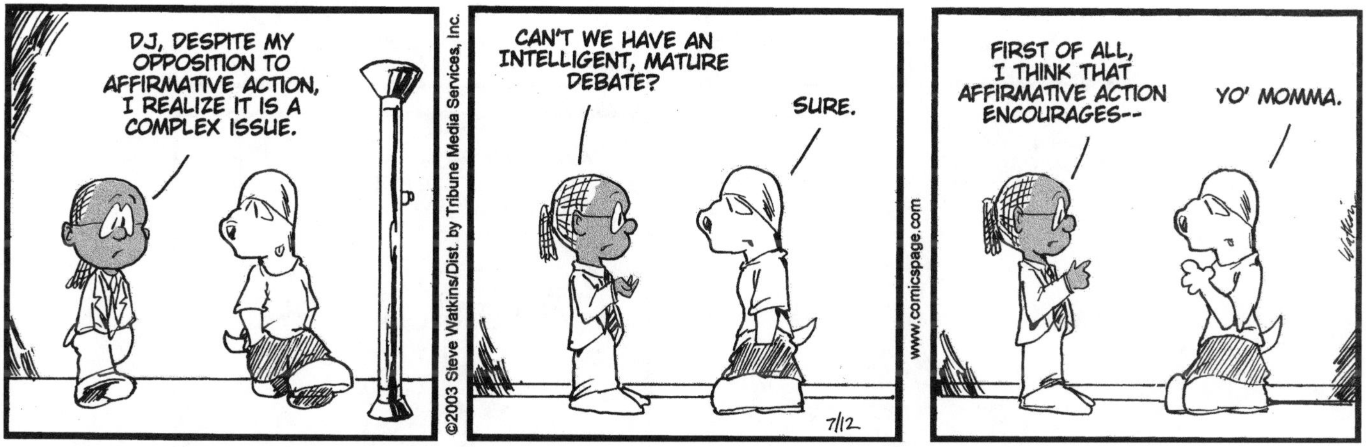
DJ, DESPITE MY OPPOSITION TO AFFIRMATIVE ACTION, I REALIZE IT IS A COMPLEX ISSUE.
©2003 Steve Watkins/Dist. by Tribune Media Services, Inc.
CAN'T WE HAVE AN INTELLIGENT, MATURE DEBATE?
SURE.
7/12
www.comicspage.com
FIRST OF ALL, I THINK THAT AFFIRMATIVE ACTION ENCOURAGES--
YO' MOMMA.
Watkins

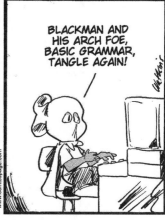

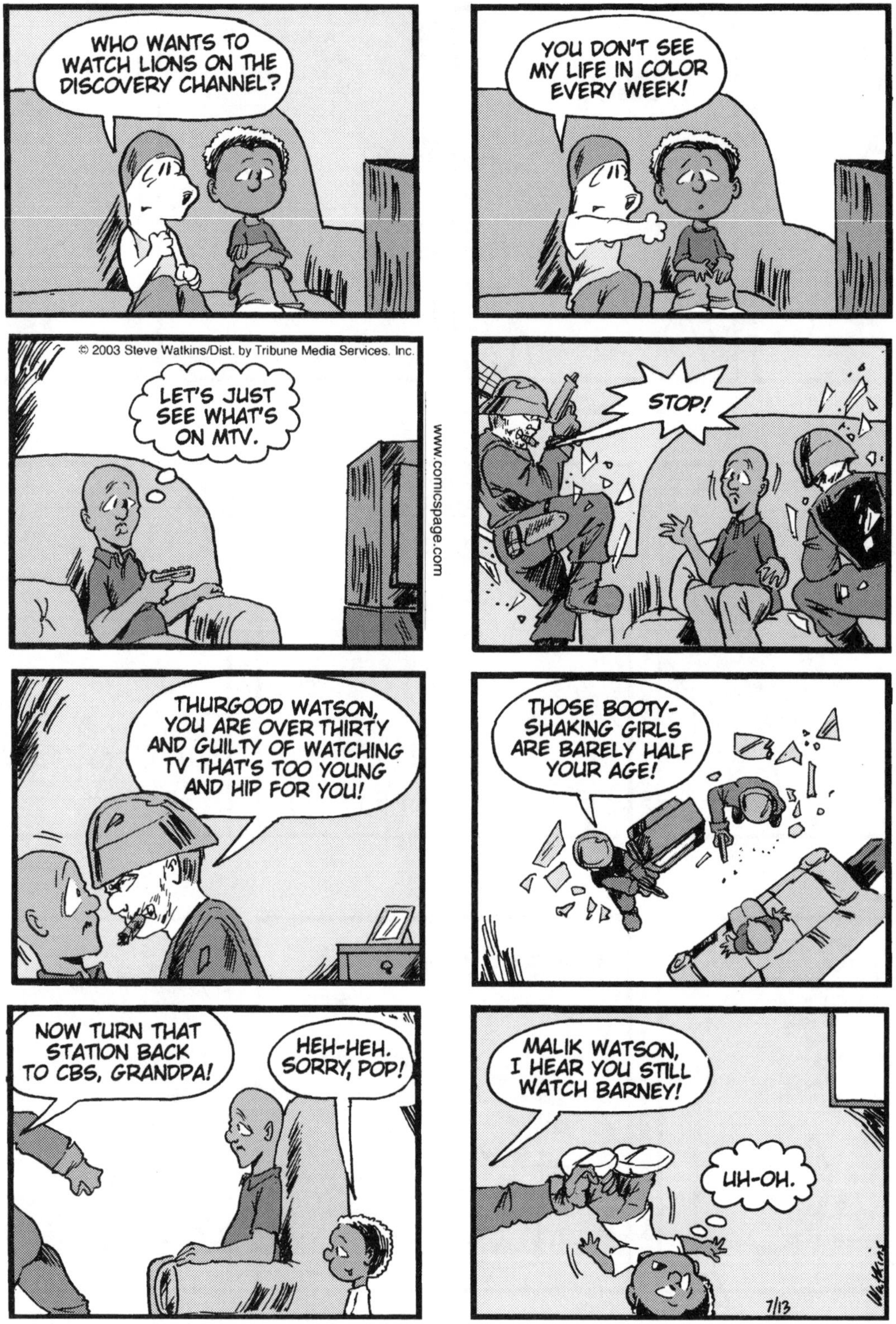

WHO WANTS TO WATCH LIONS ON THE DISCOVERY CHANNEL?
YOU DON'T SEE MY LIFE IN COLOR EVERY WEEK!
© 2003 Steve Watkins/Dist. by Tribune Media Services. Inc.
LET'S JUST SEE WHAT'S ON MTV.
www.comicspage.com
STOP!
THURGOOD WATSON, YOU ARE OVER THIRTY AND GUILTY OF WATCHING TV THAT'S TOO YOUNG AND HIP FOR YOU!
THOSE BOOTY-SHAKING GIRLS ARE BARELY HALF YOUR AGE!
NOW TURN THAT STATION BACK TO CBS, GRANDPA!
HEH-HEH. SORRY, POP!
MALIK WATSON, I HEAR YOU STILL WATCH BARNEY!
UH-OH.
7/13

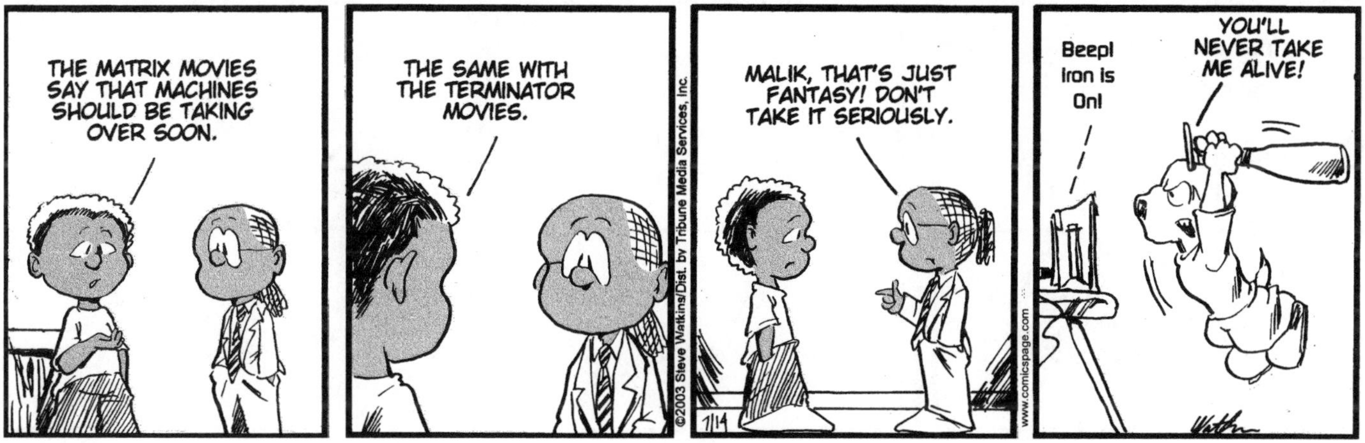
THE MATRIX MOVIES SAY THAT MACHINES SHOULD BE TAKING OVER SOON.
THE SAME WITH THE TERMINATOR MOVIES.
©2003 Steve Watkins/Dist. by Tribune Media Services, Inc.
MALIK, THAT'S JUST FANTASY! DON'T TAKE IT SERIOUSLY.
7/14
www.comicspage.com
Beep! Iron Is On!
YOU'LL NEVER TAKE ME ALIVE!

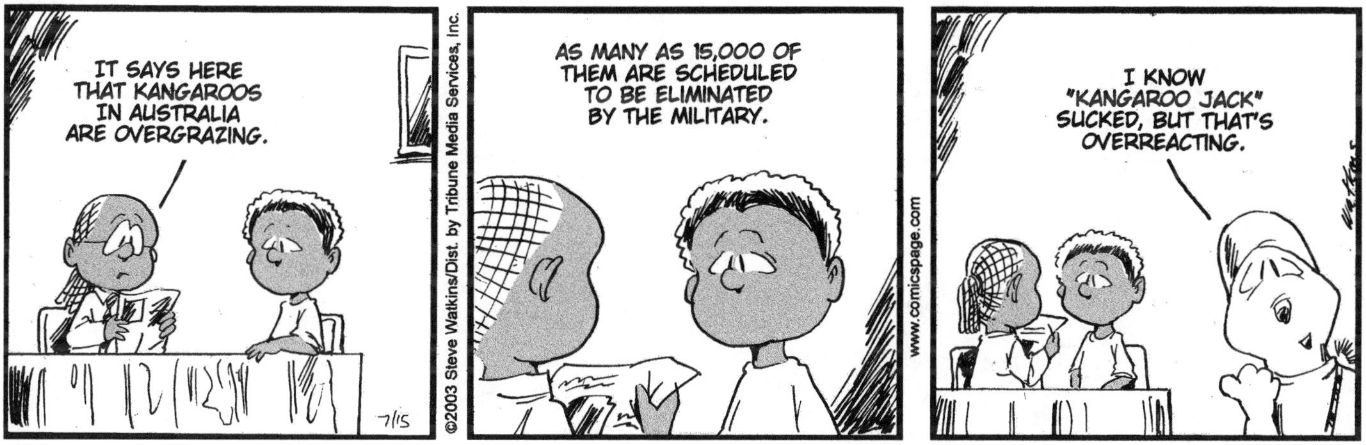
IT SAYS HERE THAT KANGAROOS IN AUSTRALIA ARE OVERGRAZING.
7/15
©2003 Steve Watkins/Dist. by Tribune Media Services, Inc.
AS MANY AS 15,000 OF THEM ARE SCHEDULED TO BE ELIMINATED BY THE MILITARY.
www.comicspage.com
I KNOW "KANGAROO JACK" SUCKED, BUT THAT'S OVERREACTING.

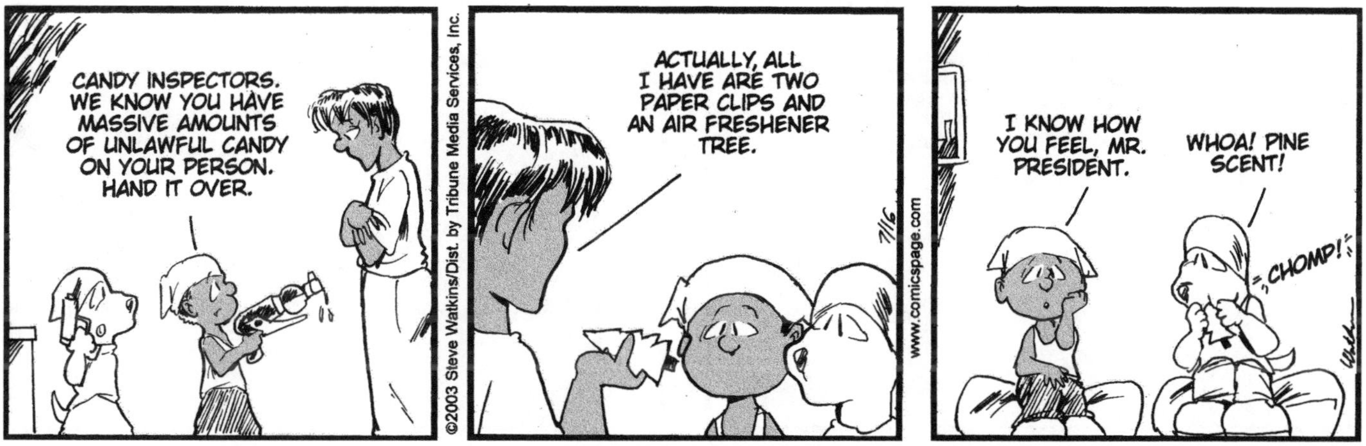
CANDY INSPECTORS. WE KNOW YOU HAVE MASSIVE AMOUNTS OF UNLAWFUL CANDY ON YOUR PERSON. HAND IT OVER.
©2003 Steve Watkins/Dist. by Tribune Media Services, Inc.
ACTUALLY, ALL I HAVE ARE TWO PAPER CLIPS AND AN AIR FRESHENER TREE.
7/16
www.comicspage.com
I KNOW HOW YOU FEEL, MR. PRESIDENT.
WHOA! PINE SCENT!
CHOMP!

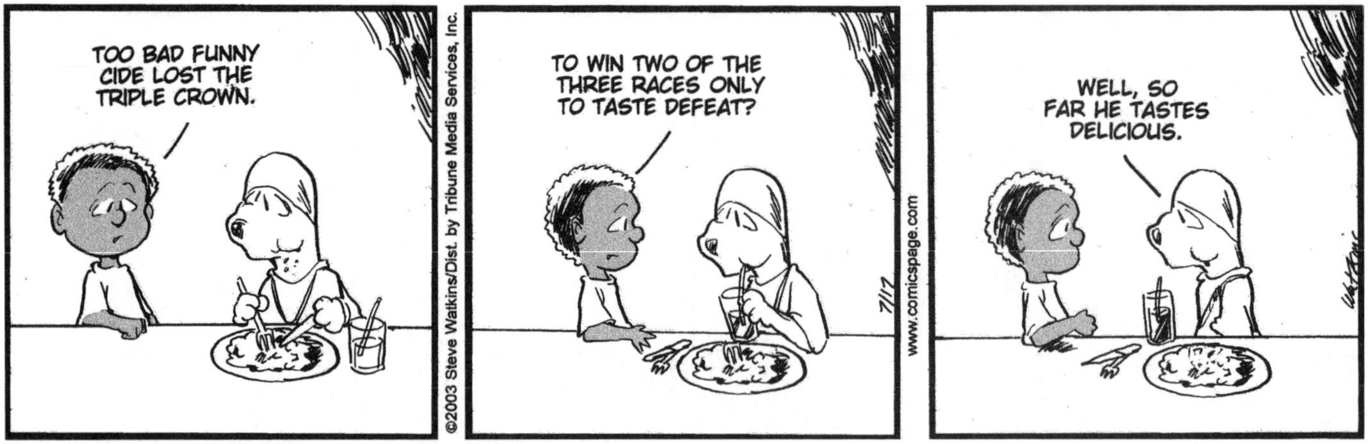
TOO BAD FUNNY CIDE LOST THE TRIPLE CROWN.
TO WIN TWO OF THE THREE RACES ONLY TO TASTE DEFEAT?
WELL, SO FAR HE TASTES DELICIOUS.
7/17
www.comicspage.com

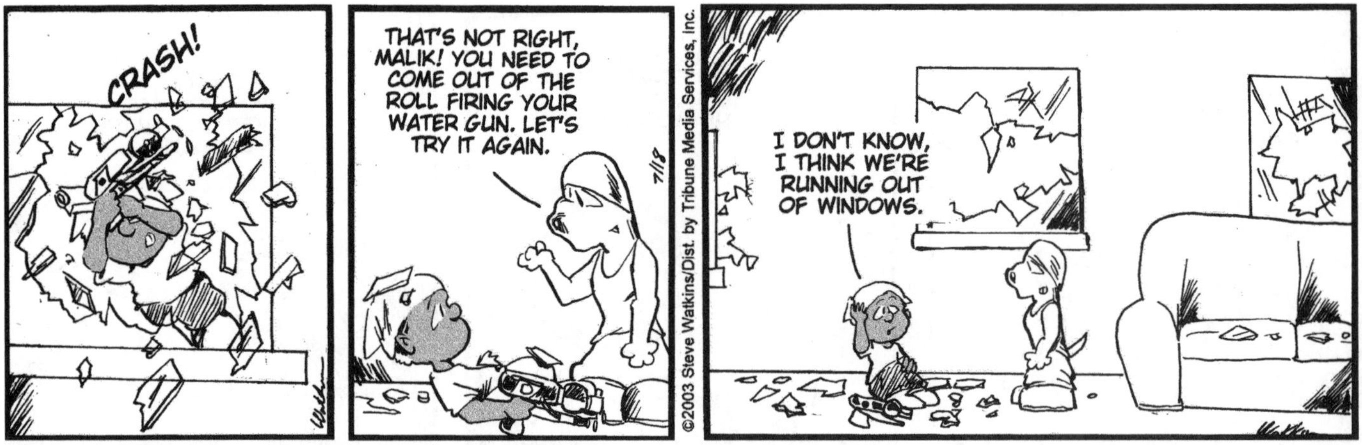
CRASH!
THAT'S NOT RIGHT, MALIK! YOU NEED TO COME OUT OF THE ROLL FIRING YOUR WATER GUN. LET'S TRY IT AGAIN.
7/18
I DON'T KNOW, I THINK WE'RE RUNNING OUT OF WINDOWS.

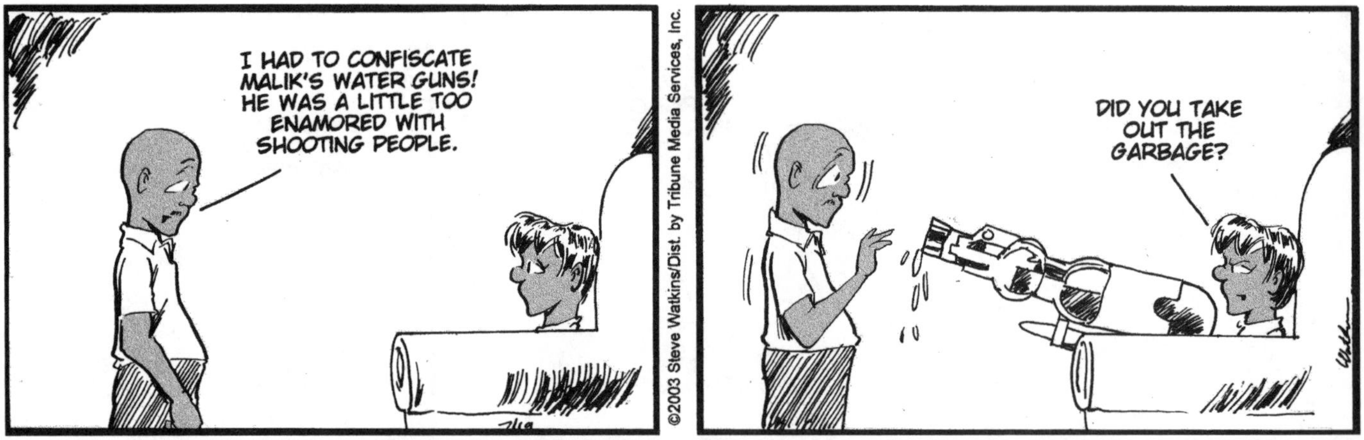
I HAD TO CONFISCATE MALIK'S WATER GUNS! HE WAS A LITTLE TOO ENAMORED WITH SHOOTING PEOPLE.
DID YOU TAKE OUT THE GARBAGE?

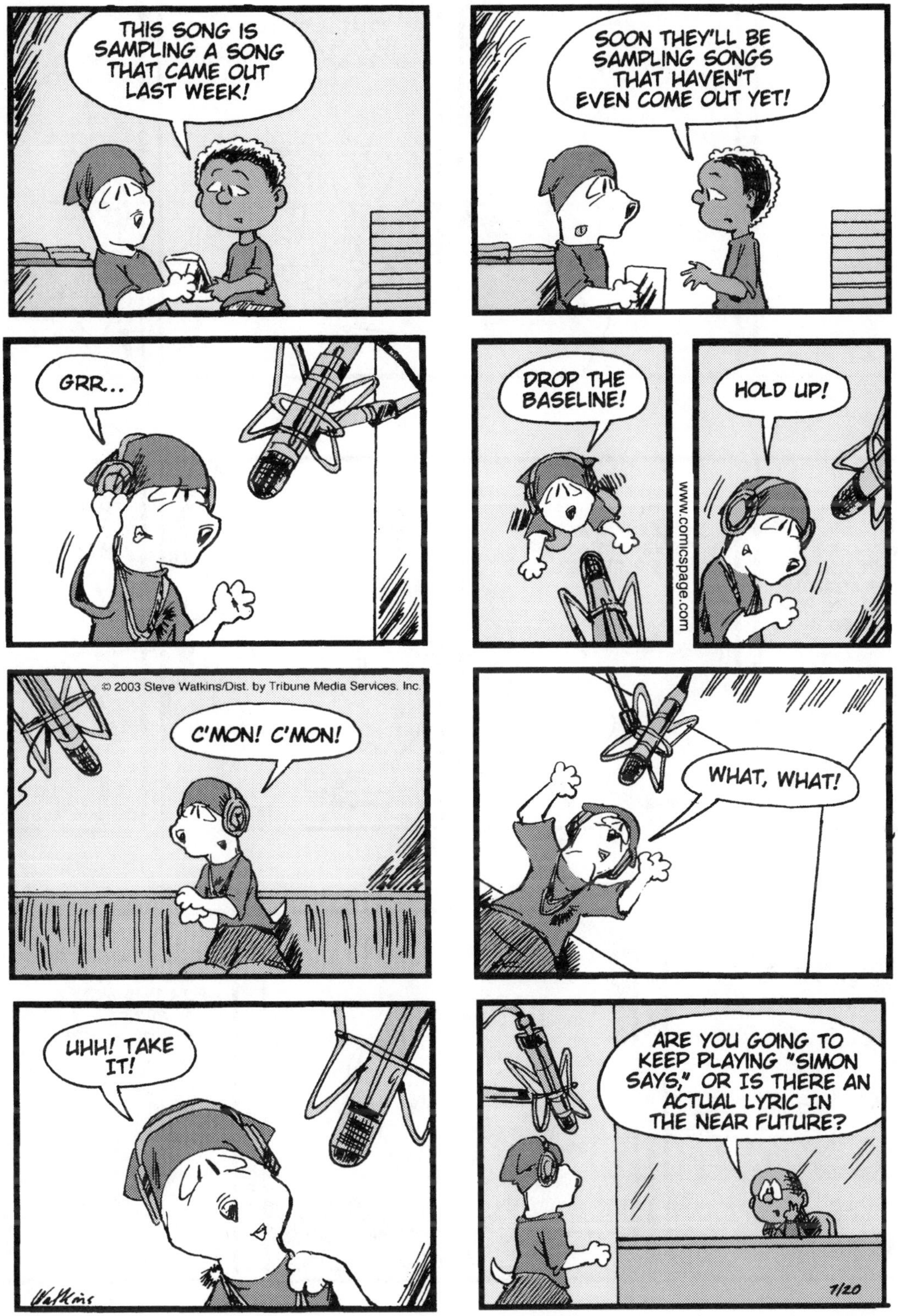
THIS SONG IS SAMPLING A SONG THAT CAME OUT LAST WEEK!
SOON THEY'LL BE SAMPLING SONGS THAT HAVEN'T EVEN COME OUT YET!
GRR...
DROP THE BASELINE!
HOLD UP!
www.comicspage.com
© 2003 Steve Watkins/Dist. by Tribune Media Services, Inc.
C'MON! C'MON!
WHAT, WHAT!
UHH! TAKE IT!
ARE YOU GOING TO KEEP PLAYING "SIMON SAYS," OR IS THERE AN ACTUAL LYRIC IN THE NEAR FUTURE?
Watkins
7/20

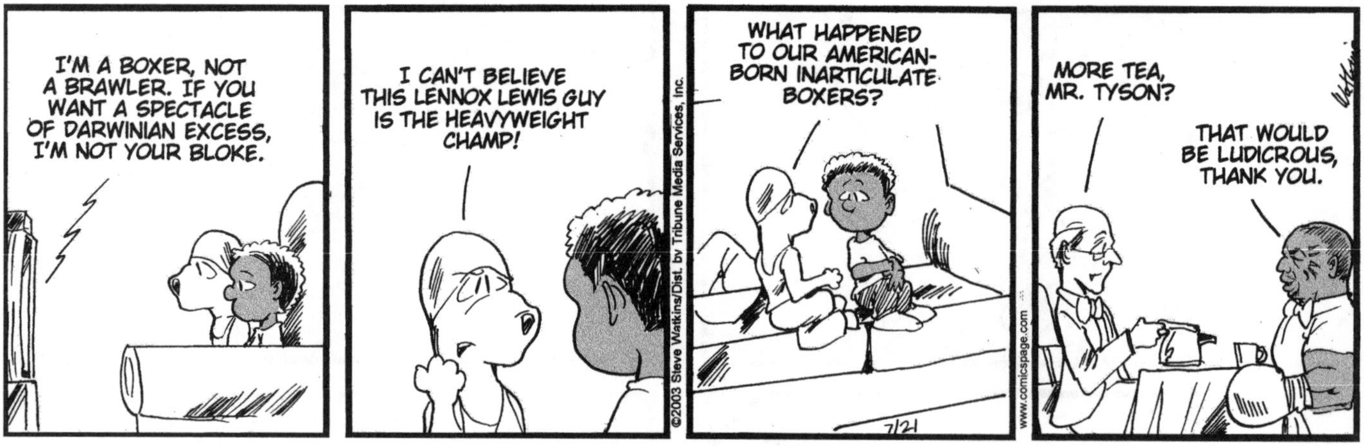
I'M A BOXER, NOT A BRAWLER. IF YOU WANT A SPECTACLE OF DARWINIAN EXCESS, I'M NOT YOUR BLOKE.
I CAN'T BELIEVE THIS LENNOX LEWIS GUY IS THE HEAVYWEIGHT CHAMP!
©2003 Steve Watkins/Dist. by Tribune Media Services, Inc.
WHAT HAPPENED TO OUR AMERICAN-BORN INARTICULATE BOXERS?
7/21
www.comicspage.com
MORE TEA, MR. TYSON?
THAT WOULD BE LUDICROUS, THANK YOU.

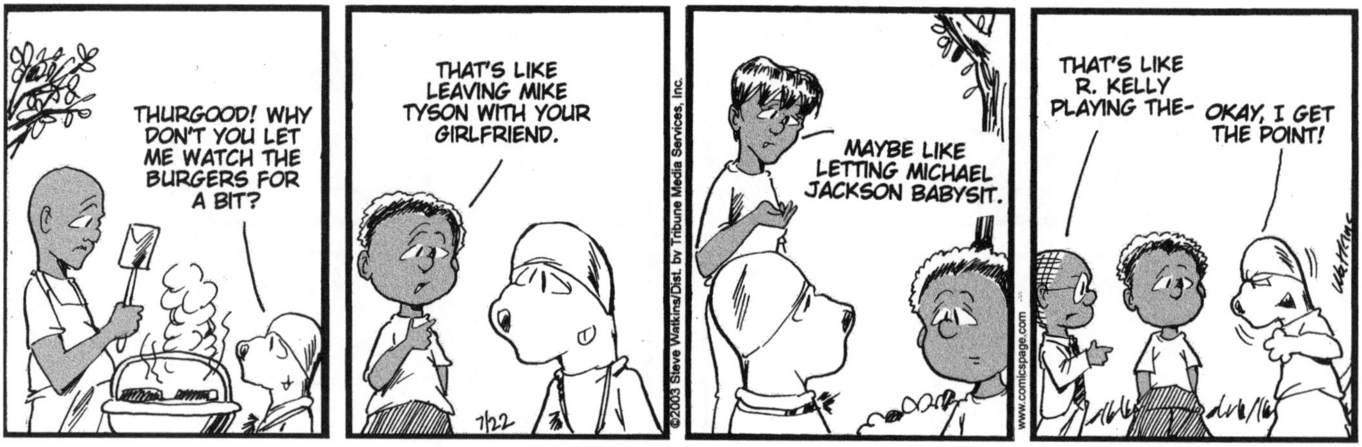
THURGOOD! WHY DON'T YOU LET ME WATCH THE BURGERS FOR A BIT?
THAT'S LIKE LEAVING MIKE TYSON WITH YOUR GIRLFRIEND.
7/22
©2003 Steve Watkins/Dist. by Tribune Media Services, Inc.
MAYBE LIKE LETTING MICHAEL JACKSON BABYSIT.
www.comicspage.com
THAT'S LIKE R. KELLY PLAYING THE-
OKAY, I GET THE POINT!

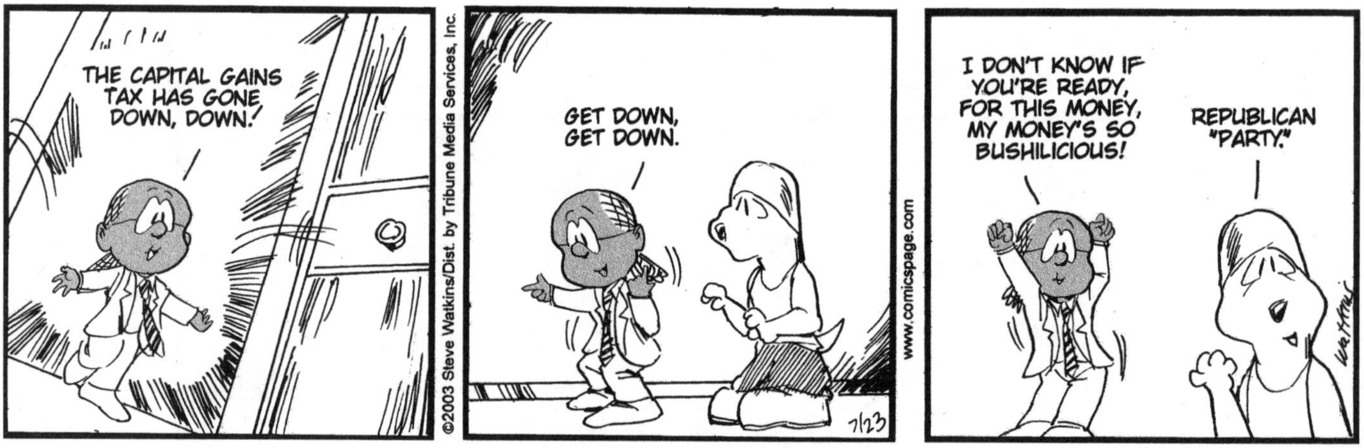
THE CAPITAL GAINS TAX HAS GONE DOWN, DOWN!
©2003 Steve Watkins/Dist. by Tribune Media Services, Inc.
GET DOWN, GET DOWN.
7/23
www.comicspage.com
I DON'T KNOW IF YOU'RE READY, FOR THIS MONEY, MY MONEY'S SO BUSHILICIOUS!
REPUBLICAN "PARTY."

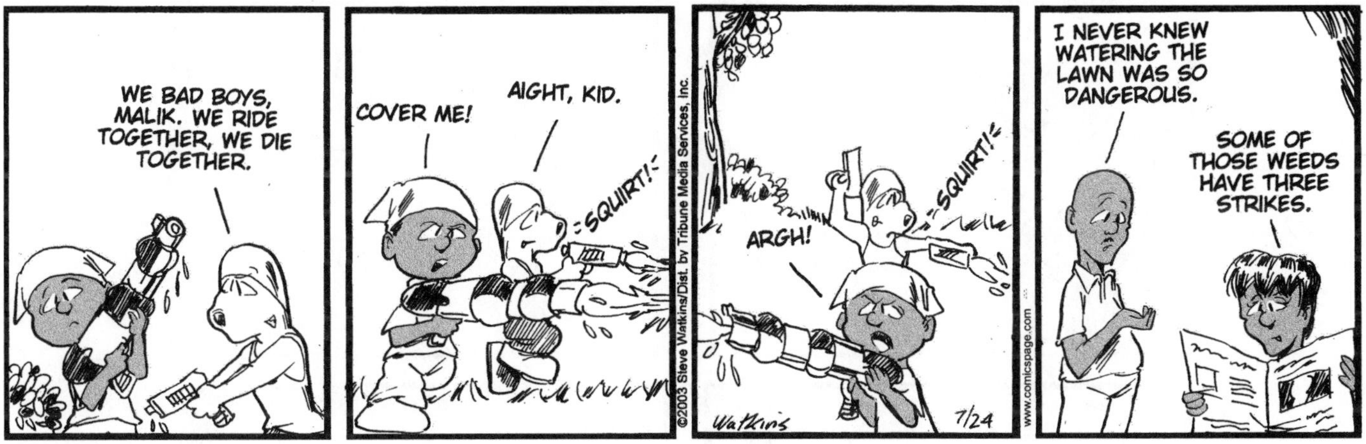
WE BAD BOYS, MALIK. WE RIDE TOGETHER, WE DIE TOGETHER.
COVER ME!
AIGHT, KID.
SQUIRT!
©2003 Steve Watkins/Dist. by Tribune Media Services, Inc.
ARGH!
SQUIRT!
Watkins
7/24
www.comicspage.com
I NEVER KNEW WATERING THE LAWN WAS SO DANGEROUS.
SOME OF THOSE WEEDS HAVE THREE STRIKES.

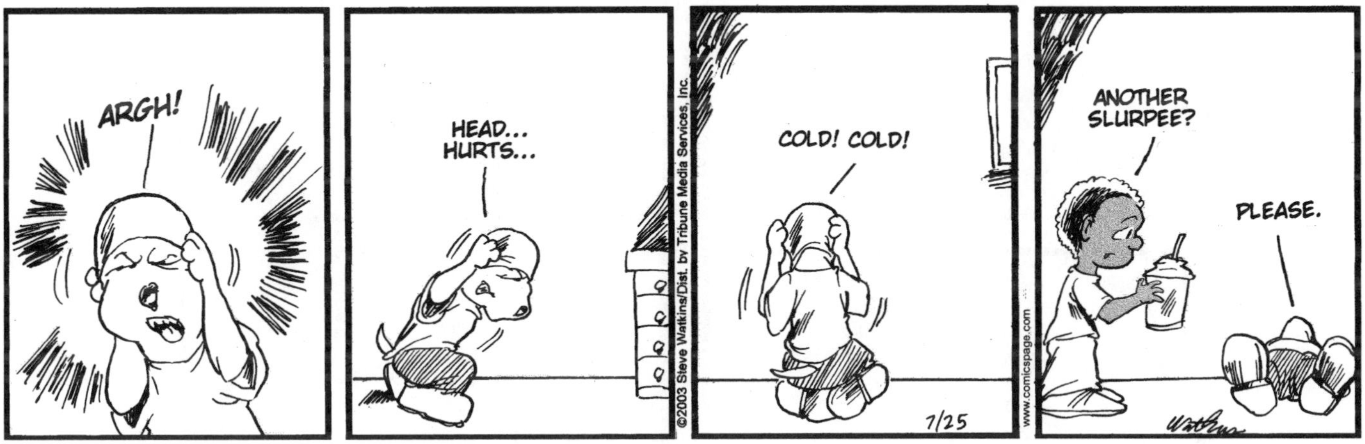
ARGH!
HEAD... HURTS...
©2003 Steve Watkins/Dist. by Tribune Media Services, Inc.
COLD! COLD!
7/25
www.comicspage.com
ANOTHER SLURPEE?
PLEASE.

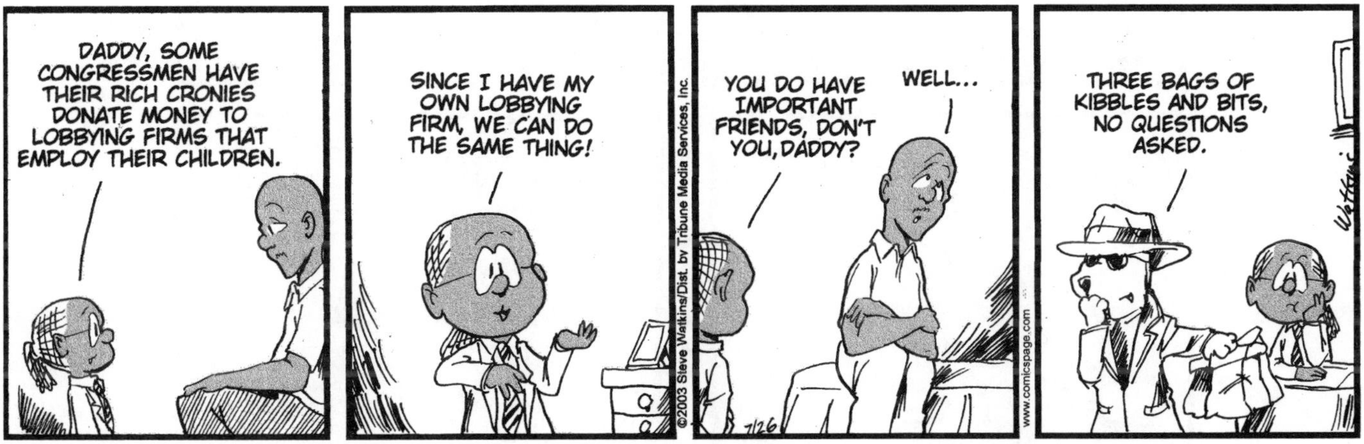
DADDY, SOME CONGRESSMEN HAVE THEIR RICH CRONIES DONATE MONEY TO LOBBYING FIRMS THAT EMPLOY THEIR CHILDREN.
SINCE I HAVE MY OWN LOBBYING FIRM, WE CAN DO THE SAME THING!
©2003 Steve Watkins/Dist. by Tribune Media Services, Inc.
YOU DO HAVE IMPORTANT FRIENDS, DON'T YOU, DADDY?
WELL...
7/26
www.comicspage.com
THREE BAGS OF KIBBLES AND BITS, NO QUESTIONS ASKED.

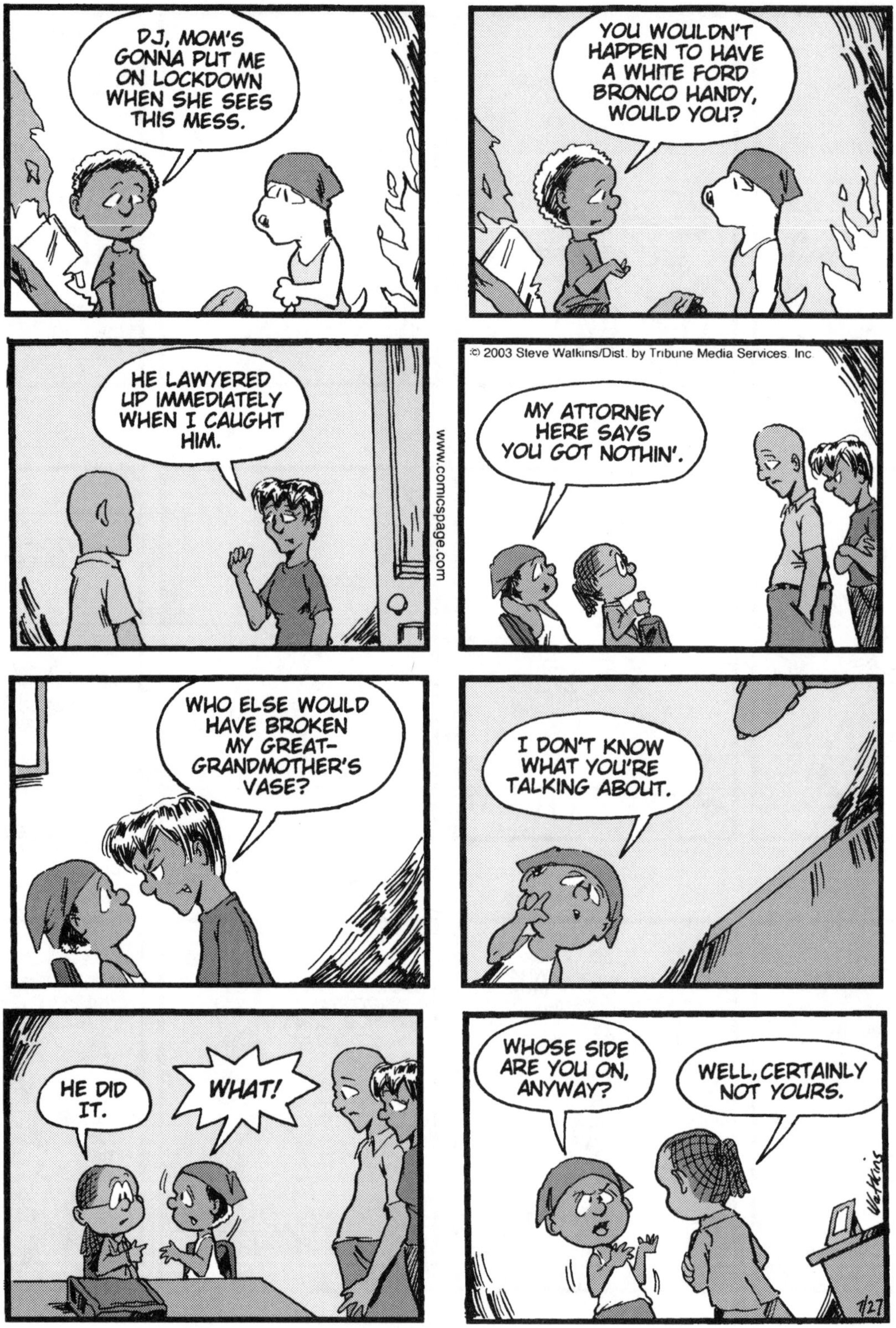
DJ, MOM'S GONNA PUT ME ON LOCKDOWN WHEN SHE SEES THIS MESS.
YOU WOULDN'T HAPPEN TO HAVE A WHITE FORD BRONCO HANDY, WOULD YOU?
HE LAWYERED UP IMMEDIATELY WHEN I CAUGHT HIM.
www.comicspage.com
© 2003 Steve Watkins/Dist. by Tribune Media Services. Inc.
MY ATTORNEY HERE SAYS YOU GOT NOTHIN'.
WHO ELSE WOULD HAVE BROKEN MY GREAT-GRANDMOTHER'S VASE?
I DON'T KNOW WHAT YOU'RE TALKING ABOUT.
HE DID IT.
WHAT!
WHOSE SIDE ARE YOU ON, ANYWAY?
WELL, CERTAINLY NOT YOURS.
Watkins
7/27

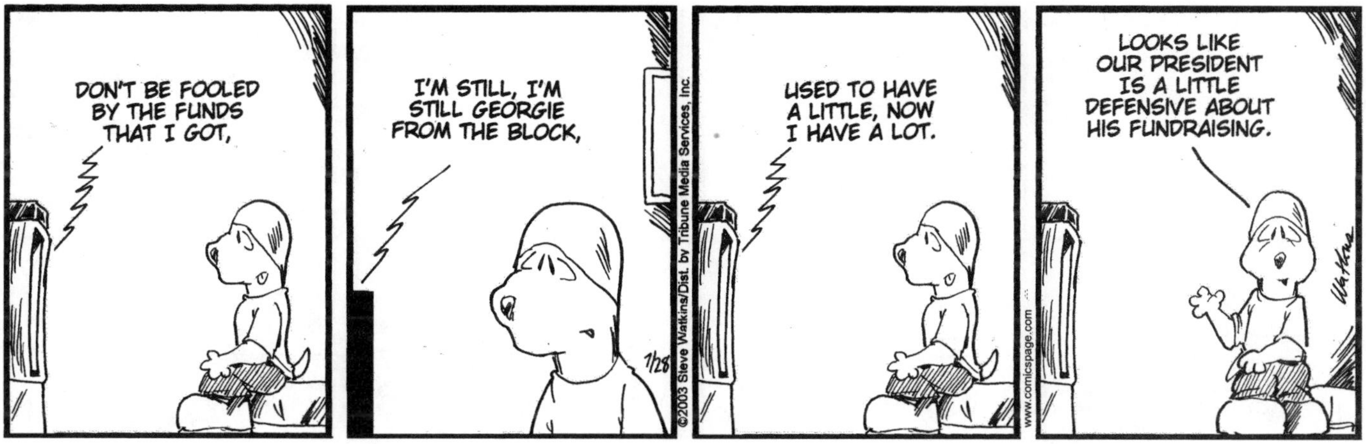
DON'T BE FOOLED BY THE FUNDS THAT I GOT,
I'M STILL, I'M STILL GEORGIE FROM THE BLOCK,
USED TO HAVE A LITTLE, NOW I HAVE A LOT.
LOOKS LIKE OUR PRESIDENT IS A LITTLE DEFENSIVE ABOUT HIS FUNDRAISING.
7/28
©2003 Steve Watkins/Dist. by Tribune Media Services, Inc.
www.comicspage.com

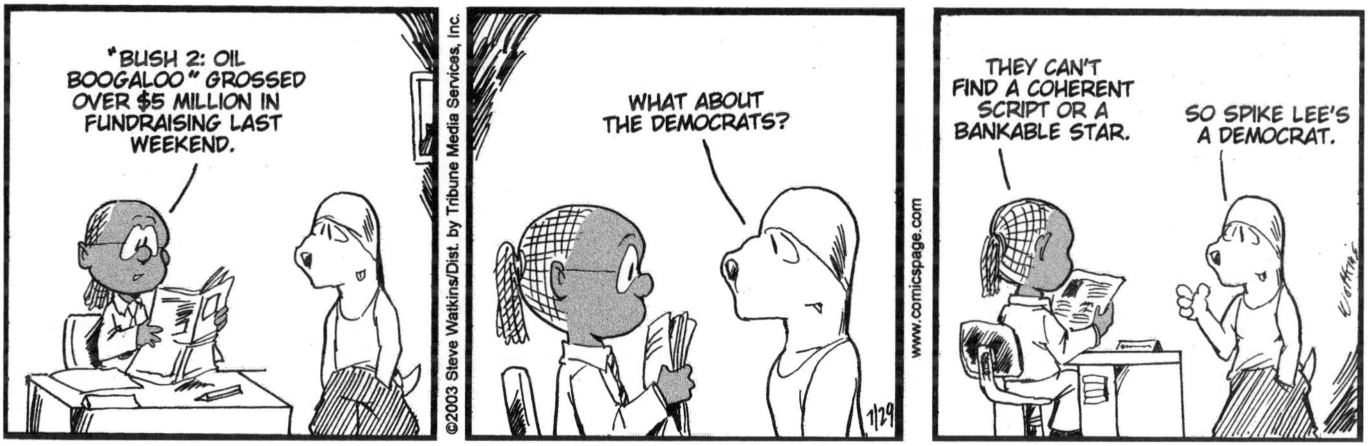
"BUSH 2: OIL BOOGALOO" GROSSED OVER $5 MILLION IN FUNDRAISING LAST WEEKEND.
WHAT ABOUT THE DEMOCRATS?
THEY CAN'T FIND A COHERENT SCRIPT OR A BANKABLE STAR.
SO SPIKE LEE'S A DEMOCRAT.
7/29
©2003 Steve Watkins/Dist. by Tribune Media Services, Inc.
www.comicspage.com

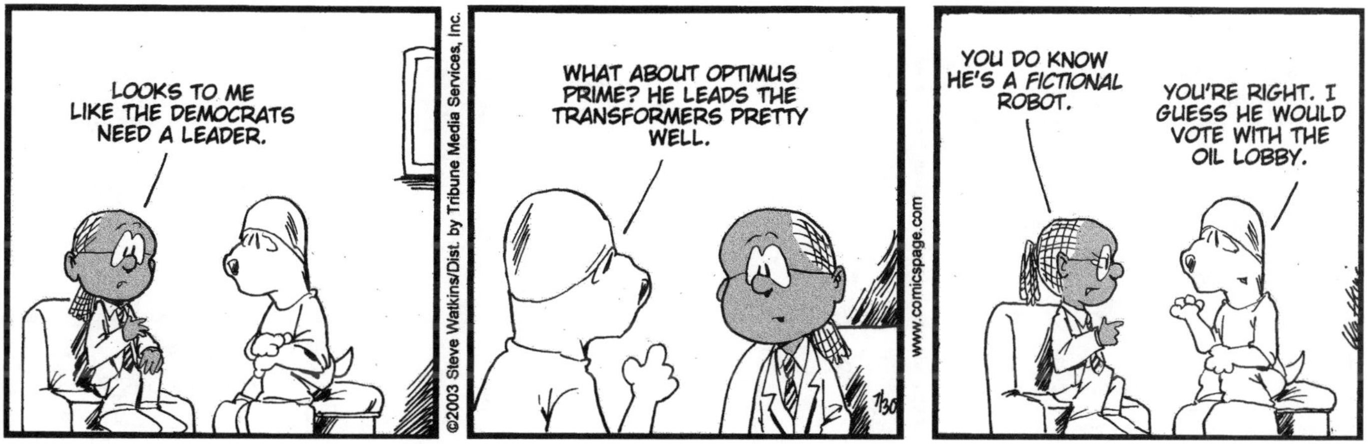
LOOKS TO ME LIKE THE DEMOCRATS NEED A LEADER.
WHAT ABOUT OPTIMUS PRIME? HE LEADS THE TRANSFORMERS PRETTY WELL.
YOU DO KNOW HE'S A *FICTIONAL* ROBOT.
YOU'RE RIGHT. I GUESS HE WOULD VOTE WITH THE OIL LOBBY.
7/30
©2003 Steve Watkins/Dist. by Tribune Media Services, Inc.
www.comicspage.com

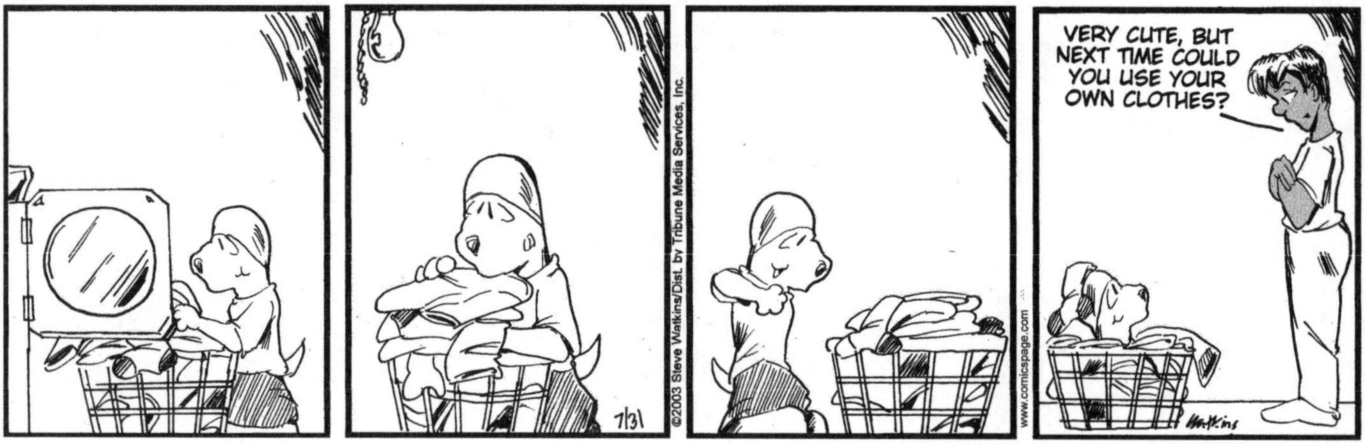
VERY CUTE, BUT NEXT TIME COULD YOU USE YOUR OWN CLOTHES?
7/31
©2003 Steve Watkins/Dist. by Tribune Media Services, Inc.
www.comicspage.com
Watkins

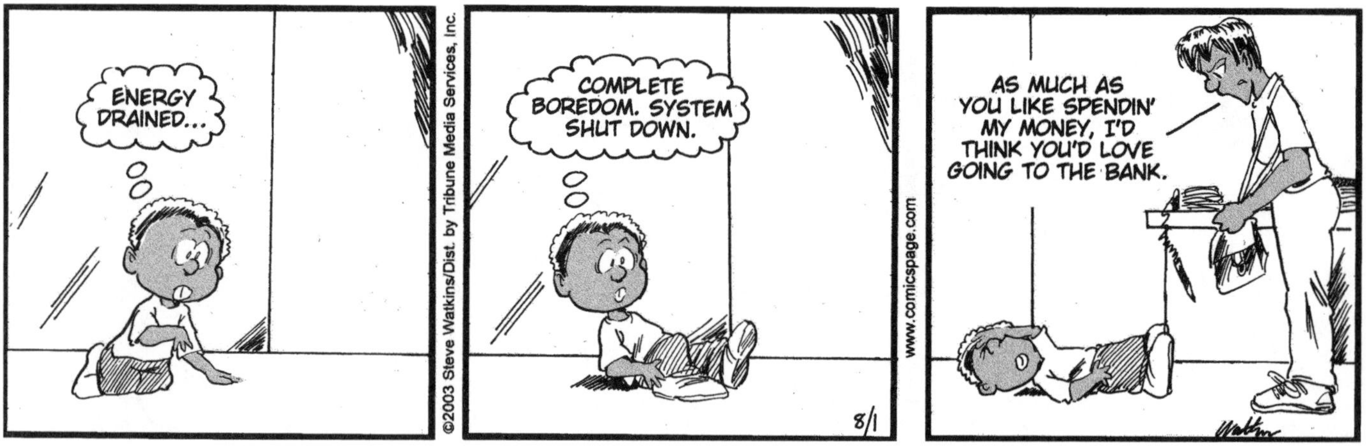
ENERGY DRAINED...
COMPLETE BOREDOM. SYSTEM SHUT DOWN.
AS MUCH AS YOU LIKE SPENDIN' MY MONEY, I'D THINK YOU'D LOVE GOING TO THE BANK.
8/1
©2003 Steve Watkins/Dist. by Tribune Media Services, Inc.
www.comicspage.com

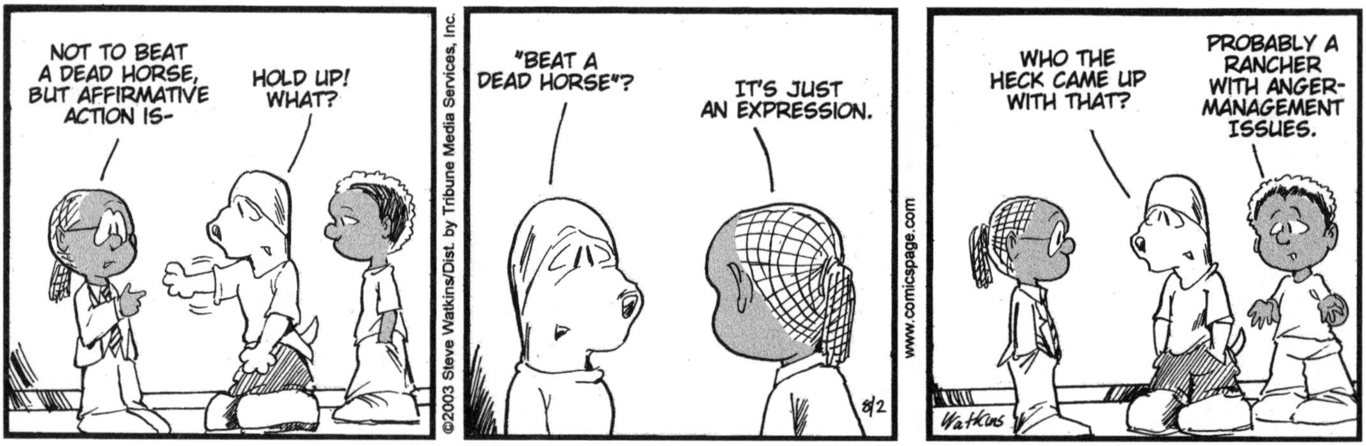
NOT TO BEAT A DEAD HORSE, BUT AFFIRMATIVE ACTION IS-
HOLD UP! WHAT?
"BEAT A DEAD HORSE"?
IT'S JUST AN EXPRESSION.
WHO THE HECK CAME UP WITH THAT?
PROBABLY A RANCHER WITH ANGER-MANAGEMENT ISSUES.
8/2
©2003 Steve Watkins/Dist. by Tribune Media Services, Inc.
www.comicspage.com
Watkins

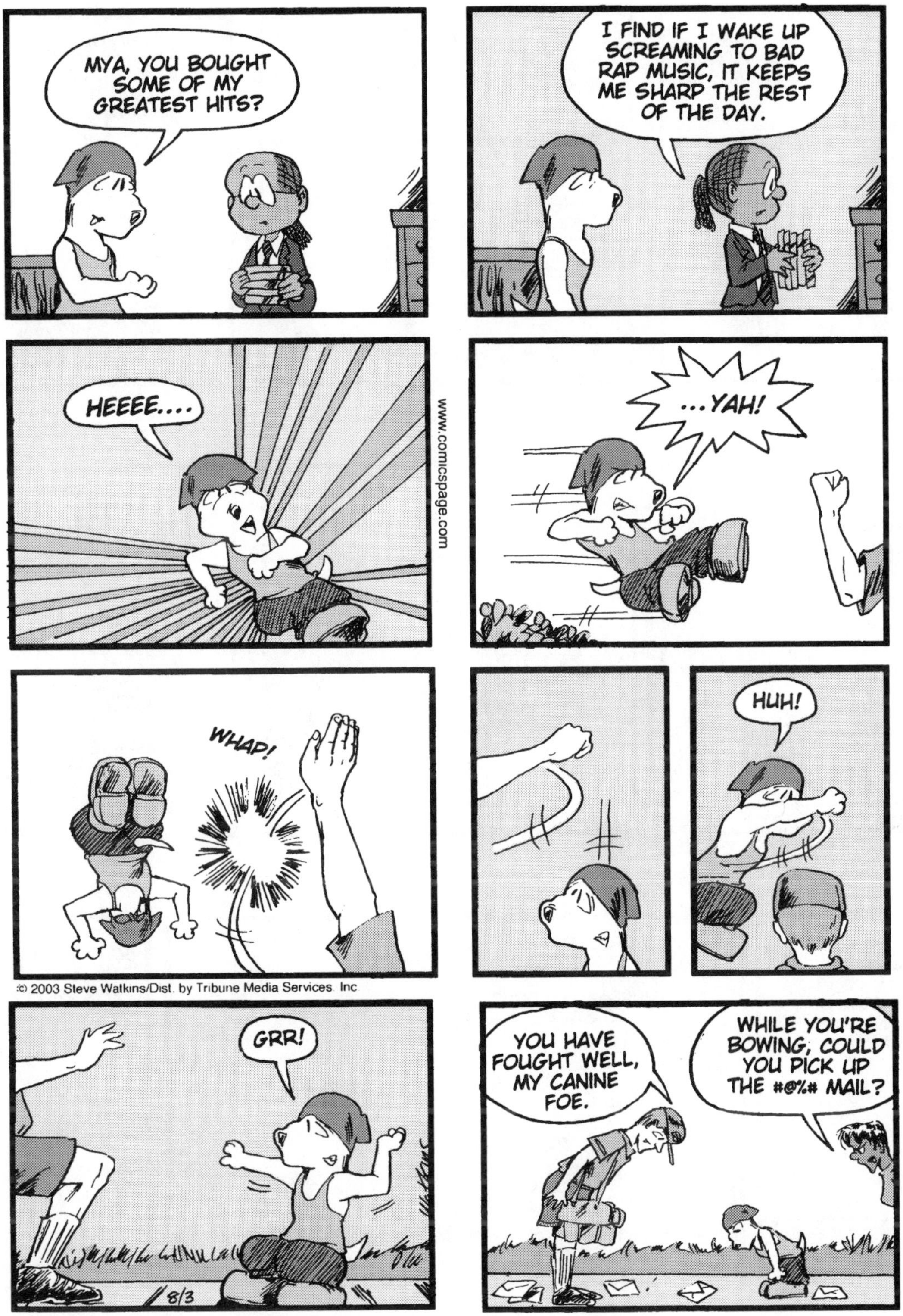
MYA, YOU BOUGHT SOME OF MY GREATEST HITS?
I FIND IF I WAKE UP SCREAMING TO BAD RAP MUSIC, IT KEEPS ME SHARP THE REST OF THE DAY.
www.comicspage.com
HEEEE....
...YAH!
WHAP!
HUH!
GRR!
8/3
YOU HAVE FOUGHT WELL, MY CANINE FOE.
WHILE YOU'RE BOWING, COULD YOU PICK UP THE #@%# MAIL?

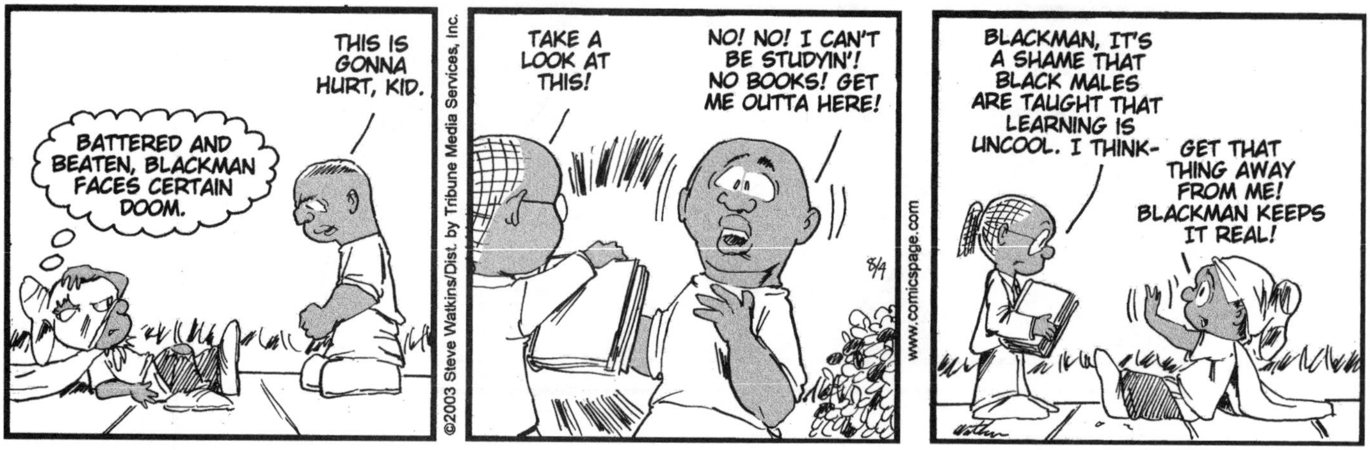
BATTERED AND BEATEN, BLACKMAN FACES CERTAIN DOOM.
THIS IS GONNA HURT, KID.
©2003 Steve Watkins/Dist. by Tribune Media Services, Inc.
TAKE A LOOK AT THIS!
NO! NO! I CAN'T BE STUDYIN'! NO BOOKS! GET ME OUTTA HERE!
8/4
www.comicspage.com
BLACKMAN, IT'S A SHAME THAT BLACK MALES ARE TAUGHT THAT LEARNING IS UNCOOL. I THINK-
GET THAT THING AWAY FROM ME! BLACKMAN KEEPS IT REAL!

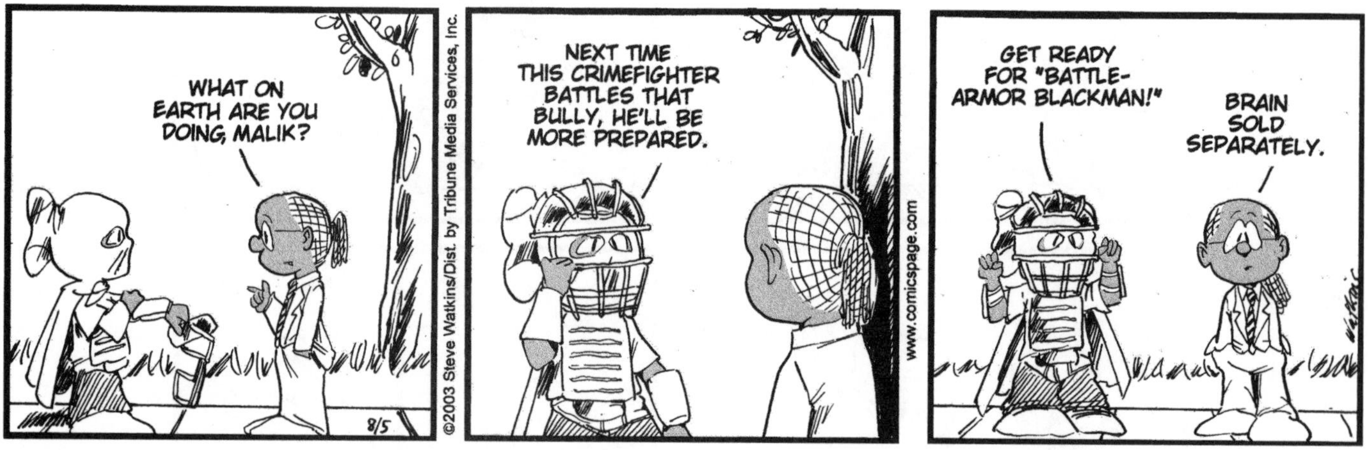
WHAT ON EARTH ARE YOU DOING, MALIK?
8/5
©2003 Steve Watkins/Dist. by Tribune Media Services, Inc.
NEXT TIME THIS CRIMEFIGHTER BATTLES THAT BULLY, HE'LL BE MORE PREPARED.
www.comicspage.com
GET READY FOR "BATTLE-ARMOR BLACKMAN!"
BRAIN SOLD SEPARATELY.

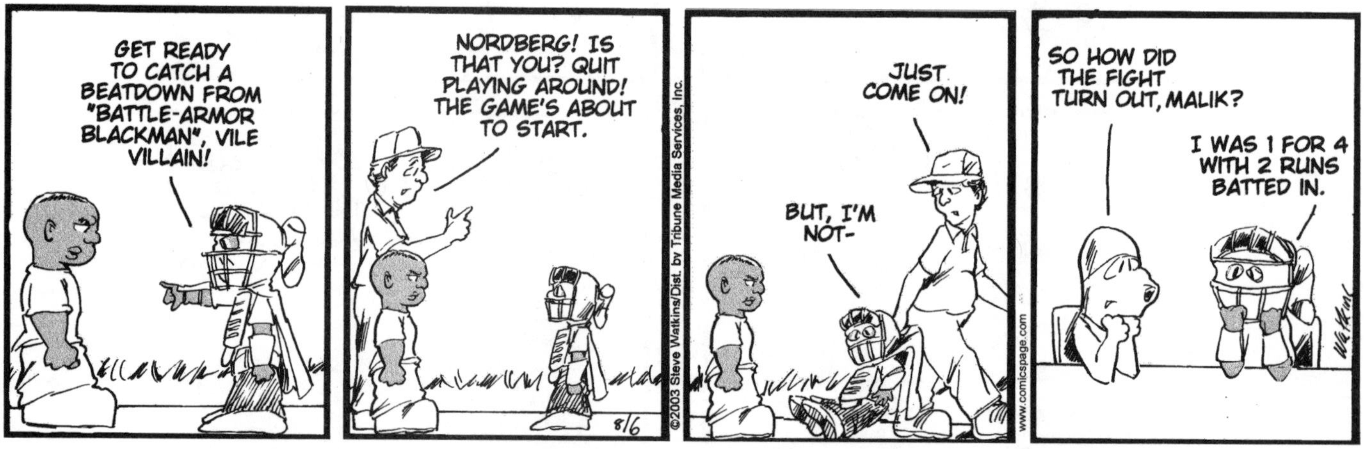
GET READY TO CATCH A BEATDOWN FROM "BATTLE-ARMOR BLACKMAN", VILE VILLAIN!
NORDBERG! IS THAT YOU? QUIT PLAYING AROUND! THE GAME'S ABOUT TO START.
8/6
©2003 Steve Watkins/Dist. by Tribune Media Services, Inc.
JUST COME ON!
BUT, I'M NOT-
www.comicspage.com
SO HOW DID THE FIGHT TURN OUT, MALIK?
I WAS 1 FOR 4 WITH 2 RUNS BATTED IN.

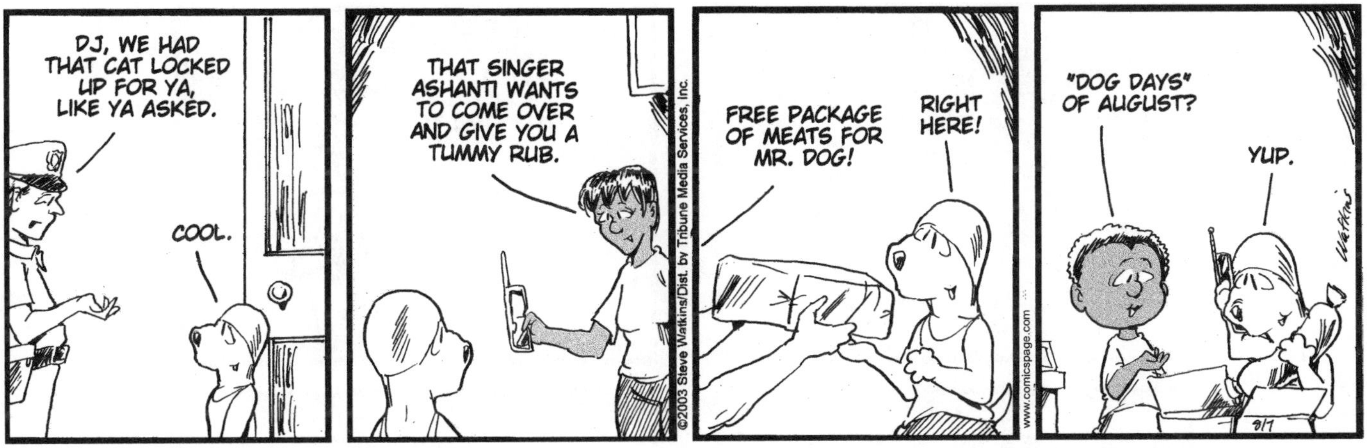
DJ, WE HAD THAT CAT LOCKED UP FOR YA, LIKE YA ASKED.
COOL.
THAT SINGER ASHANTI WANTS TO COME OVER AND GIVE YOU A TUMMY RUB.
©2003 Steve Watkins/Dist. by Tribune Media Services, Inc.
FREE PACKAGE OF MEATS FOR MR. DOG!
RIGHT HERE!
www.comicspage.com
"DOG DAYS" OF AUGUST?
YUP.
8/7

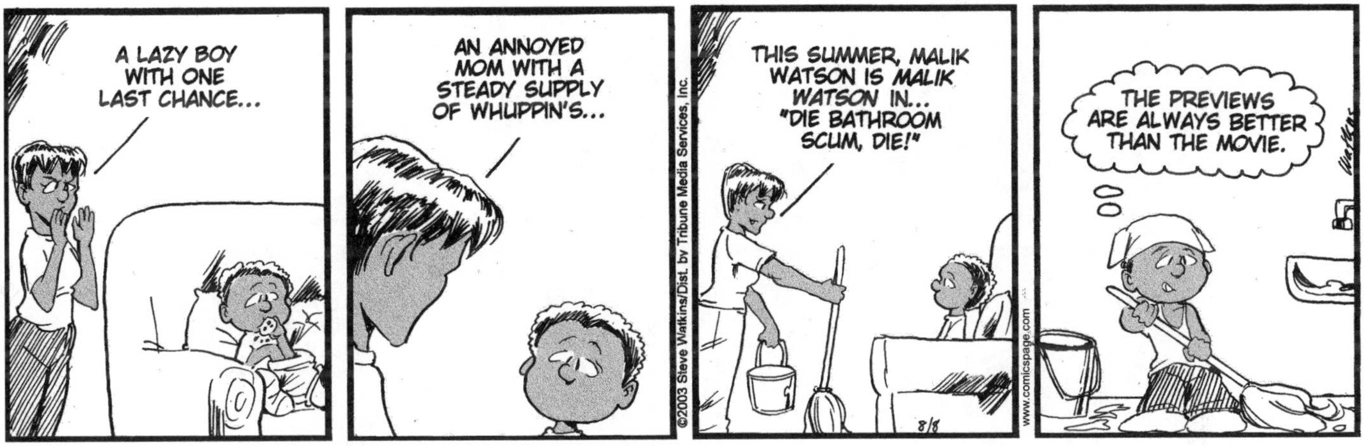
A LAZY BOY WITH ONE LAST CHANCE...
AN ANNOYED MOM WITH A STEADY SUPPLY OF WHUPPIN'S...
©2003 Steve Watkins/Dist. by Tribune Media Services, Inc.
THIS SUMMER, MALIK WATSON IS *MALIK WATSON* IN... "DIE BATHROOM SCUM, DIE!"
8/8
www.comicspage.com
THE PREVIEWS ARE ALWAYS BETTER THAN THE MOVIE.

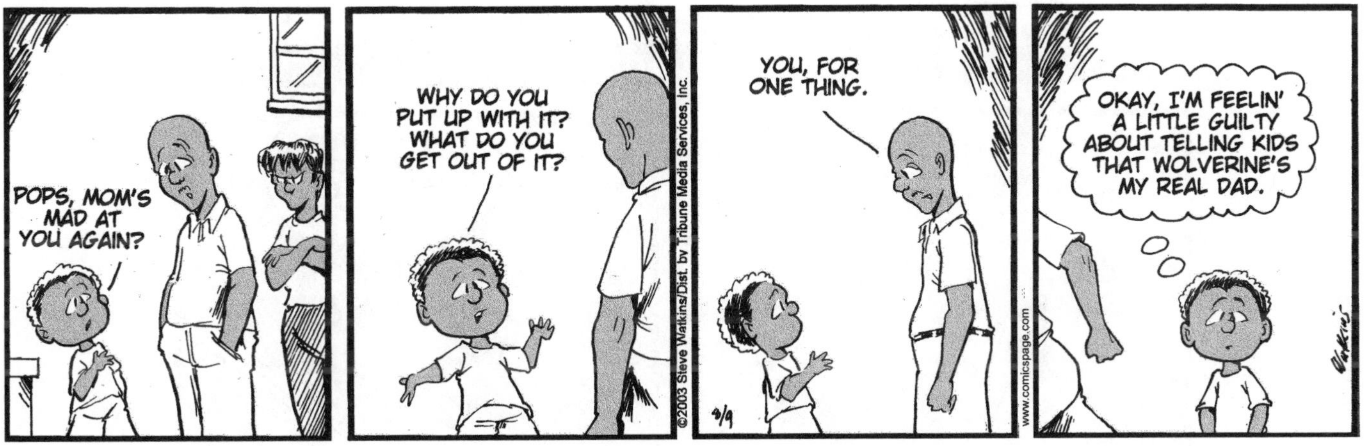
POPS, MOM'S MAD AT YOU AGAIN?
WHY DO YOU PUT UP WITH IT? WHAT DO YOU GET OUT OF IT?
©2003 Steve Watkins/Dist. by Tribune Media Services, Inc.
YOU, FOR ONE THING.
8/9
www.comicspage.com
OKAY, I'M FEELIN' A LITTLE GUILTY ABOUT TELLING KIDS THAT WOLVERINE'S MY REAL DAD.

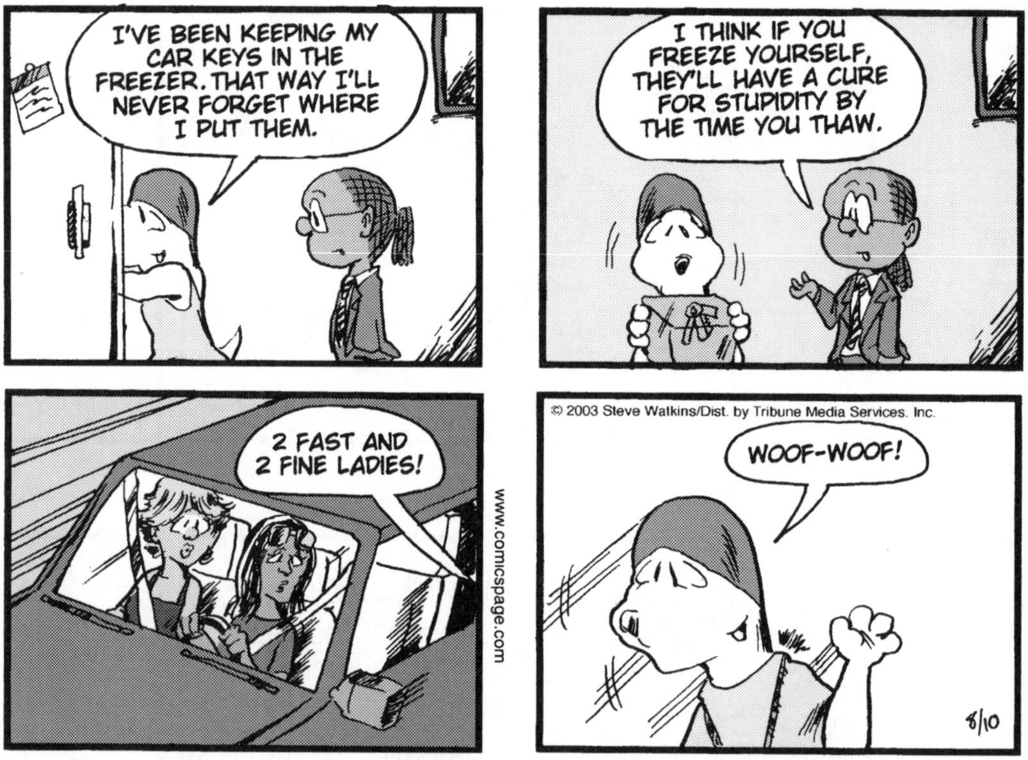
I'VE BEEN KEEPING MY CAR KEYS IN THE FREEZER. THAT WAY I'LL NEVER FORGET WHERE I PUT THEM.
I THINK IF YOU FREEZE YOURSELF, THEY'LL HAVE A CURE FOR STUPIDITY BY THE TIME YOU THAW.
2 FAST AND 2 FINE LADIES!
www.comicspage.com
© 2003 Steve Watkins/Dist. by Tribune Media Services. Inc.
WOOF-WOOF!
8/10

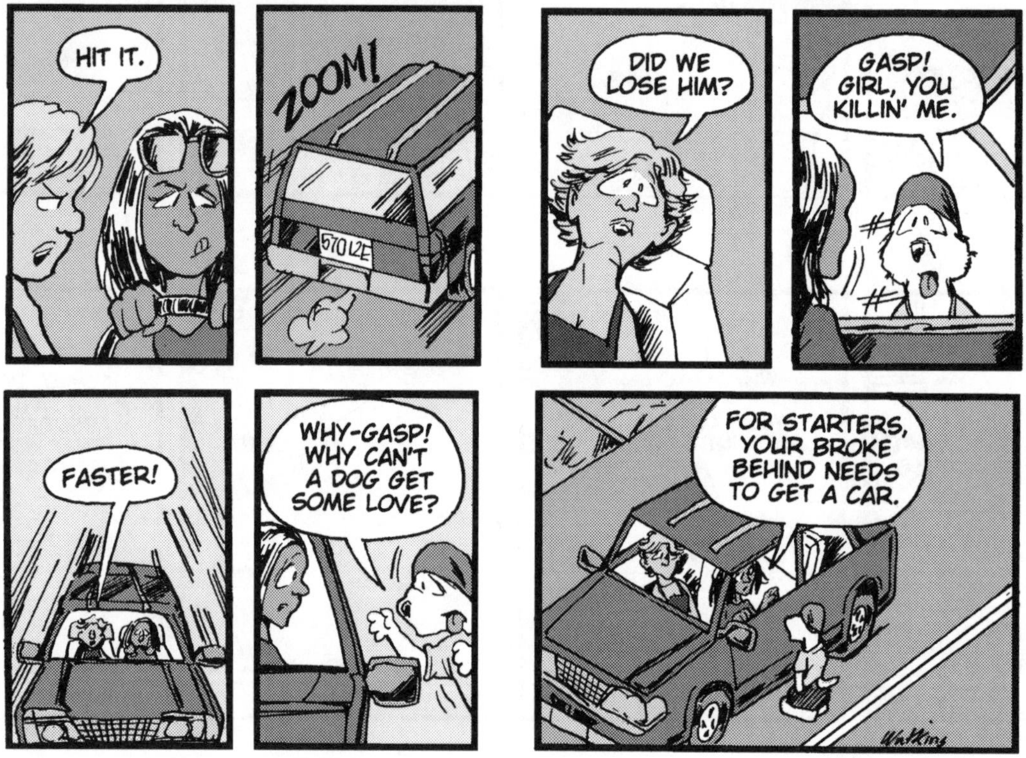
HIT IT.
ZOOM!
570 L2E
DID WE LOSE HIM?
GASP! GIRL, YOU KILLIN' ME.
FASTER!
WHY-GASP! WHY CAN'T A DOG GET SOME LOVE?
FOR STARTERS, YOUR BROKE BEHIND NEEDS TO GET A CAR.
Watkins

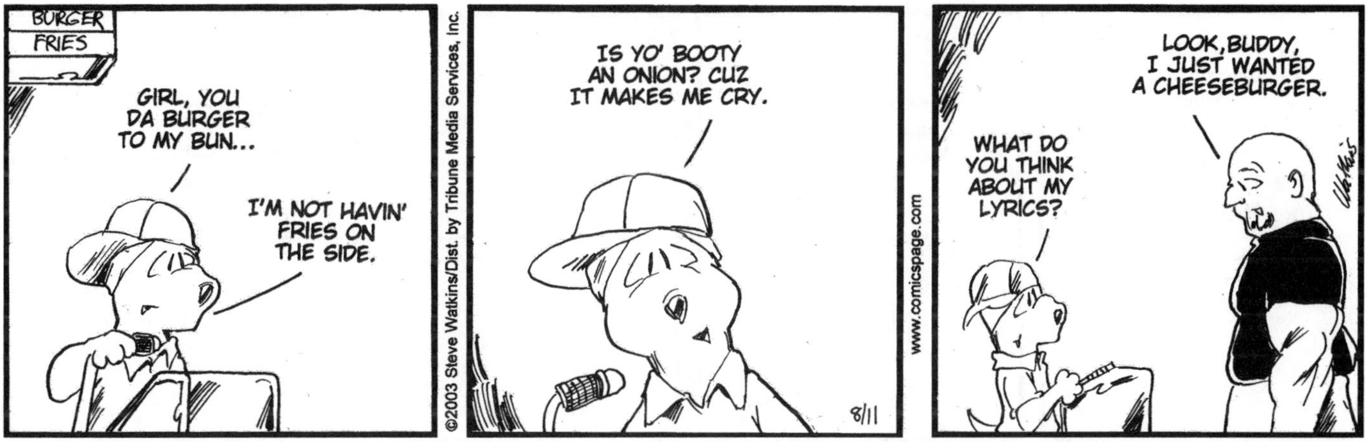
BURGER
FRIES
GIRL, YOU DA BURGER TO MY BUN...
I'M NOT HAVIN' FRIES ON THE SIDE.
©2003 Steve Watkins/Dist. by Tribune Media Services, Inc.
IS YO' BOOTY AN ONION? CUZ IT MAKES ME CRY.
8/11
www.comicspage.com
WHAT DO YOU THINK ABOUT MY LYRICS?
LOOK, BUDDY, I JUST WANTED A CHEESEBURGER.

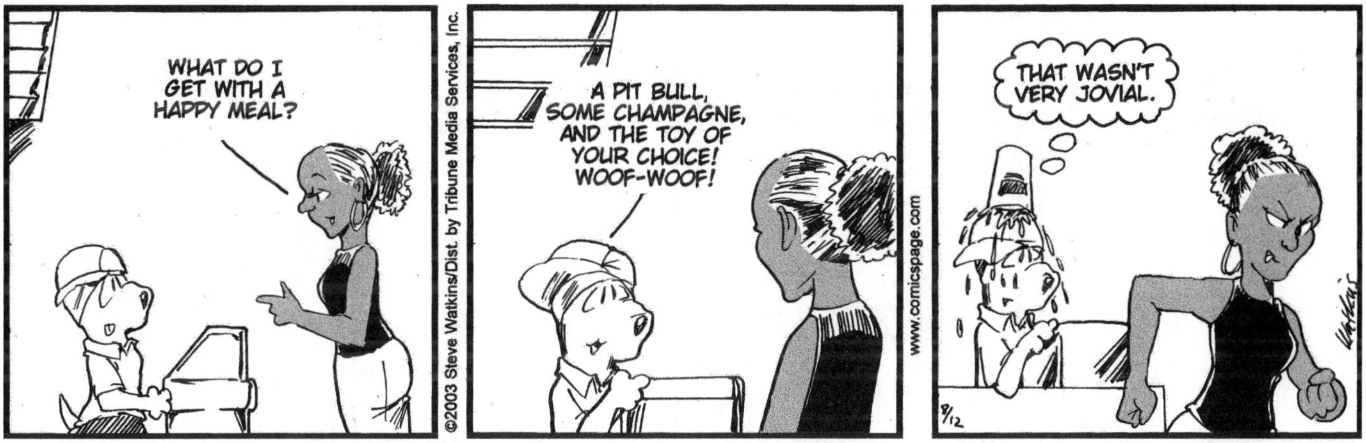
WHAT DO I GET WITH A HAPPY MEAL?
©2003 Steve Watkins/Dist. by Tribune Media Services, Inc.
A PIT BULL, SOME CHAMPAGNE, AND THE TOY OF YOUR CHOICE! WOOF-WOOF!
www.comicspage.com
THAT WASN'T VERY JOVIAL.
8/12

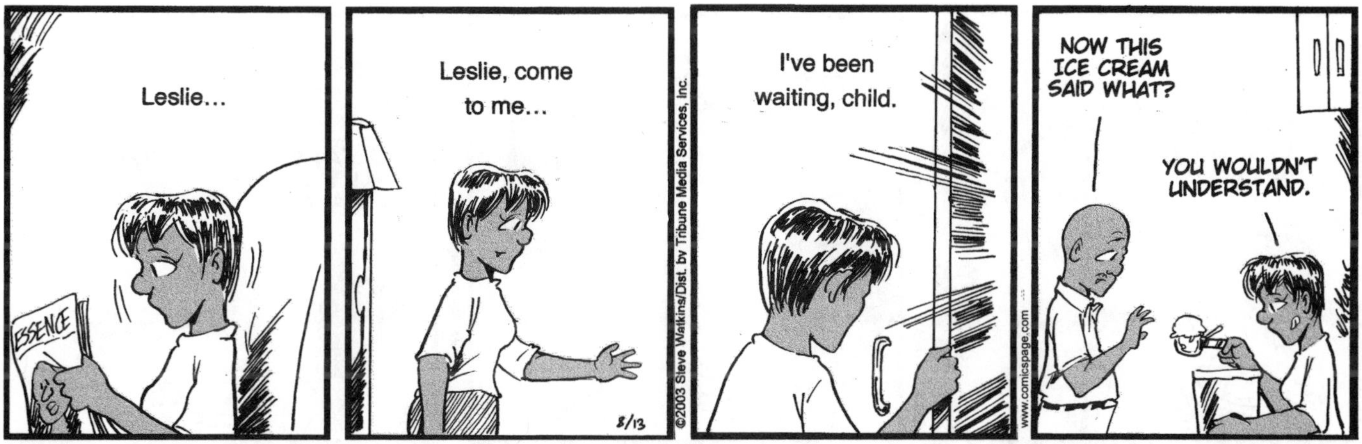
Leslie...
ESSENCE
Leslie, come to me...
8/13
©2003 Steve Watkins/Dist. by Tribune Media Services, Inc.
I've been waiting, child.
www.comicspage.com
NOW THIS ICE CREAM SAID WHAT?
YOU WOULDN'T UNDERSTAND.

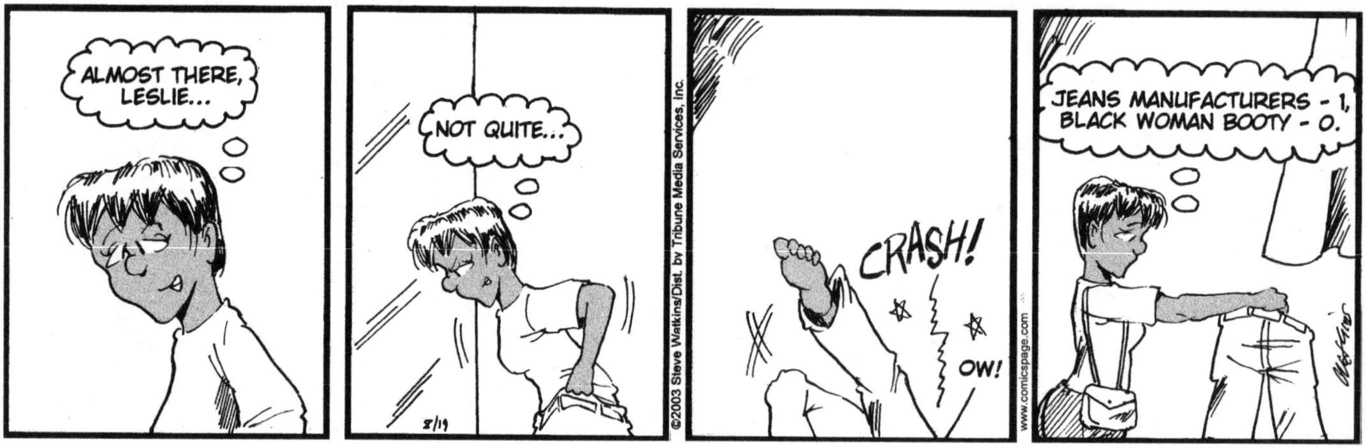
ALMOST THERE, LESLIE...
NOT QUITE...
8/19
©2003 Steve Watkins/Dist. by Tribune Media Services, Inc.
CRASH!
OW!
www.comicspage.com
JEANS MANUFACTURERS - 1, BLACK WOMAN BOOTY - 0.

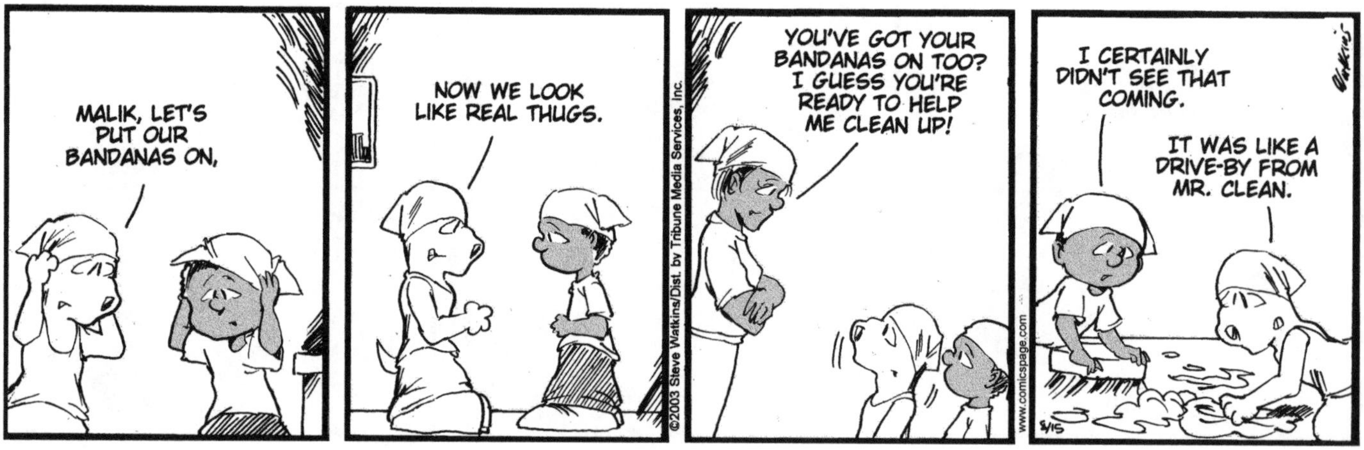
MALIK, LET'S PUT OUR BANDANAS ON.
NOW WE LOOK LIKE REAL THUGS.
©2003 Steve Watkins/Dist. by Tribune Media Services, Inc.
YOU'VE GOT YOUR BANDANAS ON TOO? I GUESS YOU'RE READY TO HELP ME CLEAN UP!
www.comicspage.com
I CERTAINLY DIDN'T SEE THAT COMING.
IT WAS LIKE A DRIVE-BY FROM MR. CLEAN.
8/15

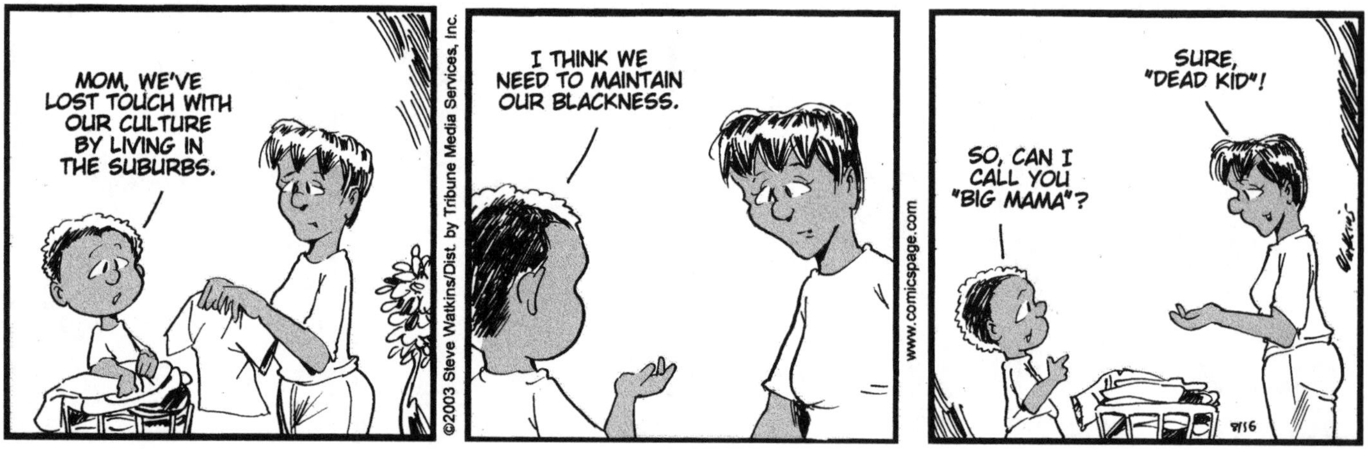
MOM, WE'VE LOST TOUCH WITH OUR CULTURE BY LIVING IN THE SUBURBS.
©2003 Steve Watkins/Dist. by Tribune Media Services, Inc.
I THINK WE NEED TO MAINTAIN OUR BLACKNESS.
www.comicspage.com
SO, CAN I CALL YOU "BIG MAMA"?
SURE, "DEAD KID"!
8/16

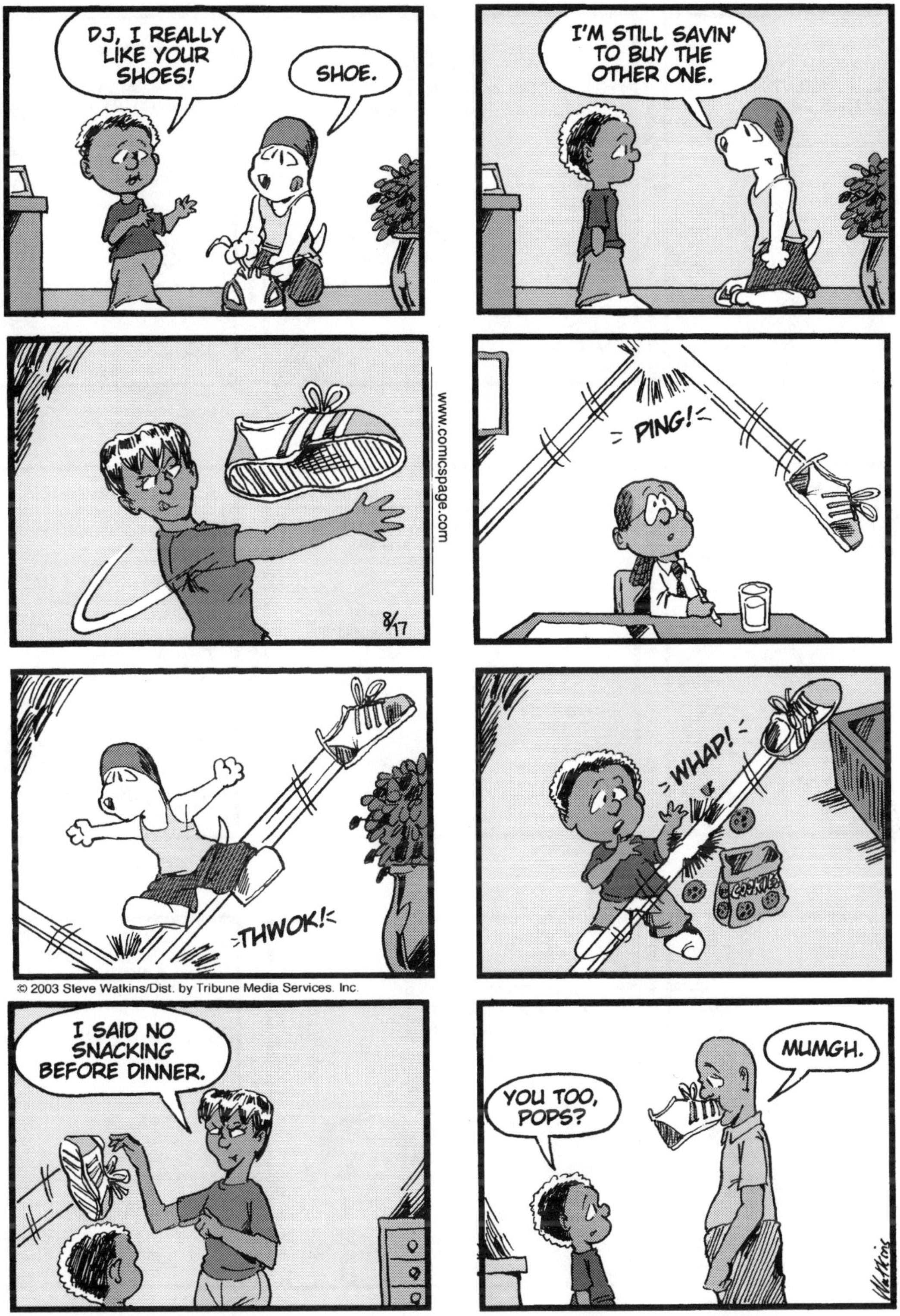
DJ, I REALLY LIKE YOUR SHOES!
SHOE.
I'M STILL SAVIN' TO BUY THE OTHER ONE.
www.comicspage.com
8/17
PING!
THWOK!
WHAP!
COOKIES
I SAID NO SNACKING BEFORE DINNER.
YOU TOO, POPS?
MUMGH.
Watkins

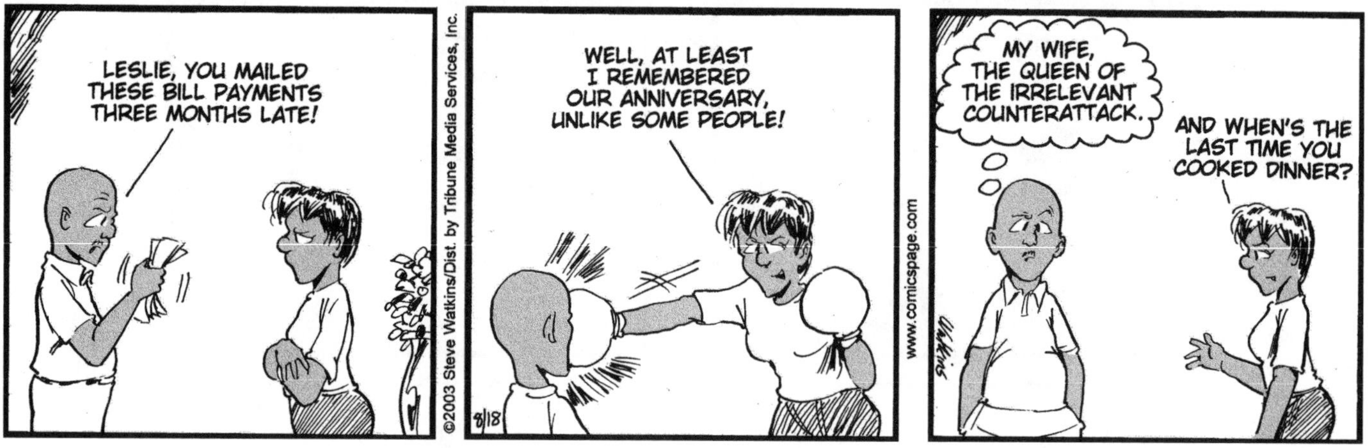
LESLIE, YOU MAILED THESE BILL PAYMENTS THREE MONTHS LATE!
©2003 Steve Watkins/Dist. by Tribune Media Services, Inc.
WELL, AT LEAST I REMEMBERED OUR ANNIVERSARY, UNLIKE SOME PEOPLE!
8/18
www.comicspage.com
MY WIFE, THE QUEEN OF THE IRRELEVANT COUNTERATTACK.
AND WHEN'S THE LAST TIME YOU COOKED DINNER?

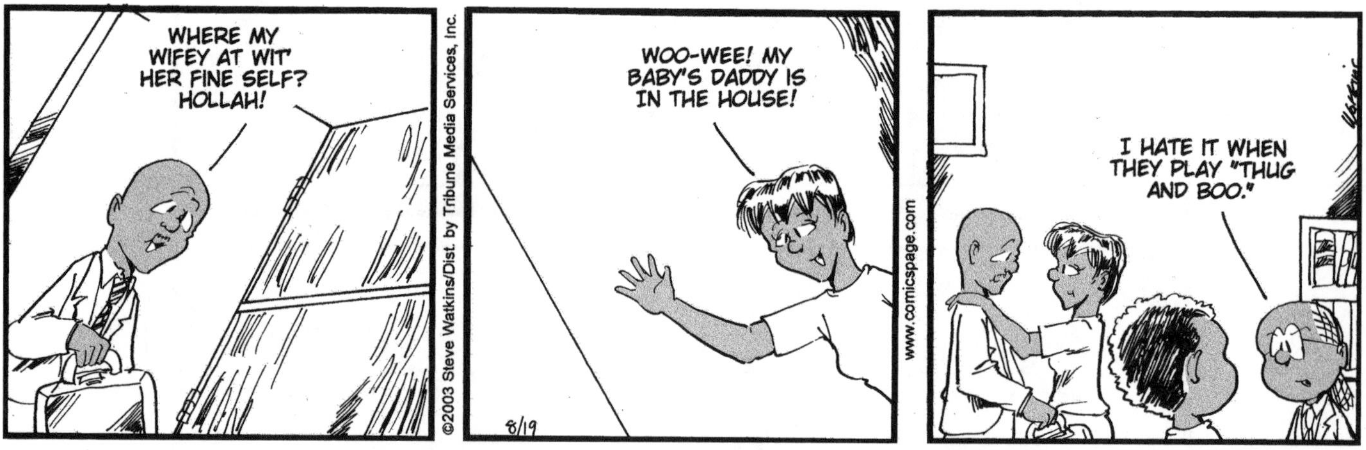
WHERE MY WIFEY AT WIT' HER FINE SELF? HOLLAH!
©2003 Steve Watkins/Dist. by Tribune Media Services, Inc.
WOO-WEE! MY BABY'S DADDY IS IN THE HOUSE!
8/19
www.comicspage.com
I HATE IT WHEN THEY PLAY "THUG AND BOO."

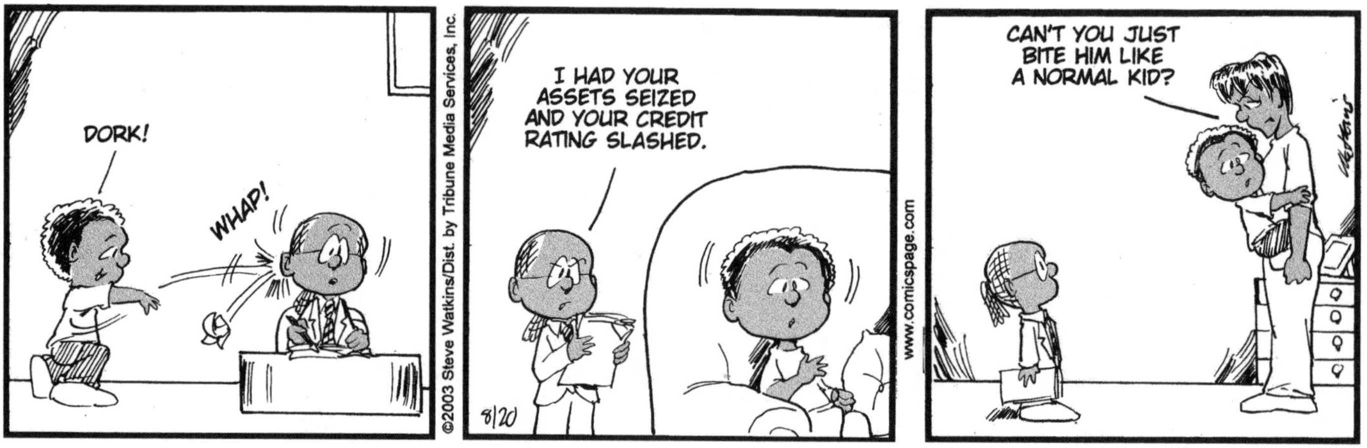
DORK!
WHAP!
©2003 Steve Watkins/Dist. by Tribune Media Services, Inc.
I HAD YOUR ASSETS SEIZED AND YOUR CREDIT RATING SLASHED.
8/20
www.comicspage.com
CAN'T YOU JUST BITE HIM LIKE A NORMAL KID?

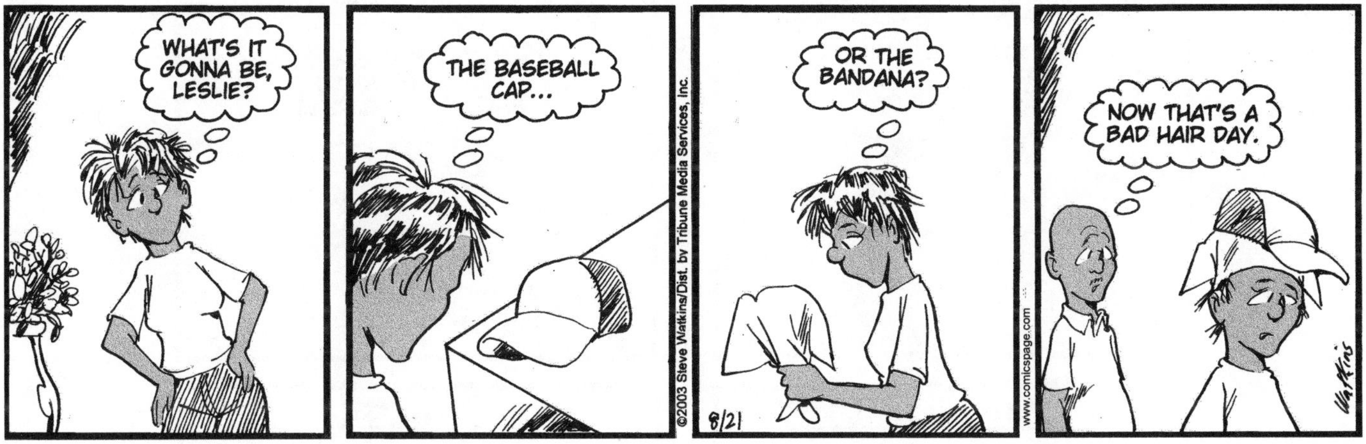
WHAT'S IT GONNA BE, LESLIE?
THE BASEBALL CAP...
©2003 Steve Watkins/Dist. by Tribune Media Services, Inc.
OR THE BANDANA?
8/21
www.comicspage.com
NOW THAT'S A BAD HAIR DAY.
Watkins

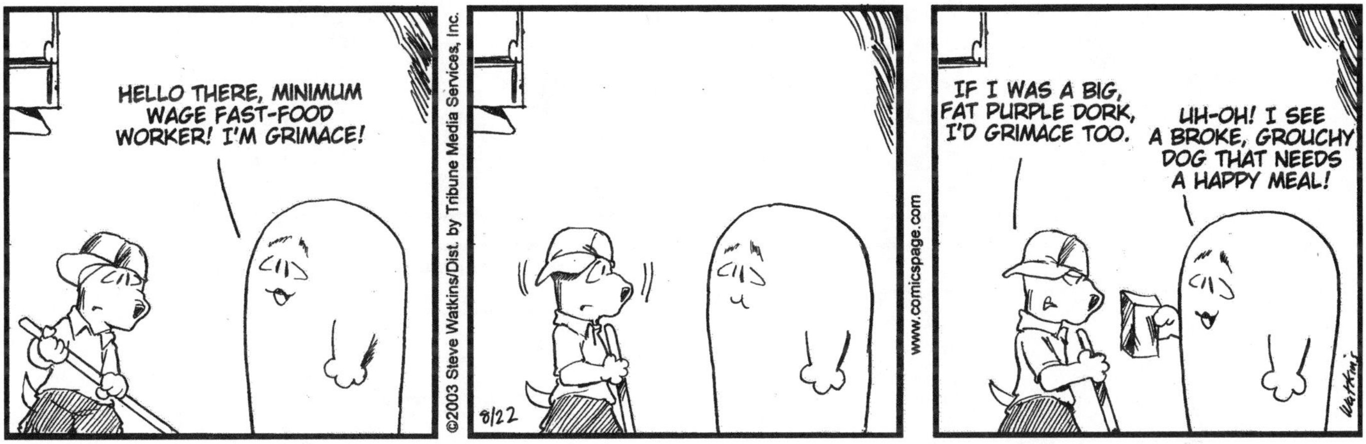
HELLO THERE, MINIMUM WAGE FAST-FOOD WORKER! I'M GRIMACE!
©2003 Steve Watkins/Dist. by Tribune Media Services, Inc.
8/22
www.comicspage.com
IF I WAS A BIG, FAT PURPLE DORK, I'D GRIMACE TOO.
UH-OH! I SEE A BROKE, GROUCHY DOG THAT NEEDS A HAPPY MEAL!
Watkins

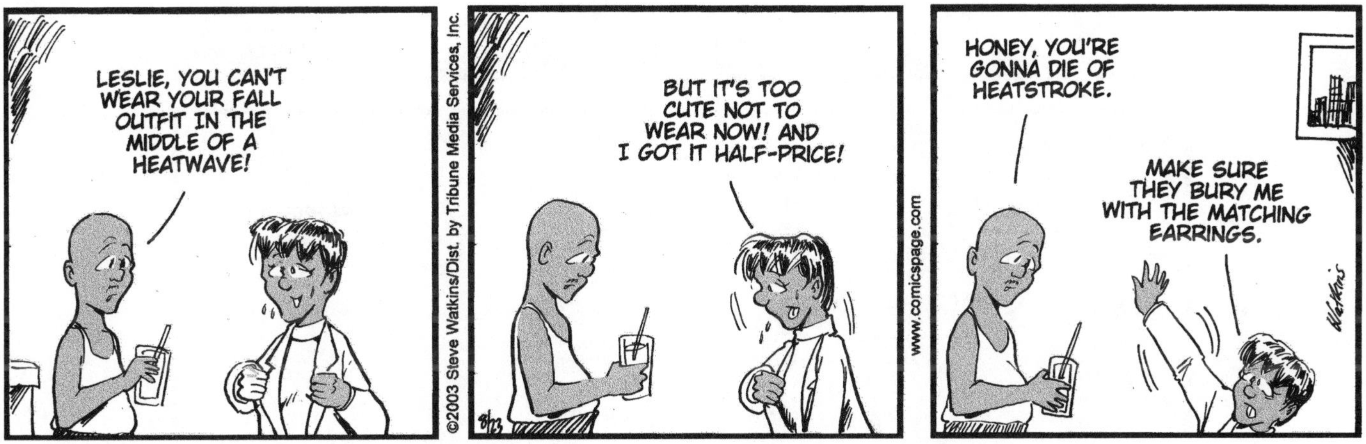
LESLIE, YOU CAN'T WEAR YOUR FALL OUTFIT IN THE MIDDLE OF A HEATWAVE!
©2003 Steve Watkins/Dist. by Tribune Media Services, Inc.
BUT IT'S TOO CUTE NOT TO WEAR NOW! AND I GOT IT HALF-PRICE!
www.comicspage.com
HONEY, YOU'RE GONNA DIE OF HEATSTROKE.
MAKE SURE THEY BURY ME WITH THE MATCHING EARRINGS.
Watkins

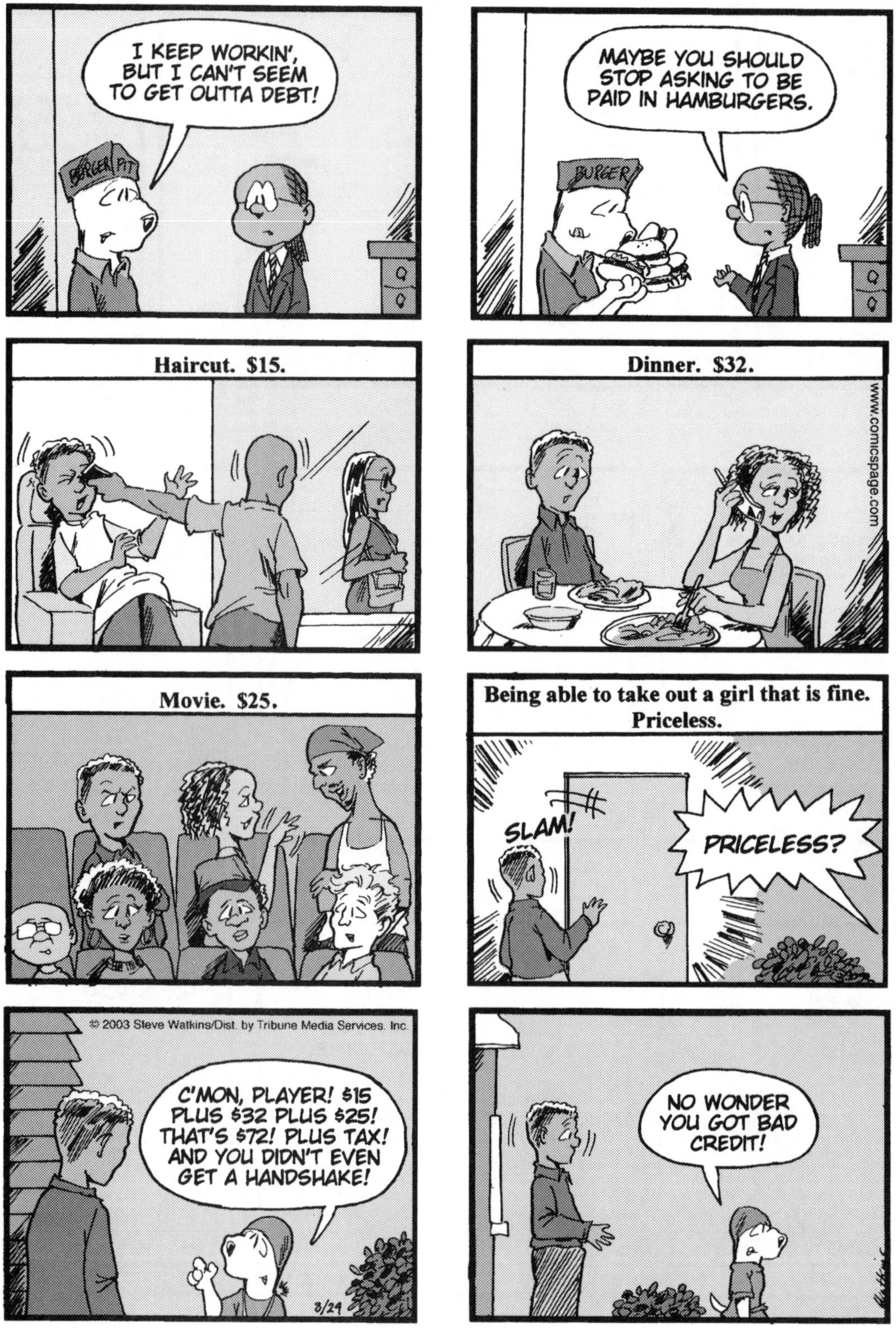
I KEEP WORKIN', BUT I CAN'T SEEM TO GET OUTTA DEBT!
BURGER PIT
MAYBE YOU SHOULD STOP ASKING TO BE PAID IN HAMBURGERS.
BURGER
Haircut. $15.
Dinner. $32.
www.comicspage.com
Movie. $25.
Being able to take out a girl that is fine. Priceless.
SLAM!
PRICELESS?
© 2003 Steve Watkins/Dist. by Tribune Media Services, Inc.
C'MON, PLAYER! $15 PLUS $32 PLUS $25! THAT'S $72! PLUS TAX! AND YOU DIDN'T EVEN GET A HANDSHAKE!
3/24
NO WONDER YOU GOT BAD CREDIT!

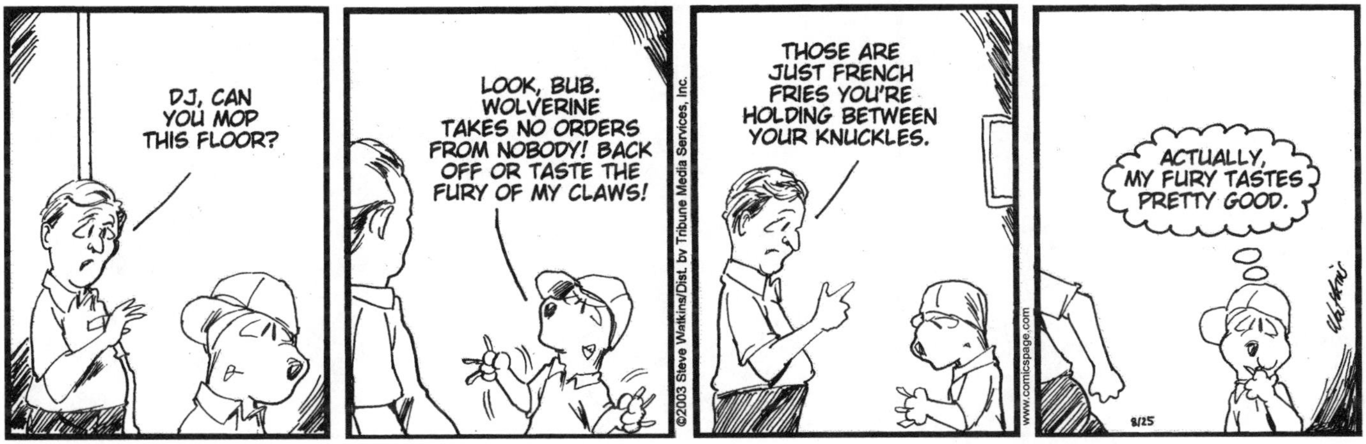
DJ, CAN YOU MOP THIS FLOOR?
LOOK, BUB. WOLVERINE TAKES NO ORDERS FROM NOBODY! BACK OFF OR TASTE THE FURY OF MY CLAWS!
THOSE ARE JUST FRENCH FRIES YOU'RE HOLDING BETWEEN YOUR KNUCKLES.
ACTUALLY, MY FURY TASTES PRETTY GOOD.
©2003 Steve Watkins/Dist. by Tribune Media Services, Inc.
www.comicspage.com
8/25

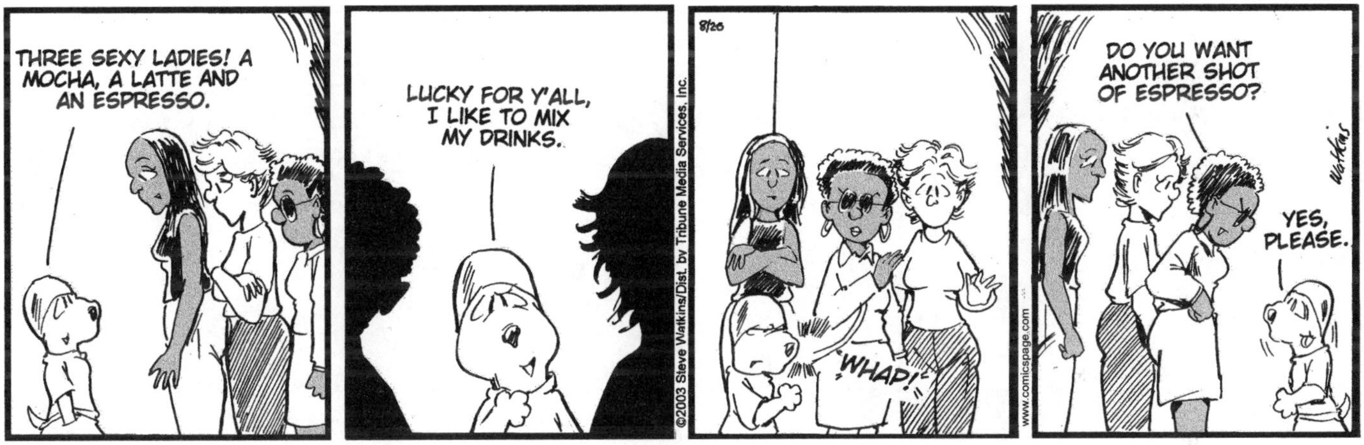
THREE SEXY LADIES! A MOCHA, A LATTE AND AN ESPRESSO.
LUCKY FOR Y'ALL, I LIKE TO MIX MY DRINKS.
WHAP!
DO YOU WANT ANOTHER SHOT OF ESPRESSO?
YES, PLEASE.
©2003 Steve Watkins/Dist. by Tribune Media Services, Inc.
www.comicspage.com
8/26

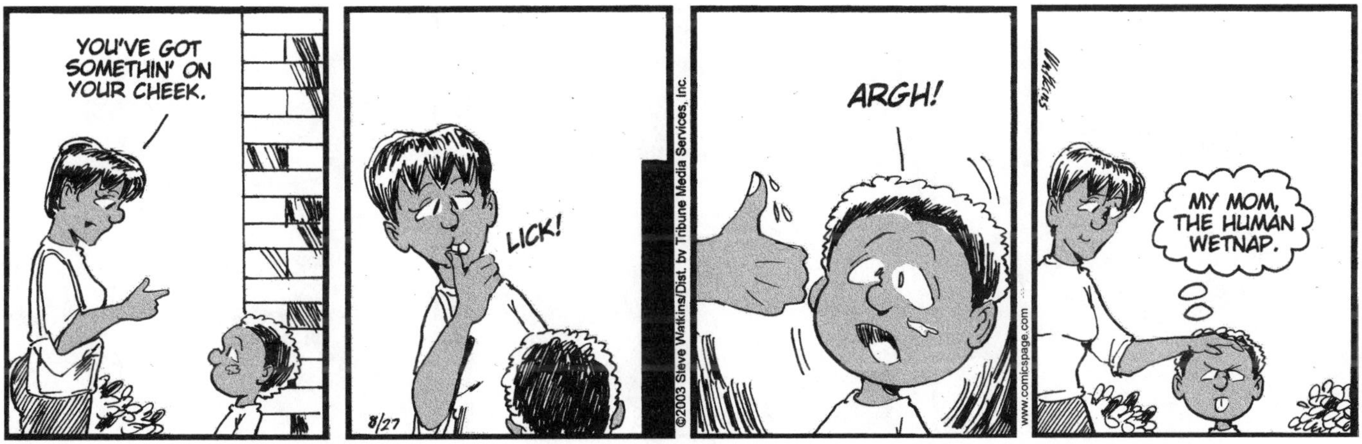
YOU'VE GOT SOMETHIN' ON YOUR CHEEK.
LICK!
ARGH!
MY MOM, THE HUMAN WETNAP.
©2003 Steve Watkins/Dist. by Tribune Media Services, Inc.
www.comicspage.com
8/27

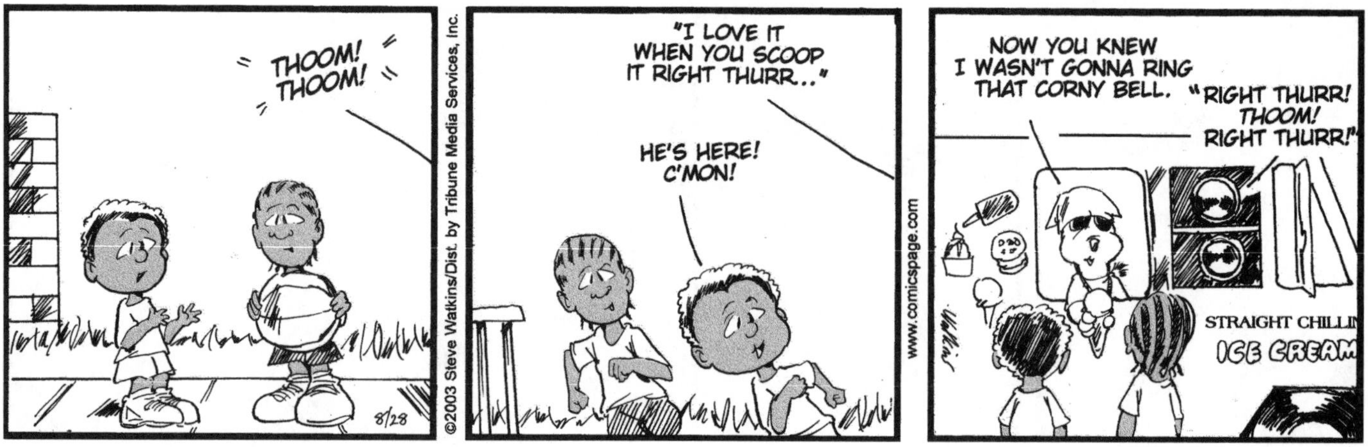
THOOM! THOOM!
8/28
©2003 Steve Watkins/Dist. by Tribune Media Services, Inc.
"I LOVE IT WHEN YOU SCOOP IT RIGHT THURR..."
HE'S HERE! C'MON!
www.comicspage.com
NOW YOU KNEW I WASN'T GONNA RING THAT CORNY BELL.
"RIGHT THURR! THOOM! RIGHT THURR!"
STRAIGHT CHILLIN
ICE CREAM

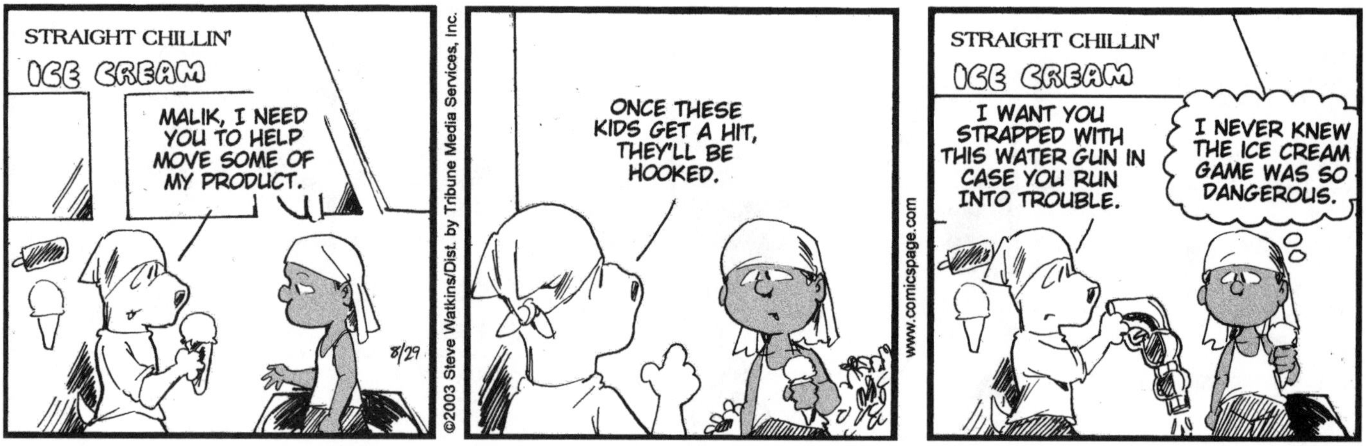
STRAIGHT CHILLIN'
ICE CREAM
MALIK, I NEED YOU TO HELP MOVE SOME OF MY PRODUCT.
8/29
©2003 Steve Watkins/Dist. by Tribune Media Services, Inc.
ONCE THESE KIDS GET A HIT, THEY'LL BE HOOKED.
www.comicspage.com
STRAIGHT CHILLIN'
ICE CREAM
I WANT YOU STRAPPED WITH THIS WATER GUN IN CASE YOU RUN INTO TROUBLE.
I NEVER KNEW THE ICE CREAM GAME WAS SO DANGEROUS.

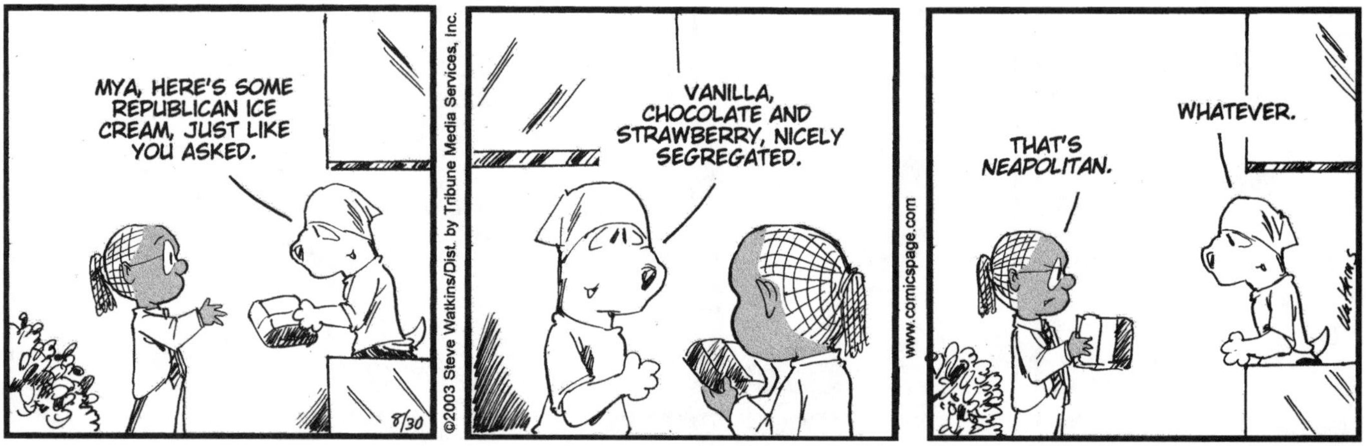
MYA, HERE'S SOME REPUBLICAN ICE CREAM, JUST LIKE YOU ASKED.
8/30
©2003 Steve Watkins/Dist. by Tribune Media Services, Inc.
VANILLA, CHOCOLATE AND STRAWBERRY, NICELY SEGREGATED.
www.comicspage.com
THAT'S NEAPOLITAN.
WHATEVER.

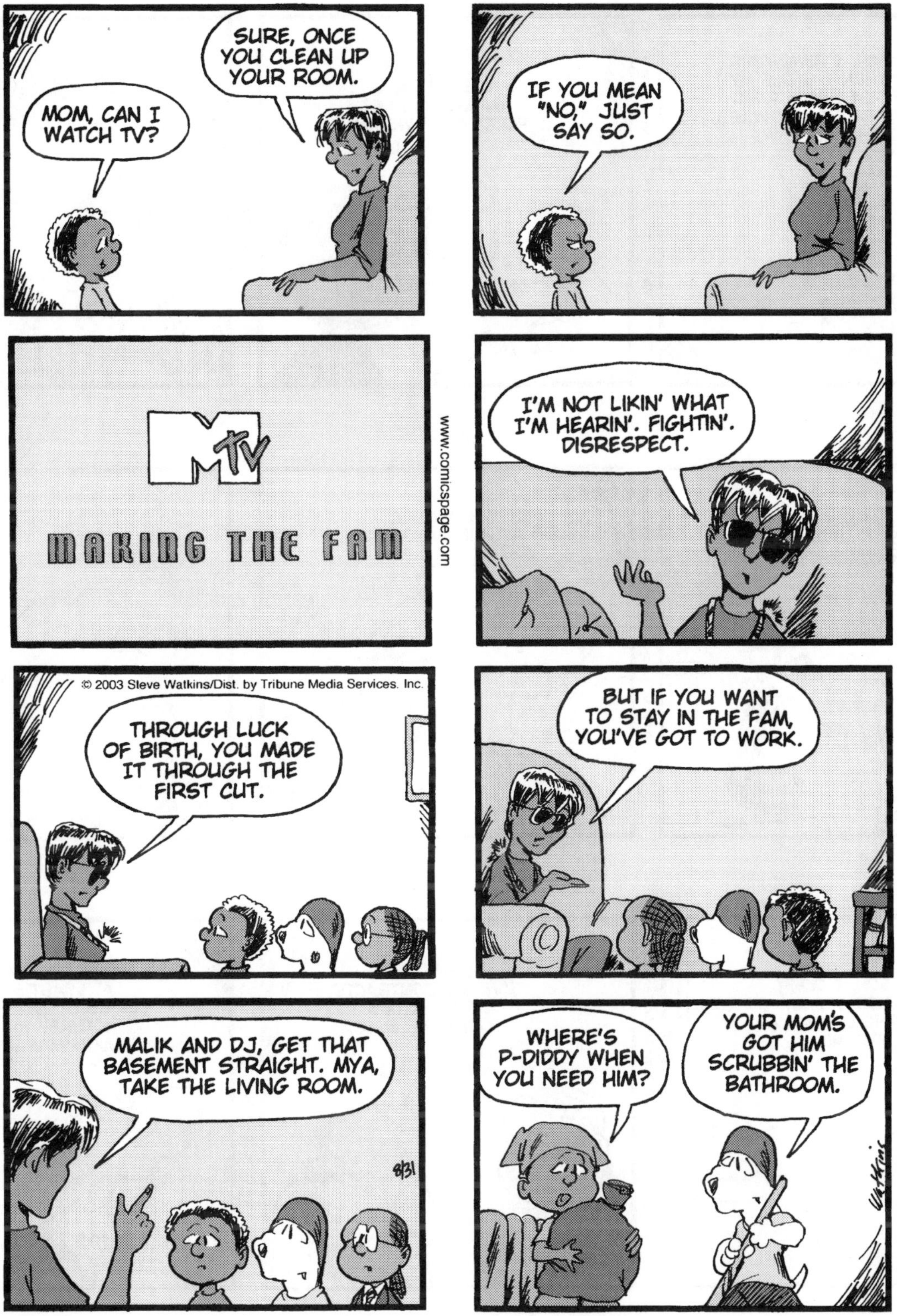
MOM, CAN I WATCH TV?
SURE, ONCE YOU CLEAN UP YOUR ROOM.
IF YOU MEAN "NO," JUST SAY SO.
MTV
MAKING THE FAM
www.comicspage.com
I'M NOT LIKIN' WHAT I'M HEARIN'. FIGHTIN'. DISRESPECT.
© 2003 Steve Watkins/Dist. by Tribune Media Services. Inc.
THROUGH LUCK OF BIRTH, YOU MADE IT THROUGH THE FIRST CUT.
BUT IF YOU WANT TO STAY IN THE FAM, YOU'VE GOT TO WORK.
MALIK AND DJ, GET THAT BASEMENT STRAIGHT. MYA, TAKE THE LIVING ROOM.
8/31
WHERE'S P-DIDDY WHEN YOU NEED HIM?
YOUR MOM'S GOT HIM SCRUBBIN' THE BATHROOM.

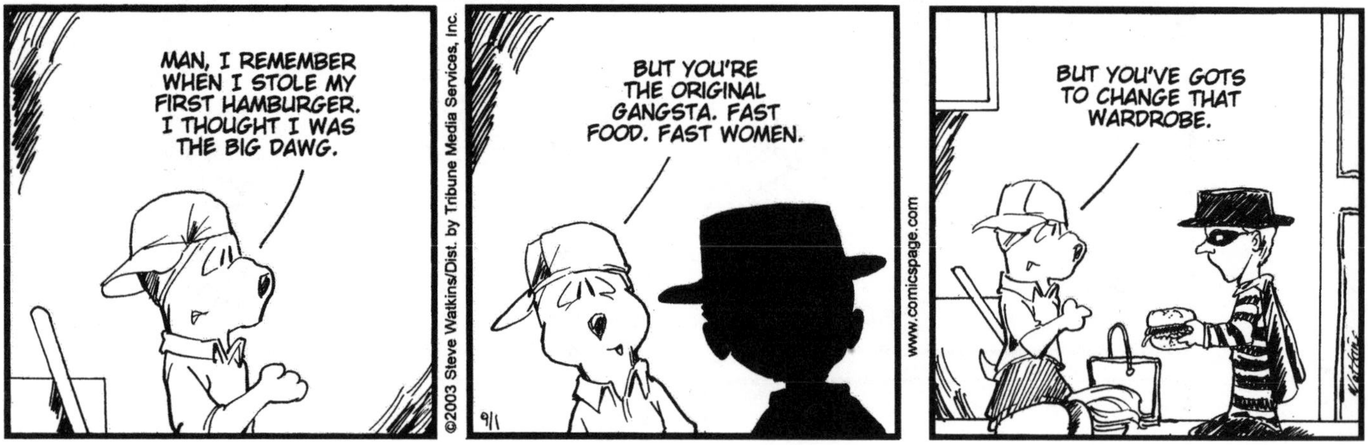
MAN, I REMEMBER WHEN I STOLE MY FIRST HAMBURGER. I THOUGHT I WAS THE BIG DAWG.
©2003 Steve Watkins/Dist. by Tribune Media Services, Inc.
BUT YOU'RE THE ORIGINAL GANGSTA. FAST FOOD. FAST WOMEN.
9/1
www.comicspage.com
BUT YOU'VE GOTS TO CHANGE THAT WARDROBE.

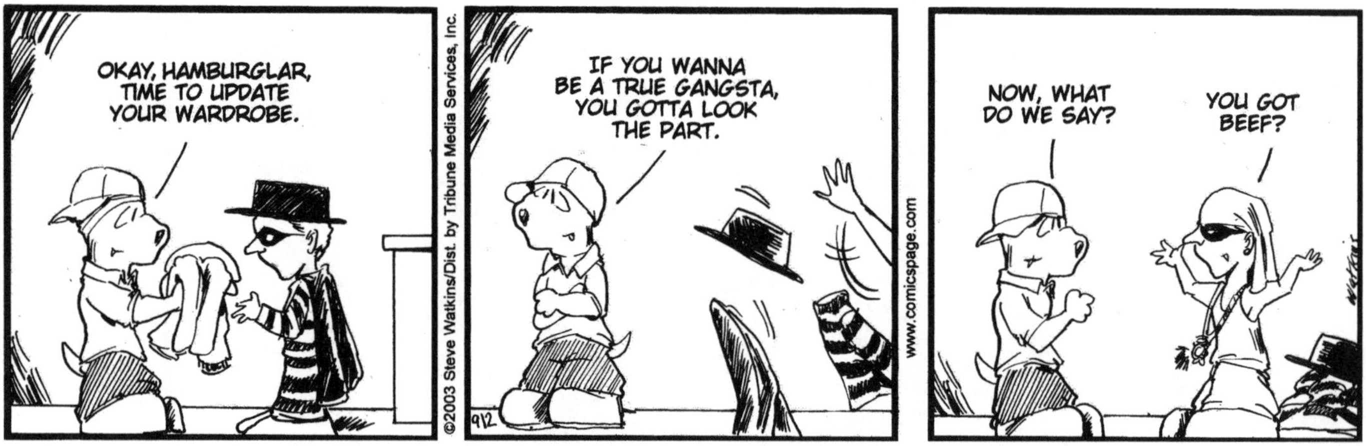
OKAY, HAMBURGLAR, TIME TO UPDATE YOUR WARDROBE.
©2003 Steve Watkins/Dist. by Tribune Media Services, Inc.
IF YOU WANNA BE A TRUE GANGSTA, YOU GOTTA LOOK THE PART.
9/2
www.comicspage.com
NOW, WHAT DO WE SAY?
YOU GOT BEEF?

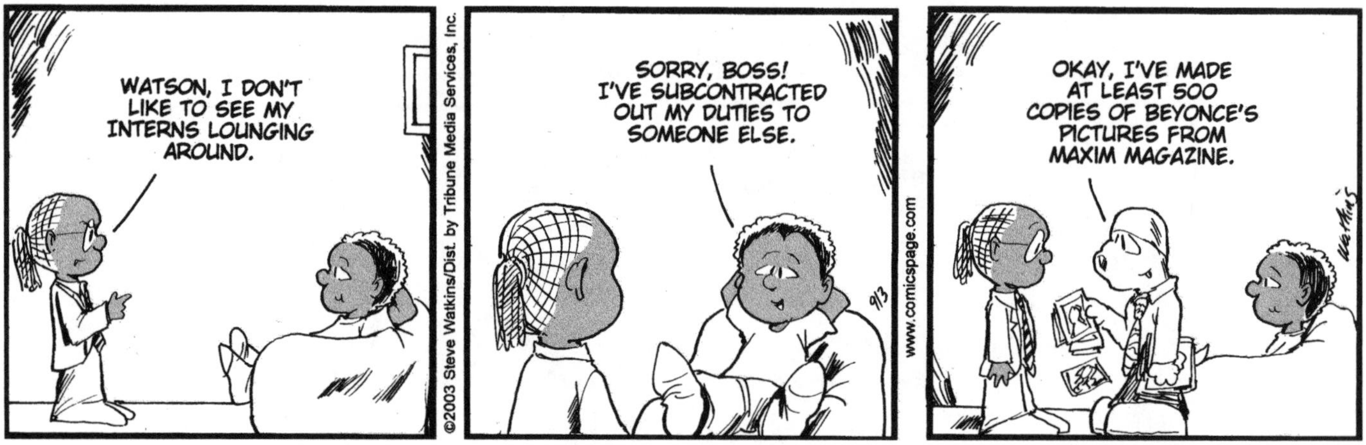
WATSON, I DON'T LIKE TO SEE MY INTERNS LOUNGING AROUND.
©2003 Steve Watkins/Dist. by Tribune Media Services, Inc.
SORRY, BOSS! I'VE SUBCONTRACTED OUT MY DUTIES TO SOMEONE ELSE.
9/3
www.comicspage.com
OKAY, I'VE MADE AT LEAST 500 COPIES OF BEYONCE'S PICTURES FROM MAXIM MAGAZINE.

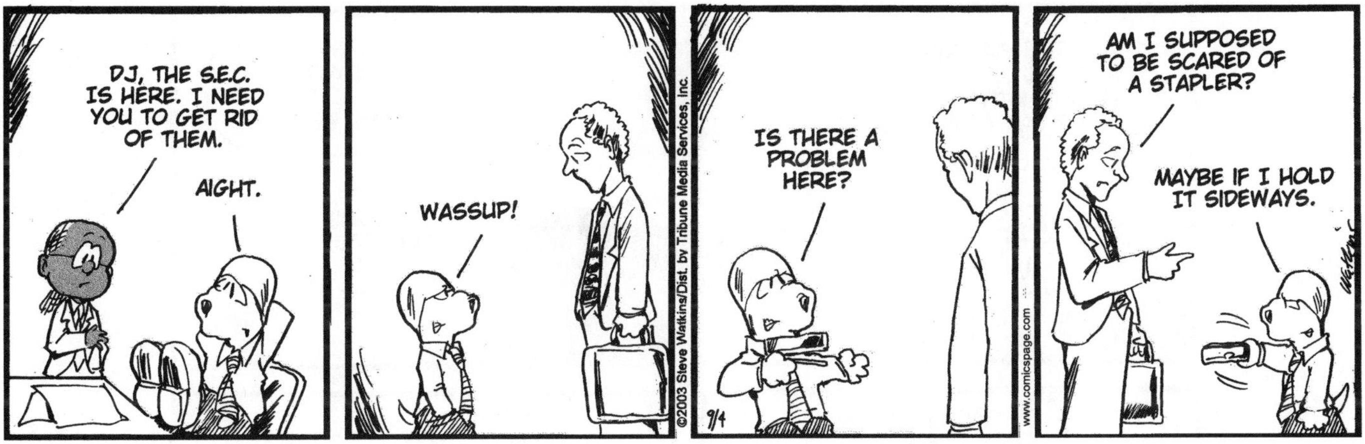
DJ, THE S.E.C. IS HERE. I NEED YOU TO GET RID OF THEM.
AIGHT.
WASSUP!
©2003 Steve Watkins/Dist. by Tribune Media Services, Inc.
IS THERE A PROBLEM HERE?
9/4
www.comicspage.com
AM I SUPPOSED TO BE SCARED OF A STAPLER?
MAYBE IF I HOLD IT SIDEWAYS.
Watkins

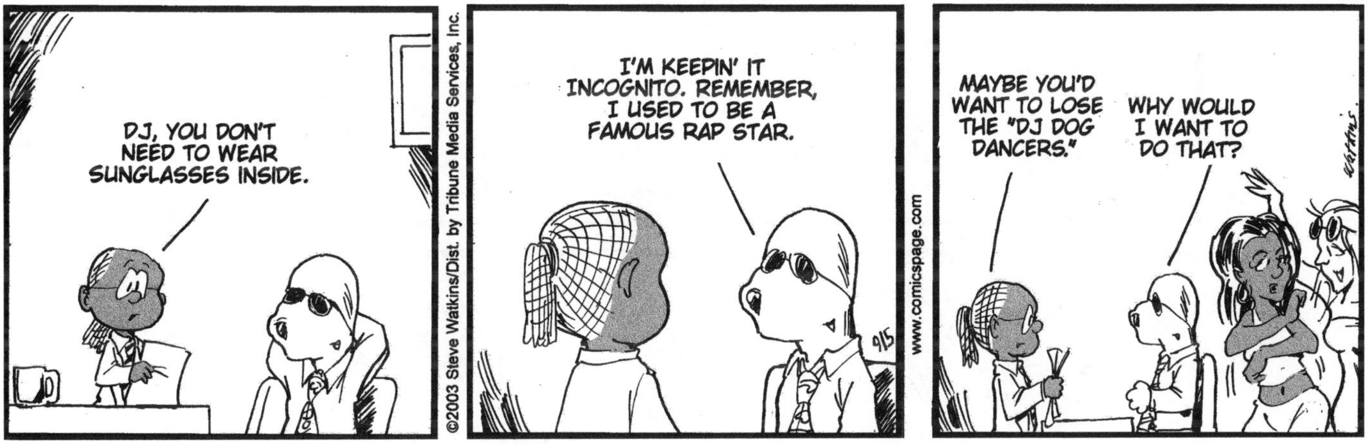
DJ, YOU DON'T NEED TO WEAR SUNGLASSES INSIDE.
©2003 Steve Watkins/Dist. by Tribune Media Services, Inc.
I'M KEEPIN' IT INCOGNITO. REMEMBER, I USED TO BE A FAMOUS RAP STAR.
9/5
www.comicspage.com
MAYBE YOU'D WANT TO LOSE THE "DJ DOG DANCERS."
WHY WOULD I WANT TO DO THAT?
Watkins

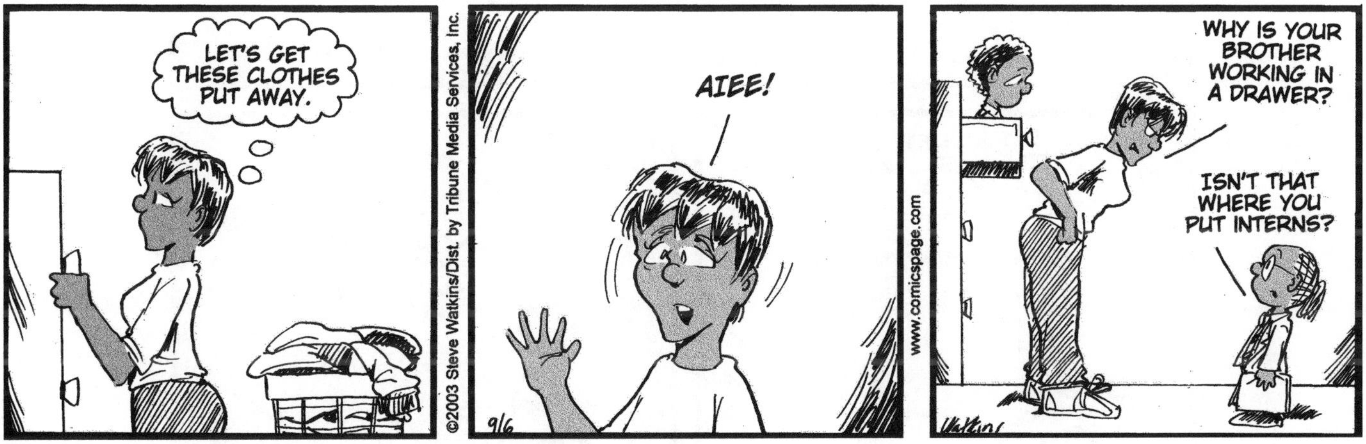
LET'S GET THESE CLOTHES PUT AWAY.
©2003 Steve Watkins/Dist. by Tribune Media Services, Inc.
AIEE!
9/6
www.comicspage.com
WHY IS YOUR BROTHER WORKING IN A DRAWER?
ISN'T THAT WHERE YOU PUT INTERNS?
Watkins

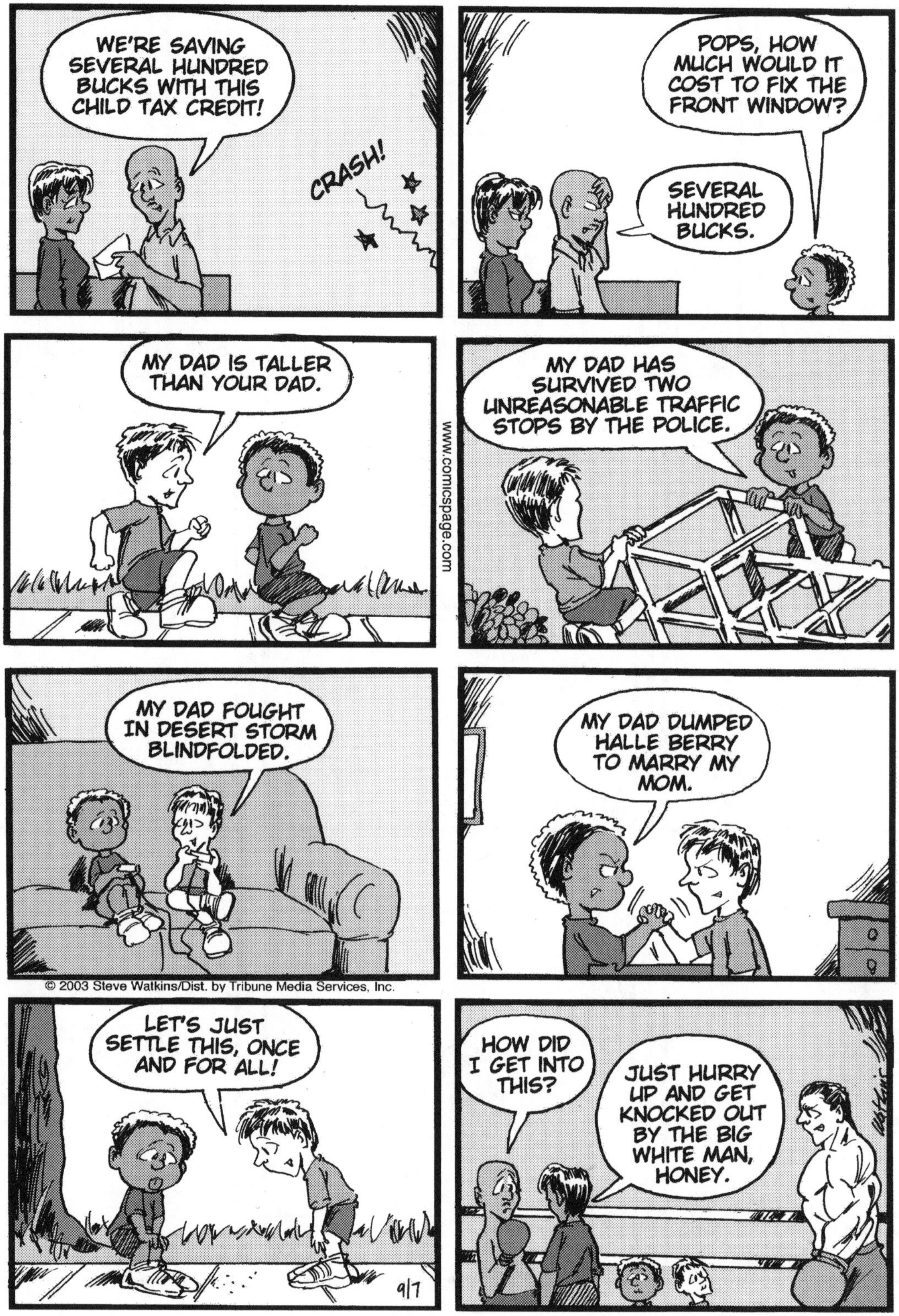
WE'RE SAVING SEVERAL HUNDRED BUCKS WITH THIS CHILD TAX CREDIT!
CRASH!
POPS, HOW MUCH WOULD IT COST TO FIX THE FRONT WINDOW?
SEVERAL HUNDRED BUCKS.
MY DAD IS TALLER THAN YOUR DAD.
www.comicspage.com
MY DAD HAS SURVIVED TWO UNREASONABLE TRAFFIC STOPS BY THE POLICE.
MY DAD FOUGHT IN DESERT STORM BLINDFOLDED.
MY DAD DUMPED HALLE BERRY TO MARRY MY MOM.
© 2003 Steve Watkins/Dist. by Tribune Media Services, Inc.
LET'S JUST SETTLE THIS, ONCE AND FOR ALL!
9/7
HOW DID I GET INTO THIS?
JUST HURRY UP AND GET KNOCKED OUT BY THE BIG WHITE MAN, HONEY.
Watkins

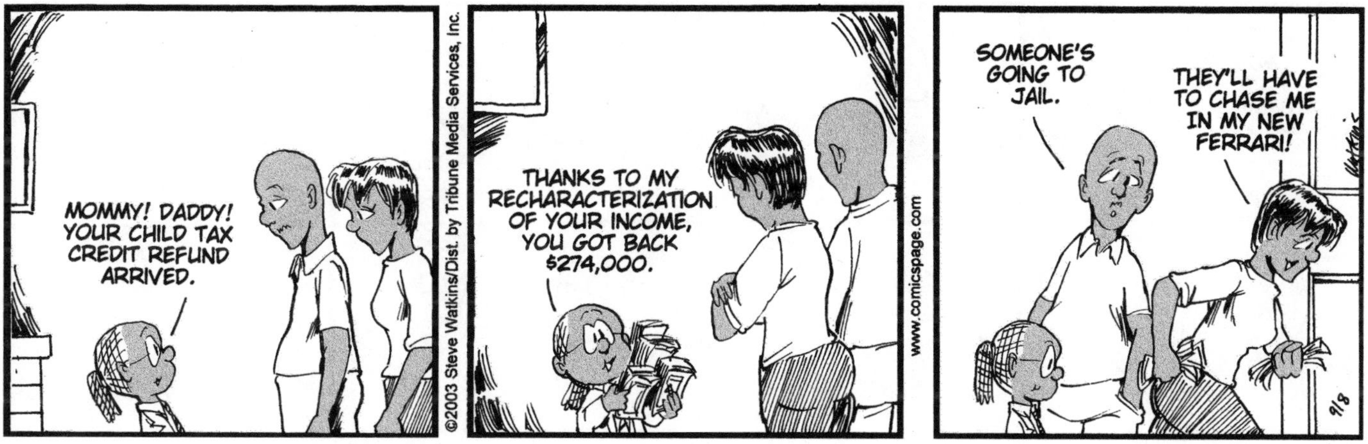
MOMMY! DADDY! YOUR CHILD TAX CREDIT REFUND ARRIVED.
©2003 Steve Watkins/Dist. by Tribune Media Services, Inc.
THANKS TO MY RECHARACTERIZATION OF YOUR INCOME, YOU GOT BACK $274,000.
www.comicspage.com
SOMEONE'S GOING TO JAIL.
THEY'LL HAVE TO CHASE ME IN MY NEW FERRARI!
9/8

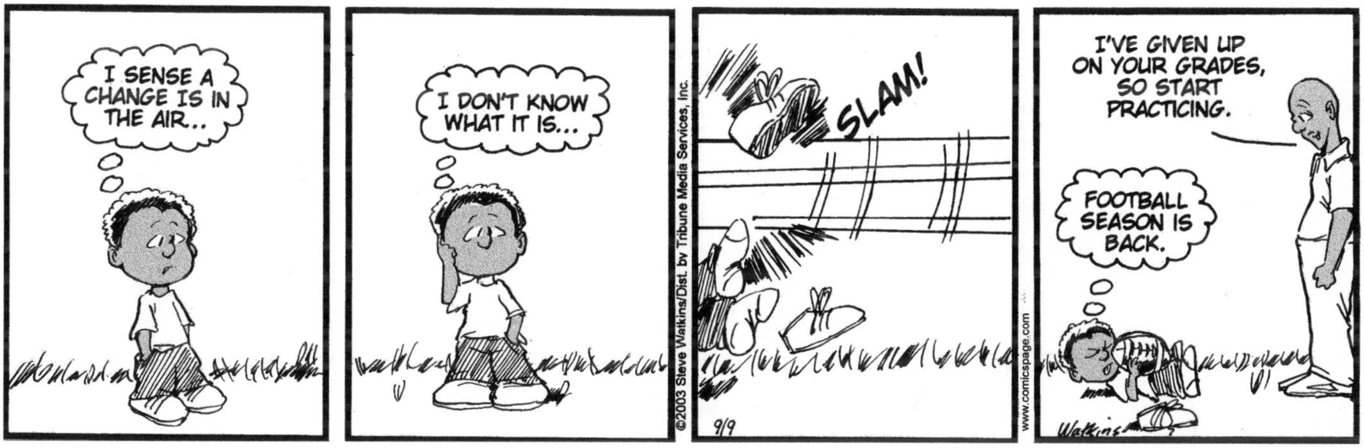
I SENSE A CHANGE IS IN THE AIR...
I DON'T KNOW WHAT IT IS...
©2003 Steve Watkins/Dist. by Tribune Media Services, Inc.
SLAM!
9/9
www.comicspage.com
I'VE GIVEN UP ON YOUR GRADES, SO START PRACTICING.
FOOTBALL SEASON IS BACK.
Watkins

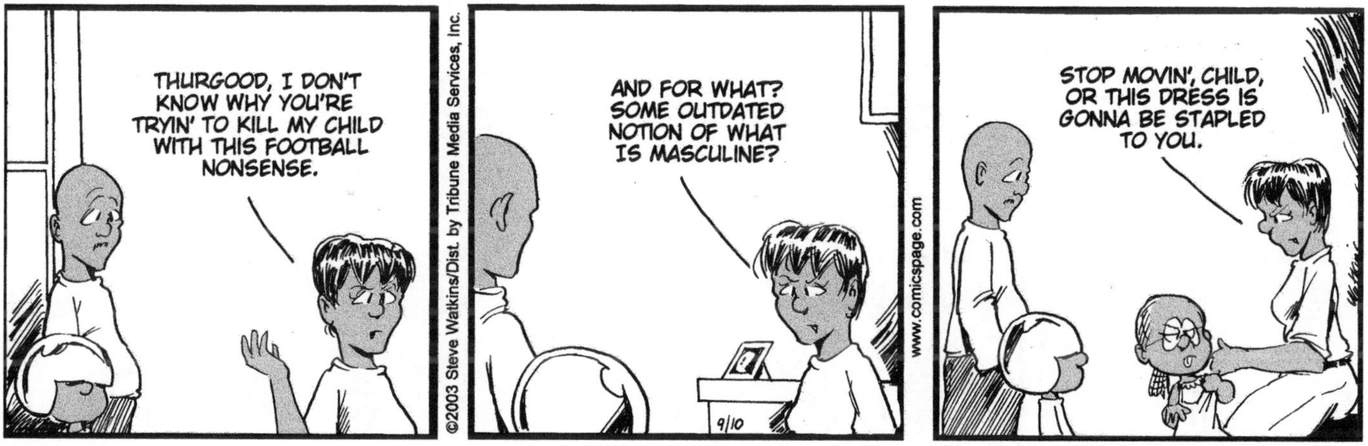
THURGOOD, I DON'T KNOW WHY YOU'RE TRYIN' TO KILL MY CHILD WITH THIS FOOTBALL NONSENSE.
©2003 Steve Watkins/Dist. by Tribune Media Services, Inc.
AND FOR WHAT? SOME OUTDATED NOTION OF WHAT IS MASCULINE?
9/10
www.comicspage.com
STOP MOVIN', CHILD, OR THIS DRESS IS GONNA BE STAPLED TO YOU.

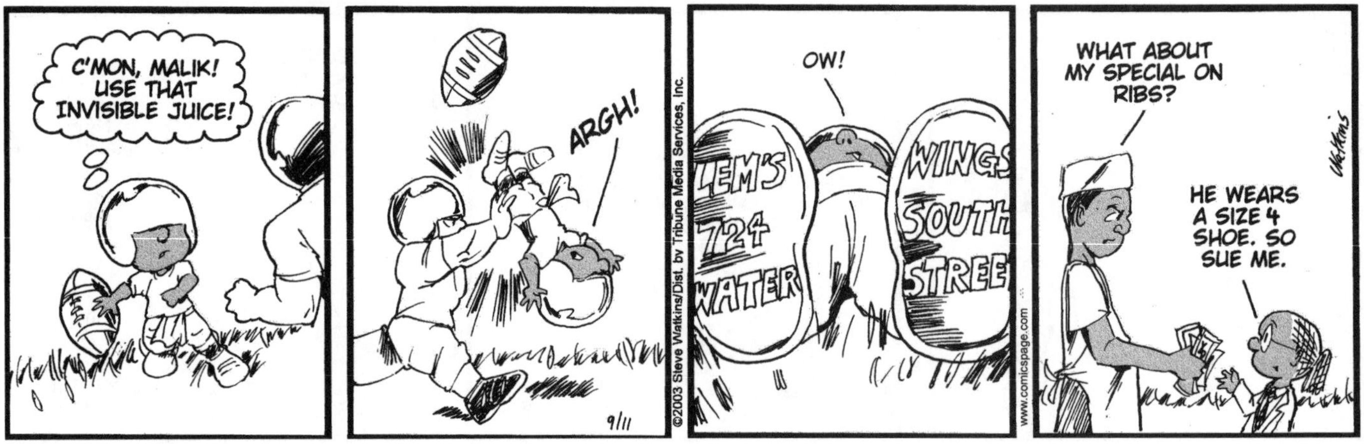
C'MON, MALIK! USE THAT INVISIBLE JUICE!
ARGH!
9/11
©2003 Steve Watkins/Dist. by Tribune Media Services, Inc.
OW!
LEM'S 724 WATER
WINGS SOUTH STREE
www.comicspage.com
WHAT ABOUT MY SPECIAL ON RIBS?
HE WEARS A SIZE 4 SHOE. SO SUE ME.
Watkins

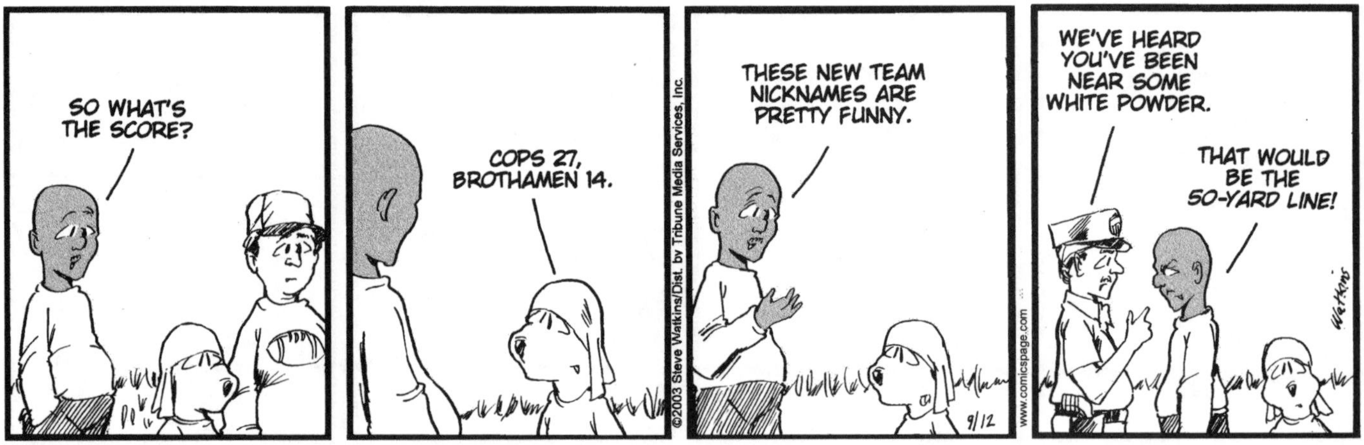
SO WHAT'S THE SCORE?
COPS 27, BROTHAMEN 14.
©2003 Steve Watkins/Dist. by Tribune Media Services, Inc.
THESE NEW TEAM NICKNAMES ARE PRETTY FUNNY.
9/12
www.comicspage.com
WE'VE HEARD YOU'VE BEEN NEAR SOME WHITE POWDER.
THAT WOULD BE THE 50-YARD LINE!
Watkins

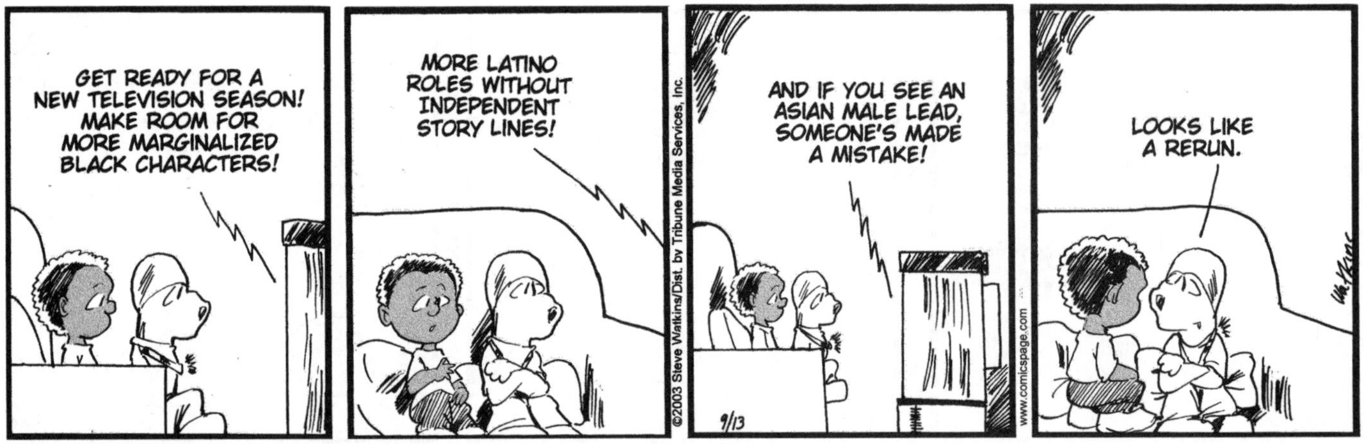
GET READY FOR A NEW TELEVISION SEASON! MAKE ROOM FOR MORE MARGINALIZED BLACK CHARACTERS!
MORE LATINO ROLES WITHOUT INDEPENDENT STORY LINES!
©2003 Steve Watkins/Dist. by Tribune Media Services, Inc.
AND IF YOU SEE AN ASIAN MALE LEAD, SOMEONE'S MADE A MISTAKE!
9/13
www.comicspage.com
LOOKS LIKE A RERUN.
Watkins

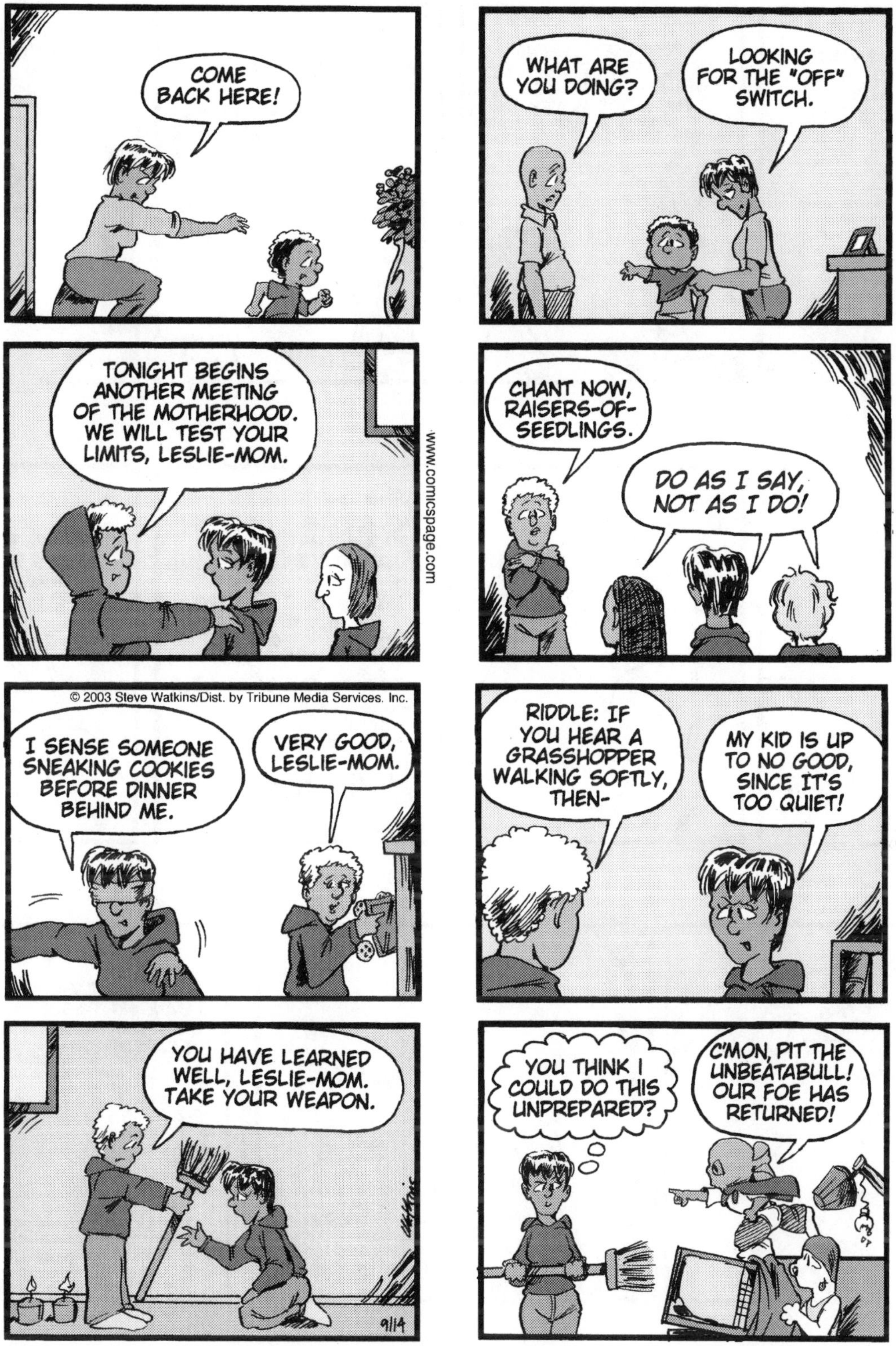
COME BACK HERE!
WHAT ARE YOU DOING?
LOOKING FOR THE "OFF" SWITCH.
TONIGHT BEGINS ANOTHER MEETING OF THE MOTHERHOOD. WE WILL TEST YOUR LIMITS, LESLIE-MOM.
www.comicspage.com
CHANT NOW, RAISERS-OF-SEEDLINGS.
DO AS I SAY, NOT AS I DO!
© 2003 Steve Watkins/Dist. by Tribune Media Services, Inc.
I SENSE SOMEONE SNEAKING COOKIES BEFORE DINNER BEHIND ME.
VERY GOOD, LESLIE-MOM.
RIDDLE: IF YOU HEAR A GRASSHOPPER WALKING SOFTLY, THEN-
MY KID IS UP TO NO GOOD, SINCE IT'S TOO QUIET!
YOU HAVE LEARNED WELL, LESLIE-MOM. TAKE YOUR WEAPON.
9/14
YOU THINK I COULD DO THIS UNPREPARED?
C'MON, PIT THE UNBEATABULL! OUR FOE HAS RETURNED!

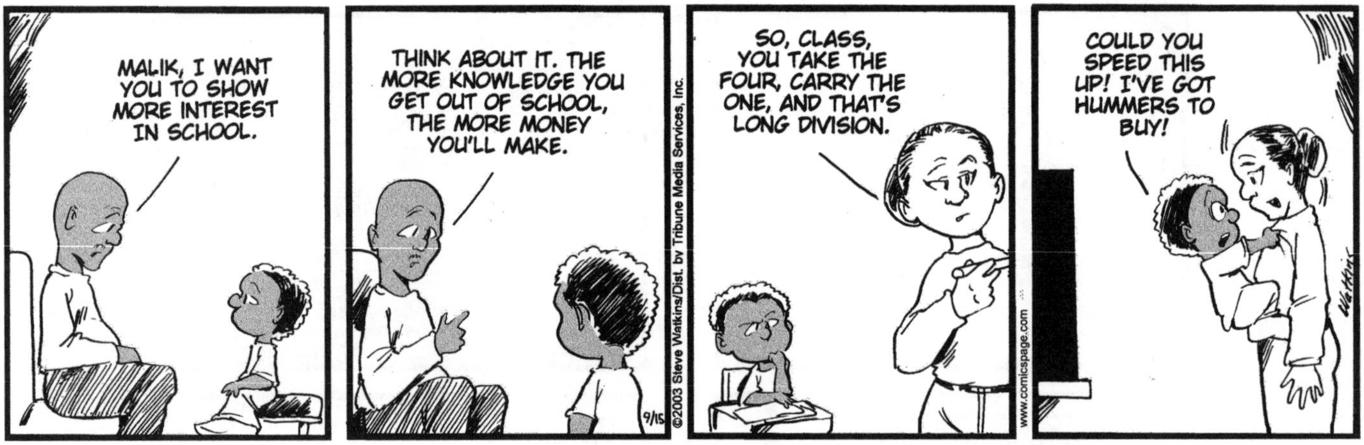
MALIK, I WANT YOU TO SHOW MORE INTEREST IN SCHOOL.
THINK ABOUT IT. THE MORE KNOWLEDGE YOU GET OUT OF SCHOOL, THE MORE MONEY YOU'LL MAKE.
9/15
©2003 Steve Watkins/Dist. by Tribune Media Services, Inc.
SO, CLASS, YOU TAKE THE FOUR, CARRY THE ONE, AND THAT'S LONG DIVISION.
www.comicspage.com
COULD YOU SPEED THIS UP! I'VE GOT HUMMERS TO BUY!

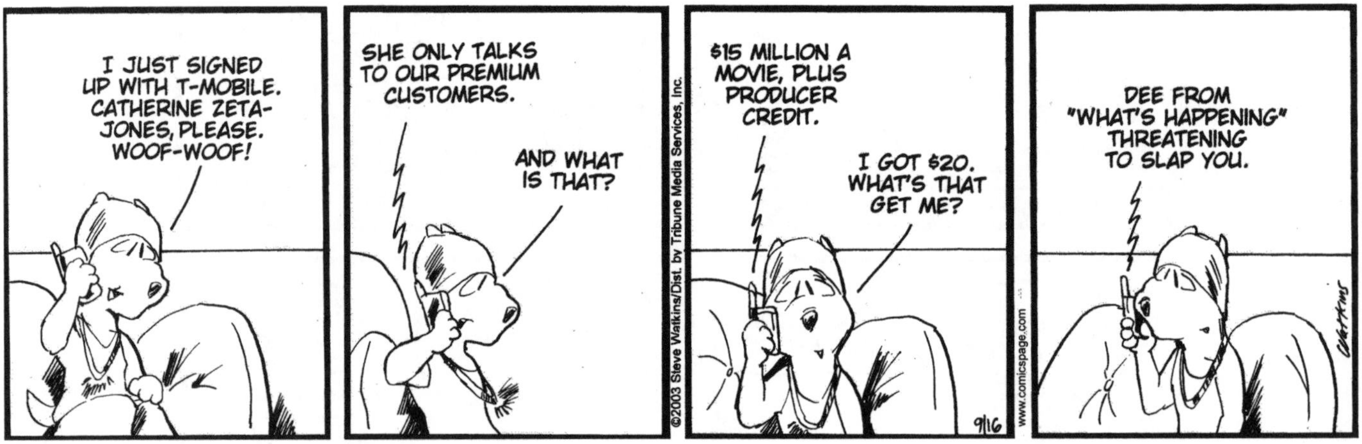
I JUST SIGNED UP WITH T-MOBILE. CATHERINE ZETA-JONES, PLEASE. WOOF-WOOF!
SHE ONLY TALKS TO OUR PREMIUM CUSTOMERS.
AND WHAT IS THAT?
©2003 Steve Watkins/Dist. by Tribune Media Services, Inc.
$15 MILLION A MOVIE, PLUS PRODUCER CREDIT.
I GOT $20. WHAT'S THAT GET ME?
9/16
www.comicspage.com
DEE FROM "WHAT'S HAPPENING" THREATENING TO SLAP YOU.

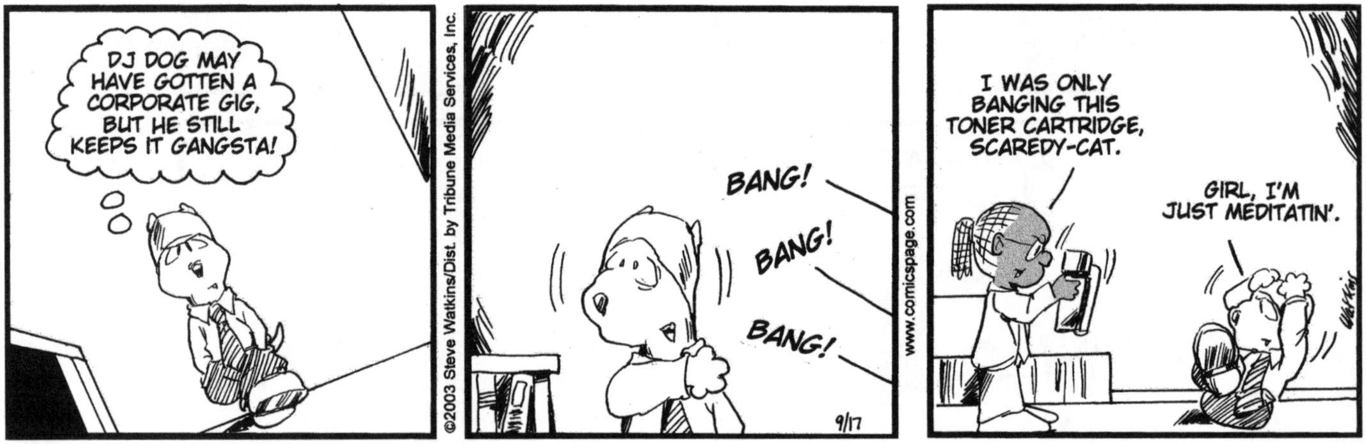
DJ DOG MAY HAVE GOTTEN A CORPORATE GIG, BUT HE STILL KEEPS IT GANGSTA!
©2003 Steve Watkins/Dist. by Tribune Media Services, Inc.
BANG!
BANG!
BANG!
9/17
www.comicspage.com
I WAS ONLY BANGING THIS TONER CARTRIDGE, SCAREDY-CAT.
GIRL, I'M JUST MEDITATIN'.

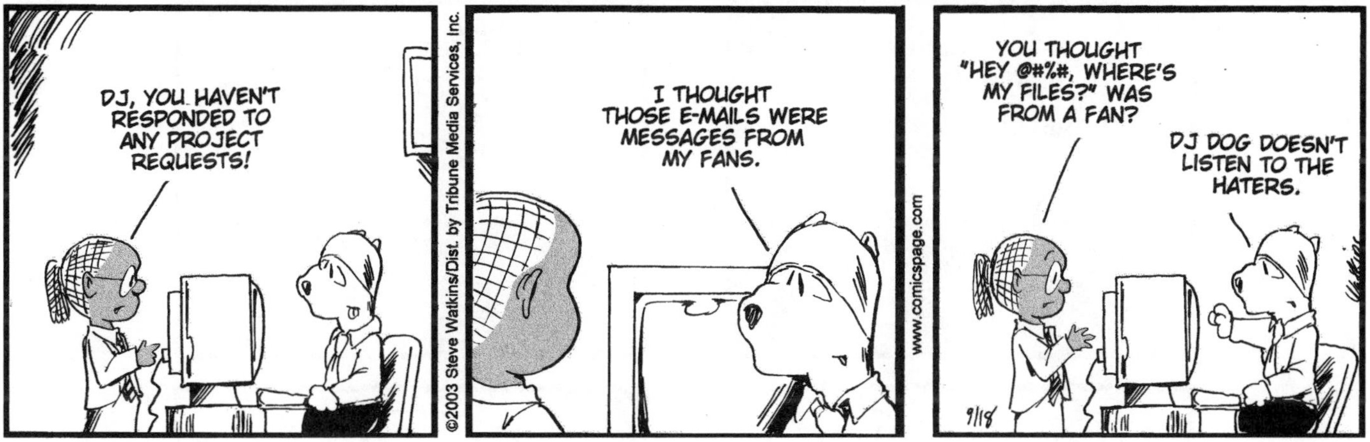
DJ, YOU HAVEN'T RESPONDED TO ANY PROJECT REQUESTS!
©2003 Steve Watkins/Dist. by Tribune Media Services, Inc.
I THOUGHT THOSE E-MAILS WERE MESSAGES FROM MY FANS.
www.comicspage.com
YOU THOUGHT "HEY @#%#, WHERE'S MY FILES?" WAS FROM A FAN?
DJ DOG DOESN'T LISTEN TO THE HATERS.
9/18

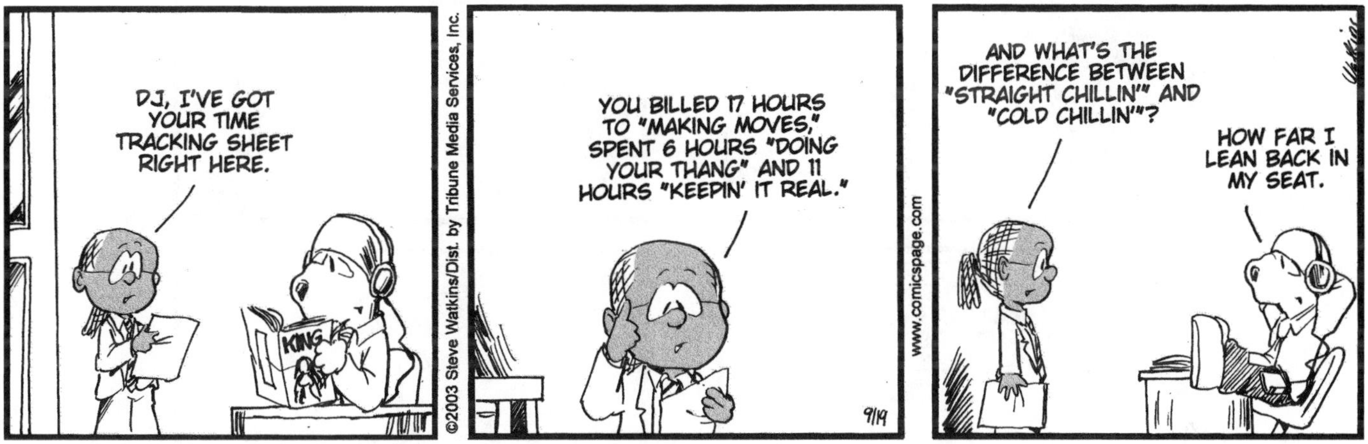
DJ, I'VE GOT YOUR TIME TRACKING SHEET RIGHT HERE.
KING
©2003 Steve Watkins/Dist. by Tribune Media Services, Inc.
YOU BILLED 17 HOURS TO "MAKING MOVES," SPENT 6 HOURS "DOING YOUR THANG" AND 11 HOURS "KEEPIN' IT REAL."
9/19
www.comicspage.com
AND WHAT'S THE DIFFERENCE BETWEEN "STRAIGHT CHILLIN'" AND "COLD CHILLIN'"?
HOW FAR I LEAN BACK IN MY SEAT.

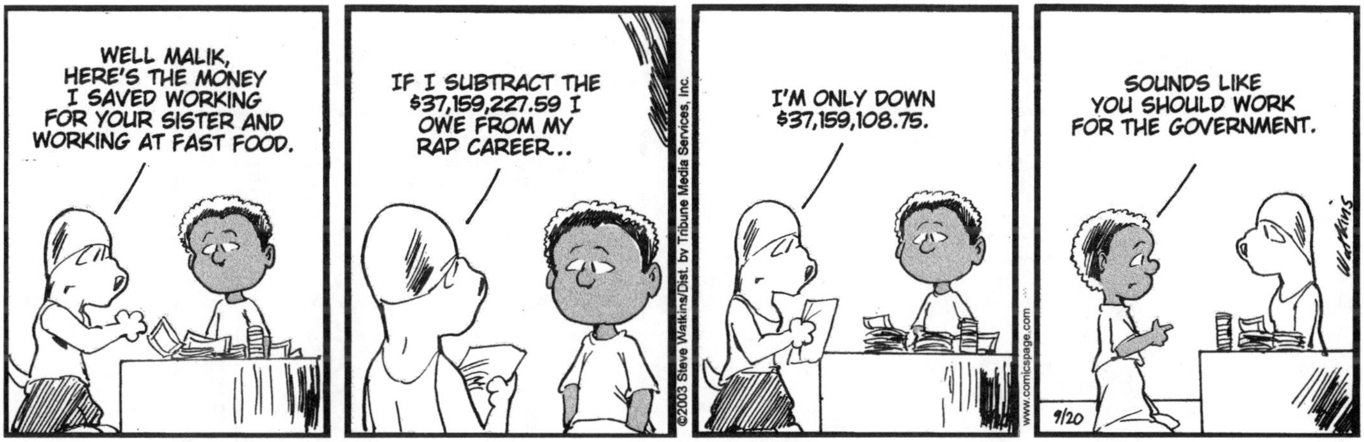
WELL MALIK, HERE'S THE MONEY I SAVED WORKING FOR YOUR SISTER AND WORKING AT FAST FOOD.
IF I SUBTRACT THE $37,159,227.59 I OWE FROM MY RAP CAREER...
©2003 Steve Watkins/Dist. by Tribune Media Services, Inc.
I'M ONLY DOWN $37,159,108.75.
www.comicspage.com
SOUNDS LIKE YOU SHOULD WORK FOR THE GOVERNMENT.
9/20

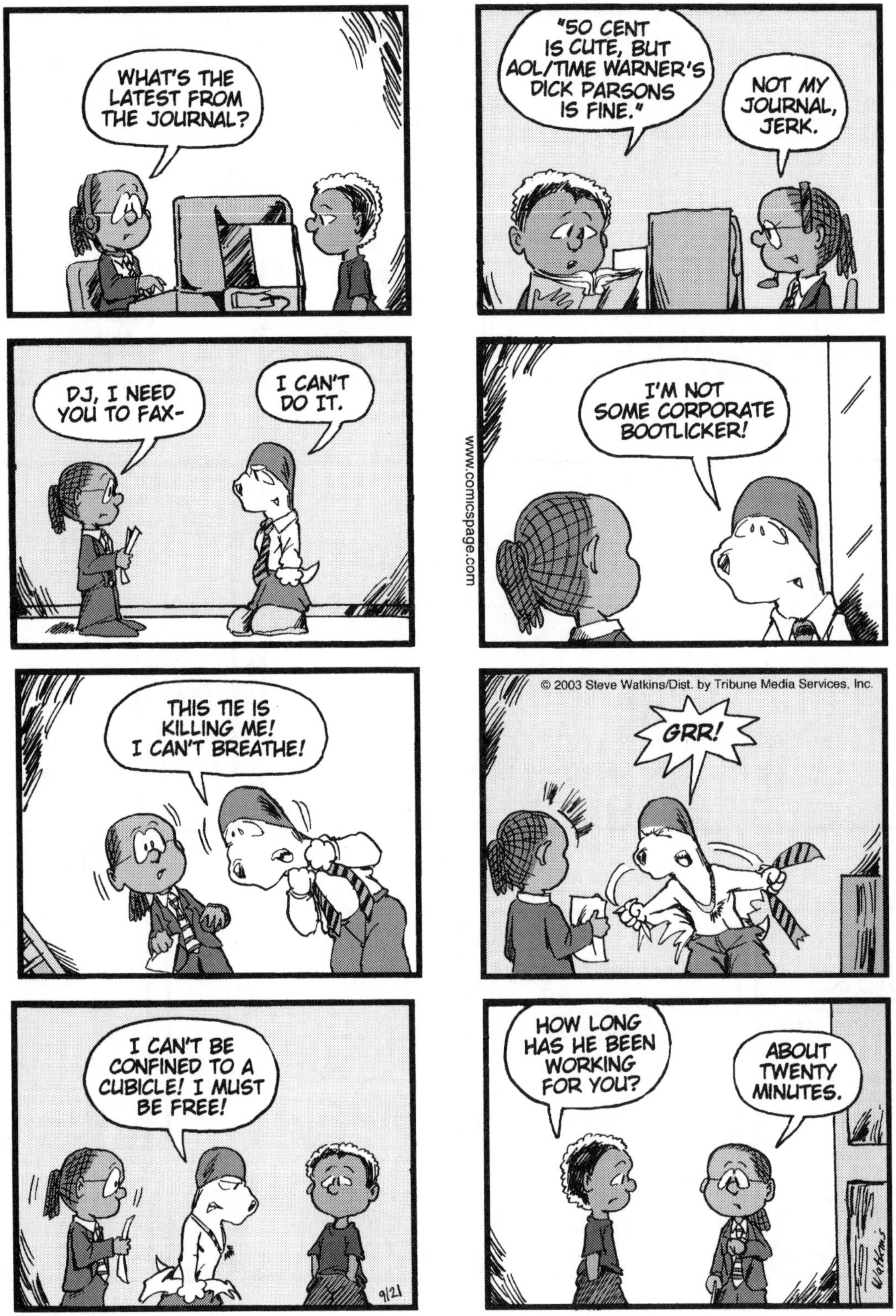
WHAT'S THE LATEST FROM THE JOURNAL?
"50 CENT IS CUTE, BUT AOL/TIME WARNER'S DICK PARSONS IS FINE."
NOT MY JOURNAL, JERK.
DJ, I NEED YOU TO FAX-
I CAN'T DO IT.
www.comicspage.com
I'M NOT SOME CORPORATE BOOTLICKER!
THIS TIE IS KILLING ME! I CAN'T BREATHE!
© 2003 Steve Watkins/Dist. by Tribune Media Services, Inc.
GRR!
I CAN'T BE CONFINED TO A CUBICLE! I MUST BE FREE!
9/21
HOW LONG HAS HE BEEN WORKING FOR YOU?
ABOUT TWENTY MINUTES.

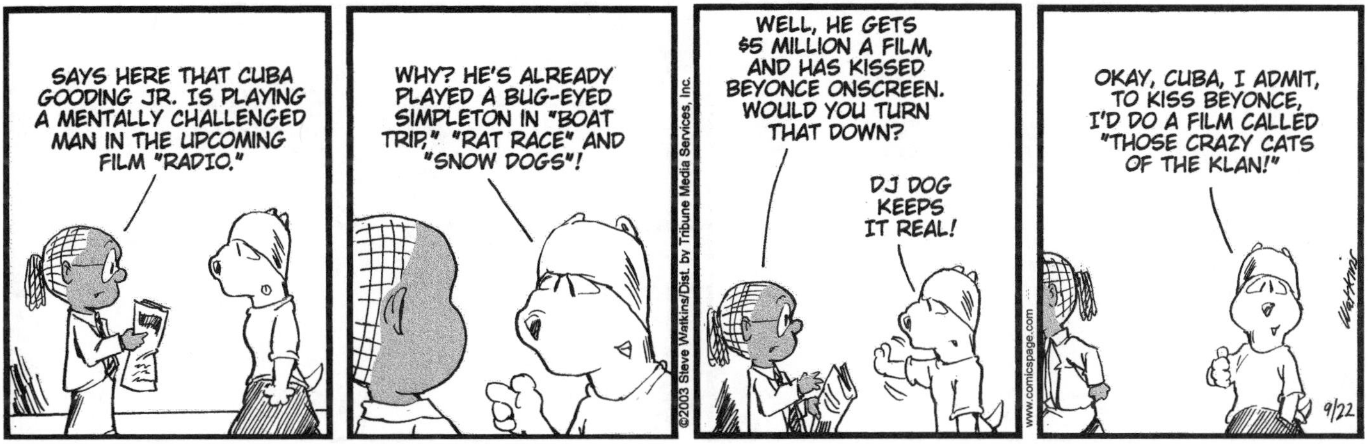
SAYS HERE THAT CUBA GOODING JR. IS PLAYING A MENTALLY CHALLENGED MAN IN THE UPCOMING FILM "RADIO."
WHY? HE'S ALREADY PLAYED A BUG-EYED SIMPLETON IN "BOAT TRIP," "RAT RACE" AND "SNOW DOGS"!
©2003 Steve Watkins/Dist. by Tribune Media Services, Inc.
WELL, HE GETS $5 MILLION A FILM, AND HAS KISSED BEYONCE ONSCREEN. WOULD YOU TURN THAT DOWN?
DJ DOG KEEPS IT REAL!
www.comicspage.com
OKAY, CUBA, I ADMIT, TO KISS BEYONCE, I'D DO A FILM CALLED "THOSE CRAZY CATS OF THE KLAN!"
Watkins
9/22

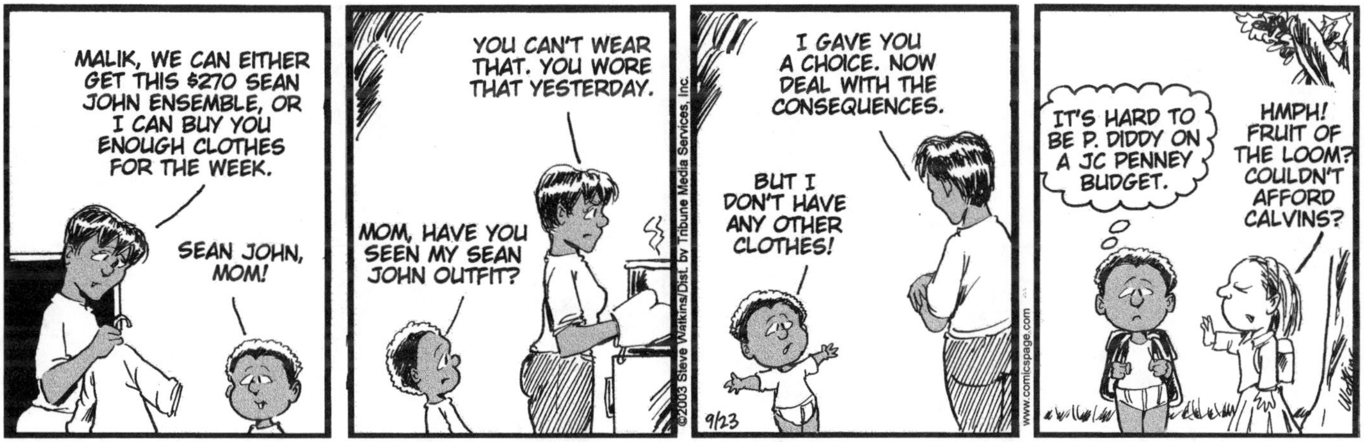
MALIK, WE CAN EITHER GET THIS $270 SEAN JOHN ENSEMBLE, OR I CAN BUY YOU ENOUGH CLOTHES FOR THE WEEK.
SEAN JOHN, MOM!
MOM, HAVE YOU SEEN MY SEAN JOHN OUTFIT?
YOU CAN'T WEAR THAT. YOU WORE THAT YESTERDAY.
©2003 Steve Watkins/Dist. by Tribune Media Services, Inc.
9/23
I GAVE YOU A CHOICE. NOW DEAL WITH THE CONSEQUENCES.
BUT I DON'T HAVE ANY OTHER CLOTHES!
www.comicspage.com
IT'S HARD TO BE P. DIDDY ON A JC PENNEY BUDGET.
HMPH! FRUIT OF THE LOOM? COULDN'T AFFORD CALVINS?

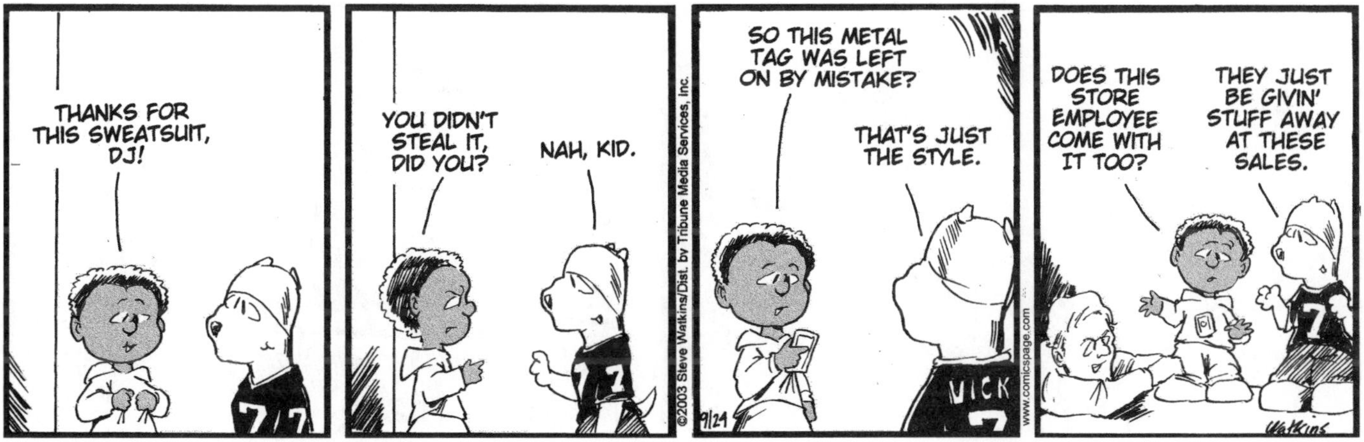
THANKS FOR THIS SWEATSUIT, DJ!
YOU DIDN'T STEAL IT, DID YOU?
NAH, KID.
©2003 Steve Watkins/Dist. by Tribune Media Services, Inc.
9/24
SO THIS METAL TAG WAS LEFT ON BY MISTAKE?
THAT'S JUST THE STYLE.
VICK
www.comicspage.com
DOES THIS STORE EMPLOYEE COME WITH IT TOO?
THEY JUST BE GIVIN' STUFF AWAY AT THESE SALES.
Watkins

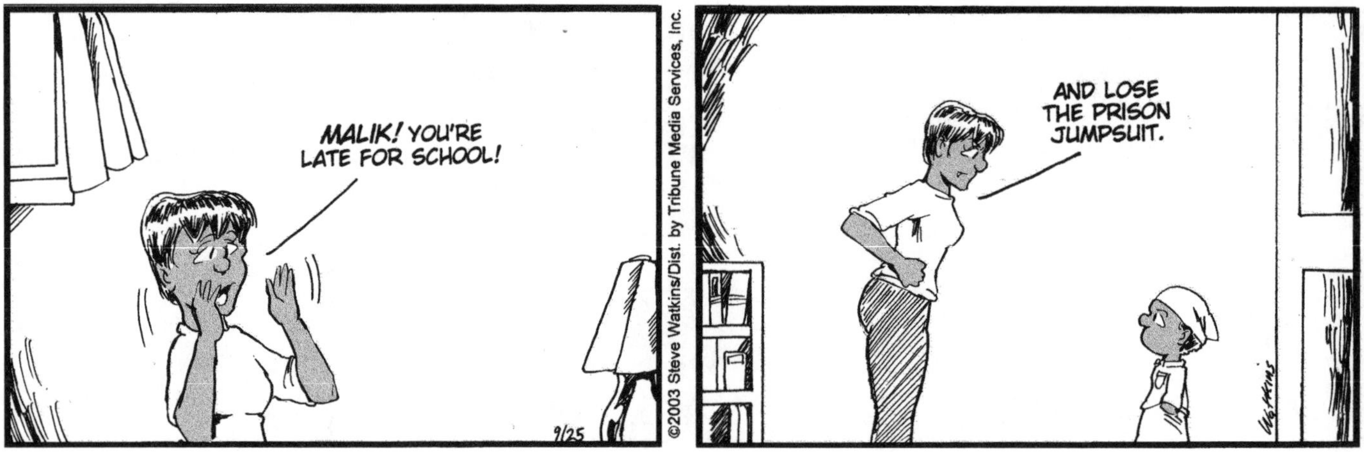
MALIK! YOU'RE LATE FOR SCHOOL!
AND LOSE THE PRISON JUMPSUIT.
9/25
©2003 Steve Watkins/Dist. by Tribune Media Services, Inc.

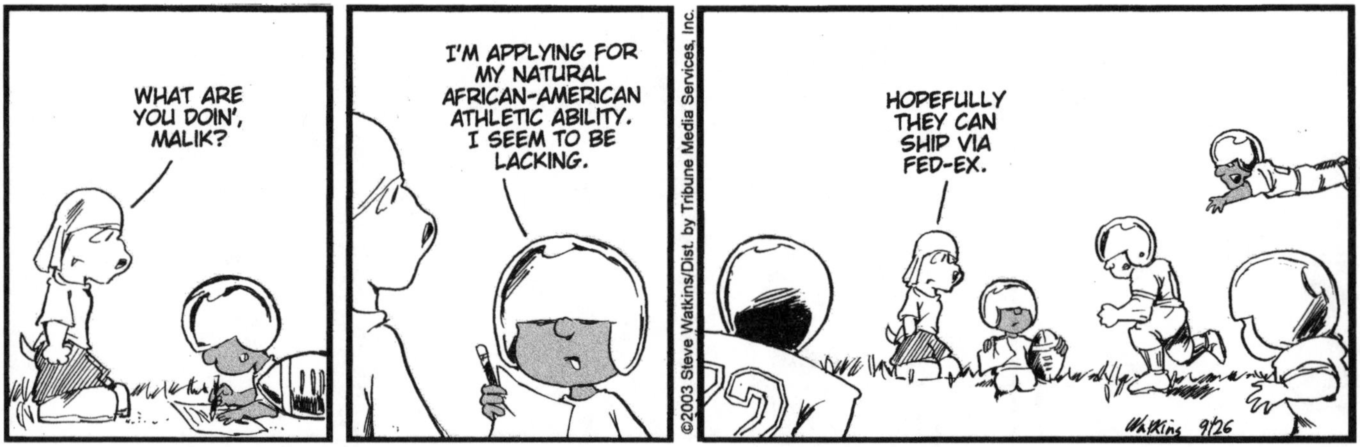
WHAT ARE YOU DOIN', MALIK?
I'M APPLYING FOR MY NATURAL AFRICAN-AMERICAN ATHLETIC ABILITY. I SEEM TO BE LACKING.
HOPEFULLY THEY CAN SHIP VIA FED-EX.
Watkins 9/26
©2003 Steve Watkins/Dist. by Tribune Media Services, Inc.

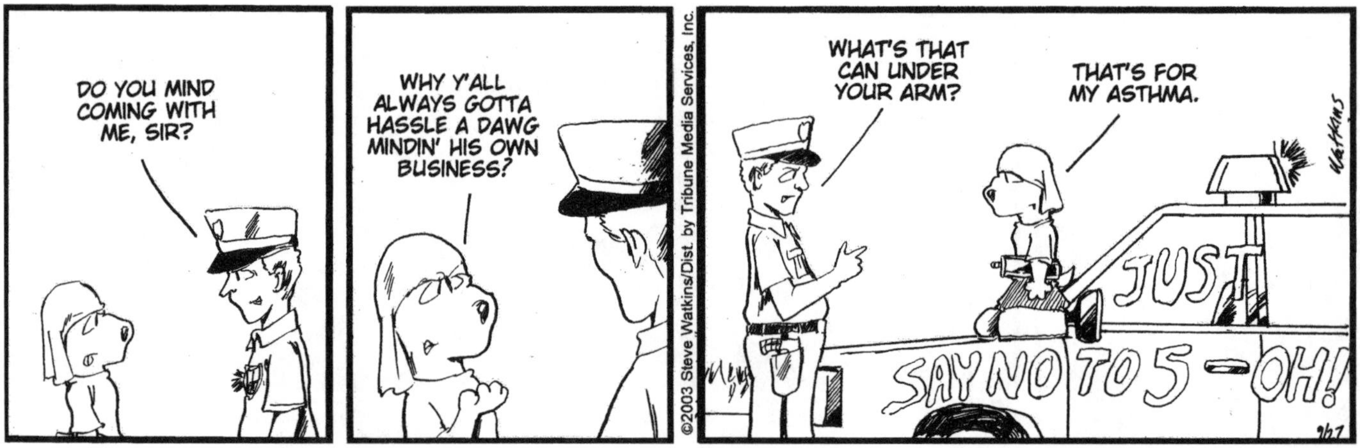
DO YOU MIND COMING WITH ME, SIR?
WHY Y'ALL ALWAYS GOTTA HASSLE A DAWG MINDIN' HIS OWN BUSINESS?
WHAT'S THAT CAN UNDER YOUR ARM?
THAT'S FOR MY ASTHMA.
JUST
SAY NO TO 5-OH!
©2003 Steve Watkins/Dist. by Tribune Media Services, Inc.

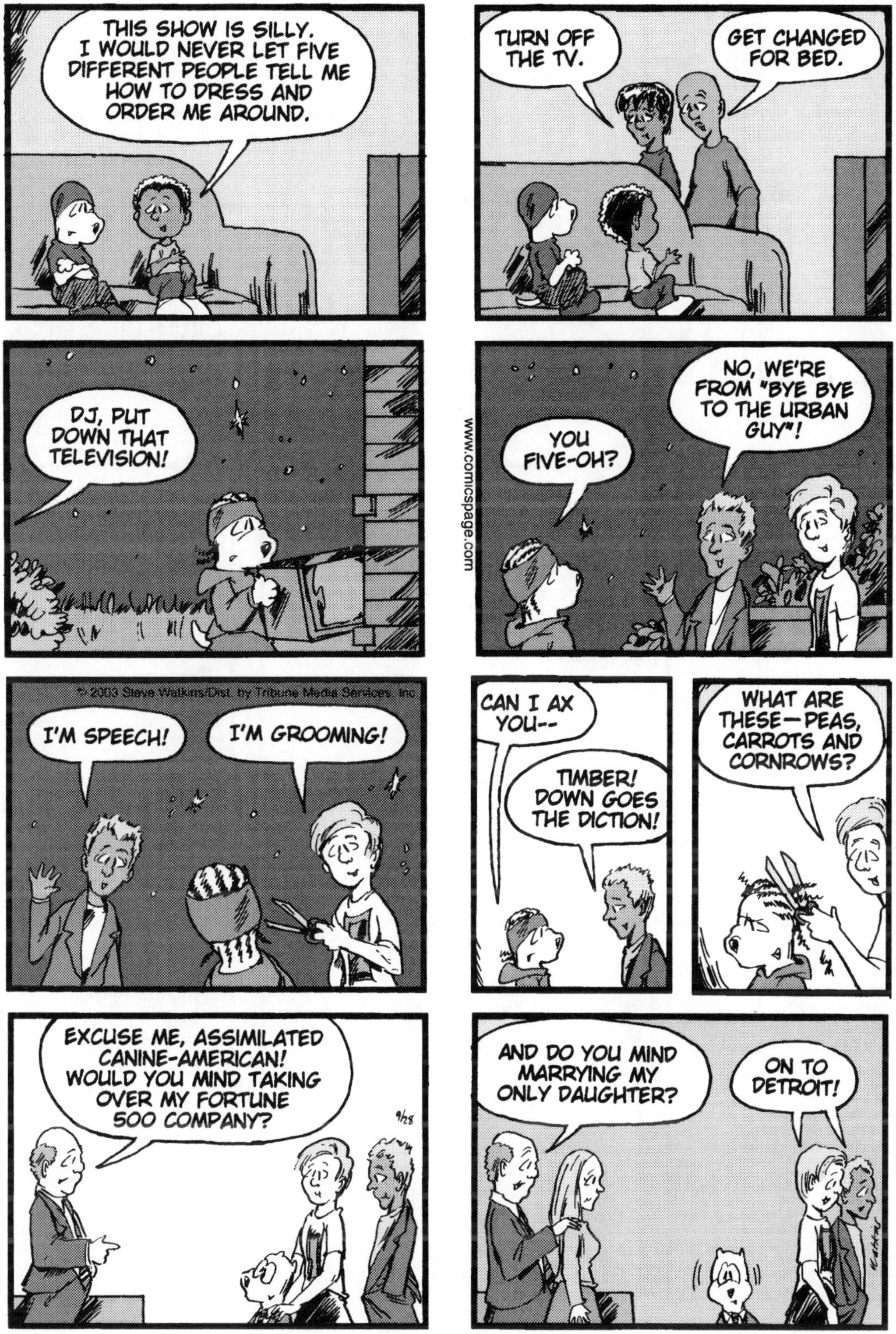
THIS SHOW IS SILLY. I WOULD NEVER LET FIVE DIFFERENT PEOPLE TELL ME HOW TO DRESS AND ORDER ME AROUND.
TURN OFF THE TV.
GET CHANGED FOR BED.
DJ, PUT DOWN THAT TELEVISION!
www.comicspage.com
YOU FIVE-OH?
NO, WE'RE FROM "BYE BYE TO THE URBAN GUY"!
© 2003 Steve Watkins/Dist. by Tribune Media Services, Inc.
I'M SPEECH!
I'M GROOMING!
CAN I AX YOU--
TIMBER! DOWN GOES THE DICTION!
WHAT ARE THESE—PEAS, CARROTS AND CORNROWS?
EXCUSE ME, ASSIMILATED CANINE-AMERICAN! WOULD YOU MIND TAKING OVER MY FORTUNE 500 COMPANY?
9/28
AND DO YOU MIND MARRYING MY ONLY DAUGHTER?
ON TO DETROIT!

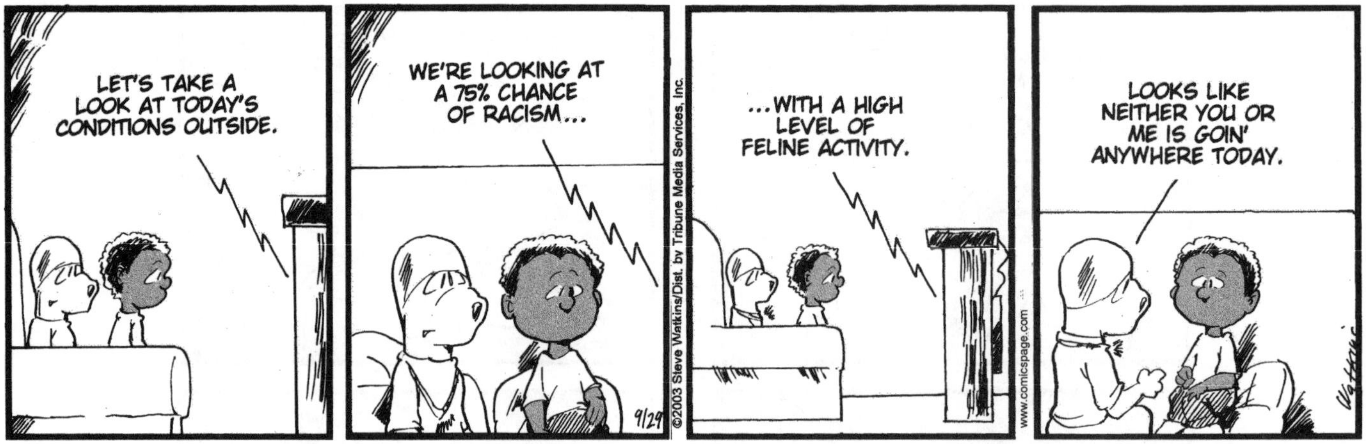
LET'S TAKE A LOOK AT TODAY'S CONDITIONS OUTSIDE.
WE'RE LOOKING AT A 75% CHANCE OF RACISM...
9/29
©2003 Steve Watkins/Dist. by Tribune Media Services, Inc.
...WITH A HIGH LEVEL OF FELINE ACTIVITY.
www.comicspage.com
LOOKS LIKE NEITHER YOU OR ME IS GOIN' ANYWHERE TODAY.
Watkins

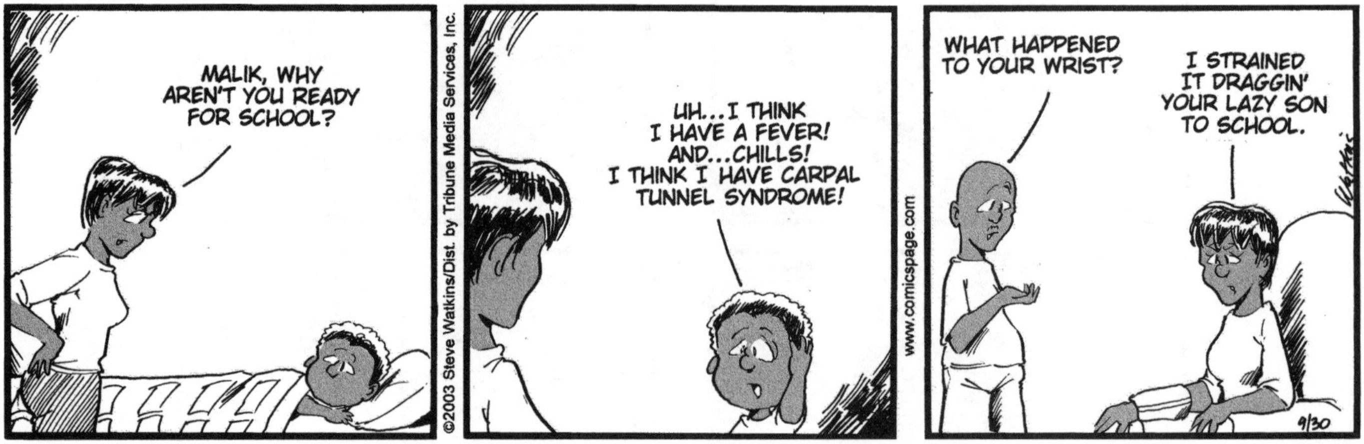
MALIK, WHY AREN'T YOU READY FOR SCHOOL?
©2003 Steve Watkins/Dist. by Tribune Media Services, Inc.
UH...I THINK I HAVE A FEVER! AND...CHILLS! I THINK I HAVE CARPAL TUNNEL SYNDROME!
www.comicspage.com
WHAT HAPPENED TO YOUR WRIST?
I STRAINED IT DRAGGIN' YOUR LAZY SON TO SCHOOL.
9/30

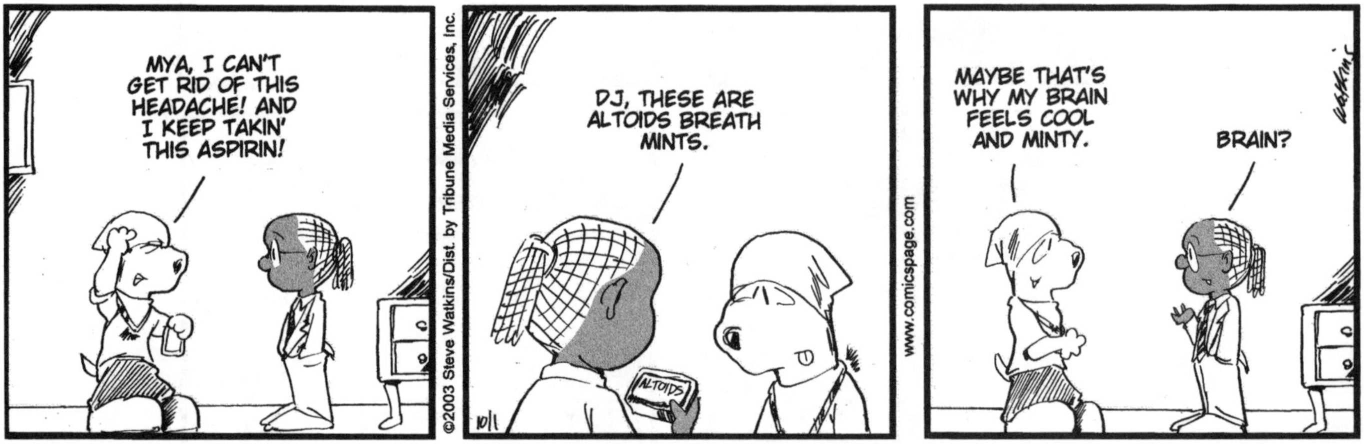
MYA, I CAN'T GET RID OF THIS HEADACHE! AND I KEEP TAKIN' THIS ASPIRIN!
©2003 Steve Watkins/Dist. by Tribune Media Services, Inc.
DJ, THESE ARE ALTOIDS BREATH MINTS.
ALTOIDS
10/1
www.comicspage.com
MAYBE THAT'S WHY MY BRAIN FEELS COOL AND MINTY.
BRAIN?
Watkins

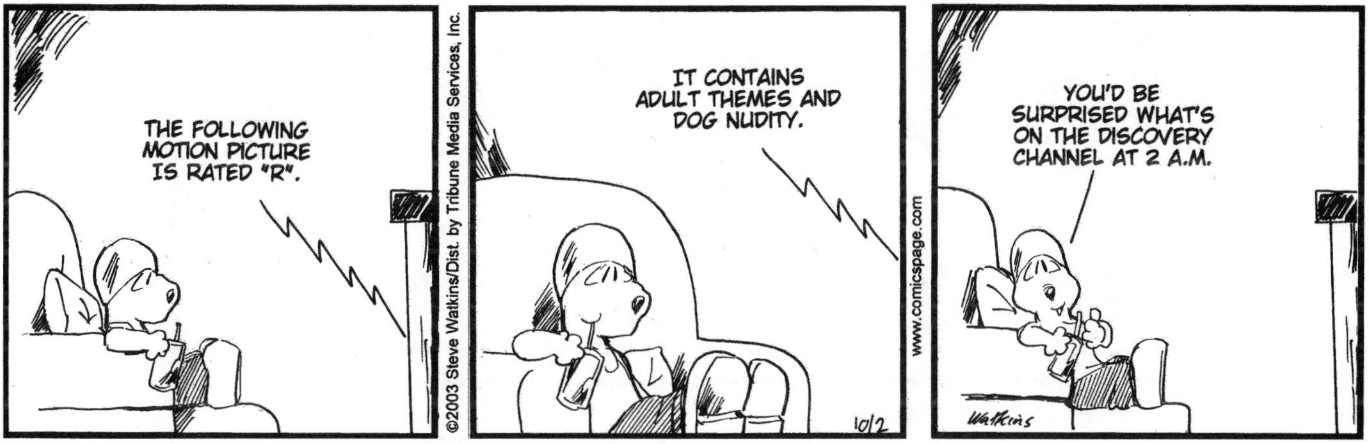
THE FOLLOWING MOTION PICTURE IS RATED "R".
IT CONTAINS ADULT THEMES AND DOG NUDITY.
YOU'D BE SURPRISED WHAT'S ON THE DISCOVERY CHANNEL AT 2 A.M.
10/2
WATKINS

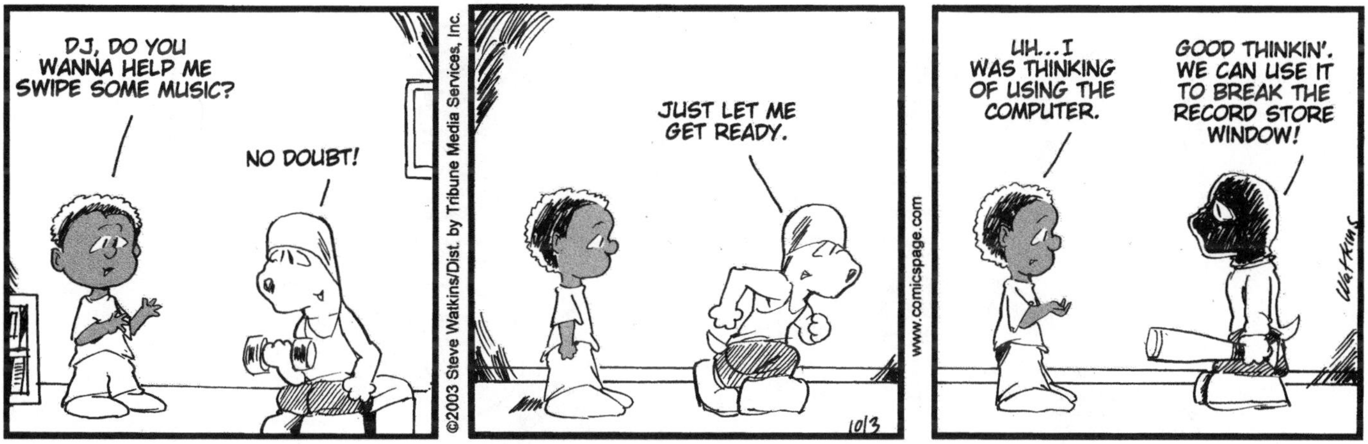
DJ, DO YOU WANNA HELP ME SWIPE SOME MUSIC?
NO DOUBT!
JUST LET ME GET READY.
UH...I WAS THINKING OF USING THE COMPUTER.
GOOD THINKIN'. WE CAN USE IT TO BREAK THE RECORD STORE WINDOW!
10/3
WATKINS

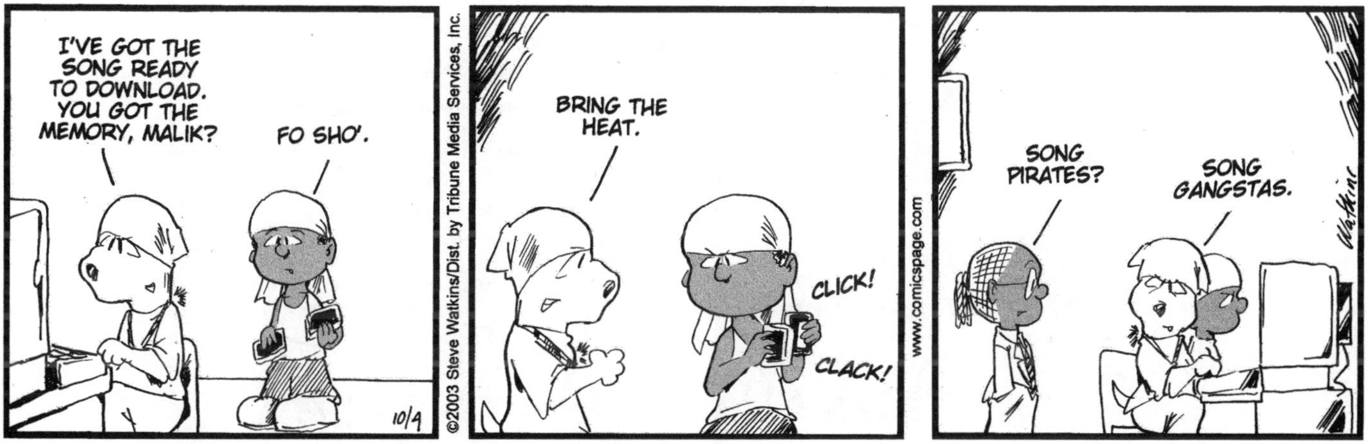
I'VE GOT THE SONG READY TO DOWNLOAD. YOU GOT THE MEMORY, MALIK?
FO SHO'.
BRING THE HEAT.
CLICK!
CLACK!
SONG PIRATES?
SONG GANGSTAS.
10/4
WATKINS

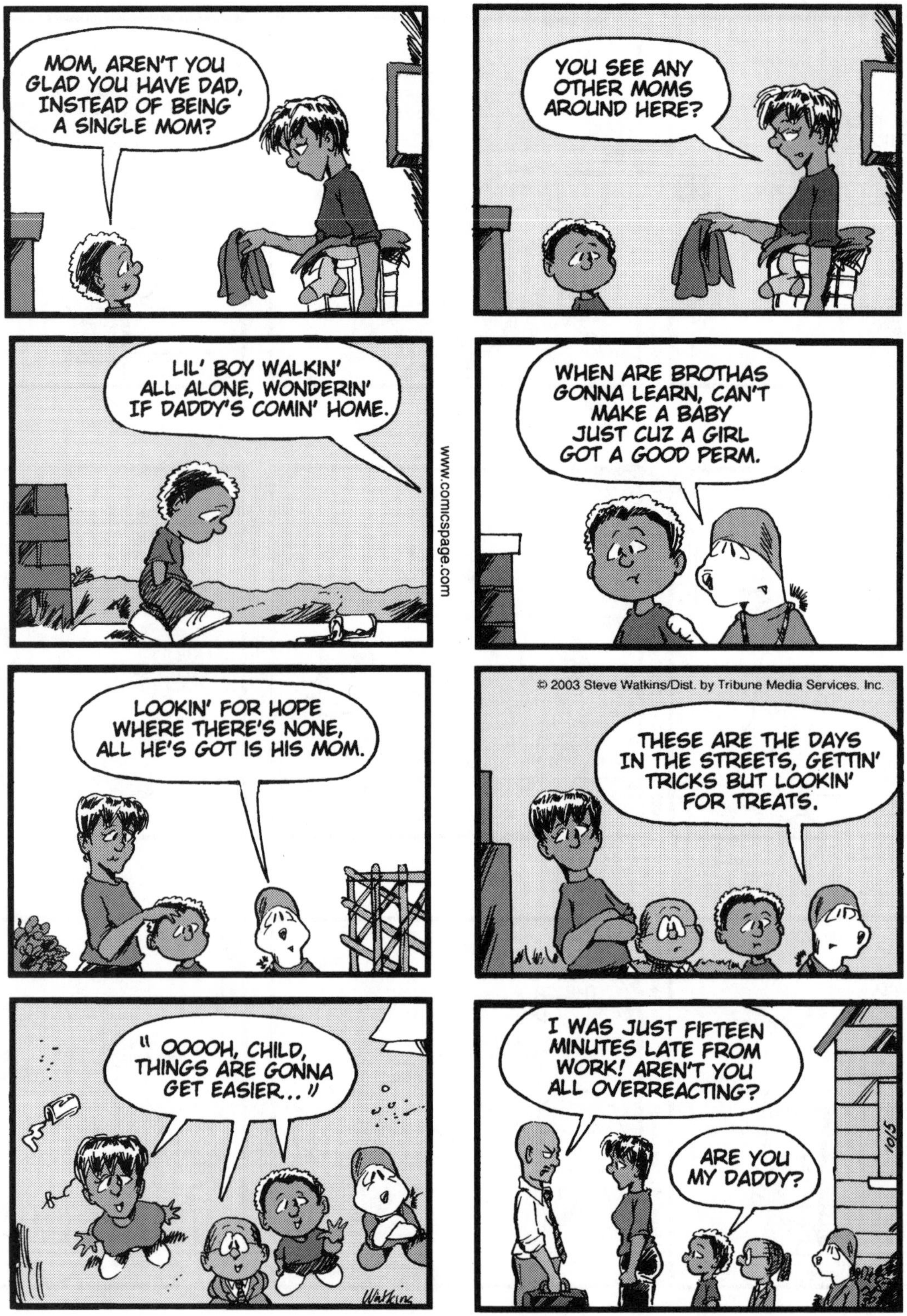
MOM, AREN'T YOU GLAD YOU HAVE DAD, INSTEAD OF BEING A SINGLE MOM?
YOU SEE ANY OTHER MOMS AROUND HERE?
LIL' BOY WALKIN' ALL ALONE, WONDERIN' IF DADDY'S COMIN' HOME.
WHEN ARE BROTHAS GONNA LEARN, CAN'T MAKE A BABY JUST CUZ A GIRL GOT A GOOD PERM.
LOOKIN' FOR HOPE WHERE THERE'S NONE, ALL HE'S GOT IS HIS MOM.
THESE ARE THE DAYS IN THE STREETS, GETTIN' TRICKS BUT LOOKIN' FOR TREATS.
" OOOOH, CHILD, THINGS ARE GONNA GET EASIER..."
I WAS JUST FIFTEEN MINUTES LATE FROM WORK! AREN'T YOU ALL OVERREACTING?
ARE YOU MY DADDY?
Watkins
10/5

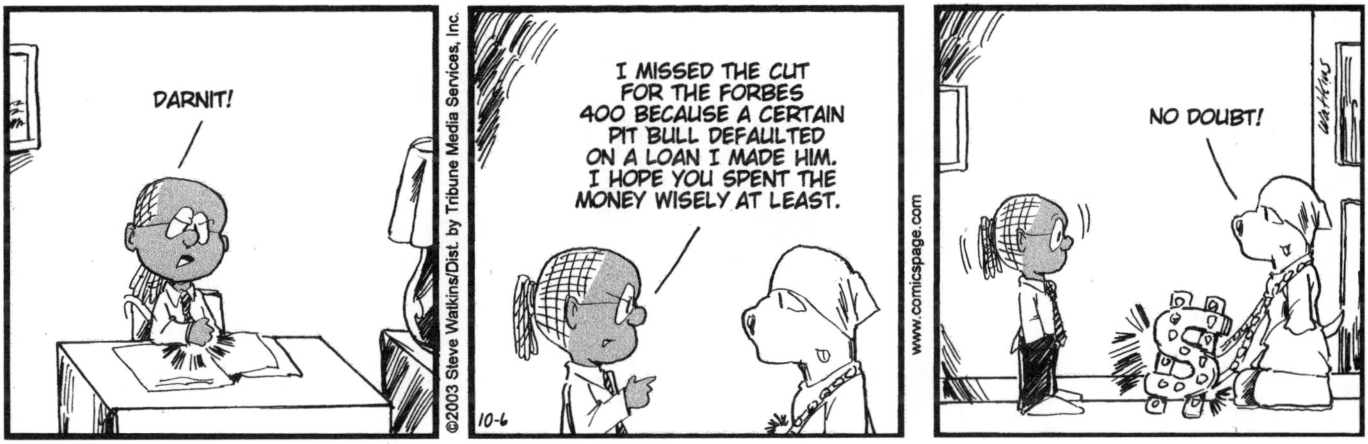
DARNIT!
I MISSED THE CUT FOR THE FORBES 400 BECAUSE A CERTAIN PIT BULL DEFAULTED ON A LOAN I MADE HIM. I HOPE YOU SPENT THE MONEY WISELY AT LEAST.
NO DOUBT!
©2003 Steve Watkins/Dist. by Tribune Media Services, Inc.
www.comicspage.com
10-6

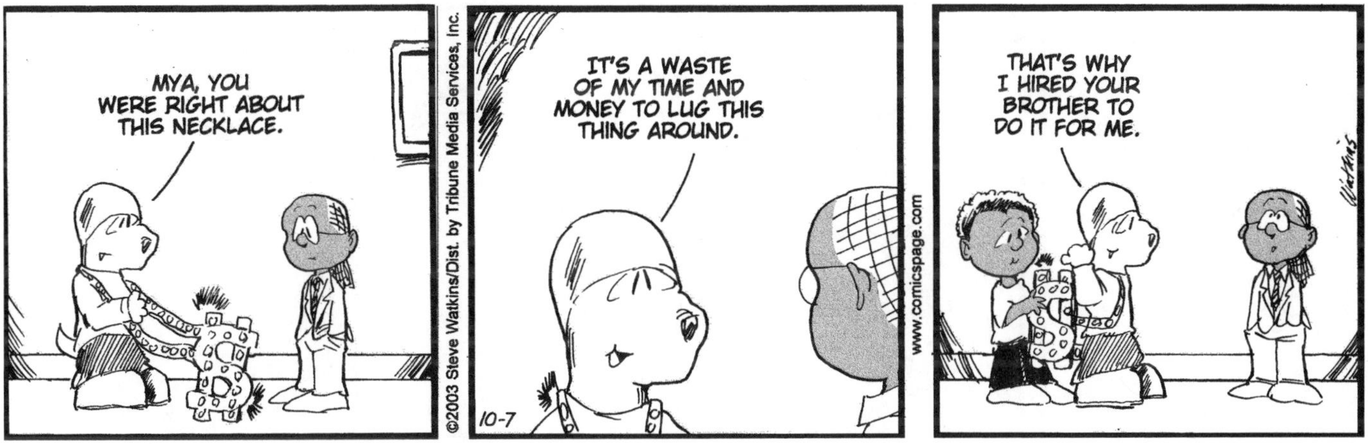
MYA, YOU WERE RIGHT ABOUT THIS NECKLACE.
IT'S A WASTE OF MY TIME AND MONEY TO LUG THIS THING AROUND.
THAT'S WHY I HIRED YOUR BROTHER TO DO IT FOR ME.
©2003 Steve Watkins/Dist. by Tribune Media Services, Inc.
www.comicspage.com
10-7

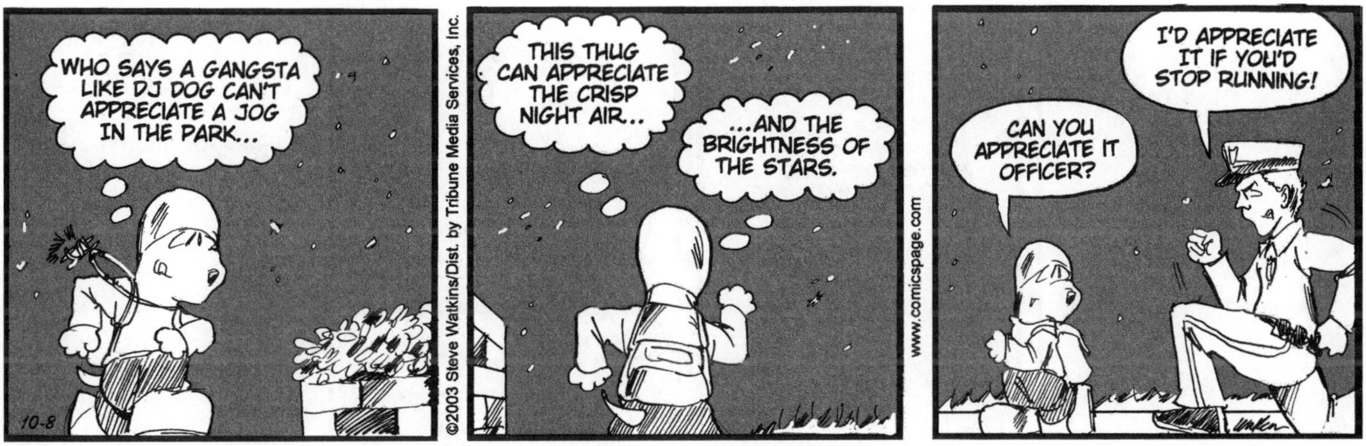
WHO SAYS A GANGSTA LIKE DJ DOG CAN'T APPRECIATE A JOG IN THE PARK...
THIS THUG CAN APPRECIATE THE CRISP NIGHT AIR...
...AND THE BRIGHTNESS OF THE STARS.
CAN YOU APPRECIATE IT OFFICER?
I'D APPRECIATE IT IF YOU'D STOP RUNNING!
©2003 Steve Watkins/Dist. by Tribune Media Services, Inc.
www.comicspage.com
10-8

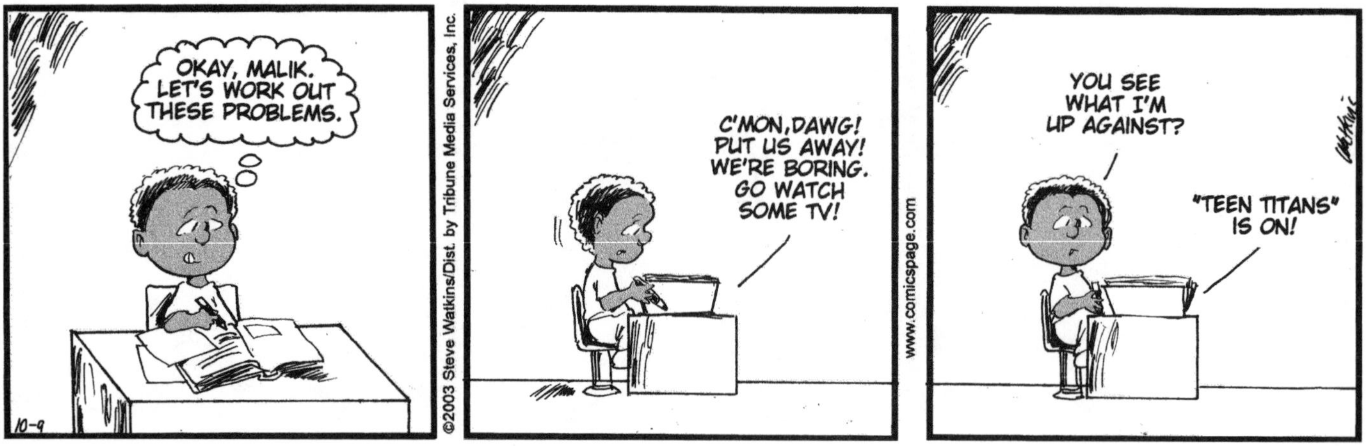
OKAY, MALIK. LET'S WORK OUT THESE PROBLEMS.
10-9
©2003 Steve Watkins/Dist. by Tribune Media Services, Inc.
C'MON, DAWG! PUT US AWAY! WE'RE BORING. GO WATCH SOME TV!
www.comicspage.com
YOU SEE WHAT I'M UP AGAINST?
"TEEN TITANS" IS ON!

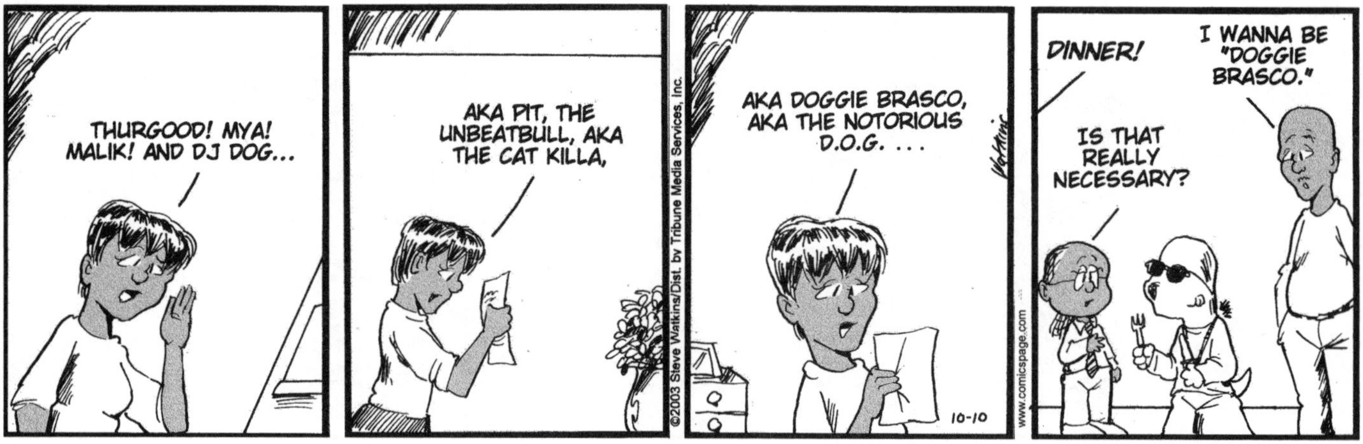
THURGOOD! MYA! MALIK! AND DJ DOG...
AKA PIT, THE UNBEATBULL, AKA THE CAT KILLA,
©2003 Steve Watkins/Dist. by Tribune Media Services, Inc.
AKA DOGGIE BRASCO, AKA THE NOTORIOUS D.O.G. . . .
10-10
www.comicspage.com
DINNER!
I WANNA BE "DOGGIE BRASCO."
IS THAT REALLY NECESSARY?

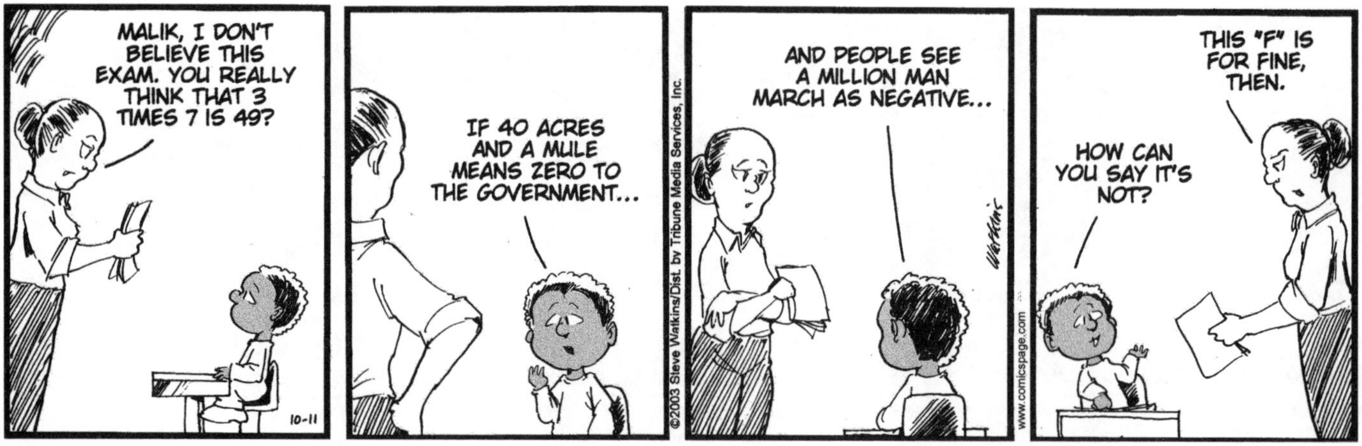
MALIK, I DON'T BELIEVE THIS EXAM. YOU REALLY THINK THAT 3 TIMES 7 IS 49?
10-11
IF 40 ACRES AND A MULE MEANS ZERO TO THE GOVERNMENT...
©2003 Steve Watkins/Dist. by Tribune Media Services, Inc.
AND PEOPLE SEE A MILLION MAN MARCH AS NEGATIVE...
www.comicspage.com
HOW CAN YOU SAY IT'S NOT?
THIS "F" IS FOR FINE, THEN.

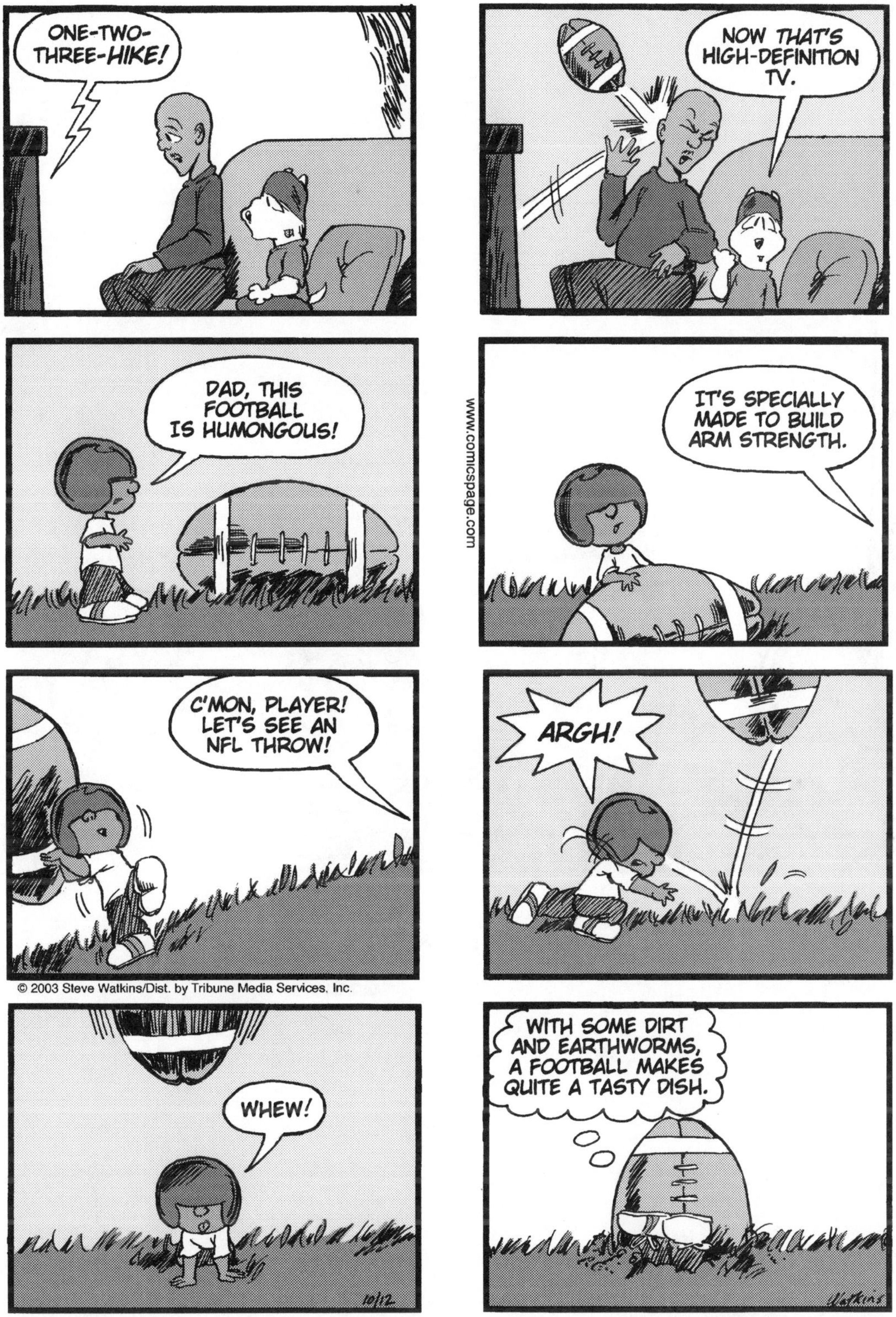
ONE-TWO-THREE-HIKE!
NOW THAT'S HIGH-DEFINITION TV.
DAD, THIS FOOTBALL IS HUMONGOUS!
IT'S SPECIALLY MADE TO BUILD ARM STRENGTH.
C'MON, PLAYER! LET'S SEE AN NFL THROW!
ARGH!
WHEW!
WITH SOME DIRT AND EARTHWORMS, A FOOTBALL MAKES QUITE A TASTY DISH.

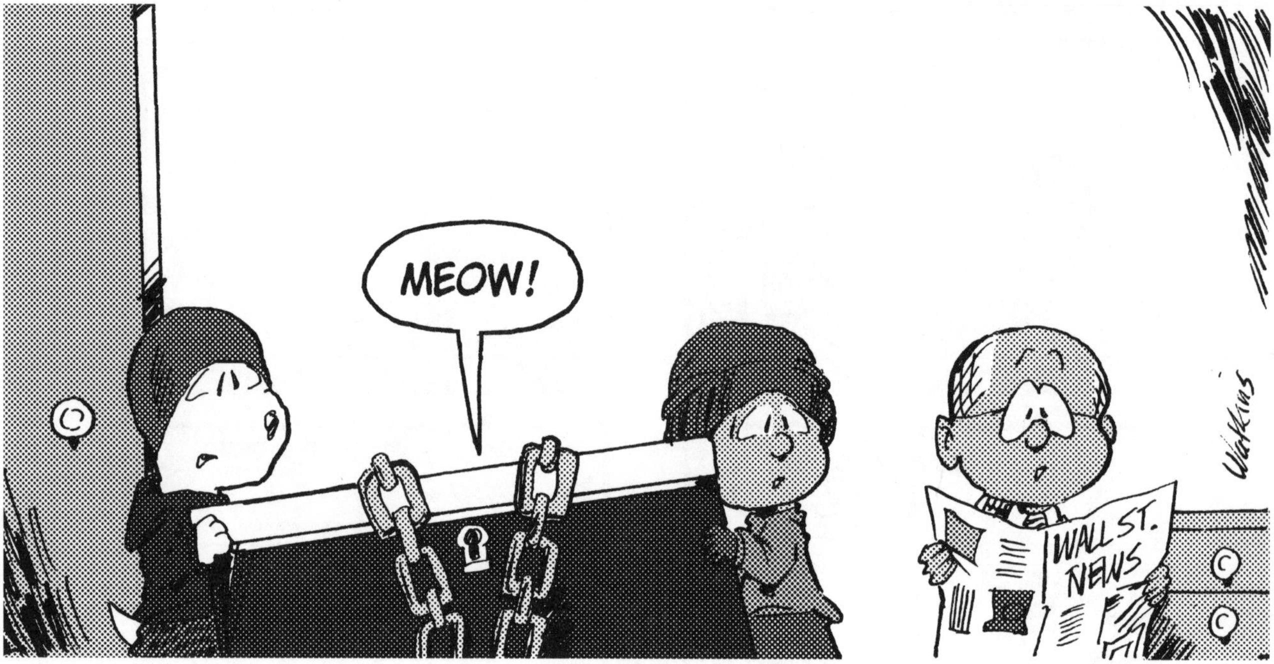
MEOW!
WALL ST. NEWS
Watkins

THE END